2010
CAREER SOURCEBOOK TWO

L I V I N G   A N D   W O R K I N G
I N   T H E
T W E N T Y - F I R S T   C E N T U R Y

Compiled and edited by Raynor Cannastra Associates

FUTURETALK
The Vocabulary of Science Fiction

Ansible is a device invented by Ursula K. LeGuin in *The Dispossessed*, used for instant communication between two points, no matter how far apart. Cousin to the ansible is James Blish's Dirac Communicator, invented in the story, "Beep," and named after the theoretical physicist Paul Dirac.

FTL, of faster than light travel and communication, circumvents Einstein's theory of relativity and other "establishment" physics. The problem is, a message sent FTL will get where it's going even before it's sent.

First contact is that critical maiden meeting between earthlings and their neighbors, if any, from outer space. That communication and the form it should take—linguistic, musical, mathematical, lasers—serves as the base for SF speculation from *A Martian Odyssey* to *Close Encounters of the Third Kind.*

Media landscape is the farthest extension of SF speculation about a world filled with communication gadgetry—holograms, videotelephones, satellites, computers.

Psi powers, or mind over matter, represent a whole group of phenomena tied to extrasensory perception. Science fiction writers and parapsychologists postulate that psi powers can manage communication and travel phenomena from precognition and telepathy to teleportation and telekinesis.

Library of Congress Cataloging in Publication Data

2010, career sourcebook two.

  Includes index.
  1. Occupations—Forecasting—Addresses, essays, lectures. 2. Twenty-first century—Forecasts—Addresses, essays, lectures. 3. Vocational guidance—Addresses, essays, lectures. 4. Career changes—Addresses, essays, lectures. I. Raynor Cannastra Associates. II. Title: 2010, career sourcebook 2.
HF5382.A14 1984   331.7′02   84-13768
ISBN 0-931032-18-0

Produced by Edison Electric Institute for the Library Grant Program.
© 1984, Edison Electric Institute

USING 2010:
CAREER SOURCEBOOK TWO

2010: Career Sourcebook Two, primarily a resource for career planning, presents timely, lively, and authoritative articles from a variety of sources describing what it will be like to live and work in the future.

Like its predecessor, *Career Sourcebook I, Sourcebook Two* will be useful to high school students, college students, and those who are exploring career changes or entering the work force later in their lives.

Career Sourcebook I introduced career planners and job hunters to the methods and resources of career development. *Sourcebook Two* reveals what work will be like in the future, and which careers and occupations offer the greatest promise.

Career Sourcebooks are brought to you by your local electric company and Edison Electric Institute, who encourage you to think of electric power as you explore careers and occupations. Our industry requires more of tomorrow's skills than many other industries, and the opportunities are great.

PART ONE

LIVING
IN THE
FUTURE

FUTUREVISION 1

The instrument he handed over . . . was nothing more than a television receiver with an elaborate set of controls for determining coordinates in time and space . . . One had merely to adjust the controls, and a window into the past opened up. Almost the whole of human history for the past five thousand years became accessible in an instant.

—*Arthur C. Clarke,* Childhood's End

FUTURISTICS:
MAKING SENSE OF TOMORROW

INTRODUCTION AND OVERVIEW

Democratic nations care little for what has been, but are haunted by visions of what will be; in this direction, their unbounded imagination grows and dilates beyond all measure.
—Alexis de Tocqueville, *Democracy in America*

With the approach of a new century, humans become fascinated, even obsessed, with the future. Their fascination and obsession have given birth to Utopian thought, science fiction, superstition, and sometimes mass hysteria.

As the second millenium approaches, the fascination with the future has been institutionalized in Western societies as both an art and a science—as futurism, or futurology. Its practitioners include scientists, social scientists, writers, film makers and others.

As Alvin Toffler, the author of *Future Shock*, sees it, futurists have a very important role to play:

Every society faces not merely a succession of probable futures, but an array of possible futures, and a conflict over preferable futures. The management of change is the effort to convert certain possibles into probables, in pursuit of agreed-on preferables. Determining the probable calls for a science of futurism. Defining the preferable calls for a politics of futurism.

Futurism has become not only a science and an art, but a profession and an industry. In many centers around the world, futurists—including economists, sociologists, mathematicians, biologists, physicists, operations researchers and others—are engaged in the assessment of probabilities. At what date could aquaculture feed half the world's population? What are the odds that electric cars will replace gas-driven automobiles in the next 15 years? What changes are most probable in leisure patterns, urban government, race relations?

TREND EXTRAPOLATION

"The most reliable way to anticipate the future," writes futurist John Naisbitt, "is by understanding the present." One way of forecasting is to identify current trends, assessing their strength and staying-power, projecting them into the future, and judging their likely impact. This method is known as trend analysis, or trend extrapolation.

Trend analysis and other methods of forecasting are explained in the readings included in Chapter 1. Trend analysis, the method favored by Naisbitt and many other futurists, is a method that you might keep in mind as you read the articles in Chapters 2 and 3. Many of these readings are based on the extrapolation of trends that may or may not prove to be correct.

Because many personal decisions, especially career choices, depend on trend analysis, you should try to develop your own instincts for judging the soundness of such extrapolations, and their relevance to your choices. If, for example, you wish to become a teacher you should be aware that the school population will continue to decline in the 1980s. At the same time, however, certain regions of the country are growing faster than average and may offer good opportunities in teaching. Depending on where you live, the national trend may or may not be relevant to your plans.

Among the many trends that futurists say will have an important influence on our lives are the following:

- the emergence of a global, interdependent economy;

- overpopulation and growing political instability in the overpopulated regions of the world;

- the acceleration of the arms race;

- the move from the old industrial cities of the North to the South and the West;

- the transition from an industrial society to an information society;

- the weakening of hierarchical structures in favor of informal networks;

- the rediscovery of innovation—acting from the bottom up to achieve results—by governments, corporations, and other groups;

- the shift from institutional help to more self-reliance in all aspects of our lives.

SCIENCE FICTION: LIFE IMITATES ART

"Determining the possible calls for an art of futurism," writes Toffler. Futurism depends on the insights of creative artists, as well as scientists.

It was science fiction writer Arthur C. Clarke who first conceived of the communications satellite. It was Clarke, too, who suggested in *2001: Space Odyssey* that a space ship might use the enormous gravitational field of Jupiter to produce a "slingshot effect," accelerating the ship in the second lap of its journey. This same maneuver was used in the Voyager space probes of 1979, permitting the first detailed reconnaisance of Jupiter and Saturn.

Science fiction writers are interested not only in gadgetry, but in ideas. What will it be like to live in the future? What role will technology play? Given the crises of the present—diminished resources, finite food supply, growing population—will technology be part of the problem or part of the solution?

Besides science fiction writers, many other creative professionals and artists contribute to the imaginative effort that is basic to futurism. Lewis Thomas, the distinguished biologist who heads the Sloan-Kettering Cancer Institute, suggests in the *New England Journal of Medicine* that humans use Bach to introduce themselves in that critical "first contact" with other worlds.

Composer Anthony Braxton experiments with music to be played by four orchestras composed of 160 musicians in revolving chairs. He calls it "multi-orchestralism" and says it's "directly related to intergalactic creative possibilities." NASA reports that musicians already are inquiring about a spot on the space shuttle so that they can improvise outside the earth's atmosphere.

For the first time in history, scientists are marrying the insights of artists, poets, dramatists, and novelists to statistical analysis and operations research, in the hope of better understanding the future. Their methods and findings are the subject of the readings that follow.

THE READINGS

"Planting Seeds for the Future" outlines the brief history of futurism, its methods, and the issues that futurists see as critical.

"An Image of the Future" is a description of the emerging framework of post-industrial society by the prominent Japanese futurist Yoneji Masuda.

"Further Adventures of Vik and Viora" is a short story revealing one science fiction writer's vision of telecommunications tomorrow.

REFERENCES

Megatrends: Ten New Directions Transforming Our Lives, by John Naisbitt, has been described by Senator Gary Hart as "an insightful analysis of the political, societal, and economic currents that will shape our future." Warner Books paperback, 1982.

2010: Odyssey Two, by Arthur C. Clarke, is a sequel to *2001: Space Odyssey.* Carl Sagan describes *2010* as "a daring romp through the solar system and a worthy successor to *2001.*"

The Futurist is a "journal of forecasts, trends, and ideas about the future," published by the World Future Society: An Association for the Study of Alternative Futures, 4916 St. Elmo Avenue, Bethesda, MD 20814-5089. Copies of *The Futurist* may be available in your library.

PLANTING SEEDS FOR THE FUTURE

Whether the future turns out to be as bright as futurists hope or as dark as they sometimes fear depends on our ability to manage the human enterprise with greater foresight than we have used in the past. Such foresight depends, in turn, on our ability to understand the world of tomorrow, a world that rapid social change has made even more enigmatic than it was in the past.

The study of the future

In 1902, the British writer H. G. Wells suggested that there might be a science of the future which might enable us to discover what would happen in the years and decades ahead. Today's futurists do not believe that the study of the future is an exact science that will allow people to know what is going to happen. They believe instead that we are all active participants in the creation of the future. Enormous endeavors such as the Manhattan Project during World War II and the space program during the 1960s demonstrated that human beings can indeed shape the future.

Since neither "the future" nor "the world of the future" actually exists, they cannot be studied directly. We can only study *ideas* about what the world may be like in the future. Thus when we "study the future" what we are really doing is studying ideas developed largely from our perceptions of the past and the present. And the *reason* for studying the future is *not* so that we can learn what may happen, but rather to help us decide what kind of future we want and develop ways to achieve it.

The modern futurist movement, which began developing rapidly during the 1960s, appears to be gradually forming a coherent philosophy or world view. Among the emerging principles of this world view are: (1) the unity or interconnectedness of reality, (2) the crucial importance of time, and (3) the importance of ideas, especially ideas about the future.

The unity of the universe is a unity of time as well as space. In emphasizing the importance of time, futurists stress that decisions made now will shape the world that we will experience in the future. But decisions reached today may take years to implement fully. The importance of time is clear in the differences between an acorn and an oak tree. There is no way to pass a magic wand over an acorn and turn it into an oak. Only time can perform that miracle.

Some futurists claim that almost anything can be done in 20 years! This statement seems outrageous—until one recalls that, once the decisions were made, unleashing the power of the atom took only four years and putting a man on the moon took only eight. Because time is so important, futurists insist that the more distant future must be an integral consideration in making current decisions. Only too often we make decisions with little concern about their impact on the longer-term future.

People think that they base their actions on past events and present realities, but images of the future may play a more critical role. We use these images of the future as blueprints in constructing our lives. And the blueprints may determine our success and happiness more than do the materials we work with (our bodies, families, financial resources, etc.).

Just as a building can be built if people believe it will be built, a desirable world might be created if people can collectively imagine what that world would be like and how it might be achieved. Futurists believe that to develop such a consensus, ideas about the future world should be systematically generated and studied. The study of the future would thus become a major human activity.

Methods of forecasting

Many people never realize that they do a great deal of forecasting in their everyday lives. Here are three methods of forecasting:

Trend extrapolation. One of the simplest assumptions that we can make about the future is that it will be like the past: things will remain as they are. The next simplest assumption is that things will change just as they have changed in the past: if the population of a city, for example, has been increasing at the rate of two percent a year, we can extrapolate this trend and calculate future populations for the city. This method of forecasting is used not only by people in their everyday lives but also by city planners, economists, demographers, and all the other specialists who first identify a trend and then make a projection suggesting where that trend will lead.

Scenarios. A scenario is simply a series of events that we imagine happening in the future. Our everyday thinking continuously takes ventures into the mysterious world of next week or next year. We may begin a scenario by asking, "What would happen if we went to the theatre on Saturday night?" With the question posed, we can begin to imagine the various consequences of the action. First it would require certain preparations: for example, transportation to the theatre would be needed. Then if the event does occur, further consequences might arise, such as missing a relative who comes unexpectedly for a visit.

A scenario awakens us to potential problems that might accompany the proposed action. It helps us to decide whether we want to do something and how to do it. Many policy analysts working for various governments now use scenarios to explore alternative policies that their governments might pursue. In effect, a scenario provides us with a way to shape our futures more intelligently.

Using experts. When we consider taking an important course of action, we usually solicit the advice of other people—often people who have some special knowledge of our proposed venture. These people will give us their judgments of what will likely happen in response to our actions. In effect these people make forecasts for us based on their own knowledge, and this counsel helps us to understand what we may encounter in the future and how we can deal with it. Top leaders in business and government use this forecasting technique. For example, the President of the United States may describe a number of alternative courses of action to his cabinet and get their views on the consequences of each.

Scholars in research institutes ("think tanks") use the above methods, plus others, to explore the future. In recent years, they have made many improvements in the naive methods of forecasting that most of us use. Yet the basic principles remain the same.

Critical issues of the future

Will the trends that have characterized our civilization over the past few centuries continue or will they change in the years ahead? No one knows. Some futurists feel that environmental constraints are beginning to limit the long-term trend of economic progress and many other basic trends will soon undergo radical change. These futurists note that the earth's bounty of fossil fuels and easily exploited minerals is disappearing and that the supply of arable land not already under cultivation has dwindled while the number of mouths to feed has climbed. Even more ominously, the natural environment no longer appears able to withstand the ever-growing assaults from man's technology and its byproducts.

Other futurists disagree with this pessimistic view, holding that the world's per capita income can continue to increase during the coming decades. They argue that advances in technology have historically enabled man to exploit resources that earlier were inaccessible. In the petroleum industry, for example, new technology has allowed oil men to drill deeper and deeper into the earth, even beneath the ocean. If the technology can be perfected, virtually inexhaustible quantities of metals lie waiting in the oceans.

The "technological optimists" and "technological pessimists" are now engaged in a lively debate. In general the technological pessimists argue for drastic population control measures, the simplification of life-styles (eating less meat, reducing automobile travel, etc.), and organic farming (to reduce the need for chemicals).

The technological optimists usually concede that technology has many unwanted side effects, but they argue that technology is crucial to a high quality of life. Without modern technology, they argue, man would quickly return to barbarism. In their view, the opponents of modern technology are romantics who fantasize about the joys of simple rural living while forgetting the brutal realities of singlehandedly wresting a living from the soil.

Other critical issues we face in the future revolve around the maintenance of world peace, the proper use of new technology, the increase and proper distribution of wealth, etc.

Here are a few examples of the innumerable problems that the world will seek to resolve in the years ahead:

Preventing World War III. The possibility of a third world war remains ever-present. The Soviet Union and the United States maintain a vast system of missiles, aircraft, and vessels that can be quickly armed with nuclear or thermonuclear explosives. A nuclear "exchange" between the superpowers would be so horrible as to defy description, yet no way has yet been found to resolve once and for all this terrifying situation. In recent years nuclear weapons have spread slowly but steadily to additional nations. What can be done to remove the menace of war—especially a thermonuclear conflict involving the major powers?

Overpopulation. Some countries are doing little to reduce the birthrate of their people with the result that they are increasingly overpopulated. With more and more mouths to feed, the food supply inevitably runs out. If a nation refuses to curb its population growth, is the international community required to try to alleviate the resulting starvation? Meanwhile, many new birth control techniques will become available. Will their use be mandatory? Will parents have to be "licensed"? By whom?

The distribution of wealth. Living standards have risen greatly during the 20th century, but wealth remains unequally distributed. To equalize distribution many governments tax the wealthy heavily and provide subsidies for the poor, but when this is done both the rich and the poor may work less because additional leisure seems preferable to the meager benefits that could be obtained from working. Should governments intensify their efforts to achieve equality even if it leads to a reduction in the total amount of wealth available for distribution?

Disorder in the financial world. Rampant inflation and the declining dollar have led to widespread uncertainty in international finance. Billions of dollars race back and forth across national frontiers beyond the control of central banks. A sudden movement somewhere could trigger an international economic crisis. What can be done to restore order in the world's financial markets?

Terrorism. Many groups have discovered that they can get their way through bombings, assassinations, and kidnappings. How can terrorism be curbed?

Energy. Energy is essential to modern civilization, but traditional fuels like petroleum, natural gas, and coal are becoming increasingly expensive. Nuclear power has recognized dangers, while alternate possible technologies each pose their own problems. What mix of energy sources should be used in the coming decades so that the world can have adequate energy without unacceptable costs and risks?

Restrictions on imports. Many workers find that their jobs are threatened by imported goods, but when restrictions are placed on imports, consumers are deprived of the opportunity to buy cheaper goods. What can be done to protect the interests of workers whose jobs are threatened by imports? Or is such protection unhealthy to a developing global economy?

Health costs. Modern medicine is achieving spectacular results in curing many sick people, but medical costs keep rising. Should the patient bear the cost, or society at large? What should be done about people who destroy their own health through overindulgence in food, drugs, and tobacco if society must pay for the damage they do to themselves?

Control of the oceans. Nations have been extending their claims to ocean areas off their shores. If the current trend continues, the coastal nations will eventually have the oceans divided up among themselves. Traditionally, maritime nations have maintained a "freedom-of-the-seas" principle, but if oceans are to be developed, ocean farmers (aquaculturists) and others need to have their property protected. Who will assume this responsibility? On what basis?

Choosing the sex of one's children. Physicians are currently developing various means whereby parents can decide whether to have a boy or a girl. But should parents make such a choice? What can be done to prevent the sex-ratio from becoming unbalanced so that there are far more women than men—or vice versa?

Intergroup tensions. Most countries contain a number of racial and/or cultural groups. Tension—even violence—often occurs between such groups: for example, between Protestants and Catholics in Northern Ireland, Basques and non-Basques in Spain, French-speakers and English-speakers in Canada, etc. What should be done to make intergroup relations more harmonious?

Decline of the family. The family has traditionally had the function of producing and rearing tomorrow's citizens. Many trends—including a huge increase in divorces and unwed mothers—suggest that the family now is experiencing major difficulties. Should the government move to strengthen the family? If so, how? If not, how will tomorrow's children be raised?

Water shortages. As population rises, conflicts over water supplies tighten in many areas. Farmers want water for crops; city residents want water for household use. How should water supplies be allocated? Who should bear the cost—the people who use the water, the local community, the state, or the nation? And what about control of weather?

Space industrialization. Space offers enormous economic possibilities. Satellites are already proving their value in communications, weather forecasting, and other areas; the moon, planets, and asteroids are rich in minerals that could be used on earth. Should more effort go into exploring and developing space? Who should control the use of the moon and other objects in space?

Reforming education. Despite rising expenditures for education, increasing numbers of young people lack the basic skills required to function effectively in modern society. How can the educational system be improved? What else can be done to increase individual competence?

The burden of government regulation. In recent decades, governments have imposed more and more regulations on business in order to protect consumers from dangerous products, workers from accidents, and the general public from pollution. Companies now spend billions of dollars to satisfy government regulations—and the cost is passed on to consumers in higher prices. Government red tape also delays the introduction of innovative technology that could be used to improve productivity and enhance human life. How can government regulations be made less costly without reducing their effectiveness in areas where controls are needed?

Reducing crime. Social thinkers once believed that education and jobs would wipe out crime. But the crime rate has risen—not fallen—during a period when society has provided additional schools and better economic conditions. What can be done to reduce crime?

Credentials for work. Many employers insist that prospective employees have certain educational credentials, such as a high school diploma or a college degree. As a result, many people who would have been excellent workers are excluded from certain jobs. Should it be illegal to discriminate on the grounds of educational deficiencies if these have no clear bearing on job performance?

Information overload. More and more people find that they simply cannot keep up with all the information they need to make decisions, including the decision about which candidates to support in an election. What can be done to help individuals cope with the information explosion and modern communications barrage?

A sense of community. In a world where space travel will become a reality and advanced telecommunications make earth one neighborhood, how will people satisfy their longing to belong to a community and to have a sense of significance? And if extra-terrestrial life is discovered, what will the impact be on people's view of the meaning of existence?

The world in the year 2000

hould recent trends continue—and the *if* must be stressed—the world of the year 2000 will differ from today's world by being:

More unified. Improved comminications and transportation will bind people together into an increasingly integrated world community.

Less organized around family and kin. People will change mates more frequently and fewer children will live with their parents.

Longer lived. Life expectancy will continue to rise on a worldwide scale. However, life spans in the industrialized countries may not be significantly higher unless breakthroughs come from current efforts to discover how to halt or retard the aging process.

More mobile. People will travel with increasing frequency—both for business and pleasure.

The foregoing trends do not reveal the exact nature of the future, but they do suggest in which directions the world has been moving toward the year 2000.

AN IMAGE OF THE FUTURE

The information epoch being brought about by computer-communication technology will not simply have a big socio-economic impact upon contemporary industrial society, it will demonstrate a force of societal change powerful enough to bring about the transformation of society into a completely new type of human society—an information society.

The innovational technology of the past was concerned with material-productive power and material values. The future information society will be built within a completely new framework. The accompanying table was developed by putting the components of the information society together piece by piece, using an historical analogy from the industrial society. Of course the entire picture of the future information society cannot be given at this stage, but this table may help the reader understand the basic elements and their relationships.

Three Stages of Change

Generally speaking, innovational technology changes social and economic systems through three stages:

Stage 1—technology does work previously done by humans

Stage 2—technology makes possible work that humans have never been able to do before

Stage 3—the existing social and economic structures are transformed into new social and economic systems.

The three stages of technological innovation, as they apply to the revolution in computer and communications technology, may be defined as:

1) **Automation,** in which human mental labor is accomplished through the application of computer technology.

2) **Knowledge creation,** which entails the amplification of human mental labor.

3) **System innovation,** a set of political, social and economic tranformations resulting from the impact of the first two developmental stages.

Automation

The social impact of automation has both bright and dark potential.

▶ There will be increasing emancipation from labor for subsistence, permitting more free time to expend on personal satisfaction.

▶ The replacement of subsistence labor may result in unemployment.

▶ There is a concern for privacy as thousands of data banks contain massive amounts of information on individuals and enterprises.

▶ Computer-communications technology could be used to create a managed society. Ruling elites could guide the 'managed' (persons and things), using information networks as control mechanisms.

Knowledge Creation

Knowledge creation includes problem solving and opportunity development. Problem solving is a method of eliminating risks that stand in the way of accomplishing an aim.

One of the most advanced problem-solving systems of this kind is the forecasting, evaluating and warning system. This system allows for:

▶ quick discovery of problems in rapidly changing circumstances

▶ forecasting a future trend

▶ evaluating the degree of danger due to these problems

▶ issuing a warning when danger appears.

Opportunity development is research and development of possibilities of future time usage or creating new values in rapidly changing environmental conditions. Opportunity development is encouraged by the existence of the information utility, which will come into being when information becomes a public commodity, similar to water and electricity, which one can obtain as needed. Such a utility will have impact in two ways.

1 There will be an increase in opportunity for education. Education will be freed from the restrictions of income, time and place.

2 There will be an increase in opportunities for work. People will be able to obtain much more information relating to the possibilities for new work and they will have many opportunities for choice when selecting future work. A new industry, the opportunity industry, will develop.

The main sectors of the opportunity industry will be the education industry, the information industry, the mass communication industry, and the consultation industry; and industries concerned with psychosomatic medicine and molecular biology, for example, will also have their part. There may even emerge something resembling religious activities, as religion in various forms again becomes a day-to-day factor in life in the 21st century.

System Innovation

When epoch-making technological innovation occurs, changes take place in the existing society and a new society emerges.

Some typical examples of major and basic transformations are a change in our value system from material value to time value; from a system of free competition to a synergetic economic system; from parliamentary democracy to participatory democracy.

A most dramatic societal change will be the transformation of the education system.

1 Education will be lifted out of the restrictions of formal schools through the open educational environment of knowledge networks.

2 A personal type of education will be introduced. A wide range of educational opportunities will allow people to move on to advanced courses, irrespective of age.

3 Self-learning will become the leading form of education. Teachers will act as advisors or counsellors.

4 Knowledge-creative education will replace memorizing lists of information and training in techniques.

5 Lifetime education will become necessary to enable adults and elderly people to adapt themselves to the changes of the information society.

The radical change in the educational system will be of great significance to the development of human history—an historical transition from the industrial society, in which the natural environment has been unilaterally transformed and materials consumption expanded, to the information society which seeks coexistence with nature through humankind's own transformation and innovation of new socio-economic systems.

A Vision of Computopia

Looking back over the history of human society, we see that as the traditional society of the Middle Ages was drawing to a close, the curtain was rising on the new industrial society. Thomas More, Robert Owen, Saint Simon, Adam Smith and other prophets arose with a variety of visions portraying the emerging society. The one that is of special interest to me is Adam Smith's vision of a universal opulent society, which he sets out in *The Wealth of Nations*. Smith's universal affluent society conceives the condition of plenty for the people, economic conditions that should free the people from dependence and subordination, and enable them to exercise true independence of spirit in autonomous actions.

Smith's vision of people having material wealth in plenty is partially accomplished, at least in the advanced countries. As the 21st century approaches, the possibility of a universally opulent society being realized has appeared in the sense that Smith envisioned, and the information society (futurization society) that will emerge from the computer-communications revolution will be a society that actually moves toward a universal society of plenty.

The most important point I would make is that the information society will function around the axis of information values rather than material values—cognitive and action-selective information. In addition, the information utility, the core organization for the production of information, will have the fundamental character of an infrastructure, and knowledge capital will predominate over material capital in the structure of the economy.

We are moving toward the 21st century with the very great goal of building a Computopia on earth, the historical monument of which will be only several chips one inch square in a small box. But that box will store many historical records, including the record of how four billion world citizens overcame the energy crisis and the population explosion; achieved the abolition of nuclear weapons and complete disarmament; conquered illiteracy; and created a rich symbiosis of God and man without the compulsion of power or law, but by the voluntary cooperation of the citizens to put into practice their common global aims.

Accordingly, the civilization to be built as we approach the 21st century will not be a material civilization symbolized by huge constructions, but a virtually invisible civilization. Precisely, it should be called an "information civilization." Homo sapiens, who stood at the dawn of the first material civilization at the end of the last glacial age, is now standing at the threshold of the second, the information civilization, after ten thousand years. ■

A NEW FRAMEWORK

		INDUSTRIAL SOCIETY	INFORMATION SOCIETY
Innovational Technology	Core	Steam engine (power)	Computer (memory, computation, control)
	Basic function	Replacement, amplification of physical labor	Replacement, amplification of mental labor
	Productive Power	Material productive power (increase in per capita production)	Information productive power (increase in optimal action-selection capabilities)
Socio-economic structure	Products	Useful goods and services	Information, technology, knowledge
	Production center	Modern factory (machinery, equipment)	Information utility (information networks, data banks)
	Market	New world, colonies, consumer purchasing power	Increase in knowledge frontiers, information space
	Leading industries	Manufacturing industries (machinery industry, chemical industry)	Intellectual industries, (information industry, knowledge industry)
	Industrial structure	Primary, secondary, tertiary industries	Matrix industrial structure (primary, secondary, tertiary, quaternary/systems industries)
	Economic Structure	Commodity economy (division of labor, separation of production and consumption)	Synergetic economy (joint production and shared utilization)
	Socio-economic principle	Law of price (equilibrium of supply and demand)	Law of goals (principle of synergetic feedforward)
	Socio-economic subject	Enterprise (private enterprise, public enterprise, third sector)	Voluntary communities (local and informational communities)
	Socio-economic system	Private ownership of capital, free competition, profit maximization	Infrastructure, principle of synergy, precedence of social benefit
	Form of society	Class society (centralized power, classes, control)	Functional society (multicenter, function, autonomy)
	National goal	GNW (gross national welfare)	GNS (gross national satisfaction)
	Form of government	Parliamentary democracy	Participatory democracy
	Force of social change	Labor movements, strikes	Citizens' movements, litigation
	Social problems	Unemployment, war, fascism	Future shock, terror, invasion of privacy
	Most advanced stage	High mass consumption	High mass knowledge creation
Values	Value standards	Material values (satisfaction of physiological needs)	Time-value (satisfaction of goal-achievement needs)
	Ethical standards	Fundamental human rights, humanity	Self-discipline, social contribution
	Spirit of the times	Renaissance (human liberation)	Globalism (symbiosis of man and nature)

FURTHER ADVENTURES OF VIK AND VIORA IN THE 21ST CENTURY

"I touched in a four-digit number on our home com center system and the quiet woodland scene on the far wall dissolved into a dazzling old-time disco scene from the 1970s. Then the fun began."

Chapter One

"It's 9:30. You've overslept." The voice of the bedcom took on a slightly more urgent tone than the softer 9 o'clock "warning" and the softest 8 o'clock "first call."

Other parts of the apartment were already awake and functioning. In the kitchen, Rikki finished his morning duties with his usual cool efficiency.

That part I liked. What I didn't like was his insufferable air of self-importance and the condition breakfast arrived at bedside each morning—rubbery eggs and tepid coffee.

But on this particular morning my condition wasn't so hot either. Last night's party was loud, long, and liquid.

"Today is Wednesday, December 13, 2043," a second voice intoned. "Today Vik has a 3 o'clock dentist appointment. You both are meeting the Montagues at noon for lunch. Today is the Winguths' anniversary, and tonight you are giving a party in honor of Thonda Penworthy's birthday. It is raining. . . ."

I plopped my hand on the touchpad to turn off the babbling bedcom while seeking Viora with the other. She was already up, struggling with a stubborn wristcom clasp, when Astar nosed open the bedroom door and made a flying leap into the center of the bed—occupied by my prone and now flattened form.

"We've got to get his affection level reprogrammed," I protested from under the sprawling syndoggy.

"Don't be silly, Darling," Viora laughed. "Just be firm."

I raised a badly quivering hand.

"Down, Astar," she commanded.

I pressed on. "I don't think this head could survive what dentists do. Let's skip the appointment and do some Christmas shopping instead."

"On one condition."

"Which is?"

"We forego the convenience of the teleshopper. I haven't seen Fifth Avenue in ages."

Chapter Two

Late that afternoon, I touched in our ID number and the door of the apartment slid open with a swish.

I deposited the holiday packages on the couch and headed for the kitchen and my favorite headache remedy—Scotch on the rocks.

Viora was still congratulating herself on how clever she was to have recorded each friend's brand of perfume on our personal teledata file. I had to admit it did speed up the shopping ordeal, and, besides, the packages were much easier to manage than last year's round of holograph projectors.

"That's strange," Viora exclaimed.

"What's strange?"

"The heat and the lights. They activated on when we came in. Rikki must have gone out."

"Not quite," I called from the kitchen. "He's in here, and it looks like he had company."

Chapter Three

I disengaged the medic-diag unit. "This thing says the body functions stopped about 20 minutes ago. The guy who zapped him can't be too far away."

"You mean *gal*," Viora countered.

"*Gal?*"

"Yes, haven't you noticed the smell in here? *Celestique*—lovely, but *not* mine."

"And definitely not mine, but I'd lay odds it belongs to someone we know, or Rikki would never have let her in without setting off the security sensors."

"But why would anyone want to destroy him?"

"Maybe she heard about his breakfasts," I offered.

"Darling, this is hardly the time for foolishness. Maybe we didn't really know him. You never did check his references, even though he gave you his personal data access code."

"I think this is a good time to check those references," I said. "Where's that number?"

"While you're looking it up, I'm going to the telefile and check our Christmas list again. Someone who wears *Celestique* has been a naughty, naughty girl."

Chapter Four

The glass that held my second Scotch was glowing empty when the guests began to arrive. Arno, a temporary replacement for Rikki, hustled over to freshen my drink. I touched-in a four digit number on our home com center system and the quiet woodland scene on the far wall dissolved into a dazzling old-time disco scene from the 1970s. Then the fun began.

Neither Viora nor I mentioned the distressing event of the afternoon or what we learned from our respective telesearches—that, surprisingly, Rikki's last position was as a cook at the Women's Interplanetary Correctional Institution, and that, not surprisingly, three of our guests tonight—including Thonda—wore *Celestique*.

Thonda, true to form, was the last to arrive, eschewing her usual conservative banker behavior for something more theatrical.

"Darling," she bussed Viora, missing her cheek and breezily kissing the air next to her ear. "This is the loveliest thing anyone has *ever* done for me!"

Without waiting for a response, she swooped over to where I was sitting. Affecting a little girl pout, she singled out a lock of my hair and wrapped it around her finger. "You're not going to avoid me again tonight are you, Handsome?"

Viora caught my eye, screwed up her face and crossed her eyes.

"Nobody ever ignores you, Sweetheart," I said, extricating my hair from her finger. "What are you drinking?"

"You always do. Just coffee, thanks. I overdid the celebrating this afternoon. Did you hear? I was made a vice president of the bank today."

Chapter Five

"Thonda, you haven't even touched your coffee," Viora said. "It'll get cold."

"That's the way I like it, Honey," she said.

I went in for the kill. "As do most past, present, and future residents of good old WIPCI," I said casually.

Thonda's face went pale, her pupils dilated, and her voice came in a croak. "The what?"

"You know. The pen, the big house, stir. For obvious reasons, you can't get a cup of really hot coffee when you're behind bars. But, of course, you know all about that."

Thonda's face turned scarlet. "That's perfectly ludicrous. I haven't the foggiest notion of what you're talking about."

"Rikki must have. Isn't that why he got you to come to our apartment this afternoon? He recognized you from the good old days and put a price tag on his discretion. But you didn't buy it. What were you in for, embezzlement?"

Thonda's face turned a pretty color I'd never seen before. "I had to do it. Don't you see? The bank would never understand a conviction for embezzlement."

"I still say your measures were a little extreme."

"I couldn't let that little jerk destroy everything I'd worked so hard for. That promotion was damned important to me, and no little creep was going to undo it. Whatever gave me away?"

"Your taste in perfume and coffee."

Chapter Six

I awoke to the wonderful aroma of steaming hot coffee. Viora was at the vis-screen, deeply involved in a game of telebridge. "You've found a replacement for Rikki?" I asked.

"Not really, Darling," she said, touching-in her bid. "I took him in to the shop for an estimate. They said they could repair the damage and disconnect the blackmail program for only 4,000 credits. Obviously some corrupt guard or prison official was using Rikki for extra-curricular activities and failed to set him straight when he moved on. Anyway, Thonda will pick up the tab."

"But the coffee's hot."

"This guy from Peru is one dumb dummy. How do you suppose he got programmed into this league?"

"The coffee?" I pressed.

"Well, my Sweet, as long as they were in there messing around with his programs, I suggested they might as well tune up his breakfast skills. What do you think?"

"I think the eggs are rubbery."

TWO INDUSTRIAL REVOLUTIONS:
HISTORIC PARALLELS AND PERSPECTIVES

INTRODUCTION AND OVERVIEW

From this foul drain the greatest stream of human industry flows out to fertilize the whole world. From this filthy sewer pure gold flows. Here humanity attains its most complete development and its most brutish; here civilization works its miracles and civilized man is turned almost into a savage.
— Alexis de Tocqueville on Manchester, 1835

Sometime in the 1780s, for the first time in human history, the shackles on productivity were broken. Human societies became capable of the constant, rapid multiplication of goods and services.

Between 1780 and 1840 the Industrial Revolution harnessed the power of a million horses in Britain's steam engines, turned out two million yards of cotton cloth each year on 17 million mechanical spindles, dug almost fifty million tons of coal, and served as the basis for a lucrative worldwide trade twice as great as that of Britain's nearest rival, France.

ENTER MR. EDISON

A second phase of the Industrial Revolution began in the 1880s with the shift from steam power to electricity—a great transformation in the history of technology. Until then the Industrial Revolution had been based primarily on water power and the steam engine. The new electric age, which was born with the dynamo, is associated with such things as alloys, synthetics, elasticity, electronics, and automation.

In the steam age, the machine was a super beast of burden, requiring the physical degradation of humans and the environment for its success. With electricity, the machine came to be seen as a benevolent super-human that increased leisure and physical comfort.

The technology of steam had polluted the American Eden, but the electricity-based technologies promised a new paradise. "The conviction grew," writes literary critic Wyn Wachhorst, "that the fallen American Adam, having lost the Garden of Eden in the age of steam, could now reenter Paradise astride the machine."

Thomas A. Edison is rightly regarded as the father of the electrical age. His phonograph was the first of all modern forms of mechanical memory. His light bulb and "Edison effect" were the forerunners of the vacuum tube, the basis of electronics. And his system of power distribution took the machine from the exclusive hands of producers and put it in the hands of everyday consumers.

It was American dominance in the new electricity-based technologies that led to the emergence of the United States as a super power at the turn of the century. In the last two decades of the nineteenth century alone, electrification had harnessed the power of ten million horses in American generators. By 1900, American industry surpassed England's, and Andrew Carnegie could write in *Triumphant Democracy*:

The old nations of the earth creep on at a snail's pace; the Republic thunders past with the rush of the express. The United States has already reached the foremost rank among nations, and is destined to go on to outdistance all others in the race.

FROM ENIAC TO THE COMPUTER-ON-A-CHIP

A third phase of the Industrial Revolution began about 40 years ago. Electrical engineer J. Presper Eckert, Jr., physicist John W. Mauchly, and helpers laboriously built the world's first electronic digital computer. Their ENIAC (electronic numerical integrator and computer) was a temperamental monster that weighed thirty tons and ran on 18,000 vacuum tubes—when it ran. But it started the computer revolution.

A second computer revolution began in 1972, with the invention of an electronic data processing machine so small that it could be lost in the socket of one of ENIAC's tubes. This remarkable machine is the microcomputer, also called the "computer-on-a-chip." Even a medium strength microcomputer can perform 100,000 calculations a second, 20 times as many as ENIAC could.

In its importance, the microcomputer rivals its illustrious predecessors, the vacuum tube, the transistor, and the integrated-circuit logic chip. So far, only a fraction of its potential uses have reached production stage. In 1980 there were about 200,000 digital computers in the world. By 1990, thanks to the microcomputer, there may be 20 million.

FORECASTING THE IMPACT

Microelectronic silicon chips, which contain as much circuitry as room-sized computers once contained, are the electronic brains of pocket calculators, computers, industrial robots, word processors, computerized supermarket checkout systems, and guided missiles. The development of these chips already has shrunk the size of electronic equipment, increased the power and flexibility of small computers, slashed the cost of storing and using information, and led to major changes in industrial production.

As machinery incorporating microelectronics becomes more widely adopted, it could bring changes just as sweeping as those that accompanied the Industrial Revolution. On the international level, some futurists foresee the possibility of "information wars" in which countries and corporations fight for supremacy in the new technologies and markets.

On the national level, some futurists foresee a restructuring of government, business, and other activities as a result of the second computer revolution. With the computer to keep track of people and information, it is no longer necessary for organizations to be structured as hierarchies. "The computer will smash the pyramid," writes John Naisbitt. "We created the hierarchical, pyramidal, managerial system because we needed it to keep track of people and the things people did. With the computer to keep track, we can restructure our institutions horizontally."

On the personal level, futurists have shown that the second computer revolution will affect patterns of employment, change skill requirements, alter the nature of many jobs, and pose severe challenges to industrial relations.

Earlier phases of the Industrial Revolution offer parallels with all of the trends we observe today. As always, studying the past offers perspectives on the future. That is the lesson revealed in the readings that follow.

THE READINGS

"People and Machines: The Possible Dream" traces the human fascination with technology as it is reflected in literature.

"The Second Industrial Revolution" reviews the brief history of the microelectronics revolution and speculates on its impact on our society and economy.

"The Promise of Neo-Industrialization" describes many of the innovative ways in which electricity-based technologies can be used to boost American productivity.

REFERENCES

The Big Change: America Transforms Itself, 1900-1950, by Frederick Lewis Allen, is a popular and lively account of the various forces, including electrification, that reshaped our society. Harper & Row hardcover, 1952.

Future Shock, by Alvin Toffler, describes the emerging super-industrial world and its impact on culture, life styles, human relationships, business and work. Bantam paperback, originally published in 1970.

PEOPLE AND MACHINES: THE POSSIBLE DREAM

BIBLE

So when the woman saw that the tree was good for food, and that it was a delight to the eyes, and that the tree was to be desired to make one wise, she took of its fruit and ate; and she also gave some to her husband, and he ate. Then the eyes of both were opened...

GENESIS 3:6-7

CULKIN

We don't know who discovered water, but we're certain it wasn't a fish.

JOHN CULKIN

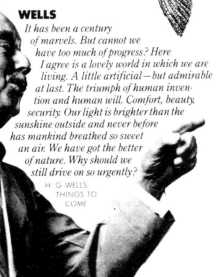

WELLS

It has been a century of marvels. But cannot we have too much of progress? Here I agree is a lovely world in which we are living. A little artificial—but admirable at last. The triumph of human invention and human will. Comfort, beauty, security. Our light is brighter than the sunshine outside and never before has mankind breathed so sweet an air. We have got the better of nature. Why should we still drive on so urgently?

H. G. WELLS
THINGS TO
COME

When Aldous Huxley prepared a new introduction to *Brave New World,* he said that if he were rewriting the book at that moment, he would offer his beleaguered Savage a third alternative. To be sure, the original *Brave New World* offers a rather cheerless vision of the future. In the book, the poor Savage must choose between a dehumanized, state-manipulated "utopian" world or a cruelly primitive one. Years later, though, Huxley apparently saw a third alternative. In that alternative, he said, "Science and technology would be used as though, like the Sabbath, they had been made for man, not as though man were to be adapted to and enslaved by them."

Huxley is gone now, never to know if the third alternative will come to pass. But, those of us living in the last stages of the 20th century must confess to casting a wary eye at science and technology. We are still unsure who is enslaved by whom.

The suspicion is rooted in a long and honorable tradition. It was, after all, Adam and Eve who got humankind summarily tossed out of the Garden of Eden simply by giving in to the temptation to know. Perhaps it's our collective guilt over that one act that sends schoolchildren everywhere trudging off to Teacher with the notorious apple.

But, literature has immortalized an entire procession of poor fools who aspired to know more than was seemly. Mythology gives us Icarus, who dared test his new wings too near the sun. Because he was a man, held aloft only by wax and feathers, the sun did its damage and Icarus plunged into the sea. Marlowe, Goethe, and others gave us Dr. Faustus, who willingly traded his soul to the devil for an entire harvest from the tree of knowledge and the love of one woman. "Sweet Analytics, 'tis thou hast ravished me,"

DA VINCI

Although human subtlety makes a variety of inventions... it will never devise an invention more beautiful more simple or more direct than does nature, because in her inventions, nothing is lacking and nothing is superfluous.

LEONARDO DA VINCI

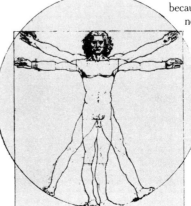

Marlowe's Faustus cries among his books and crucibles, moments before the devil gets his due. Even Prospero, Shakespeare's gentle island magician, living alone with his daughter, his spirits, and his books, must give up his staff, symbol of his knowledge and the magic he works with it, to rejoin the company of other men.

Surely today's wonders, brought to us courtesy of science and technology, are more dazzling than anything that ever tempted Faustus and friends. The real accomplishments of science—longer, healthier, more comfortable lives—dwarf the dreams of times gone by. While alchemists struggled to make gold, Leonardo (and generations of scientists who followed him) turned Icarus' madness into sanity. Man can fly.

When Saturn-bound Pioneer II reached its destination in the late summer of 1979, it had travelled more than six years and two billion miles. Even so, its pilots back on earth could guide the craft so easily—by means of a communications system—that it could pass in and out of Saturn's rings unimpeded. Considering that Pioneer II's collision with even one rock, no bigger than a baseball, could have destroyed the craft, such a communications system becomes less an act of providence and more an awesome example of flawless, professional engineering.

Meanwhile, back on earth, we perfectly ordinary mortals balance our checkbooks with a computing device that costs considerably less than half a sack of groceries. Yet, that same device is so sophisticated in its capabilities that no one but the maddest prophet could have predicted a generation ago we would one day tuck it in purse or pocket.

Telephony has more than kept pace with other technologies. If our telephones are already served by an electronic switching system, our calls can cheerfully follow us wher-

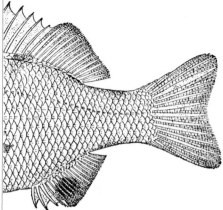

POGO
Thank goodness modern convenience is a thing of the remote future.
POGO

CLARKE
We must not, however, commit the only too common mistake of equating mere physical expansion or even increasing scientific knowledge with 'progress,' however that may be defined. Only little minds are impressed by sheer size and number. There would be no virtue in possessing the Universe if it brought neither wisdom nor happiness. Yet possess it we must, at least in spirit, if we are ever to answer the questions that men have asked in vain since history began.
ARTHUR C. CLARKE

CLARKE
Any smoothly functioning technology will have the appearance of magic.
ARTHUR C. CLARKE

MARLOWE
"Sweet Analytics, 'tis thou hast ravished me."
CHRISTOPHER MARLOWE, DR FAUSTUS

EINSTEIN

My religion consists of a humble admiration of the illimitable superior spirit who reveals himself in the slight details we are able to perceive with our frail and feeble mind.

ALBERT EINSTEIN

SHAKESPEARE

Now my charms are all o'erthrown, And what strength I have's mine own, Which is most faint.

WILLIAM SHAKESPEARE, PROSPERO IN *THE TEMPEST*

BRADBURY

At base, science is no more than an investigation of a miracle we can never explain, and art is an interpretation of that miracle.

RAY BRADBURY, *THE MARTIAN CHRONICLES*

ever we go. Long distance rates have become so reasonable that the weekly call to Grandma is a far more economic indulgence than a decent ice cream soda.

And yet, and yet . . . What does all this progress buy us? An unparalleled standard of living, more time to spend with friends and family. That's what some argue. Just in this century, we've moved from a standard six-day work week to five days.

Another faction argues with equal vehemence that what some technology has bought us is a befouled environment, a crushing lack of privacy, and a gnawing fear that our jobs could be taken over tomorrow by R2D2 and his cohorts.

Nonsense, the other side reasons back. Don't condemn science for social problems. Ask the survivors of New York's Lower East Side at the turn of this century about "privacy." Read up on sewage problems and air pollution of coal-fired cities a century ago.

Some have given up the argument altogether. They eschew chemicals in favor of compost, universities in favor of solitary reading by candlelight, and indoor plumbing in favor of privies under the stars. Others don't see a fight at all. Economic realities dictate, they insist, that we push ahead uncovering more and more, regardless of the consequences.

But for many, there's another, a middle ground, much like the third alternative Huxley wanted to present to the Savage: Science and technology ought to serve people. Properly exploited, technology should solve problems, not create them. If technology has posed terrible riddles about the environment, then surely it holds the answers. And, if a job can be replaced by a machine, perhaps that job is not a uniquely human job. Should people be wasted on jobs that can be performed by gadgets and circuits?

In some ways, telecommunications technology occupies

BRADBURY

So we wait quietly for the day when
the machines are dented junk and then
we hope to walk by and say, here we are,
to those who survive this war, and we'll
say, "Have you come to your senses now?
Perhaps a few books will do you
some good."

RAY BRADBURY, *FAHRENHEIT 451*

DE SAINT-EXUPERY

It is only with the
heart that one can see
rightly; what is
essential is in-
visible to
the eye.

ANTOINE
DE SAINT-EXUPERY,
THE LITTLE PRINCE

VONNEGUT

Makes you feel kind of creepy,
don't it . . . watching them keys go
up and down? You can almost
see a ghost sitting there playing
his heart out.

KURT VONNEGUT, *PLAYER PIANO*

a more comfortable position than most: It's clean and it's energy-efficient. More importantly, telephony is a technology of choice. For people desiring only the basics, POTS (plain old telephone service, in the Bell System) will always be available. But for those who want more, today's technology—and tomorrow's—offer a dazzling array of sophisticated services.

And, even the most cursory examination of the possibilities telecommunications offers for the future suggests solutions to some of today's most pressing problems. As many work, shopping, and education functions are managed from home "communications centers," the bumper-to-bumper, rush hour traffic jam could become an endangered species. More flexibility about where we perform what functions could help solve child care problems. The list (See "The Wired Home," "The Wired Office," and "The Wired World" in this booklet) goes on and on.

Bell Labs' Dean Gillette calls telecommunications an interactive technology because it simply allows other forces to have an impact on people. "Telephony, by itself, is not centralizing or decentralizing. It is simply a facilitator." The telephone business' traditional role has been putting people together to do whatever they needed or wanted to do. In a world where misunderstandings and missed communications can be cataclysmic, that facilitator's role has never been more critical.

Advances in data communications point to a future alive with possibilities. And those possibilities suggest new and different ways for people to live, work, and play.

Will those ways be better? They certainly could be. "We are" says Prospero, at *Tempest's* end, "such stuff as dreams are made on." As far as the imagination can see, telecommunications holds the promise of pleasant dreams.

LINDBERGH

*If we can combine our
knowledge of science
with the wisdom of
wildness, if we can
nurture civilization
through roots in the
primitive, man's poten-
tialities appear to be
unbounded.*

CHARLES LINDBERGH

THE SECOND INDUSTRIAL REVOLUTION

by GENE BYLINSKY *November, 1975*

Less than thirty years ago, electrical engineer J. Presper Eckert Jr. and physicist John W. Mauchly, and helpers, laboriously built the world's first electronic digital computer. Their ENIAC (Electronic Numerical Integrator and Computer) was a fickle monster that weighed thirty tons and ran on 18,000 vacuum tubes—when it ran. But it started the computer revolution.

Now under way is a new expansion of electronics into our lives, a second computer revolution that will transform ordinary products and create many new ones. The instrument of change is an electronic data-processing machine so tiny that it could easily have been lost in the socket of one of those ENIAC tubes. This remarkable device is the microcomputer, also known as the computer-on-a-chip. In its basic configuration, it consists of just that—a complex of circuits on a chip of silicon about the size of the first three letters in the word ENIAC as printed here. Yet even a medium-strength microcomputer can perform 100,000 calculations a second, twenty times as many as ENIAC could.

This smallest of all data-processing machines was invented six years ago, but its mass applications are just beginning to explode, setting off reverberations that will affect work and play, the profitability and productivity of corporations, and the nature of the computer industry itself. For the microcomputer provides an awesome amount of computer power in a package that in its simplest form costs less than $10 bought in quantity and easily fits inside a matchbox.

Unlike the familiar older computers that come in their own boxes, the microcomputer is mounted on a small board that can be made to fit easily and unobtrusively into a corner of an electric typewriter, a butcher's scale, a cash register, a microwave oven, a gas pump, a traffic light, a complex scientific instrument such as a gas chromatograph, and any of a myriad other devices whose capabilities already are being enhanced by these slices of electronic brainpower. Soon microcomputers will start replacing wheels, gears, and mechanical relays in a variety of control applications, because it's more efficient to move electrons around than mechanical parts.

To cite these applications and capabilities, as well as many other uses to come in the home, the factory, and the automobile, is to do only pale justice to this marvelous invention. What sets any computer apart from every other kind of machine is its stored and alterable program, which allows one computer to perform many different tasks in response to program changes. Now the microcomputer imparts this power, in a compact form and at a low price, to many other machines and devices.

In the most common form of microcomputer, furthermore, a user can change the program simply by unplugging a tiny memory chip and putting a new one in its place. To show off this versatility, Pro-Log Corp. of Monterey, California, built a demonstration apparatus that in its original version is a digital clock; when a program chip that runs the clock is removed and another is put in its place, the thing suddenly starts belting out a tinny version of the theme from *The Sting*.

Besides providing versatility for users, the microcomputer makes possible large economies in manufacturing. Now a manufacturer can buy a standard microcomputer system for many different products and use a different program chip with each. Furthermore, a microcomputer that replaces, say, fifty integrated circuits does away with about 1,800 interconnections—where most failures occur in electronics. The microcomputer, in other words, is one of those rare innovations that at the same time reduces the cost of manufacturing *and* enhances both the capabilities and value of the product.

The microcomputer is the logical end result of the electronics industry's drive to miniaturize. The industry has galloped through three generations of components in as many decades. In the late 1950's, the transistor replaced the vacuum tube. Within a few years, the transistor itself gave way to "large-scale integration," or LSI, the technique that now places thousands of tiny transistors—an integrated circuit—on a sliver of silicon only a fraction of an inch on a side. LSI made possible the suitcase-sized minicomputer.

The semiconductor logic circuit, of course, contained the seed of the microcomputer, since the chip had logic elements on it—the transistors. But the

individual chips were designed to perform limited tasks. Accordingly, the central processing units of large computers were made up of hundreds, or thousands, of integrated circuits.

Logic chips were also employed for control or arithmetic functions in specialized applications. In what became known as "hard-wired logic" systems, chips and other individual components were soldered into a rigid pattern on a so-called printed-circuit board. The fixed interconnections served as the program.

The electronic calculator, in all but the latest versions, uses hard-wired logic. The arithmetic functions, or the operating program instructions, are embedded in the chips, while the application program is in the user's head—his instructions yield the desired calculations.

What Hoff saw

A young Intel engineer, M. E. Hoff Jr., envisioned a different way of employing the new electronic capabilities. In 1969 he found himself in charge of a project that Intel took on for Busicom, a Japanese calculator company. Busicom wanted Intel to produce calculator chips of Japanese design. The logic circuits were spread around eleven chips and the complexity of the design would have taxed Intel's capabilities—it was then a small company.

Hoff saw a way to improve on the Japanese design by making a bold technological leap. In the intricate innards of a memory chip, Hoff knew, it was possible to store a program to run a minuscule computing circuit.

In his preliminary design, Hoff condensed the layout onto three chips. He put the computer's "brain," its central processing unit, on a single chip of silicon. That was possible because the semiconductor industry had developed a means of inscribing very complex circuits on tiny surfaces. A master drawing, usually 500 times as large as the actual chip, is reduced photographically to microminiature size. The images are transferred to the chip by a technique similar to photoengraving.

The central processing unit on a chip became known as the microprocessor. To the

Research associate: Alicia Hills Moore

The big companies rushed to get on board by "second-sourcing" —i.e., copying—Intel's microcomputers.

Chips to help the blind

microprocessor Hoff attached two memory chips, one to move data in and out of the CPU and one to provide the program to drive the CPU. Hoff now had in hand a rudimentary general-purpose computer that not only could run a complex calculator but also could control an elevator or a set of traffic lights, and perform many other tasks, depending on its program. The microcomputer was slower than minicomputers, but it could be mass-produced as a component, on the same high-volume lines where Intel made memory chips—a development that would suddenly put the semiconductor company into the computer business.

After other Intel engineers who took over the detailed design work got through with it, Hoff's invention contained 2,250 microminiaturized transistors on a chip slightly less than one-sixth of an inch long and one-eighth of an inch wide, and each of those microscopic transistors was roughly equal to an ENIAC vacuum tube. Intel labeled the microprocessor chip 4004, and the whole microcomputer MCS-4 (microcomputer system 4). "The 4004 will probably be as famous as the ENIAC," says an admiring Motorola executive. Despite its small size, the 4004 just about matched ENIAC's computational power. It also matched the capability of an I.B.M. machine of the early 1960's that sold for $30,000 and whose central processing unit took up the space of an office desk.

Replacing hardware with words

For logic and systems designers the appearance of the microcomputer brought with it a dramatic change in the way they employed electronics. They could now replace all those rigid hard-wired logic systems with microcomputers, because they could store program sequences in the labyrinthine circuits of the memory chip instead of using individual logic chips and discrete components to implement the program. Engineers thus could substitute program code words for hardware parts.

At first the semiconductor industry showed surprisingly little interest in this great leap in its technology. Semiconductor manufacturers had made so many extravagant promises in the past that the industry seemed to have become immune to claims of real advances. To speed the adoption of microcomputers, Intel undertook to recast the thinking of the industrial-design engineers—the company taught 5,000 engineers the use of the microcomputer in the early Seventies and another 5,000 or so later on.

Once these engineers started ordering the tiny computers in some quantity, the big companies rushed to get on board by "second-sourcing"—i.e., copying—Intel's microcomputers. Second-sourcing is a common practice in the semiconductor industry, widely accepted by the companies involved. It works to the benefit of the user in establishing a competitive source for the component as well as a backup for the original manufacturer. In fact, users normally demand second-sourcing.

Second-sourcing microcomputers proved to be a complex task, however. What's more, Intel kept moving. It followed up the 4004 with a more capacious 8008 model in 1972, and toward the end of 1973 brought out its second-generation microcomputer, the 8080. This was twenty times faster than the 4004. Even then most competitors had no microcomputers of their own to offer. The first real competition to the 8080 was Motorola's 6800, which came a year afterward. The late starters finally began to catch up this year.

They are battling for a market that so far is fairly small—this year it will amount to only about $50 million. But it is expected to expand to $150 million next year, and to reach $450 million by 1980.* One estimate is that consumer-product uses will account for about one-third of that market. Microcomputers are expected to start appearing in automobiles. Ford Motor Co. has found that microcomputer-run controls can cut fuel consumption by as much as 20 percent under test conditions. In the home, microcomputer controls could result in savings on electric and heating bills.

*The current estimate for 1980 is $550 million.

For the military, the tiny computers promise the evolution of more versatile weapons. In medical electronics, they open up possibilities for compact and less costly diagnostic instruments. There are indications that in conjunction with complex optical and mechanical devices, microcomputers could help restore vision for some of the blind. In one project, a microprocessor chip will be embedded in an eyeglass frame to decode visual information from artificial "eyes" and send it to the brain.

From 200,000 to 20 million

There seems to be little disagreement that the microcomputer is close to being an ultimate semiconductor circuit and that it now sets the direction for semiconductor technology. Everyone agrees, furthermore, that there will be a whole spectrum of microcomputers aimed at different applications, with many companies sharing the anticipated big market.

The ability of users to operate a whole hierarchy of computers, from a big host machine to the microcomputer far down in the organization, will speed the trend toward "distributed" computer power. Texas Instruments, one of the late starters in the game, sees as a result a computer world polarized into giant machines and huge numbers of microcomputers, with medium-sized computers diminishing in importance. Some specialists see computers of the future evolving into modular processor systems based on microcomputers, with many of their programs embedded in microcomputer memories, replacing expensive software.

In its impact, the microcomputer will rival its illustrious predecessors, the vacuum tube, the transistor, and the integrated-circuit logic chip. So far, probably no more than 10 percent of the tiny computer's potential applications have reached production stage. Today, nearly thirty years after the debut of the ENIAC, there are about 200,000 digital computers in the world. Ten years from now, thanks to the microcomputer, there may be 20 million. ▣

THE PROMISE OF NEOINDUSTRIALIZATION

By Mary H. Wayne

Much as a severe wood shortage prompted the development of coal-based technologies in the early 1800s and gave rise to that society-transforming phenomenon known as the Industrial Revolution, recent changes in the supply and price of raw materials are spurring the development of new electricity-based production technologies. In the first two parts of this three-part series on neoindustrialization, author Mary Wayne examined this similarity and explained why these emerging technologies may foreshadow a second revolution—a "neoindustrial" revolution. In this final article, she explores how such a revolution could transform society.

"Neoindustrialization" describes a new type of economic growth beginning to occur in the United States and other advanced nations. Accompanied by the soft hum of computers rather than the noisy hiss and clatter of steam engines, it promises to boost manufacturing output in ways that are quieter, cleaner, and far more efficient than earlier production methods.

The resource base of neoindustrial production is diverse. It moves beyond heavy dependence on fossil fuels and on the raw materials used in the past. Many neoindustrial technologies will be powered by electricity generated from a growing variety of power sources: not only from traditional fuels such as coal, but from renewable resources such as the sun, the wind, and the movement of water.

The new production methods are similarly diverse, especially those that are electricity-based. Many can be fine-tuned to their special applications. Industrial production methods in the future likely will display a flexibility that contrasts sharply with the unwieldy steam power methods of the industrial age.

Just as shifts in the resource base and in production methods have marked major socioeconomic shifts in the past, neoindustrial society may be quite different from the industrial society in which most Americans have grown up. To supply a framework for speculating about what may lie ahead, let us look back for a moment at the Industrial Revolution and the transformations it brought.

Features of Industrial Society

One of the first changes was the centralization of work under the factory system. To find gainful employment, people left their pursuits on the land and presented themselves at the place where the capital and the concentrated energy sources necessary to run high-volume industrial production came together: the factory.

This centralization of work in the factory led inevitably to centralization of life in the city. In all nations since England's early example, urban growth has been a direct consequence of industrial production methods. In a traditional industrial system, it has been axiomatic that labor, like capital and energy, must be concentrated in one place for production to occur.

Standardization was another consequence of industrial technology. The cheapest way to do things with these technologies was uniformly, and on a large scale. Both products and manufacturing methods became increasingly standardized as industry expanded. This uniformity eventually extended far beyond the factory, pervading styles of housing, dress, education, speech, and entertainment—in short, the entire industrial culture.

The need for concentration of capital meant those who had worked at home as independent producers under the preindustrial system of domestic manufacture could no longer do so. Access

Mary H. Wayne, a free-lance writer based in San Francisco, specializes in energy issues.

Reprinted from *Electric Perspectives*, Spring 1983, Edison Electric Institute.

to ownership of the expensive new power machinery required wealth. Under such a highly capital-intensive system of production, most people were excluded; they had no choice but to become wage workers in the employ of those who owned the machines. This became a feature of industrial societies regardless of their economic or political structure—that is, regardless of whether the machinery belonged to individuals, to groups, or to the state.

A certain increase in environmental pollution was another inevitable consequence of the new production methods. Intensive burning of fossil fuels was so much a part of the industrial system that the belching smokestack came to symbolize prosperity. As soot-showering factories turned out more and better goods for the average citizen, most people seemed willing to accept some dirt as the price of progress. It was not until much later, during the 1960s, that environmental preservation became a major topic of public concern.

Industrial society, then, can be characterized very roughly in terms of these five broad tendencies: centralization of work in factories and other production facilities; urbanization of the population; standardization of products and procedures for large-scale production; exclusion of many would-be small producers from the system; and gradual pollution of the environment. Some observers believe that all these tendencies are likely to be challenged by the advent of neoindustrial society —by what various thinkers are calling "the technetronic age," "postindustrial society," or "the third wave."[1]

Already the arrival of a mature industrial economy has signaled certain shifts. Today's workers enjoy far more leisure than their nineteenth-century forebears did and still maintain a far higher standard of living. If we take the 1890 workweek as a standard, the modern worker can be viewed as receiving a four-month paid vacation every year. The average American workweek has fallen from nearly 62 hours in the 1890s to around 40 hours or less today. The result is about 1200 extra hours of free time per worker per year.[2]

What's more, people begin working later in life today, after years of extended schooling. And they have more leisure years in retirement. Producing

goods and services, even at rising levels, no longer requires the full-time life-long effort it once did.

Part of the reason is a fundamental shift in the way work is accomplished. Back in the 1890s, 90 percent of all Americans still worked with their hands. Today, various estimates place that figure between 20 and 40 percent —in any case, a massive decline. According to management theorist Peter F. Drucker, "The substitution of knowledge for manual effort as the productive resource in work is the greatest change in the history of work. . . . This change is still in progress, but in the industrially advanced countries, especially in the United States, it has already completely changed society."[3]

The emergence of knowledge workers as the predominant type in the labor force of a mature industrial economy presages greater changes to come, according to author Alvin Toffler. He is among the futurists who foresee neo-industrial production methods promoting the evolution of radically new workstyles. He envisions major work changes occurring in the factory, the office, and—perhaps most important of all—the home.

The Factory of the Future

The factory of the future, in Toffler's view, will be very much like the high-technology Hewlett-Packard electronics production facility he visited in Colorado. This factory is staffed about 40 percent by knowledge workers: engineers, programmers, technicians, and managerial and clerical personnel. It is quiet and filled with greenery. The workers have flexible hours and dress as they wish on this very unusual factory floor.

"As I entered the building," Toffler writes, "I remembered again the factories in which I had once worked, with all their clatter and roar, their dirt, smoke, and suppressed anger. . . . My old companions in their heavy steel-tipped shoes, dirty overalls, and workingmen's caps would find it difficult, I believe, to think of the place as a factory at all."[4]

The very nature of blue-collar work is expected to change in these new factories. Physical strain and danger will be almost eliminated, but greater mental effort will be required. Gone will be

The very nature of blue collar work is expected to change in these new factories.

the days when a worker could perform routine tasks with his hands while his mind was free for conversation or daydreaming. Operating and monitoring computerized control panels for industrial robots, which will do most of the heavy physical work, will call for advanced skills and intensified concentration. Even the factory production worker will thus become a knowledge worker.[5]

The trend in this direction received a recent push when IBM unveiled its new industrial robot system featuring a computer-controlled arm that can move in as many as six directions. The arm, mounted in a rectangular frame, is versatile in its applications. It has already been used to insert electronic parts into circuit boards, assemble mechanical parts for word processors and printers, drill holes in aircraft components, and test the wiring of large mainframe computers.[6] Furthermore, the computer's ability to integrate all the diverse operations involved in producing a particular item—say, a camera or a motorcycle—can transform conventional production methods. The computer can allocate resources, speed materials flow, and schedule operations, in addition to directing much of the actual production work.

But innovative manufacturing operations such as the Colorado plant are still rare in the United States. This is so despite the fact that much of the technology that makes these operations possible was first developed here. Foreign nations have taken the lead in applying new electrotechnology, especially computerized systems, to the manufacturing process.

A West German company that uses computer-integrated methods to produce titanium parts for Tornado fighter planes has been called the most advanced and flexible machine system in the world today.[7] About 75 to 80 percent of the cutting work is handled by machines, in contrast to the usual 15 to 30 percent in a conventional operation. And the plane is produced in 18 months rather than 30, with fewer machine tools and fewer skilled machinists required.

But most of all it is the Japanese who are forging ahead with new manufacturing applications in a way that has become increasingly worrisome to

their American competitors. Several Japanese companies run their plants 24 hours a day, with only computer-controlled machines at work during the night shift. Further, some are close to perfecting computerized systems that can operate around the clock.

Factory work will become much less labor-intensive and much more knowledge-intensive. Industrial robots will man the production lines, and workers will operate and monitor the robots.

Whereas the conventional factory achieves only about 15 percent utilization of its capital equipment, the 24-hour unmanned system being developed by the Japanese is expected to provide utilization in the vastly improved range of 75 to 80 percent.[8]

The first patents for industrial robots were filed in the United States around 1954, but again, the Japanese have taken the lead in applying robot technology. By the early 1980s, Japan had roughly 14,000 programmable industrial robots in operation, compared with only 3500 to 4000 working in the United States. Japanese companies typically make their own robots, tailoring them to the needs of their particular manufacturing systems. For example, Yamaha makes arc-welding robots that work on its motorcycle assembly lines. Seiko makes robots that assemble watches. Pentel builds robots that put together felt-tip pens, and Okamura's robots assemble office furniture. These specialized robots are often sold to other members of the same industry once their usefulness has been established.[9]

An American management consultant who has studied Japanese industrial practices emphasizes the critical role of adapting new technologies—not only computers and robots, but lasers and the great variety of other manufacturing innovations—to American industry's very basic problems with productivity and cost control. "It's precisely in those . . . areas," says consultant Ira Magaziner, "that we in this country have been so weak—that is, in taking new inventions and applying them to existing industries for existing problems."[10]

In the United States, several companies are offering industry the latest in applied electrotechnology: packages of factory automation products and services. For example, General Electric offers its new GEnet, a local communications network for signaling and data-sharing between computers and other electronics equipment, as "the spinal cord and central nervous system of an automated factory."[11] The slogan GE has been using to stir industrial customers is "automate, emigrate, or evaporate."

Hughes Aircraft Company, for example, is spending $240 million over the next five years on computer-aided manufacturing systems. This capital investment is part of a $1.5 billion program for expansion and modernization to improve productivity. According to Hughes, computer-aided manufacturing is improving productivity in the electronics business by as much as a factor of ten.

But market resistance in the United States to new capital spending for such systems has remained stiff, especially in a recessionary economy. The investment in existing systems is huge, and the risk of switching is substantial in terms of lost production time or uncertain product quality. The tendency has been to patch and upgrade conventional systems rather than risk investment in something new.

So the neoindustrial factory will probably come slowly to the United States, though many experts consider its eventual arrival inevitable. Meanwhile, electrotechnology on a smaller scale is penetrating the office environment at a rapid pace. The investment in new computers, word processors, optical scanners, and telecommunications systems is less costly than an investment in manufacturing equipment. And the payoff in increased office productivity is almost immediate.

The Paperless Office

Conventional office productivity increased a bare 4 percent during the entire decade of the 1970s.[12] At the same

Hughes Aircraft expects computer-aided design and manufacturing systems to increase productivity significantly—perhaps by as much as a factor of ten.

time, computers developed the ability to perform a great variety of office functions at a steadily decreasing cost per function. Taking advantage of these advances in electrotechnology, particularly for the information transactions estimated to consume the bulk of the workday for most office personnel, has become the obvious way to boost the efficiency of office operations.

By 1983, about five million computers or data terminals were installed in American offices. The first applications have been to computerize repetitious, routine tasks such as taking inventories or managing payrolls. And now, the electronic word processor is moving in to replace the conventional typewriter. So far, only about 10 percent of the typewriters in the nation's largest corporations have been replaced, but the trend is unmistakable. The word processors linked to the company's computers become part of one big electronic network that can carry communications almost instantly, not only within a single office but among different offices and organizations. Wall-sized two-way videoconferencing screens are expected to make travel to meetings unnecessary.

The "paperless" office of the future might, for example, microfilm all incoming information and store it for computer retrieval. Paper documents could then be discarded. Information generated within the office would never see paper at all. The person originating a memo or report could feed it into an electronic word processor, either by using the keyboard available on today's systems or by dictating into the voice-recognition attachment that is now under development. Then, instead of the communication being printed and mailed out, it could be transmitted directly to the recipient's word processing terminal via the growing telecommunications network that uses telephone lines to move the data electronically.

As Toffler points out, the new equipment can record a communication, correct it, duplicate it, send it, and file it automatically on the machine's tape or disk storage system "in what amounts virtually to a single process. Speed increases. Costs go down. And the five steps are compressed into one."[13]

The development of the new office technology naturally raises some questions about who will be doing what in the future. Will executives actually learn to type so they can key some of their communications directly into the network and be able to tap information from that network, without having to rely on an intermediary? Will that traditional intermediary, the secretary, then become a technically skilled administrator of electronic systems? These and other questions attend the prospect of increasingly automated work procedures in both office and factory. What will happen to all the people who perform repetitious manual tasks when "smart" machines have taken over the work?

Indications on this point are equivocal. When automation was first introduced on a limited scale several decades ago, there was fear of massive unemployment. But employment in the high-technology nations actually expanded. In the United States and in Japan, investment in new technology during the 1960s and early 1970s correlated with growth in employment. Great Britain, which had the lowest investment in new machinery among economically advanced nations during that period, showed the greatest loss in jobs.[14]

New technology may eventually create as many jobs as it destroys. It can, in fact, give birth to whole new industries. The computer industry is a case in point. Millions of people are now employed manufacturing, selling, servicing, and programming the machines that did not even exist outside the research laboratory a few short decades ago. As our growing level of technology supports ever higher living standards, the demand for previously unavailable goods and services likely will create more such jobs in the future.

The snag for today's displaced workers is that qualifying for these jobs will often require skills that they do not have. The consequent need for retraining is probably going to be a fact of life for the neoindustrial workforce.

As technology expands to offer new work options, many people will have to accept the necessity for career changes to escape the decline of certain types of employment. Probably hardest hit will be production workers in

The development of new office technology naturally raises some questions about who will be doing what in the future.

traditional manufacturing fields. In Ohio's now depressed Mahoning Valley, long a steel center, the cost squeeze on combustion steel-making has idled some 50,000 workers. And in California, the closing of at least 400 automobile, steel, and other heavy industrial plants since 1980 has forced another 73,000 workers out of their jobs.

The trend toward fewer jobs in the smokestack industries is nationwide. Because these industries need to automate to survive in the face of foreign competition, many of these jobs will never return, even in an economic upswing. The main hope for displaced workers will be retraining, either to upgrade their skills for the increasingly computerized new jobs in their own industries or to take advantage of emerging opportunities in other fields.

The Electronic Cottage

An attractive and increasingly viable option for many people is the prospect of working at home. Parents who need to care for small children during working hours, physically disabled people, and many other people who simply prefer not to commute to an office every day are finding that they can still work through computer terminals located in their homes. Many are already receiving regular paychecks from their companies for performing tasks such as bookkeeping or computer programming in these electronic extensions of the company office. Banks and insurance companies, as information-processing enterprises, are some of the first to experiment with this new workstyle.

Toffler refers to this phenomenon as the "electronic cottage"—"a return to cottage industry on a new, higher, electronic basis."[15] And he believes that this trend need not be limited to office work. The parallel shift from industrial to neoindustrial technologies in manufacturing will also reduce the number of production workers who have to manipulate physical goods. "This means," says Toffler, "that even in the manufacturing sector an increasing amount of work is being done that —given the right configuration of telecommunications and other equipment—could be accomplished anywhere, including one's own living room."[16]

He cites the case of an electronics manufacturing firm in which fully half the employees now handle information rather than physical components. Managers estimate that 25 percent of their employees could work at home today with existing technology, and that in a few more years virtually all the manufacturing firm's knowledge workers, or about 50 percent of the regular payroll, could make their contributions to the manufacture of electronic switching gear directly from their homes. Since knowledge workers in all fields are a growing segment of the work force, the possibility for both business and industrial employees to work at home seems increasingly realistic.

The workplace, then, is expected to be revolutionized by neoindustrial technology. Factories will not look, sound, smell, or feel like traditional factories as the new electrotechnologies gradually replace the throbbing steam boilers and noisy, heavy machinery of the past. In the office, the sound of clattering typewriters will give way to the quiet hum of electronic word processing equipment. And more and more homes will have computer terminals where the inhabitants can not only play games or analyze their budgets, but also perform work to earn a living.

Factories will not look, sound, smell, or feel like traditional factories. . . .

Notes
1. Alvin Toffler, *The Third Wave* (New York: Bantam Books, 1981), p. 9.
2. Juanita M. Kreps and Joseph J. Spengler, "The Leisure Component of Economic Growth," in Howard R. Bowen and Garth L. Mangum, eds., *Automation and Economic Progress* (Englewood Cliffs, New Jersey: Prentice-Hall, 1966), p. 128–129.
3. Peter F. Drucker, *Technology, Management, and Society* (New York: Harper and Row, 1970), p. 81.
4. See Toffler, pp. 179–181.
5. Daniel Goleman, "The Electronic Rorschach," *Psychology Today*, February 1983, pp. 40–41.
6. "IBM Is Ready to Ship Its 7565 Robot System. . . ," *The Wall Street Journal*, January 25, 1983, p. 12.
7. American Association of Engineering Studies, position paper on productivity and innovation, as reviewed by Lucien E. Smartt, *Public Utilities Fortnightly*, October 14, 1982, p. 8.
8. See Smartt, p. 8.
9. "Nipponese Know-How," *Science News*, November 6, 1982, p. 299.
10. Ira Magaziner, as quoted in "Nipponese Know-How," p. 297.
11. Lauro Landro, "GE Promotes Factory Automation. . . ." *The Wall Street Journal*, October 21, 1982, p. 33.
12. See Toffler, p. 187.
13. See Toffler, p. 189.
14. See Toffler, p. 192.
15. See Toffler, p. 194.
16. See Toffler, p. 196.

HIGH TECHNOLOGY:
THE NEW SHAPE OF LIFE AND LIVING

INTRODUCTION AND OVERVIEW

TECHNETRONIC: A society shaped by the impact of technology and electronics, and especially by the impact of computers and communications on its structure, culture, psychology, and economics.
—Webster's New Collegiate Dictionary

"O mama, come into the drawing room; there is a man in there playing the piano with his hands."
—John Philip Sousa, "The Menace of Mechanical Music," 1906

"Have you seen Michael Jackson's new song?"
—American teen-ager, circa 1984

In 1946 there was only one of them—ENIAC. Ten years later, there were 600 computers. By 1966 there were 30,000; by 1976, 400,000; and today, more than six million. It is estimated that by 1990 half of all American households will have a computer. New technologies—but especially computers and telecommunications—will create a totally new human environment.

Computer and communication technologies have joined together to produce new hybrid technologies that deliver home-based information services. Sometime in the 1990s we will have access to a new band of frequencies—the 30/20 GigaHertz (GHz) frequencies. We will also be able to build more powerful satellites and less expensive earth stations. These advances will allow almost every business, school, community center, and hospital to install satellite receiving stations, giving them access to the new satellites efficiently and cheaply.

Satellite technology offers several advantages over the telephone as a communication system. Communication from one location can be sent via satellite to multiple locations simultaneously. The system is simple, requiring only an earth station at each location in the network. And communication costs do not vary with distance.

A NEW HUMAN ENVIRONMENT

Among the possible results of advances in hybrid computer-telecommunications technologies are these:

- Social institutions, including business and government, could be restructured horizontally, rather than vertically.

- The "electronic cottage" could restructure family relationships—permitting, for example, both parents to be part-time workers and part-time parents.

- Telecommuting may promote the decentralization of government and business, enabling many persons to work at home.

- More goods and services will be purchased using the telephone and interactive cable television, requiring consumers to develop new skills.

Computers could have an equalizing and democratizing effect on society because they can be used anywhere, even in remote areas. A student in a rural community can plug into a satellite and retrieve information from a public library or private data base in New York City or Los Angeles. Potentially, computers could mean equal access to useful information.

But at the same time, there is the possibility that grave new inequalities could be created—a social division between those who possess computer literacy and those who do not. One of these two possibilities —equality and inequality—is obviously preferable to the other. One of the challenges facing our society today is to promote the development of the preferable option.

The readings that follow describe the contours of the emerging technetronic society, its promise, and its challenges.

THE READINGS

"Home, Office, Society" is a vision of a not-so-distant future in which reality is indistinguishable from science fiction.

"The Computer Moves In" is an account of the thousands of quiet revolutions occurring on the farm, in the factory, office, and home as a result of the second computer revolution.

"Reinventing the Computer" describes the effort by countries and companies to exploit a faster, smarter technology in hopes of dominating a $500 billion-a-year industry.

"Tomorrow's Computer May Reproduce Itself" documents the effort by computer scientists to prove that someday it will be possible to create an organic computer, or "biochip."

"The Born-Again Technology" details the revolution in telecommunications and the efforts by governments to help their industries capture new world markets.

"Sounding the Battle Cry" describes the economic and social impact of the revolution in telecommunications, as well as the status of world competition since the breakup of AT&T on January 1, 1984.

"TV's Higher Tech Future" identifies new developments in television technology, including high definition television (HDTV) and digital processing.

"How Teletext and Videotex Will Shape Society" explains the use of two new telecommunications technologies, and speculates on their impact on life and work.

"Future Energy Technologies" describes several long-range programs now under way to develop new technologies for generating the electricity our nation needs.

"The Next Step into Space" outlines NASA's plans for a permanent manned space station, and the uses that are foreseen for it.

"Robots Are Playing New Roles as They Take a Hand in Our Affairs" documents 20 years of achievement in robotics, and the optimism that characterizes the field today.

REFERENCES

The Electronic Cottage, by John Deken, describes everyday living with personal computers, emphasizing what *you* will be able to do with them. William Morrow & Company paperback, 1982.

Understanding Media: The Extensions of Man, by Marshall McLuhan, explores the unintended, largely misunderstood, impact of the media on our lives. McGraw-Hill paperback, originally published in 1964.

Engines of the Mind: A History of the Computer, by Joel M. Shurkin, is a popularized, clearly written history of computing. Norton hardcover, 1984.

HOME, OFFICE, SOCIETY

Imagine Corbusier's machine for living come to life! Imagine a complex communications system of home management, an on-line design to feed, clean, warm, cool, and entertain the entire household from a single set of controls. Imagine all that and still, tomorrow's surface is barely scratched. For instance:

Food, glorious food

Breakfast in bed? Why not? Use the bedside phone to turn on the coffee, warm the sweet rolls, and send the oranges through the juicer. Then, all it takes is a sleepy volunteer to bring it upstairs. (Unless, of course, you've programmed your electronic housekeeper to load the tray and bring it bedside). Oh, and while you've got the phone handy, turn on the stereo. Let's have Frank Sinatra join us for breakfast—or Kiss or Leontyne Price.

It's beginning to look a lot like Christmas

 Shopping at home has replaced a lot of temper-fraying holiday trips to the stores. Dad summons up the L. L. Bean catalogue to shop for Mom. He finds a pair of fishing boots he thinks she'll like, asks the system to turn them this way and that so he can get all views, asks to see them on a model. Then, when he's satisfied, orders them wrapped and delivered. Oh, yes, he also pays for them, punching in his checking account number, and the funds are automatically transferred.

Neither rain nor snow nor

While he's at the screen, he might just as well pay the rest of the bills. So, Dad calls up the last two weeks' mail, looks at each bill on the screen, and orders up the right amount of money to be moved from the family's account to Macy's, his credit cards, the mortgage company, and the dentist. He needs records of some of these transactions for tax purposes, so he asks for, and gets instantly, hard copy. To his surprise, the bank signals him that there's something left in the account. So, he dials up his brokerage account and places an order for the hot prospect Mom's had her eye on.

I bid two hearts

 Though all four members of the family are home tonight, Sue's the only bridge player in the gang. Oh, Mom and Joe fool around with it, but they're hardly any challenge to her. So, milk and cookies in hand, she rings up telebridge. Because telebridge knows exactly how Sue's played her last 1500 hands, she's instantly matched with three other players in the system of equal ability. The fact that one happens to be a New Yorker, one a Georgian, one a Canadian, and one an Australian with insomnia hardly matters. They're all looking at the same hand on the screen; play commences. Sue plays the hand smashingly, but if she'd bombed out, she could have opted to get out of the game after a single hand.

That's entertainment

 An argument is brewing at home. Mom says there's never been a Tracy Lord like Katherine Hepburn in the original *Philadelphia Story.* Dad counters with Grace Kelly's later performance in the musical version, *High Society*. Susan argues, all modesty aside, that she was a terrific Tracy Lord herself at the Pumpkin Corners Little Theater in summer stock last year. How to settle the argument? Simple. Retrieve all three performances instantly from a centralized entertainment library. One phone call, one request, and all three Tracy Lords appear, one after another, on the family screen.

School days, school days, good old electronic rule days

That whole silly argument Mom and Dad and Sue had about *Philadelphia Story* gets Joe thinking about the variety of rituals people perform to get married. An inspiration comes to him for his term paper in sociology. Joe calls the Library of Congress and asks for everything they've got on modern American wedding rituals. He scans 75 book and article titles, selects half a dozen, and settles in to read those in full.

The weather outside is frightful, but the house is so delightful

 Who wants to come home to a cold house? Interconnected communications and home environment systems have made it possible to come home to a house already heated or cooled to the temperature of your choice. Half an hour or so before you're ready to come home, you dial a prearranged code. Twenty-one, say, turns on the heat, 22 turns on the air conditioner, and if you're a sybaritic Californian, 23 turns on the heater in the hot tub.

Over the river and through the woods

I remember, says Dad as the family reassembles, when I was a boy (Sue and Joe sigh, roll their eyes to the ceiling; some things never change), we used to read Dickens' *A Christmas Carol* together. Your grandmother did a wonderful ghost of Christmas past. To indulge Dad, the family decides to beam up Grandma on the family screen to join them for a family reading once again. Grandma isn't at home, but she has programmed her communications system to call-forward selected callers. Quickly, the family reaches her on a houseboat in India. Goodnaturedly, she summons up her copy of *A Christmas Carol* on her portable video screen. And, at the appropriate moment, the family watches and listens as Grandma, with perfect Dickensian intonation, solemnly says, "I am the ghost of Christmas past." And, though it would be nice to have her there in the den, it does seem more like the holidays to bring her so near.

Imagine an approach to city planning that abandons the struggle to unravel the fender-bending, horn-honking 25-mile-per-hour, twice-daily mass movement of people to and from their places of work, and concerns itself instead with equally mass movements of information at electronic speeds to people at home.

Imagine an office system that hands the beastly drudgery of the paper blizzard over to machines, thereby eliminating yet another obstacle to the challenge of making work more interesting, productive, and meaningful.

Imagine all this and you've got a vision of an entire smorgasbord of office telecommunications possibilities, including:

Can you picture this?

Your video phone of the future has a built-in feature that lets you switch to a high-resolution screen for transmitting and receiving highly-detailed documents you wish to discuss. Be it a memo, a draft of a report, or a drawing, such documents are either transmitted by the sender or summoned from a central memory source where it is in storage. Among the system's many advantages is the virtual elimination of risks associated with two people discussing different documents when they thought they were discussing the same one.

Whither thou goest

When you're making your rounds, whether through an office building or on the factory floor, you can arrange to have your calls follow you wherever you roam. The pager you carry alerts you to an incoming call and all you have to do is pick up the nearest phone. Conversely, you can also dial a common nationwide number when you shop for particular products sold through distributors, and automatically you will be connected with the nearest dealer.

How to cut paper without scissors

Electronics is greatly reducing your paper work—electronic mail, memos, messages, cash transfers, and reports. Instead of overflowing file drawers, access to information and memory via display terminals hooked into data centers puts materials into your own electronic data bank. Hard copies are summoned only on an as-needed basis.

Take my letter . . . please

Need a letter typed? Speak right into your tele-dictation machine. It transmits your letter via telephone line to an agency that, in turn, transmits it to the first available secretary's home terminal, where it goes on a recording. The secretary types your letter on a machine that, for ease of correcting and revising, stores it on a memory unit, such as a cartridge, a card, or a disk. The work is then relayed back to you on your monitor for your approval, and you either accept it as is, or you make changes. When letter perfect, you can send it either by electronic or conventional mail.

Taking all your coffee breaks at home

By transferring the biggest piece of the work load to the home terminals of their staff members, some companies operate almost entirely without offices. As a manager in one of these companies, you communicate with your "remote staff" by dialing into the computers they use, and, after reviewing their work and progress, you send comments and instructions to them via their home terminals. Pay is in accordance with units of work completed.

You oughta be in pictures

The *Picturephone®* Meeting Service is already here, and while it can't promise the advantages of "pressing the flesh," it can provide good old-fashioned eye-to-eye contact for several groups of six to eight people separated by long distances. The per-hour costs, while expensive, are nothing compared with the costs of transporting large groups of people to central destinations—not to mention the wear and tear on the people as they travel to those destinations. Voice activated cameras, video tubes, and small microphones offer all the comforts of being there.

Fun with committee reports

Committees have been defined as "groups of people who can't get together on Thursday." With everyone having his or her very own home terminal, however, time conflicts no longer count as valid excuses for not getting reports in on time. Using home terminals, the committee authors send their contributions to a distant memory machine that each member has access to. Then, at each member's leisure, the committee accesses all or pieces of the report "draft" to restructure, modify, correct, or, if they don't like it, attempt to throw the whole thing out. When, or if, the committee reaches a consensus on a final draft, the authors can elect to instruct the terminals to print clean copies or they can leave the report in the memory machine until needed.

No more sittin' here, waiting on the busy signal blues

Your office telephone exchange is loaded with new features such as calling you back when a number you've been trying to get is no longer busy and giving you a distinctive ring to let you know an incoming call is from the outside. Further down the line is a voice-activated phone that dials or answers at the sound of your own voice. And even further down the line is a service that will take your voice dictation in English and translate it into a hard copy in the language of your choice.

Imagine a world where information, goods, and services move instantly from one spot to another, across town, across a continent, across the world. Imagine a society where the best resources—education, medicine, the arts—are available, accessible, and affordable. Imagine that, and you begin to comprehend the possibilities of the wired world. For instance:

Pardon me, boy, is this the Pennsylvania Station?

 Yes, sir, beeps back the train. A combination of microprocessors and a sophisticated communications system has resulted in self-operating trains, subways, automobiles. Programming enables cars to move to selected destinations, reading signs along the way, avoiding other vehicles, and adapting to road conditions.

Sherlock Holmes never had it so good

Telecommunications links, hooking homes and offices to security agencies, make life a lot safer than it used to be. Smoke, heat, and movement sensors automatically trigger a call to the nearest fire or police station when the occupants are away. If they're home, peacefully asleep, the call goes out and an alarm wakens them and directs them to the nearest safe exit.

You can fight city hall

Inasmuch as the end of citizen/government frustration still isn't in view, a special telecommunications link can instantly put a troubled (or confused or irate) individual in touch with an ombudsman or advocate in any governmental agency. Instant retrieval of records (tax returns, licenses, filings, and the like) and the ability to call in as many extra parties as necessary make for quick resolution of problems.

Last one out, hit the lights

More sophisticated energy conservation is possible, thanks to centralized management of home environments. Brownouts a possibility this summer? For a reduced utility rate, homeowners give electric utilities permission to automatically turn down the lights or cut back the air conditioner in their homes if the electric power supply starts running low. Centralized power management like this forestalls severe shortages altogether.

Still, there's April in Paris

Despite all the conveniences of home sweet home, the travel bug continues to bite. The pleasures of travel, however, now outweigh the pains, because airline and hotel reservations, sightseeing previews, and language lessons can all be handled ahead of time at the home communications center. And, if your wristphone is programmed with the language the natives will be speaking, so much the better.

Don't leave home without it

Microelectronics has made telecommunications part of the early morning "don't forget" litany—"Let's see, can't forget change, keys, credit cards, or wristphone." The wristphone, which features a personal computer, clock, and radio, accesses the network through radio waves transmitted to a receiver in the central office. And a special alarm button on the phone brings such immediate aid that muggers have practically gone out of business.

Cotton for corn, soybeans for silk

 A data base that stores information concerning what's been grown or manufactured when and where, turns shortages into sufficiencies and surpluses into bargaining power. Equitable management of a worldwide catalogue of goods moves the right things to the right places instantly, peaceably.

So long, bumper-to-bumper woes

Flexible workdays, home and office communications links, shortened work weeks, all add up to an end to that great metropolitan institution—the rush hour. But, should an accident or weather conditions cause an unanticipated traffic jam, a centralized traffic management system communicates with affected drivers to give them instructions or divert them to alternate paths. The mode of communications? A mobile Picturephone system or the ubiquitous wristphone.

The return of the house call

For years, house calls went the way of nickel cigars and penny candy. Doctors' time was simply too expensive to spend trekking house to house, patient to patient. But, interactive video systems connected to telephone service bring the doctor and a host of medical services into the home. Electronic data retrieval systems enable any doctor anywhere to summon up a patient's records. Then, with a two-way video system, the doctor talks with patient, performs a visual exam, or, with the aid of in-home instruments and a visiting nurse, conducts more sophisticated physical exams and monitors ongoing tests.

The world is so full of a number of things

A Shakespeare scholar on a remote island in the Pacific? Why not? With all the stored knowledge of humanity available on any subject at any time through a central data base, proximity to the right libraries is no longer relevant. And should said scholar want to argue a fine point about one of the sonnets, he or she can summon a colleague across the world with a single call. Interactive video means the scholars can look each other in the eye as they argue back and forth. And, should the arguments take place in different languages, an extra channel on the communications console provides a simultaneous translation.

THE COMPUTER MOVES IN

By the millions, it is beeping its way into offices, schools and homes

WILL SOMEONE PLEASE TELL ME, the bright red advertisement asks in mock irritation, WHAT A PERSONAL COMPUTER CAN DO? The ad provides not merely an answer, but 100 of them. A personal computer, it says, can send letters at the speed of light, diagnose a sick poodle, customtailor an insurance program in minutes, test recipes for beer. Testimonials abound. Michael Lamb of Tucson figured out how a personal computer could monitor anesthesia during surgery; the rock group Earth, Wind and Fire uses one to explode smoke bombs onstage during concerts; the Rev. Ron Jaenisch of Sunnyvale, Calif., programmed his machine so it can recite an entire wedding ceremony.

In the cavernous Las Vegas Convention Center a month ago, more than 1,000 computer companies large and small were showing off their wares, their floppy discs and disc drives, joy sticks and modems, to a mob of some 500,000 buyers, middlemen and assorted technology buffs. Look! Here is Hewlett-Packard's HP9000, on which you can sketch a new airplane, say, and immediately see the results in 3-D through holograph imaging; here is how the Votan can answer and act on a telephone call in the middle of the night from a salesman on the other side of the country; here is the Olivetti M20 that entertains bystanders by drawing garishly colored pictures of Marilyn Monroe; here is a program designed by The Alien Group that enables an Atari computer to say aloud anything typed on its keyboard in any language. It also sings, in a buzzing humanoid voice, *Amazing Grace* and *When I'm 64* or anything else that anyone wants to teach it.

As both the Apple Computer advertisement and the Las Vegas circus indicate, the enduring American love affairs with the automobile and the television set are now being transformed into a giddy passion for the personal computer. This passion is partly fad, partly a sense of how life could be made better, partly a gigantic sales campaign. Above all, it is the end result of a technological revolution that has been in the making for four decades and is now, quite literally, hitting home.

Americans are receptive to the revolution and optimistic about its impact. A new poll* for TIME by Yankelovich, Skelly and White indicates that nearly 80% of Americans expect that in the fairly

*The telephone survey of 1,019 registered voters was conducted on Dec. 8 and 9. The margin of sampling error is plus or minus 3%.

near future, home computers will be as commonplace as television sets or dishwashers. Although they see dangers of unemployment and dehumanization, solid majorities feel that the computer revolution will ultimately raise production and therefore living standards (67%), and that it will improve the quality of their children's education (68%).

The sales figures are awesome and will become more so. In 1980 some two dozen firms sold 724,000 personal computers for $1.8 billion. The following year 20 more companies joined the stampede, including giant IBM, and sales doubled to 1.4 million units at just under $3 billion. When the final figures are in for 1982, according to Dataquest, a California research firm, more than 100 companies will probably have sold 2.8 million units for $4.9 billion.

To be sure, the big, complex, costly "mainframe" computer has been playing an increasingly important role in practically everyone's life for the past quartercentury. It predicts the weather, processes checks, scrutinizes tax returns, guides intercontinental missiles and performs innumerable other operations for governments and corporations. The computer has made possible the exploration of space. It has changed the way wars are fought, as the Exocet missile proved in the South Atlantic and Israel's electronically sophisticated forces did in Lebanon.

Despite its size, however, the main-frame does its work all but invisibly, behind the closed doors of a special, climatecontrolled room. Now, thanks to the transistor and the silicon chip, the computer has been reduced so dramatically in both bulk and price that it is accessible to millions. In 1982 a cascade of computers beeped and blipped their way into the American office, the American school, the American home. The "information revolution" that futurists have long predicted has arrived, bringing with it the promise of dramatic changes in the way people live and work, perhaps even in the way they think. America will never be the same.

In a larger perspective, the entire world will never be the same. The industrialized nations of the West are already scrambling to computerize (1982 sales: 435,000 in Japan, 392,000 in Western Europe). The effect of the machines on the Third World is more uncertain. Some experts argue that computers will, if anything, widen the gap between haves and

have-nots. But the prophets of high technology believe the computer is so cheap and so powerful that it could enable underdeveloped nations to bypass the whole industrial revolution. While robot factories could fill the need for manufactured goods, the microprocessor would create myriad new industries, and an international computer network could bring important agricultural and medical information to even the most remote villages. "What networks of railroads, highways and canals were in another age, networks of telecommunications, information and computerization . . . are today," says Austrian Chancellor Bruno Kreisky. Says French editor Jean-Jacques Servan-Schreiber, who believes that the computer's teaching capability can conquer the Third World's illiteracy and even its tradition of high birth rates: "It is the source of new life that has been delivered to us."

The year 1982 was filled with notable events around the globe. It was a year in which death finally pried loose Leonid Brezhnev's frozen grip on the Soviet Union, and Yuri Andropov, the coldeyed ex-chief of the KGB, took command. It was a year in which Israel's truculent Prime Minister Menachem Begin completely redrew the power map of the Middle East by invading neighboring Lebanon and smashing the Palestinian guerrilla forces there. The military campaign was a success, but all the world looked with dismay at the thunder of Israeli bombs on Beirut's civilians and at the massacres in the Palestinian refugee camps. It was a year in which Argentina tested the decline of European power by seizing the Falkland Islands, only to see Britain, led by doughty Margaret Thatcher, meet the test by taking them back again.

Nor did all of the year's major news derive from wars or the threat of international violence. Even as Ronald Reagan cheered the sharpest decline in the U.S. inflation rate in ten years, 1982 brought the worst unemployment since the Great Depression (12 million jobless) as well as budget deficits that may reach an unprecedented $180 billion in fiscal 1983. High unemployment plagued Western Europe as well, and the multibillion-dollar debts of more than two dozen nations gave international financiers a severe fright. It was also a year in which the first artificial heart began pumping life inside a dying man's chest, a year in which millions cheered the birth of cherubic Prince William Arthur Philip Louis of Britain, and millions more rooted for a wrinkled, turtle-like figure struggling to find its way home to outer space.

There are some occasions, though, when the most significant force in a year's news is not a single individual but a process, and a widespread recognition by a whole society that this process is changing the course of all other processes. That is why, after weighing the ebb and flow of events around the world, TIME has decided that 1982 is the year of the computer. It would have been possible to single out as Man of the Year one of the engineers or entrepreneurs who masterminded this technological revolution, but no one person has clearly dominated those turbulent events. More important, such a selection would obscure the main point. TIME's Man of the Year for 1982, the greatest influence for good or evil, is not a man at all. It is a machine: the computer.

It is easy enough to look at the world around us and conclude that the computer has not changed things all that drastically. But one can conclude from similar observations that the earth is flat, and that the sun circles it every 24 hours. Although everything seems much the same from one day to the next, changes under the surface of life's routines are actually occurring at almost unimaginable speed. Just 100 years ago, parts of New York City were lighted for the first time by a strange new force called electricity; just 100 years ago, the German Engineer Gottlieb Daimler began building a gasoline-fueled internal combustion engine (three more years passed before he fitted it to a bicycle). So it is with the computer.

T he first fully electronic digital computer built in the U.S. dates back only to the end of World War II. Created at the University of Pennsylvania, ENIAC weighed 30 tons and contained 18,000 vacuum tubes, which failed at an average of one every seven minutes. The arrival of the transistor and the miniaturized circuit in the 1950s made it possible to reduce a room-size computer to a silicon chip the size of a pea. And prices kept dropping. In contrast to the $487,000 paid for ENIAC, a top IBM personal computer today costs about $4,000, and some discounters offer a basic Timex-Sinclair 1000 for $77.95. One computer expert illustrates the trend by estimating that if the automobile business had developed like the computer business, a Rolls-Royce would now cost $2.75 and run 3 million miles on a gallon of gas.

Looking ahead, the computer industry sees pure gold. There are 83 million U.S. homes with TV sets, 54 million white-collar workers, 26 million professionals, 4 million small businesses. Computer salesmen are hungrily eyeing every one of them. Estimates for the number of personal computers in use by the end of the century run as high as 80 million. Then there are all the auxiliary industries: desks to hold computers, luggage to carry them, cleansers to polish them. "The surface is barely scratched," says Ulric Weil, an analyst for Morgan Stanley.

Beyond the computer hardware lies the virtually limitless market for software, all those prerecorded programs that tell the willing but mindless computer what to do. These discs and cassettes range from John Wiley & Sons' investment analysis program for $59.95 (some run as high as $5,000) to Control Data's PLATO programs that teach Spanish or physics ($45 for the first lesson, $35 for succeeding ones) to a profusion of space wars, treasure hunts and other electronic games.

This most visible aspect of the computer revolution, the video games, is its least significant. But even if the buzz and clang of the arcades is largely a teen-age fad, doomed to go the way of Rubik's Cube and the Hula Hoop, it is nonetheless a remarkable phenomenon. About 20 corporations are selling some 250 different game cassettes for roughly $2 billion this year. According to some estimates, more than half of all the personal computers bought for home use are devoted mainly to games.

Computer enthusiasts argue that these games have educational value, by teaching logic, or vocabulary, or something. Some are even used for medical therapy. Probably the most important effect of these games, however, is that they have brought a form of the computer into millions of homes and convinced millions of people that it is both pleasant and easy to operate, what computer buffs call "user friendly." Games, says Philip D. Estridge, head of IBM's personal computer operations, "aid in the discovery process."

Apart from games, the two things that the computer does best have wide implications but are quite basic. One is simply computation, manipulating thousands of numbers per second. The other is the ability to store, sort through and rapidly retrieve immense amounts of information. More than half of all employed Americans now earn their living not by producing things but as "knowledge workers," exchanging various kinds of information, and the personal computer stands ready to change how all of them do their jobs.

▶ Frank Herringer, a group vice president of Transamerica Corp., installed an Apple in his suburban home in Lafayette, Calif., and spent a weekend analyzing various proposals for Transamerica's $300 million takeover of the New York insurance brokerage firm of Fred S. James Co. Inc. "It allowed me to get a good feel for the critical numbers," says Herringer. "I could work through alternative options, and there were no leaks."

▶ Terry Howard, 44, used to have a long commute to his job at a San Francisco stock brokerage, where all his work involved computer data and telephoning. With a personal computer, he set up his own firm at home in San Rafael. Instead of rising at 6 a.m. to drive to the city, he runs five miles before settling down to work. Says he: "It didn't make sense to spend two hours of every day burning up gas, when my customers on the telephone don't care whether I'm sitting at home or in a high rise in San Francisco."

▶ John Watkins, safety director at Harriet & Henderson Yarns, in Henderson, N.C., is one of 20 key employees whom the company helped to buy home computers and paid to get trained this year. Watkins is trying to design a program that will record and analyze all mill accidents: who was injured, how, when, why. Says he: "I keep track of all the cases that are referred to a doctor, but for every doctor case, there are 25 times as many first-aid cases that should be recorded." Meantime, he has designed a math program for his son Brent and is shopping for a word-processing program to help his wife Mary Edith write her master's thesis in psychology. Says he: "I don't know what it can't do. It's like asking yourself, 'What's the most exciting thing you've ever done?' Well, I don't know because I haven't done it yet."

▶ Aaron Brown, a former defensive end for the Kansas City Chiefs and now an office-furniture salesman in Minneapolis, was converted to the computer by his son Sean, 15, who was converted at a summer course in computer math. "I thought of computers very much as toys," says Brown, "but Sean started telling me, 'You could use a computer in your work.' I said, 'Yeah, yeah, yeah.'" Three years ago, the family took a vote on whether to go to California for a vacation or to buy an Apple. The Apple won, 3 to 1, and to prove its value, Sean wrote his father a program that computes gross profits and commissions on any sale.

Brown started with "simple things," like filing the names and telephone numbers of potential customers. "Say I was going to a particular area of the city," Brown says. "I would ask the computer to pull up the accounts in a certain zip-code area, or if I wanted all the customers who were interested in whole office systems, I could pull that up too." The payoff: since he started using the computer, he has doubled his annual sales to more than $1 million.

Brown has spent about $1,500 on software, all bound in vinyl notebooks along a wall of his home in Golden Valley, Minn., but Sean still does a lot of programming on his own. He likes to demonstrate one that he designed to teach French. *"Vive la France!"* it says, and then starts beeping the first notes of *La Marseillaise*. His mother Reatha uses the computer to help her manage a gourmet cookware store, and even Sister Terri, who originally cast the family's lone vote against the computer, uses it to store her high school class notes. Says Brown: "It's become kind of like the bathroom. If someone is using it, you wait your turn."

Reatha Brown has been lobbying for a new carpet, but she is becoming resigned to the prospect that the family will acquire a new hard-disc drive instead. "The video-cassette recorder," she sighs, pointing across the room, "that was my other carpet." Replies her husband, setting forth an argument that is likely to be replayed in millions of households in the years just ahead: "We make money with the computer, but all we can do with a new carpet is walk on it. Somebody once said there were five reasons to spend money: on necessities, on investments, on self-improvement, on memories and to impress your friends. The carpet falls in that last category, but the computer falls in all five."

By itself, the personal computer is a machine with formidable capabilities for tabulating, modeling or recording. Those capabilities can be multiplied almost indefinitely by plugging it into a network of other computers. This is generally done by attaching a desk-top model to a telephone line (two-way cables and earth satellites are coming increasingly into use). One can then dial an electronic data base, which not only provides all manner of information but also collects and transmits messages: electronic mail.

The 1,450 data bases that now exist in the U.S. range from general information services like the Source, a *Reader's Digest* subsidiary in McLean, Va., which can provide stock prices, airline schedules or movie reviews, to more specialized services like the American Medical Association's AMA/NET, to real esoterica like the Hughes Rotary Rig Report. Fees vary from $300 an hour to less than $10.

Just as the term personal computer can apply to both a home machine and an office machine (and indeed blurs the distinction between the two places) many of the first enthusiastic users of these devices have been people who do much of their work at home: doctors, lawyers, small businessmen, writers, engineers. Such people also have special needs for the networks of specialized data.

Orthopedic Surgeon Jon Love, of Madisonville, Ky., connects the Apple in his home to both the AMA/NET, which offers, among other things, information on 1,500 different drugs, and Medline, a compendium of all medical articles published in the U.S. "One day I accessed the computer three times in twelve minutes," he says. "I needed information on arthritis and cancer in the leg. It saved me an hour and a half of reading time. I want it to pay me back every time I sit down at it."

Charles Manly III practices law in Grinnell, Iowa (pop. 8,700), a town without a law library, so he pays $425 a month to connect his CPT word processor to Westlaw, a legal data base in St. Paul. Just now he needs precedents in an auto insurance case. He dials the Westlaw telephone number, identifies himself by code, then types: "Courts (Iowa) under-insurance." The computer promptly tells him there is only one such Iowa case, and it is 14 years old. Manly asks for a check on other Midwestern states, and it gives him a long list of precedents in Michigan and Minnesota. "I'm not a chiphead," he says, "but if you don't keep up with the new developments, even in a rural general practice, you're not going to have the competitive edge."

The personal computer and its networks are even changing that oldest of all home businesses, the family farm. Though only about 3% of commercial farmers and ranchers now have computers, that number is expected to rise to nearly 20% within the next five years. One who has grasped the true faith is Bob Johnson, who helps run his family's 2,800-acre pig farm near De Kalb, Ill. Outside, the winter's first snow-flakes have dusted the low-slung roofs of the six red-and-white barns and the brown fields specked with corn stubble. Inside the two-room office building, Johnson slips a disc into his computer and types "D" (for dial) and a telephone number. He is immediately connected to the Illinois Farm Bureau's newly computerized AgriVisor service. It not only gives him weather conditions to the west and the latest hog prices on the Chicago commodities exchange, but also offers advice. Should farmers continue to postpone the sale of their newly harvested corn? "Remember," the computer counsels, "that holding on for a dime or a nickel may not be worth the long-term wait."

Johnson started out playing computer games on an Apple II, but then "those got shoved in the file cabinet." He began computerizing all his farm records, which was not easy. "We could keep track of the hogs we sold in dollars, but we couldn't keep track of them by pounds and numbers at the same time." He started shopping around and finally acquired a $12,000 combination at a shop in Lafayette, Ind.: a microcomputer from California Computer Systems, a video screen from Ampex, a Diablo word printer and an array of agricultural programs.

Johnson's computer now knows the yields on 35 test plots of corn, the breeding records of his 300 sows, how much feed his hogs have eaten (2,787,260 lbs.) and at what cost ($166,047.73). "This way, you can charge your hogs the cost of the feed when you sell them and figure out if you're making any money," says Johnson. "We never had this kind of information before. It would have taken too long to calculate. But we knew we needed it."

Just as the computer is changing the way work is done in home offices, so it is revolutionizing the office. Routine tasks like managing payrolls and checking inventories have long since been turned over to computers, but now the typewriter is giving way to the word processor, and every office thus becomes part of a network. This change has barely begun; about 10% of the typewriters in the 500 largest industrial corporations have so far been replaced. But the economic imperatives are inescapable. All told, office professionals could save about 15% of their time if they used the technology now available, says a study by Booz, Allen & Hamilton, and the technology is constantly improving. In one survey of corporations, 55% said they were planning to acquire the latest equipment. This technology involves not just word processors but computerized electronic message systems that could eventually make paper obsolete, and wall-size, two-way TV teleconference screens that will obviate traveling to meetings.

The standard home computer is sold only to somebody who wants one, but the same machine can seem menacing when it appears in an office. Secretaries are often suspicious of new equipment, particularly if it appears to threaten their jobs, and so are executives. Some senior officials resist using a keyboard on the ground that such work is demeaning. Two executives in a large firm reportedly refuse to read any computer print-out until their secretaries have retyped it into the form of a standard memo. "The biggest problem in introducing computers into an office is management itself," says Ted Stout of National Systems Inc., an office design firm in Atlanta. "They don't understand it, and they are scared to death of it."

But there is an opposite fear that drives anxious executives toward the machines: the worry that younger and more sophisticated rivals will push ahead of them. "All you have to do," says Alexander Horniman, an industrial psychologist at the University of Virginia's Darden School of Business, "is walk down the hall and see people using the computer and imagine they have access to all sorts of information you don't." Argues Harold Todd, executive vice president at First Atlanta Bank: "Managers who do not have the ability to use a terminal within three to five years may become organizationally dysfunctional." That is to say, useless.

If more and more offices do most of their work on computers, and if a personal computer can be put in a living room, why should anyone have to go to work in an office at all? The question can bring a stab of hope to anybody who spends hours every day on the San Diego Freeway or the Long Island Rail Road. Nor is "telecommuting" as unrealistic as it sounds. Futurist Jack Nilles of the University of Southern California has estimated that any home computer would soon pay for itself from savings in commuting expenses and in city office rentals.

Is the great megalopolis, the marketplace of information, about to be doomed by the new technology? Another futurist, Alvin Toffler, suggests at least a trend in that direction. In his 1980 book, *The Third Wave,* he portrays a 21st century world in which the computer revolution has canceled out many of the fundamental changes wrought by the Industrial Revolution: the centralization and standardization of work in the factory, the office, the assembly line. These changes may seem eternal, but they are less than two centuries old. Instead, Toffler imagines a revived version of preindustrial life in what he has named "the electronic cottage," a utopian abode where all members of the family work, learn and enjoy their leisure around the electronic hearth, the computer. Says Vice President Louis H. Mertes of the Continental Illinois Bank and Trust Co. of Chicago, who is such a computer enthusiast that he allows no paper to be seen in his office (though he does admit to keeping a few files in the drawer of an end table): "We're talking when—not if—the electronic cottage will emerge."

Continental Illinois has experimented with such electronic cottages by providing half a dozen workers with word processors so they could stay at home. Control Data tried a similar experiment and ran into a problem: some of its 50 "alternate site workers" felt isolated, deprived of their social life around the water cooler. The company decided to ask them to the office for lunch and meetings every week. "People are like ants, they're communal creatures," says Dean Scheff, chairman and founder of CPT Corp., a word-processing firm near Minneapolis. "They need to interact to get the creative juices flowing. Very few of us are hermits."

TIME's Yankelovich poll underlines the point. Some 73% of the respondents believed that the computer revolution would enable more people to work at home. But only 31% said they would prefer to do so themselves. Most work no longer involves a hayfield, a coal mine or a sweatshop, but a field for social intercourse. Psychologist Abraham Maslow defined work as a hierarchy of functions: it first provides food and shelter, the basics, but then it offers security, friendship, "belongingness." This is not just a matter of trading gossip in the corridors; work itself, particularly in the information industries, requires the stimulation of personal contact in the exchange of ideas: sometimes organized conferences, sometimes simply what is called "the schmooze factor." Says

Sociologist Robert Schrank: "The workplace performs the function of community."

But is this a basic psychological reality or simply another rut dug by the Industrial Revolution? Put another way, why do so many people make friends at the office rather than among their neighbors? Prophets of the electronic cottage predict that it will once again enable people to find community where they once did: in their communities. Continental Illinois Bank, for one, has opened a suburban "satellite work station" that gets employees out of the house but not all the way downtown. Ford, Atlantic Richfield and Merrill Lynch have found that teleconferencing can reach far more people for far less money than traditional sales conferences.

Whatever the obstacles, telecommuting seems particularly rich with promise for millions of women who feel tied to the home because of young children. Sarah Sue Hardinger has a son, 3, and a daughter three months old; the computer in her cream-colored stucco house in South Minneapolis is surrounded by children's books, laundry, a jar of Dippity Do. An experienced programmer at Control Data before she decided to have children, she now settles in at the computer right after breakfast, sometimes holding the baby in a sling. She starts by reading her computer mail, then sets to work converting a PLATO grammar program to a disc that will be compatible with Texas Instruments machines. "Mid-morning I have to start paying attention to the three-year-old, because he gets antsy," says Hardinger. "Then at 11:30 comes *Sesame Street* and *Mr. Rogers,* so that's when I usually get a whole lot done." When her husband, a building contractor, comes home and takes over the children, she returns to the computer. "I use part of my house time for work, part of my work time for the house," she says. "The baby has demand feeding; I have demand working."

To the nation's 10 million physically handicapped, telecommuting encourages new hopes of earning a livelihood. A Chicago-area organization called Lift has taught computer programming to 50 people with such devastating afflictions as polio, cerebral palsy and spinal damage. Lift President Charles Schmidt cites a 46-year-old man paralyzed by polio: "He never held a job in his life until he entered our program three years ago, and now he's a programmer for Walgreens."

Just as the vast powers of the personal computer can be vastly multiplied by plugging it into an information network, they can be extended in all directions by attaching the mechanical brain to sensors, mechanical arms and other robotic devices. Robots are already at work in a large variety of dull, dirty or dangerous jobs: painting automobiles on assembly lines and transporting containers of plutonium without being harmed by radiation. Because a computerized robot is so easy

to reprogram, some experts foresee drastic changes in the way manufacturing work is done: toward customization, away from assembly-line standards. When the citizen of tomorrow wants a new suit, one futurist scenario suggests, his personal computer will take his measurements and pass them on to a robot that will cut his choice of cloth with a laser beam and provide him with a perfectly tailored garment. In the home too, computer enthusiasts delight in imagining machines performing the domestic chores. A little of that fantasy is already reality. New York City Real Estate Executive David Rose, for example, uses his Apple in business deals, to catalogue his 4,000 books and to write fund-raising letters to his Yale classmates. But he also uses it to wake him in the morning with soft music, turn on the TV, adjust the lights and make the coffee.

In medicine, the computer, which started by keeping records and sending bills, now suggests diagnoses. CADUCEUS knows some 4,000 symptoms of more than 500 diseases; MYCIN specializes in infectious diseases; PUFF measures lung functions. All can be plugged into a master network called SUMEX-AIM, with headquarters at Stanford in the West and Rutgers in the East. This may all sound like another step toward the disappearance of the friendly neighborhood G.P., but while it is possible that a family doctor would recognize 4,000 different symptoms, CADUCEUS is more likely to see patterns in what patients report and can then suggest a diagnosis. The process may sound dehumanized, but in one hospital where the computer specializes in peptic ulcers, a survey of patients showed that they found the machine "more friendly, polite, relaxing and comprehensible" than the average physician.

The microcomputer is achieving dramatic effects on the ailing human body. These devices control the pacemakers implanted in victims of heart diseases; they pump carefully measured quantities of insulin into the bodies of diabetics; they test blood samples for hundreds of different allergies; they translate sounds into vibrations that the deaf can "hear"; they stimulate deadened muscles with electric impulses that may eventually enable the paralyzed to walk.

In all the technologists' images of the future, however, there are elements of exaggeration and wishful thinking. Though the speed of change is extraordinary, so is the vastness of the landscape to be changed. New technologies have generally taken at least 20 years to establish themselves, which implies that a computer salesman's dream of a micro on every desk will not be fulfilled in the very near future. If ever.

Certainly the personal computer is not without its flaws. As most new buyers soon learn, it is not that easy for a novice to use, particularly when the manuals contain instructions like this specimen from Apple: "This character prevents script from terminating the currently forming output line when it encounters the script command in the input stream."

Another problem is that most personal computers end up costing considerably more than the ads imply. The $100 model does not really do very much, and the $1,000 version usually requires additional payments for the disc drive or the printer or the modem. Since there is very little standardization of parts among the dozens of new competitors, a buyer who has not done considerable homework is apt to find that the parts he needs do not fit the machine he bought.

Software can be a major difficulty. The first computer buyers tended to be people who enjoyed playing with their machines and designing their own programs. But the more widely the computer spreads, the more it will have to be used by people who know no more about its inner workings than they do about the insides of their TV sets—and do not want to. They will depend entirely on the commercial programmers. Good programs are expensive both to make and to buy. Control Data has invested $900 million in its PLATO educational series and has not yet turned a profit, though its hopes run into the billions. A number of firms have marketed plenty of shoddy programs, but they are not cheap either. "Software is the new bandwagon, but only 20% of it is any good," says Diana Hestwood, a Minneapolis-based educational consultant. She inserts a math program and deliberately makes ten mistakes. The machine gives its illiterate verdict: "You taken ten guesses." Says Atari's chief scientist, Alan Kay: "Software is getting to be embarrassing."

Many of the programs now being touted are hardly worth the cost, or hardly worth doing at all. Why should a computer be needed to balance a checkbook or to turn off the living-room lights? Or to recommend a dinner menu, particularly when it can consider (as did a $34 item called the Pizza Program) ice cream as an appetizer? Indeed, there are many people who may quite reasonably decide that they can get along very nicely without a computer. Even the most impressive information networks may provide the customer with nothing but a large telephone bill. "You cannot rely on being able to find what you want," says Atari's Kay. "It's really more useful to go to a library."

It is becoming increasingly evident that a fool assigned to work with a computer can conceal his own foolishness in the guise of high-tech authority. Lives there a single citizen who has not been commanded by a misguided computer to pay an income tax installment or department store bill that he has already paid?

What is true for fools is no less true for criminals, who are now able to commit electronic larceny from the comfort of their living rooms. The probable champion is Stanley Mark Rifkin, a computer analyst in Los Angeles, who tricked the machines at the Security Pacific National Bank into giving him $10 million. While free on bail for that in 1979 (he was eventually sentenced to eight years), he was arrested for trying to steal $50 million from Union Bank (the charges were eventually dropped). According to Donn Parker, a specialist in computer abuse at SRI International (formerly the Stanford Research Institute), "Nobody seems to know exactly what computer crime is, how much of it there is, and whether it is increasing or decreasing. We do know that computers are changing the nature of business crime significantly."

Even if all the technical and intellectual problems can be solved, there are major social problems inherent in the computer revolution. The most obvious is unemployment, since the basic purpose of commercial computerization is to get more work done by fewer people. One British study predicts that "automation-induced unemployment" in Western Europe could reach 16% in the next decade, but most analyses are more optimistic. The general rule seems to be that new technology eventually creates as many jobs as it destroys, and often more. "People who put in computers usually increase their staffs as well," says CPT's Scheff. "Of course," he adds, "one industry may kill another industry. That's tough on some people."

Theoretically, all unemployed workers can be retrained, but retraining programs are not high on the nation's agenda. Many new jobs, moreover, will require an aptitude in using computers, and the retraining needed to use them will have to be repeated as the technology keeps improving. Says a chilling report by the Congressional Office of Technology Assessments: "Lifelong retraining is expected to become the norm for many people." There is already considerable evidence that the schoolchildren now being educated in the use of computers are generally the children of the white middle class. Young blacks, whose unemployment rate stands today at 50%, will find another barrier in front of them.

Such social problems are not the fault of the computer, of course, but a consequence of the way the American society might use the computer. "Even in the days of the big mainframe computers, they were a machine for the few," says Katherine Davis Fishman, author of *The Computer Establishment*. "It was a tool to help the rich get richer. It still is to a large extent. One of the great values of the personal computer is that smaller concerns, smaller organizations can now have some of the advantages of the bigger organizations."

How society uses its computers depends greatly on what kind of computers are made and sold, and that depends, in turn, on an industry in a state of chaotic growth. Even the name of the product is a matter of debate: "microcomputer" sounds too technical, but "home computer" does not fit an office machine. "Desktop" sounds awkward, and "personal computer" is at best a compromise. Innovators are pushing off in different directions. Hewlett Packard is experimenting with machines that respond to vocal commands; Osborne is leading a rush toward portable computers, ideally no larger than a book. And for every innovator, there are at least five imitators selling copies.

There is much talk of a coming shakeout, and California Consultant David E. Gold predicts that perhaps no more than a dozen vendors will survive the next five years. At the moment, Dataquest estimates that Texas Instruments leads the low-price parade with a 35% share of the market in computers selling for less than $1,000. Next come Timex (26%), Commodore (15%) and Atari (13%). In the race among machines priced between $1,000 and $5,000, Apple still commands 26%, followed by IBM (17%) and Tandy/Radio Shack (10%). But IBM, which has dominated the mainframe computer market for decades, is coming on very strong. Apple, fighting back, will unveil its new Lisa model in January, putting great emphasis on user friendliness. The user will be able to carry out many functions simply by pointing to a picture of what he wants done rather than typing instructions. IBM is also reported to be planning to introduce new machines in 1983, as are Osborne and others.

Just across the horizon, as usual, lurk the Japanese. During the 1970s, U.S. computer manufacturers complacently felt that they were somehow immune from the Japanese combination of engineering and salesmanship that kept gnawing at U.S. auto, steel and appliance industries. One reason was that the Japanese were developing their large domestic market. When they belatedly entered the U.S. battlefield, they concentrated not on selling whole systems but on particular sectors—with dramatic results. In low-speed printers using what is known as the dot-matrix method, the Japanese had only a 6% share of the market in 1980; in 1982, they provided half the 500,000 such printers sold in the U.S. Says Computerland President Ed Faber: "About 75% of the dot-matrix printers we sell are Japanese, and almost all the monitors. There is no better quality electronics than what we see coming from Japan."

Whatever its variations, there is an inevitability about the computerization of America. Commercial efficiency requires it, Big Government requires it, modern life requires it, and so it is coming to pass. But the essential element in this sense of inevitability is the way in which the young take to computers: not as just another obligation imposed by adult society but as a game, a pleasure, a tool, a system that fits naturally into their lives. Unlike anyone over 40, these children have grown up with TV screens; the computer is a screen that responds to them, hooked to a machine that can be programmed to respond the way they want it to. That is power.

There are now more than 100,000 computers in U.S. schools, compared with 52,000 only 18 months ago. This is roughly one for every 400 pupils. The richer and more progressive states do better. Minnesota leads with one computer for every 50 children and a locally produced collection of 700 software programs. To spread this development more evenly and open new doors for business, Apple has offered to donate one computer to every public school in the U.S. —a total of 80,000 computers worth $200 million retail—if Washington will authorize a 25% tax write-off (as is done for donations of scientific equipment to colleges). Congress has so far failed to approve the idea, but California has agreed to a similar proposal.

Many Americans concerned about the erosion of the schools put faith in the computer as a possible savior of their children's education, at school and at home. The Yankelovich poll showed that 57% thought personal computers would enable children to read and to do arithmetic better. Claims William Ridley, Control Data's vice president for education strategy: "If you want to improve youngsters one grade level in reading, our PLATO program with teacher supervision can do it up to four times faster and for 40% less expense than teachers alone."

No less important than this kind of drill, which some critics compare with the old-fashioned flash cards, is the use of computers to teach children about computers. They like to learn programming, and they are good at it, often better than their teachers, even in the early grades. They treat it as play, a secret skill, unknown among many of their parents. They delight in cracking corporate security and filching financial secrets, inventing new games and playing them on military networks, inserting obscene jokes into other people's programs. In soberer versions that sort of skill will become a necessity in thousands of jobs opening up in the future. Beginning in 1986, Carnegie-Mellon University expects to require all of its students to have their own personal computers. "People are willing to spend a large amount of money to educate their children," says Author Fishman. "So they're all buying computers for Johnny to get a head start (though I have not heard anyone say, 'I am buying a computer for Susie')."

This transformation of the young raises a fundamental and sometimes menacing question: Will the computer change the very nature of human thought? And if so, for better or worse? There has been much time wasted on the debate over whether computers can be made to think, as HAL seemed to be doing in *2001*, when it murdered the astronauts who might challenge its command of the spaceflight. That answer is simple: computers do not think, but they do simulate many of the processes of the human brain: remembering, comparing, analyzing. And as people rely on the computer to do things that they used to do inside their heads, what happens to their heads?

Will the computer's ability to do routine work mean that human thinking will shift to a higher level? Will IQs rise? Will there be more intellectuals? The computer may make a lot of learning as unnecessary as memorizing the multiplication tables. But if a dictionary stored in the computer's memory can easily correct any spelling mistakes, what is the point of learning to spell? And if the mind is freed from intellectual routine, will it race off in pursuit of important ideas or lazily spend its time on more video games?

Too little is known about how the mind works, and less about how the computer might change that process. The neurological researches of Mark Rosenzweig and his colleagues at Berkeley indicate that animals trained to learn and assimilate information develop heavier cerebral cortices, more glial cells and bigger nerve cells. But does the computer really stimulate the brain's activity or, by doing so much of its work, permit it to go slack?

Some educators do believe they see the outlines of change. Seymour Papert, professor of mathematics and education at M.I.T. and author of *Mindstorms: Children, Computers and Powerful Ideas,* invented the computer language named Logo, with which children as young as six can program computers to design mathematical figures. Before they can do that, however, they must learn how to analyze a problem logically, step by step. "Getting a computer to do something," says Papert, "requires the underlying process to be described, on some level, with enough precision to be carried out by the machine." Charles P. Lecht, president of the New York consulting firm Lecht Scientific, argues that "what the lever was to the body, the computer system is to the mind." Says he: "Computers help teach kids to think. Beyond that, they motivate people to think. There is a great difference between intelligence and manipulative capacity. Computers help us to realize that difference."

The argument that computers train minds to be logical makes some experts want to reach for the computer key that says ERASE. "The last thing you want to do is think more logically," says Atari's Kay. "The great thing about computers is that they have no gravity systems. The logical system is one that you make up. Computers are a wonderful way of being bizarre."

Sherry Turkle, a sociologist now finishing a book titled *The Intimate Machine: Social and Cultural Studies of Computers and People,* sees the prospect of change in terms of perceptions and feelings. Says she: "Children define what's special about people by contrasting them with their nearest neighbors, which have always been the animals. People are special because they know how to think. Now children who work with computers see the computer as their nearest neighbor, so they see that people are special because they feel. This may become much more central to the way people think about themselves. We may be moving toward a re-evaluation of what makes us human."

For all such prophecies, M.I.T. Computer Professor Joseph Weizenbaum has answers ranging from disapproval to scorn. He has insisted that "giving children computers to play with . . . cannot touch . . . any real problem," and he has described the new computer generation as "bright young men of disheveled appearance [playing out] megalomaniacal fantasies of omnipotence."

Weizenbaum's basic objection to the computer enthusiasts is that they have no sense of limits. Says he: "The assertion that all human knowledge is encodable in streams of zeros and ones—philosophically, that's very hard to swallow. In effect, the whole world is made to seem computable. This generates a kind of tunnel vision, where the only problems that seem legitimate are problems that can be put on a computer. There is a whole world of real problems, of human problems, which is essentially ignored."

So the revolution has begun, and as usually happens with revolutions, nobody can agree on where it is going or how it will end. Nils Nilsson, director of the Artificial Intelligence Center at SRI International, believes the personal computer, like television, can "greatly increase the forces of both good and evil." Marvin Minsky, another of M.I.T.'s computer experts, believes the key significance of the personal computer is not the establishment of an intellectual ruling class, as some fear, but rather a kind of democratization of the new technology. Says he: "The desktop revolution has brought the tools that only professionals have had into the hands of the public. God knows what will happen now."

Perhaps the revolution will fulfill itself only when people no longer see anything unusual in the brave New World, when they see their computer not as a fearsome challenger to their intelligence but as a useful linkup of some everyday gadgets: the calculator, the TV and the typewriter. Or as Osborne's Adam Osborne puts it: "The future lies in designing and selling computers that people don't realize are computers at all." —*By Otto Friedrich.* *Reported by Michael Moritz/San Francisco, J. Madeleine Nash/Chicago and Peter Stoler/New York*

REINVENTING THE COMPUTER

by Tom Alexander

A WAVE of technological change is poised to sweep over the computer industry. Faster and cheaper computers will allow users to do things they can't today—operate a typewriter by voice, for example. Companies and nations alike will face the opportunities and dangers that always accompany a major innovation. The stakes are high: the new technology will affect all information-age businesses, ranging from electronic mail networks to computer manufacturing, which are expected to have worldwide revenues, in today's dollars, of up to $500 billion a year by 1993.

The transformation will be based on one fundamental idea: that the way to speed up computers is to divide the labor among many inexpensive data-processing devices rather than continue the present quest for ever faster single processors made with ever more exotic materials and techniques. Called parallel processing, the new approach is analogous to mass-producing shoes with unskilled labor on assembly lines instead of handcrafting them with skilled workmen one by one. Over the next few years, U.S., Japanese, and European industry and governments will spend some $10 billion on advanced computer research, including parallel processing.

The demand for faster but cheaper computers grows continuously. Sales of "supercomputers"—fast, specialized, hand-built, and expensive number-crunchers—have been taking off. Cray Research Inc., a Minneapolis company (1983 sales: $170 million), got orders for 25 supercomputers last year vs. 16 in 1982. The burst of sales was ignited by technological advances that made possible deep price cuts—as much as $5 million on a $10-million Cray—and put the machines within reach of more users.

Aircraft and auto manufacturers have begun to use simulations performed on supercomputers in place of wind tunnels and machines that smash parts to determine their strength and durability. Pharmaceutical companies are using computers to develop new drugs with molecules derived from quantum theory, which predicts how atoms will interact, instead of relying on the random mixing and testing of substances. Oil companies are constructing computerized 3-D models of underground oil and water movements to de-termine how to exploit oil fields. Digital Productions, a Los Angeles company that turns out feature films and TV commercials, used a Cray to simulate in vivid detail the surfaces of alien planets that appear in an upcoming Lorimar Productions movie, *The Last Starfighter*.

Today's supercomputers are too slow for many potential tasks. Some jobs now take weeks or months—for example, simulating the airflow around an entire airplane in flight. Users have identified additional applications that would take hundreds or thousands of times longer; one would create a minutely detailed three-dimensional model of a fusion reactor's interior at work.

Unfortunately, performing these tasks will be impractical as long as computer makers stick with the present dominant design—the "von Neumann architecture," named for the Hungarian-American genius John von Neumann, who helped develop it near the end of World War II. In the von Neumann approach a single main processing unit calls forth programmed instructions and data from memory in sequence, manipulates the data as instructed, and either returns the results to memory or performs other operations (see box, page 89). With only one processor at work, the pace of computation is set by the speed of the processor's electronic circuits. Circuit speeds, in turn, are limited by the agility of transistor switches, the rate at which electricity flows through wires, and the intense heat produced by tiny fast-acting chips. Conventional supercomputers require expensive cooling to keep them from burning up. The circuit boards on the forthcoming Cray-2 will be immersed in a liquid coolant to keep them at room temperature.

The big computer and semiconductor circuit makers have been exploring exotic new technologies to speed up the von Neumann computer with faster switches. This can be done by making integrated circuit chips of gallium arsenide, a semiconductor material, instead of silicon, or by using devices called Josephson junctions, named for British researcher Brian Josephson. But gallium arsenide has proved brittle and difficult to transform reliably into workable chips. Josephson junctions must be cooled to within a few degrees of absolute zero. If these technologies are employed to speed up the traditional von Neumann architecture, tomorrow's faster computer may wind up priced out of the market. That perception was behind a recent decision by IBM to scale back its Josephson junction development.

In any event, these new technologies would be inadequate for many potential computing tasks. "In my opinion, we are already within a factor of ten of the top speed achievable with a von Neumann machine," says Bill Buzbee, a computer scientist at the Los Alamos National Laboratory, one of the big buyers of supercomputers (it has five). A formidable barrier is what IBM's eminent computer scientist John Backus—inventor of the Fortran programming language among other things—has identified as the "von Neumann bottleneck." That is the single channel along which data and instructions must flow between a conventional computer's central processor and its memory. Like a constriction in a pipe feeding raw material to a factory, the von Neumann bottleneck can limit the pace of production.

The faster, smarter, cheaper alternative to von Neumann's architecture, many designers agree, is parallel processing. The latent advantages of parallelism have long been recognized; even von Neumann was impressed by discoveries in the 1940s about how animal brains process information in a parallel manner. Had electronic hardware not been so costly in his day, he might have designed a machine more like a brain.

That economic constraint no longer applies. A technology called VLSI (for "very large-scale integration") makes it possible to reproduce computer circuits with hundreds of thousands of transistors on a single tiny silicon chip almost as easily and cheaply as printing pages of a book. This capability affords designers a tantalizing way around the von Neumann bottleneck: put many processors on a single chip. Processors could operate simultaneously on different parts of a problem and even specialize in performing particular operations at great speed. Another type of parallelism, called active or associative memory, can immensely speed up certain computing tasks, such as retrieving information from data bases, by eliminating the role of the central processor in searching through memory. In essence, each piece of data would be stored with its own tiny processor, smart enough to respond when a centralized computer calls for that item.

RESEARCH ASSOCIATE *Darienne L. Dennis*

PARALLELISM will probably spawn many specialized types of computers with different species of processors connected in a variety of ways. Inherently general-purpose, the von Neumann computer relies on software programs to let it perform many different kinds of jobs. But almost any computational problem can be solved more rapidly with special-purpose hardware that uses a minimum of software. In addition, prices of hardware have plunged, but software costs have not, and software now accounts for seven of every ten dollars spent on computing. Now that the cost trade-off has swung in favor of hardware, much of the complex software may be replaced by specialized parallel machines. Certain types of machines will do the number-crunching, while others will control robots, search data bases, understand written and spoken language, and even see.

CRAY AND CONTROL DATA CORP., another Minneapolis company (1983 sales: $4.6 billion), already turn out supercomputers based partly on parallelism. The Cray-1 and Control Data Cyber 205 embody a basic von Neumann architecture to which are attached banks of simple processors that carry out arithmetic operations on large collections of similar data, called vectors and arrays. One type of vector might consist of a continuous series of readings from scientific instruments—such as barometric pressures at many points around the world, used in constructing weather maps for forecasting. In addition, several companies build array-processing attachments for general-purpose computers. One, Floating Point Systems of Beaverton, Oregon, had sales last year of more than $100 million, up 239% in the last five years. Traded on the New York Stock Exchange, Floating Point shares have been as high as $45 but like other technology stocks have been hard hit and recently sold at $28.50. With an array processor costing less than $500,000, a user can soup up his $300,000 Digital Equipment Corp. VAX computer system to about one-tenth of the $7-million Cray-1's performance—an attractive proposition for those who can't afford the Cray.

Array processors and other high-speed computing devices are leading to what Cornell physicist and Nobel laureate Kenneth Wilson calls "the computerization of science." They are replacing experimental apparatus in fusion energy, advanced physics, astronomy, biology, chemistry, and aeronautics. The trend has spilled over into industrial research and design. At General Motors, engineers study engine knock with computer models of pressure waves that occur in a car cylinder after fuel vapor ignites.

Today's number-crunchers won't work for tasks in which each processor executes a different program but nevertheless must exchange information with other processors. A machine for understanding speech, for instance, might need one processor to pick out sounds, others to identify words and parts of speech, still others to search for meaning. Each processor would constantly make guesses and compare notes with other processors to resolve the ambiguities and confusions of human expression. That way they could distinguish the different meanings of words in "Time flies like an arrow" and "Fruit flies like a banana."

A mobile robot will probably use separate processors for navigation and propulsion and for operating each joint of a manipulating arm and hand. These would have to consult with each other and with processors in charge of vision, which will dissect scenes into specific features such as color, texture, and lines, and pass the findings on to higher processors that can recognize these as the elements of known objects.

AT PRESENT, programmers must spell out in excruciating detail everything they want a computer to know and do. Some experts think parallelism will eventually make computers easier to program. But for the moment scientists are still baffled about how to program parallel machines at all. MIT computer scientist Michael Dertouzos says parallel machines can fall into a "deadly embrace," a paralysis that ensues when one processor must wait for data from another, which in turn waits for another, and so on. A parallel system caught in this predicament might wind up working more slowly than a von Neumann machine—or not at all.

And how do you break up sequential problems in mathematics or logic so that they can run concurrently on multiple processors? Just as nine women can't cooperate to produce a baby in one month, parallelism can't reduce the time it takes to solve a problem that must be approached in a series of steps taken one after the other. But other problems, including some now usually performed sequentially, can be broken into discrete parts that could be solved more quickly by a series of processors working in parallel than by one computer alone. For example, parts of a long column of figures can be distributed among processors for addition, with subtotals then being combined.

At the University of North Carolina at Chapel Hill, computer scientist Gyula Mago and others are working on parallel systems that automatically reduce a complex problem to many primitive operations that can be executed simultaneously. In Mago's reduction machine, as it is called, each processor is given a special task to perform—say, addition or multiplication. A complex formula might be fed into the computer, and as it percolates through the network each processor would perform its particular function as needed, just as specialized circuits in animal brains apparently do.

Reprogramming thousands or even millions of parallel processors to perform each new application would be impractical. So each processor might be permanently programmed to perform a limited repertory of tasks. Ultimately, programming such a machine to solve a new problem might require an operator to do no more than type in necessary equations and push the start button.

Some proponents of parallelism hope that it will make possible machines that learn things on their own—computers able to do jobs no programmer knows how to tell them to do. These proponents argue that the von Neumann computer is an awkward vehicle for biological-style intelligence. For example, computers and people do arithmetic differently. People don't actually add the numbers two and two, as a computer does; instead they associate the memorized phrase "two plus two" with the word "four." Far more complex associations probably lie at the heart of human perception, recognition, generalization, learning, and intuition—things difficult to explain even to ourselves, much less spell out for an obtuse machine. What conceivable sequence of instructions, for example, could tell a machine how to recognize a face in a crowd?

The key to association in the human mind appears to be massive parallelism in which billions of items in memory are stored in conjunction with their own specific processors—cells called neurons. Human memory consists of a vibrant network of processors comparing notes with other processors and singling out similarities, learning relationships, and generalizing about concepts. Teuvo Kohonen and his colleagues at Finland's University of Technology have imitated human memory in a machine that can distinguish human faces from one another, even faces viewed from perspectives the computer hadn't seen them from before.

OTHER RESEARCHERS have developed parallel concepts that enable computers to learn as humans do through exploration, observation, and trial and error. At the moment, these concepts take the form of simulations on conventional von Neumann computers and for that reason are limited and simple. Using only a few processors, Andrew Barto and associates at the University of Massachusetts at Amherst have simulated a neural net that learns by trial and error the various manipulations necessary to balance a broomstick on end atop a moving cart.

One ambitious active memory project is the Connection Machine, invented by Daniel Hillis, 26, an MIT graduate student. In its ultimate form, the machine would consist of perhaps a million or more processors, each with a relatively small memory and about as much power as the processor in a home computer. The links among the machine's processors can be altered to construct different parallel architectures in different applications, ranging from medical diagnosis to robot vehicles. The Connection Machine is being developed at a new private company, Thinking Machines Corp. of Waltham, Massachusetts, which has already fabricated prototypes of some necessary VLSI chips.

More brainlike still is a concept being explored by researchers Geoffrey Hinton and Scott Fahlman of Pittsburgh's Carnegie-Mellon University and Terrence Sejnowski of Johns Hopkins University. As in neuron networks, the machine they envision will have processors with memory distributed throughout the network. The researchers hope this will permit the machine to deal in "fuzzy" concepts, including generalizations and analogies, that conventional computers find difficult. Distributed memory should also provide redundancy and resiliency like that of animal nervous systems, which can suffer the loss of many memory cells without totally losing recollection of an item—the image of grandmother's face, for example.

Perceiving competitive opportunities in the potential break with conventional computing, many of the world's computer designers have raced back to the drawing boards. The Japanese were the first to understand that what's at stake is dominance of computer hardware and software. This is the industry that best exploits what advanced countries have to sell—the knowledge in the heads of highly educated people, rather than the strength of their muscles. With the fortunes of entire nations, not just companies, at risk, the race to dominate these "information technologies" has become an international competition in which governments encourage and subsidize the participants.

Japan's much publicized fifth-generation computer project is aimed at developing parallel machines that can perceive their surroundings and recognize, manipulate, and draw inferences from non-numerical symbols—words, sentences, and visual or aural patterns (see "Here Comes Computer Inc.," FORTUNE, October 4, 1982). "We're thinking about computers that will have everyday non-numerical applications—processing and understanding text, making judgments, giving advice," says Kazuhiro Fuchi, director of the project. He says that these yet to be developed computers will do many jobs secretaries do today. "The cost of having a human secretary will be greater than having a fifth-generation computer," he adds. "Only rich or high-level executives will be able to afford secretaries."

Europe also aims to seize the moment of technological transition to chop into America's computer dominance. In Britain, government, industry, and universities are collaborating on advanced computer developments. The government will put up nearly $300 million over the next five years, and companies are expected to match that sum. The European Community and some 200 Western European companies, including Siemens and Britain's General Electric, are putting together a five-year, $1.1-billion effort called the European Strategic Program for Research and Information Technologies (ESPRIT). It will cover advanced computer technology, from fundamental semiconductor research to parallel hardware and artificial intelligence software. Most of the work will be done by companies and universities.

U.S. hopes for maintaining the lead in computers depend on a variety of government and private projects. The Pentagon's Defense Advanced Research Projects Agency (DARPA) has launched a Strategic Computing program on which it plans to spend $600 million in the first five years. Nominally aimed at exploiting promising advances in microelectronics, computer concepts, and artificial intelligence, DARPA's project is also designed to stimulate broad corporate and university research in these technologies through research contracts. One of the project's goals is a robot vehicle able to navigate autonomously over roads and through woods at 35 mph, guided by artificial vision and other senses. DARPA hasn't publicly specified a mission for such a device, but

whatever uses the robot vehicle might have on land, the sensory, navigational, and computational talents involved would obviously be useful in unmanned air, space, or underwater craft with reconnaissance or destructive missions.

At the moment few parallel computers have reached the market. The Cray X-MP (the "MP" stands for "multiprocessor") merely connects two Cray-1's in the same box. The Cray-2, scheduled to appear this year, will have four processors, each more powerful than the Cray-1. Control Data recently formed a little company called ETA Systems, 90% owned by Control Data, to develop a parallel supercomputer 20 times faster than any present machine. Denelcor Inc. of Aurora, Colorado (1982 sales: $1 million), offers an ingenious design—at up to $8 million per machine—that allows users to hook together as many processors as they need. So far Denelcor has found four buyers and says it expects to sell 15 more machines this year. The company has yet to make a profit, but Denelcor stock, traded over the counter, recently sold at $8.50 a share.

Most research on parallel processing is still being done in universities where more than 70 novel concepts are being investigated. Just about every major computer maker in the U.S. is also pursuing parallel research in some form. They include such surprising participants as Goodyear Aerospace, which recently developed a 16,384-processor machine for NASA to use in processing images transmitted from earth-surveying satellites. A harbinger of new technology aborning is the recent sprouting of little companies started by university professors and defectors from old-line computer companies.

ONE REVOLUTIONARY ASPECT of parallel computing is that it will probably open many more niches for competitors to develop machines to handle specific tasks, just as Floating Point Systems has done with machines for high-speed calculations in engineering and science. Most likely it will take years for the real world to sort out which concepts are practical and economic—and which companies will make investors rich. But in the next decade specialized parallel machines will begin nibbling at the market for general-purpose computers like IBM's mainframes, giving many little contenders in many countries a shot at growing big. ∎

TOMORROW'S COMPUTER MAY REPRODUCE ITSELF

Using Protein Components And Microscopic in Size, It Might Work Wonders

Or It May Be Science Fiction

By Susan Chace
Staff Reporter of THE WALL STREET JOURNAL

It is the stuff of science fiction: Computers with elements the size of molecules and brainpower that dwarfs the most sophisticated machines known today reproduce themselves in test tubes from natural and synthetic protein.

Robots equipped with these supercomputers could conduct deep-sea rescues or fight fires. Implanted in human beings, the computers might enable the crippled to walk or the blind to see. Or they might be used to enhance perfectly healthy human faculties—such as the memory—much as a telescope augments normal sight.

Visionary? Yes. But a small number of computer scientists are engrossed in trying to prove that someday it will be possible to create an organic computer, or "biochip," an incredibly small package of computer circuits assembled from molecules. They hope that their research in molecular electronics will result in a new generation of computers that is many times smaller, faster and cheaper than today's state-of-the art machines assembled from silicon microcircuits.

The work so far is purely theoretical, and many of the researchers themselves are quick to stress that what they produce may never have commercial use, at least not in the next 30 years. Skeptics don't doubt that biochips could become a laboratory reality, but they suggest that the devices aren't likely to be reliable or efficient enough to have wide applications. Still, rudimentary prototypes of conventional silicon-chip computers that one day may be implanted to correct physical disabilities exist now. A rather cumbersome device that enabled a paraplegic woman to take a few steps captured newspaper headlines last November.

Switching Functions

In the simplest sense, computers are a vast collection of electrical switches that turn on and off to transmit or block an electrical current. A computer functions by turning its millions of switches on and off in various combinations, each pattern representing a "bit" of information. The binary code—the ones and zeros of machine language—merely reflects these on-off switching combinations.

The task of building ever more intelligent machines boils down to squeezing more computational capacity—in the form of millions of tiny switches—onto smaller and smaller circuit boards. In recent years, computer scientists have been remarkably successful in achieving such miniaturization. The capacity of a vintage-1950s room-sized computer now is contained on a silicon chip thinner than a fingernail and about the size of a match head.

But researchers working in microcircuitry say they are approaching a limit: Tiny circuits eventually may be crammed so close together that the silicon chip will "overheat" and melt.

"As switching circuits become ever smaller, it's easy to conclude that in 20 or 30 years, a computer's elementary switches will be the size of molecules," says Forrest Carter, the head of a molecular electronics research project at the Naval Research Laboratory outside Washington. "At that point, silicon will no longer be the construction material of choice. We need to start working now on new ideas."

Organic Circuits

One new theory involves trying to emulate the one-way flow of electrons that occurs during plant photosynthesis. At the University of Mississippi, researchers Robert Metzger and Charles Panetta are trying to achieve a one-way flow of charges within a single molecule, as a first step toward constructing organic logic circuits. But Mr. Metzger cautions that building an organic computer is "a long way from where I stand today."

Other researchers hope to show that certain proteins could be made to emulate a computer's on-off switching action. Noting that hemoglobin in red blood cells changes from one shape to another when the electrical charge it carries is altered, they suggest that in a biochip, one shape could represent on, and the other off.

Shrinking a computer to molecular dimensions would permit a host of new applications. The Naval Research Laboratory's Mr. Carter sees biochips eventually serving as "brains" for robots that could perform high-risk chores, like deep-sea rescues or firefighting.

"The amount of (conventional circuitry) needed to get a computer to recognize an object and to know what to do with it and be able to do it just won't fit into a reasonably sized robot," he says.

Bloodstream Computers

He also envisions minuscule computers implanted in the bloodstream to monitor body chemistry and to correct imbalances.

But computers that small couldn't be made using conventional manufacturing processes. "We just don't have tools that small," says Kevin Ulmer, the director of exploratory research of Genex Corp., a Rockville, Md., bioengineering concern.

So scientists at Genex and EMV Associ-ates—also based in Rockville—are striking out in a new direction: They hope some day to coax cell-sized computers to assemble themselves. Their research is grounded in the theory that every cell carries in its genes the formula for how it will evolve.

"How else does a carrot know to grow itself into a carrot?" says biophysicist James McAlear, the president of EMV Associates. "The carrot's formula is locked inside its genes. The end result of that cell can only be one thing—a carrot."

To explain, he draws another analogy. "It is as if in every cell there were a Tinker Toy set," he says. "But instead of holes and pegs permitting random assembly, there are only locks and keys, so the parts can only be assembled one way."

In drawing up theoretical models for self-assembling biochips, researchers are borrowing genetic engineering techniques, that create new molecules or modify existing ones.

"We know," Mr. McAlear says, "that a virus molecule can be pulled apart and that when it is thrown back into a test tube, it will reassemble itself. What we hope to do is produce new molecules that, when combined, would form a predicted structure suitable for computer circuits."

Mr. Ulmer of Genex doubts that a naturally occurring molecule suitable for computer microcircuits exists. But he adds: "It's possible today to make entirely new molecules using genetic engineering techniques. So, theoretically, we could construct an organic molecule that would have electronic properties."

Toward a Biochip

Some progress has been made in getting organic molecules to assemble themselves. EMV holds a patent on what Mr. McAlear calls a basic pattern for a biochip. It involves proteins that lock themselves together in specific and predictable ways.

Working under a grant from the National Science Foundation, EMV is looking for ways to link computers to the brain. Mr. McAlear says his company's experiments prove that living nerve cells from animal embryos could be attached to certain proteins to form a "bridge," or "wire" of living tissue connecting a computer and the brain. The aim of this research, he says, is to use such a bridge to connect a biochip implanted in the visual cortex of the brain to a visual sensor worn on a pair of glasses. It is conceivable, he says, that such a device could correct blindness caused by nerve damage.

Even with today's relatively primitive silicon-chip technology, scientists can make implantable computers to help correct physical deficiencies. A project of the University of New Mexico School of Medicine and Sandia

National Laboratories has produced an implantable computer that regulates the flow of insulin in diabetics. The implant—now being used by three patients—is the size of a deck of cards and contains electronic controls, batteries, a motor and a pump within its thin, titanium case.

Before eating, the patient calculates his insulin dose using a formula that factors in his anticipated calorie intake from the meal and his blood-sugar level. He then uses a hand-held keyboard to instruct the implanted computer to deliver the correct dosage at the proper rate.

Computerized Steps

At Wright State University in Dayton, Ohio, Dr. Jerrold Petrofsky is using computers to attempt to reactivate the legs of paraplegics. The computers send signals to electrodes attached to the legs of young accident victims. With the computer's help, some of the patients have been able to ride stationary bicycles or, in the case of one young woman, take a few steps. Dr. Petrofsky says that all his hardware—various computers strung together with old telephone switchboard wire—could eventually be packaged in microprocessors the size of postage stamps.

Some on the outer theoretical fringes of biochip research speculate what might be possible if cell-sized computers were connected to the brain as logic and memory boosters.

Says Charles Lecht, the president of New York-based Lecht Sciences Inc. and the author of "Waves of Change," a 1977 book about the future of computing: "Some of our cells carry memory composed of information dating back to the primordial soup. But the memory courses along our genetic stream of consciousness without any means of retrieval. In this stream is locked the memory of how to fly and how to live under water, and perhaps even the secret of life—how it arose, and why, or even whether it ends with the death of the individual." Mr. Lecht suggests that, with biochips, man someday might be able to tap into this primordial memory, "remembering", for example, a time when the genetic material carried in his cells was part of a prehistoric aquatic creature.

Credibility Problems

Such speculation has done little to enhance the biochip's credibility in established scientific circles. As Mr. McAlear concedes, "We've had a real problem getting them to take us seriously." But he adds: "There were people who didn't believe the Wright brothers could fly an airplane even after they did it. So you can't blame people for not believing that we can build a molecular switch that will be able to self-assemble." He, being one of the field's optimists, believes that a molecular switch that functions like a transistor could be developed within five years.

At IBM, officials soft-pedal the company's research in organic computers, stressing that no work is being done in implantable computers. But two IBM scientists hold the patent on an organic memory-device developed in the 1970s.

When asked whether an organic computer is feasible, Louis Robinson, IBM's director of university relations, replies: "In science it's foolish to say something is impossible." And to those who flinch at the idea of a man-made computer someday implanted in the human brain, he observes that "at the microcosmic level, the distinction between animate and inanimate is a difficult question. Microscopic organisms sometimes seem alive and sometimes seem like rocks."

Already, others point out, human beings habitually alter the brain's "normal" functioning—whenever they take an aspirin for a headache, smoke a cigarette or drink coffee. Such substances, Mr. Lecht says, can be regarded as "chemical implants," no less "artificial" than an implant organic computer.

THE BORN-AGAIN TECHNOLOGY

New technology is offering the world instant two-way communication—of documents and data as well as voice—from virtually anywhere to anywhere. For equipment manufacturers, the commercial aspects are dazzling; even selling telephone systems promises new riches as the industrialised countries belatedly struggle to acquire the easy access that Americans have enjoyed for decades and as the developing world strives to give its villages their first telephone.

How can governments help their national telecommunications industries to capture the new markets? The American way—dismantling monopoly to stimulate competition—has both excited and bewildered onlookers. The benefits of opening telecommunications to competition, as Mrs Thatcher's government well knows, look enormous. So do the risks. Brenda Maddox reports.

Once upon a time the world of telecommunications was cosy and boring. Few national leaders paid much attention to it and no political hostess felt her dining table adorned by the presence of a minister for posts and telephones. In most countries the telecommunications network was a state-owned monopoly or, in the United States, as near as made no difference. Quietly, between themselves, the national monopoly and its main suppliers agreed what to design and manufacture at what price. Telephone subscribers took what they were given, and manufacturers looked towards their country's traditional export markets.

All that is changed utterly. Telecommunications has moved to the top of the political agenda. New technology is breaking up the monopoly control of telecommunications; companies are begging their governments to help them to innovate so as to win new world markets.

In the United States, President Reagan is taking a personal, and predictable, hand in the seven-year struggle by the justice department, and the five-year one

by congress, to break the domination of the communications industry by the American Telephone and Telegraph Company (AT&T). Even so, AT&T, the world's biggest company in spite of being confined to the domestic market, has already formed for the first time an AT&T International. In Britain, the telecommunications business has been split off from the labour-intensive postal service and itself opened to competition. The bill making all this happen has been called (by Mr Kenneth Baker, the industry minister responsible) the single most important piece of legislation to be passed by this government.

In Brussels, the European commission is labouring to persuade the EEC member countries to relax their protectionist barriers and sell telecommunications equipment to each other. In Geneva, the United Nations International Telecommunications Union has declared 1983 Telecommunications Year, with a goal that will please manufacturers: to bring every country up to a standard of one telephone for every hundred people.

Telecommunications owes its en-

hanced political status to three separate forces:
- Governments like the British and French which have realised that their countries cannot participate in the full flowering of information technology without good telecommunications.
- The computer and telecommunications industries, each of which sees its main possibility of future growth lying in the other's traditional territory.
- Multinational companies and banks which have woken up to their need for a round-the-clock, unimpeded global flow of information and cash transfers—and to the fragility of their communications links. The big spenders (which account for more than 40% of the revenue of AT&T's Bell telephone system) want more choice and better service.

Add to these the facts that telecommunications' modernisation involves massive expenditures of government money and raises problems of redundancy and protecting domestic industries, and it is obvious that telecommunications is never going to go back to its old quiet corner.

A digital tide

Technology has created all these pressures. Digital techniques and microelectronics have rejuvenated telecommunications, giving its devices the speed, lightness and "intelligence" of computers. The distinction between telecommunications and computers is now technological nonsense. If, indeed, it ever made sense, for it was AT&T's Bell Laboratories which invented the transistor, whose ability to switch electrical current "on" and "off" in a tiny space with no moving parts, made the computer industry possible.

Today the world's telephone networks are changing over to computer language, using on-off (or digital) codes and abandoning the traditional analogue code. In analogue transmission electrical pulses mimic the rise and fall of the human voice and, travelling at 9.6 kilobits a second, woefully slow down data transmission in the telephone network. In digital form, voices, data, telex and facsimile can all travel at 64 kilobits a second, also more cheaply and more accurately.

Telephone exchanges are also going digital. The heart of any telephone system, the exchange is the place where incoming calls are accepted and routed to their destination. Even old-fashioned electro-mechanical exchanges, which

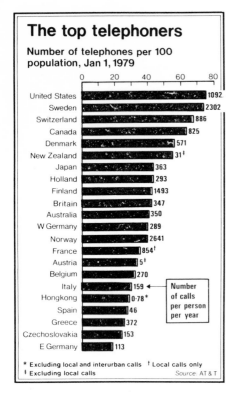

The top telephoners

Number of telephones per 100 population, Jan 1, 1979

Country	Value	Number of calls per person per year
United States		1092
Sweden		2302
Switzerland		886
Canada		825
Denmark		571
New Zealand		31‡
Japan		363
Holland		293
Finland		1493
Britain		347
Australia		350
W Germany		289
Norway		2641
France		854†
Austria		5‡
Belgium		270
Italy		159
Hongkong		0·78*
Spain		46
Greece		372
Czechoslovakia		153
E Germany		113

* Excluding local and interurban calls † Local calls only
‡ Excluding local calls   Source: AT&T

click out telephone numbers step-by-step, are now often controlled by a computer. New all-electronic digital exchanges like Britain's costly System X (see later) work without moving parts and are, in effect, computers themselves. It is not surprising that the world's largest computer is owned by a telephone company—Nippon Telegraph and Telephone.

Nor should it be surprising that computers can act as telephone exchanges. They can set up a path between two telephones, just as they can do addressing or billing or almost any office chore. Certainly they can deliver messages: IBM sees electronic mail—the high-speed delivery of printed documents—as the logical extension of its business.

The coming together of these two technologies, one new, the other old, has caused the French to invent the word "telematics", a Harvard professor to come up with "compunications" and the industry to speak of "convergence". What they all are trying to convey is that nobody—not bureaucrats, not lawyers, not customers, certainly not engineers—can say anymore where data-processing stops and message-carrying begins.

Both industries are enjoying a fall in costs and rise in capacity of about 10% a year in real terms, thanks to the benefits from large-scale integration, the packing of more and more transistors on to a single silicon chip.

The rivalry between the two industries presents a big headache for government. (IBM versus AT&T is arguably the big-gest political fight in America.) The consolation to all sides is that the converging industries may be fighting over an expanding pie that may prove more than enough for both.

Optical reality

Communications traffic travels four ways, depending on the distance it has to cover: along pairs of copper wires for local services; by microwaves (tower-to-tower) for distances about 30 miles apart; through copper coaxial cables, particularly for long-distance trunk routes over land or sea, and by satellite for very long hauls, particularly over water.

All transmission media are still expanding in capacity and speed: an AT&T subsidiary's coaxial cable being installed in California can, for example, transmit an entire 76-page newspaper from city to city in a second. Satellites are growing bigger and bigger (and earth stations correspondingly smaller and cheaper). They are considered to be a mature middle-aged technology. The first Intelsat satellite over the Atlantic carried 240 telephone conversations or two television channels. The latest Intelsat V carries 12,000—and television as well. By the end of the century the Intelsat system should be offering 700,000 international voice circuits. Satellites will be launched by shuttle, assembled in space to form clusters or erected on platforms as big as a football field. So what else is new?

Optical fibres, that's what. Five years ago the great hope for the next leap forward in terrestrial transmission lay in waveguides: hollow tubes along which pulses of laser light were to be sent, carrying telephone calls by the thousands. Both AT&T and the British Post Office (now renamed British Telecom) committed themselves wholeheartedly to waveguides. Now waveguides are dead and forgotten, killed by the surging success of the development of optical fibres.

It is now possible for two strands of high-purity glass, each thinner than a human hair, to carry 2,000 telephone calls. Four pairs can be squeezed into a cable (see the cover of this survey), whose size corresponds to that of a co-axial cable as a pencil does to the human arm. As glass is cheaper than copper, and the photons of light which carry the signals inside the fibre are cheaper than the electrical pulses which go along a coaxial cable, optical fibre requires far fewer repeaters.

Optical fibres, according to a study by Mr Malcolm Ross of Arthur D. Little, could become more economic than satellites over all but the longest distances by 1995, even on transoceanic routes. (The first transatlantic fibre optic cable is projected for 1988.)

Optical fibres are going into trunk networks now. Britain already has 4,000 miles in service, which operate at a maximum of 140m bits a second. AT&T has begun to set up a 631-mile optic link between Washington and Cambridge, Massachusetts. Nippon Telegraph and Telephone plans to introduce a commercial test in 12 cities. The French, Germans and Swiss have also begun to install optical fibres. The next step ahead (already under construction by British Telecom) will use an even finer fibre, and will

Light as hair—and 2,000 telephone calls each

carry 10,000 telephone channels.

The next obstacle looks harder: finding how to use optical fibres for local links with homes and offices. When this technique is perfected, the telephone cable will become broadband (that is, carrying a far wider spread of frequencies than narrow-band telephone wire) and therefore able to carry television into the home. It will then rival satellites and cable television as a medium for distributing pay-TV films. Right now Bell is conducting local optical experiments in Connecticut and New York, while France is embarked on an ambitious optical-wiring of homes in Biarritz.

Is there any demand for so many channels at such speed? The marketplace will tell. But technically, transmission is a problem solved. After glass hairs, there is nothing left to pursue. Except perhaps the electrical transfer of thought? "Who would want that?" asks an engineer. "Thought is awfully slow."

Satellite to home—in Blue Creek, West Virginia

Getting the goods

While debates rage about the best way to improve public telecommunications networks, the consumer goods that attach to the ends of the network are becoming so attractive that some people will buy them even if it means defying the law, as they did in Britain with citizens' band radio.

What you can buy depends on where you live, not on technology. For a start, you might consider a **satellite earth station.** About $6,000 will get you (in the United States) a 10-foot dish that will impress your neighbours and pull down 40 or more television programmes from the sky. If you live somewhere else, or don't have the money, just wait. The dishes will drop in size to a yard across and the price to about $100.

More modest gadgets include **intelligent telephones,** which will soon (even in Britain) become as commonplace as the socket and plug that allows all telephones to be moved from room to room. These can accept instructions to forward calls, wake you up, leave messages, calculate the cost of the call and remember for you the telephone numbers you frequently call.

The age of the **answering machine** is just dawning. The kind to buy is one which allows you to ring home, collect messages that have come in and change the message you leave behind. This device can act as a family message centre, collecting and delivering messages from husband, wife and children without any of them needing to be at home. (You need to send an acoustical signal into the machine to retrieve your messages; other callers will not get them.) The commercial possibilities of these machines have

hardly been tapped—as a means of communication on the day's inventory between, say, a supermarket chain and its branches or of taking orders for advertised goods and services. One improvement over older varieties is that these new machines, when delivering a stored message, begin at the beginning.

Cheaper is the **electronic answering service** which can deal with calls for thousands of subscribers, storing their messages in electronic cubbyholes. The subscriber can retrieve messages just by giving his own tone or number.

A **scribophone**, or writing telephone, enables the user to display drawings or graphs on a videoscreen attached to the telephone. By writing on a sensitised electronic pad, the speaker can alter the drawing during the conversation.

Some innovations are demanded by the public; others are thrust upon it. Time will tell whether the customers want **videotex**, a marriage of the television screen with telephone lines. Britain's Prestel was designed for home users but a number of costly years later it now seems to be finding its future among business users who want it not for retrieving general information but for transactions like exchanging information about reservations and for retrieving information in other systems' computers. Like high-speed **facsimile**, for which there is a greater demand, videotex service will be slowed up by a confusion of technical standards, for such services, before taking off commercially, must be able to interconnect with millions of others.

The **cordless telephone**, on the other hand, is gaining ground in Britain even though it is illegal and has every prospect of remaining so. This is a portable extension telephone—indispensible, once he's

tried it, to a farmer, builders' merchant or car dealer who wants to be able to receive calls when away from his single, fixed telephone. British Telecom would be happy to provide these cordless telephones; electronic goods shops do sell them (penalties against them doing so are coming soon) but the home office will not release the necessary radio frequencies.

On the move

Over the next decade, the world will spend $640 billion on telecommunications equipment, estimates the consultants, Arthur D. Little. A good share of that will go on mobile radio, including satellite-borne maritime communications, air-to-ground services and an infinite variety of forms of telephoning between cars and public exchanges.

Radio paging—one-way communication between a station and people on the move—is already a winner. Very popular in the United States and Japan, it is underdeveloped in Europe, but British Telecom expects to reach 1.6m people with its new nationwide service in a few years. Among its offerings is a "pager" made by Standard Telephones and Cables which is as small as a cigarette lighter and dispenses four tones, indicating which of four numbers to call back.

The growth of mobile communication will be aided by the increasing sophistication of **cellular radio**. This technique helps overcome the obstacle to mobile communications everywhere—the shortage of radio frequencies over which to travel through the air. Cellular radio uses low-powered base stations to communicate with mobile transmitters (or car telephones) and then links them to the public telephone system. The transmit-

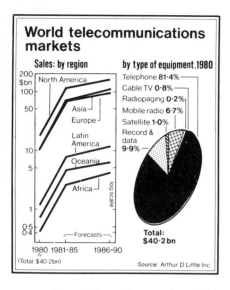

World telecommunications markets

Sales: by region

by type of equipment, 1980

200 $bn
100
50
10
5
1
0.5
0.4

North America
Asia
Europe
Latin America
Oceania
Africa

log scale

Forecasts

1980 1981-85 1986-90
(Total: $40.2bn)

Telephone 81·4%
Cable TV 0·8%
Radiopaging 0·2%
Mobile radio 6·7%
Satellite 1·0%
Record & data 9·9%

Total: $40.2bn

Source: Arthur D Little Inc

ters are located throughout a city, which is subdivided into a honeycomb of small radio zones. Thus, radio frequencies which would otherwise be occupied by a few services city-wide can be broken up and re-used over and over again in different areas—as long as two adjacent areas do not use the same frequency.

Trials of this technique are under way in Britain, continental Europe, Japan and Mexico. The Bell system is conducting a $20m field trial in Chicago. The capacity of that 2,100-square-mile patch is now about 5,000 subscribers but could, as cell sizes become progressively reduced, eventually support 300,000 car telephones—more than any but the biggest cities might require in the foreseeable future.

Cellular radio opens up the possibility of the telephone on every wrist, and the personal telephone number. Some day it will seem absurd to ring a telephone when it is the person, not the instrument, that you are trying to find.

Speak to me

What's the biggest obstacle between man and computer? The need to address it in a special language typed in on a keyboard. So the race is on to smooth the "man-machine interface". The pot of gold will go to the first company to market a machine that understands the unconstrained continuous speech of man, woman or child.

"Voice recognition" is of vital importance to telephone services, to banks and also to two other groups: the Japanese and the male sex. The Japanese because their language is fiendishly difficult to handle in office systems using a keyboard (think what the Japanese might have accomplished in exports without this handicap) and men because, by and large, they have not learned to type. If

men want to instruct a word processor (that is a typewriter and a screen connected to a computer) they have to get a secretary to type the instructions in.

It is not irrelevant to the slow advance of sophisticated telecommunications in Europe that so many businessmen are unrepentant male chauvinists. They see most office work as women's work. Even the salesmen of advanced business machines think of their new products as a superior female. "Like a good secretary", one extolled his office automation system, "it will do virtually anything you tell her to do." Or as the managing director said of his electronic switchboard: "It can do filing too—better than some little girl in cotton knickers." The irony is that women executives are resistant to word processors too, for the keyboard reminds them of secretarial work—something they have risen above.

Machine recognition of virtually any number of voices will come in 20 years or so, but it will be preceded by three other steps:

● **Character recognition.** This technique is well advanced, providing a world market of $400m a year in systems that can read text—typed, printed or handwritten. Banks and postal systems are the big customers while the most visible version is the hand-held reader used in stores to read price labels.

● **Voice response.** Starting with Texas Instruments' Speak and Spell, a growing range of electronic games vocally tells the player how well he has done and invites him to try again. The technique, spurred by large-scale integrated circuitry, will make rapid headway in both public and private telephone exchanges; in offices, it can truly do the secretary's chores of saying "out to lunch" or "on holiday until the first of the month" and the voices,

assembled from the basic elements of speech from a digital store in the computer, are becoming increasingly friendly and humanoid. (It should not be difficult to replace the robotic sound of the Bell-trained operator: "That li-on is busy.")

● **Voice identification.** Systems can already be designed to recognise the identity of a particular speaker (by matching his voice with the stored record of his voice). Eventually the technique may be used in police work to trace and match voices, like fingerprints. More immediate applications will permit selected access to paying-by-telephone, to bank statements or to security-protected buildings.

On the way to the long-term goal, the voice typewriter should emerge, turning the spoken word into printed text. Gradually, then, voice recognition machines will be able to comprehend an expanding vocabulary and an increasing variety of voices, not just their programmer's. Eventually they may supersede push-button telephones as the instrument of communication. The manager will then be able to shout instructions at the computer instead of at the secretary and the industrial worker can sit and talk to his machine.

First, choose your switchboard

Business, not the home, will lead the drive for new telecommunications products and the essential piece of equipment for any company interested in joining the information revolution is a computer-controlled switchboard. Saddled with an ugly label—PABXs (for private automatic branch exchanges)—electronic versions give companies a chance to create a superb internal telephone network, connecting branches with head office, and offering, in addition, automatic retrying of engaged numbers, call forwarding, conference calls, itemised billing, night answering service and even data-processing. (The 300-line PABX just installed at the Dorchester Hotel by Philips Business Systems, for example, not only handles all telephones but prepares the customers' bills and supplies the hotel's pay-TV service.) Their most conspicuous advantage is to cram the kind of switchboard equipment that used to fill an eight-by-five room into a space the size of a briefcase.

Their eventual applications seem boundless. PABXs can control machinery remotely; they can "manage" energy, in the sense that they can turn electricity on and off in specified locations, carry burglar and fire alarm signals and they can connect word-processors. Simply automating message-taking might

Beautiful!

Operators fall in love with it.

And so will you.
Phone Phil Astill for a demonstration on 0784 51488.

make it worth a company's while to invest in a big electronic PABX, for today only one in four telephone calls reaches the intended person at first try and to eliminate the time wasted in waiting and transferring calls would mean a big jump in office productivity.

But only if a company can buy what it wants. Telephone monopolies are very jealous about what may be attached to their networks. IBM found that the PABX marked the front-line between the rival computer and communications industries when in 1968 it tried to introduce its first digital-controlled switchboard in Europe. For a long time it could not get permission from the British Post Office, for example, to install it.

The fact is that, apart from public telephone exchange equipment, PABXs are where the big money now lies and telecommunications monopolies tend to favour their national suppliers, and to control installation and maintenance themselves.

One of the most powerful forces leading to the demolition of British Telecom's monopoly was the rage and frustration of British businesses waiting for 18 months or more for British Telecom (or the old Post Office) to give them a switchboard. Theirs is a diluted victory, however. British Telecom will not have to surrender its monopoly on small PABXs (that is, those with under 100 lines) for three years. In that period, if British businesses want to buy themselves the Canadian Mitel PABX (available abroad for about £90 a line) they will have to take the version British Telecom is manufacturing under licence—at a higher price.

X marks the question

Don't be deceived by the new gadgetry. Public telephone equipment is what accounts for 50% of the world market for telecommunications equipment of all kinds. As Britain has learned to its cost. It was the world leader in exports until 1963, then lost its lead because of a disastrous misjudgment about the kind of exchange to replace the old electro-mechanical system that was the backbone of everybody's prewar telephone network.

Britain is now trying to recapture that lead with a digital exchange called System X. It is not going to succeed. What is clear to anybody outside British Telecom and the consortium of its three big suppliers (Plessey, GEC and STC) which were paid to do the development, System X will make about as much impact on world markets as the Concorde. Not that the exchange won't work. It will, and well. System X simply is too late, and too over-

System X: overdue and over-smart

engineered to overtake its rivals.

Every major manufacturer is now scouring the world for new markets, with its own model of digital exchange as its standard-bearer, complete with soft loans from its government and promises of local manufacture as bait. Even Western Electric, AT&T's wholly owned supplier, which already has 80% of the American market (and is likely to hold on to it no matter how the justice department's antitrust suit against AT&T comes out) is looking for contracts abroad. Japan is best placed to scoop up many of the new markets in Asia (which will constitute a market 20% bigger than Europe's) by 1990. Among the European contenders, Sweden's L.M. Ericsson probably has the lead in digital exchanges; its AXE system has been sold to 27 countries, including Ireland. Belgium-based ITT's System 12 is doing well and CIT-Alcatel and Thomson-CSF of France, both spurred by that country's massive investment programme, have each sold their respective digital exchanges in about 20 countries. The fattest contracts have gone to groups: Philips, Ericsson and Bell Canada captured Saudi Arabia's contract while Thomson and Siemens of Germany are handling the £2 billion modernisation of Egypt's telephones.

So far System X, unveiled in Geneva two years ago, has not got a single international customer, although there are some nibbles which the suppliers (working through a joint marketing group for exports) call promising. There are high hopes that India will bite. At home Britain already has one System X exchange working, and should have eight in place in the domestic network by the mid-1980s.

Only eight? That is not fast enough to pull Britain into the mainstream of digital

telephony. By then System X's benefits, like the long overdue itemised telephone bill, will be available only piecemeal—at extra cost, probably a high one. France will be installing nothing but digital exchanges. The Bell system electronic exchanges already offer some subscribers the kind of enhanced telephone service enjoyed in Britain only by owners of big PABXs.

Mr Michael Corby of the Telecommunications' Users Association advises: "For planning purposes, for the next five to 10 years, unless you are in an exceptional area, you can forget about System X." Until more than half of all subscribers are connected, it will not bring overall improvement to the British network— and not even then unless British Telecom also manages to revitalise its leaky cable networks under the streets.

The worst thing about System X lies in its development cost, although any foreign buyers will be shielded from that. Claiming that System X is the only digital exchange in the world to have been financed virtually entirely by the telephone authority, not the manufacturers, British Telecom will not deny that £400m has been spent and its critics think that £1 billion is nearer the mark.

Its design weakness—which British Telecom has now told the engineers to try to cure in the second generation—is that it incorporates too much "intelligence" in the exchange, making it slow to develop and costlier than necessary. Business customers will already have paid for such information-processing services in their terminal equipment. Where to concentrate intelligence, or computer power, is a general problem in network design. The current philosophy is to diffuse it to the ends of the system—where the customers will pay for it—and to leave the central exchange as simple as possible. System X is too clever by half—at today's telephone subscriber's expense.

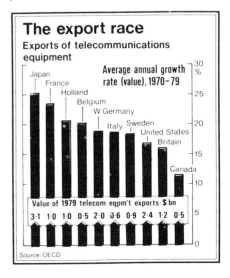

SOUNDING THE BATTLE CRY

A telecommunications revolution will bring profound economic and social changes.

The weeks leading up to the breakup of AT&T on Jan. 1 have been filled with hullabaloo and political bickering about consumer phone rates and access charges. All this shouting may have drowned out the real sounds of battle. For an enormous industrial struggle is at hand, pitting American companies against each other and American technology against Japanese and European technology. The prize is dominance of the brave new world of telecommunications, and the stakes are not only economic but social, for this competition is almost sure to bring profound changes in the way people work and how they organize their lives. "The world is going to look back on this period as the beginning of the flowering of the information economy," predicts William McGowan, chairman of MCI Communications, which won a landmark antitrust case against AT&T.

The industry is already undergoing explosive growth. More than $94 billion was spent in the American market last year for telecommunications equipment and services. Analysts estimate that the total will jump to more than $100 billion in 1984, fueled by advances in technology and the competitive free-for-all that will follow the AT&T breakup. Independents stand to reap a huge windfall. Local Bell telephone companies will no longer necessarily buy equipment from AT&T's giant manufacturing arm, Western Electric, opening the market to other companies. And new telecommunication services are proliferating. "A lot of companies will seize a piece of the action," says Fritz Ringling, telecommunications analyst for the Gartner Group.

The toughest battles in the telecommunications-equipment market will be fought over the sales of huge network switches—actually very large computers—that the local telephone companies use to operate their systems. There will also be intense competition over sales of PBX's, the electronic switchboards that form the heart of office networks. Traditionally, Western Electric has had the lion's share of the $12 billion market for telephone-company switching gear, but ITT, Siemens, Sweden's L.M. Ericsson, GTE and Canadian-based Northern Telcom hope to come on strong.

Dismembering AT&T will open up huge markets for specialized telecommunications services—long-distance voice and data communications, cellular radio (cordless phones for use in cars and briefcases), teleconferencing, electronic mail and information-retrieval services. In the long-distance voice and data-communications markets, AT&T's chief competitors will be MCI, GTE, ITT and Satellite Business Systems, a partnership backed by IBM, Comsat and Aetna Insurance. McGowan predicts that data markets alone will grow at 25 percent annually.

Electronic Mail: Cellular radio is just beginning; the first system began operation in Chicago in October. Local telephone companies will control half of the U.S. market, while the rest will be served by an array of companies including MCI, Metromedia, Graphic Scanning and The Washington Post Company (NEWSWEEK's parent company). In the emerging teleconferencing business, AT&T, SBS and hotel chains will be the main competitors. Another new telecommunications service is electronic mail—a way to bypass postal or express services by sending messages directly from computer to computer. GTE's Telenet has the largest market share, MCI has just announced a huge electronic-mail system and Federal Express and other companies are expected to follow suit.

This enormous growth in the telecommunications industry is being powered by dramatic technological advances and a decline in the cost of computer intelligence and communications. Microelectronics have transformed a wide spectrum of products—from telephones to video games. The machine world is beginning to use the same universal language—the digital codes of computers. Information once stored on paper and physically transported from one location to another now exists in digitized form and can be transported electronically. Even the machinist's skill has been captured digitally in the growing robotics industry.

The digital revolution is changing the nature of the telephone network, which once carried only analog voice communications. "There is no medium where digital is not less expensive," says Solomon J. Buchsbaum of Bell Laboratories. "That drives the networks to digital, and once the networks are digital, you mix up things like voice and video and send them along in one stream." Some critics of the AT&T breakup, however, worry that the technical integrity of the evolving telecommunications network will ultimately suffer—leaving it prone to the equivalent of potholes or bridge collapses.

Social Changes: The social impact of these technological changes has only just begun. For one thing, many jobs are likely to be eliminated or transformed. An enormous number of people are simply human message switches, says McGowan. "When you get all through examining that equation, you realize, considering how much space they take up, and cost, and air conditioning and heat, you can easily figure out how you can do it far less expensively, far quicker, automatically. So there are going to be major structural changes in the way business is organized." Social changes will also be brought by dramatic shifts in telecommunications costs: big corporations may benefit at the expense of small users.

Clearly, there is no end in sight to the rapid pace of innovation in microelectronics and telecommunications technologies. True believers like McGowan are confident that the transformation wrought by the new age in telecommunications will invigorate the American economy. "The new battle on the frontier is not over who's going to make steel cheaper," he says. "The real competition is what country, what system can best handle the marriage of computering power with information and telecommunications. I happen to believe we have a natural system for it." He may be right. The most important impact of the breakup of the Bell system next week will probably have little to do with the telephone and everything to do with the Information Age now aborning.

WILLIAM D. MARBACH with WILLIAM J. COOK
and CHRISTOPHER MA in Washington and
JENNET CONANT in New York

TV'S HIGHER-TECH FUTURE

More than 40 years ago, a group of 168 engineers and executives met to hammer out technical standards for the exotic new technology known as television. At the time there were only a few thousand television sets in the entire United States. Today, nearly every home has one and electronic technology has raced ahead, but American television still broadcasts at the same 525-line signal standard the National Television Standards Committee (NTSC) adopted in March 1941—leaving viewers with a picture quality not substantially better than it was at the industry's birth. "That was as far as we knew how to go in those days," says Joseph Flaherty, chief engineer for CBS Laboratories. "But now we're getting close to wringing the last bit out of 525 lines. It's time to take the next big step."

As demands on television technology grow, so does impatience with the existing standard. TV no longer just serves the simple function it did in the days of Howdy Doody and Ed Sullivan. "People are using TV's for more things now—for their computer, VCR, laser-disc player, video-game machine," says Lee Isgur, electronics-industry analyst for Paine Webber. "They need higher resolution." Just what new standards will emerge is not yet clear, but in comparison with the hazy, dull visual quality of today's television, the new technologies offer dramatic improvements. "Once you've experienced [high-definition television], it's hard to go back to the old product," says Yasuhiko Kuroda of Sony Corp.

Crisp Images: A television image is created by an electron beam scanning rapidly across a phosphorcoated screen. In the United States and Japan, the broadcast signal carries 525 lines of information. The more lines the signal carries, the greater the resolution—and the higher the quality of the picture. Western European broadcasters, who did not adopt a television-transmission standard until 1967, chose a 625-line standard, and as a result enjoy distinct-

ly better picture quality. In the United States, however, most viewers do not even get the full benefit of the NTSC standard: most sets display only about 300 lines; the rest of the information is lost. By refining the technology—using special line-comb filters—manufacturers have been able to achieve much crisper images, up to 500 lines, on high-priced television sets and monitors.

A major technological leap forward will occur with the advent of digital television, which should appear on the market in 1984. ITT, Matsushita, RCA, Philips and others are developing powerful semiconductor chips that will replace much of the circuitry in conventional sets. Digital TV sets will receive the 525-line broadcast signals in analog form—as continuous waves—but will break both audio and video into digital data—the same code of zeros and ones used by computers. Digital processing should permit several important technical feats: the sets will be able to store the image in memory for a split second—editing out extraneous ghosts, colors and other artifacts before the image is displayed, thereby producing purer color and sharper detail. Digital should also make it possible for the home user to split the screen and zoom in for close-ups.

Digital may be only a transition, however. Some engineers would like to take a much bolder step into the future. "Now with the state of technology it is possible to double the resolution and widen the screen and to deliver cinematography quality in the home," says Flaherty. High-definition television—HDTV, as it is called—would break the stranglehold of the 525-line NTSC standard and offer wider-screen pictures with much higher resolution, 800 lines or more. Doubling the resolution makes the detail, depth and clarity of the picture startling.

HDTV is a huge gamble. Initially, it was developed at the Tokyo laboratories of NHK, Japan's public-broadcasting system. In the late 1960s, NHK engineers considered proposals

for television with three-dimensional images, even for a TV that emitted smells, but decided instead to try to create television images with quality as good as or better than 35-mm film. They succeeded beautifully: NHK's HDTV uses 1,125 scanning lines and a wider screen, virtually eliminating screen flicker. NHK hopes that the ambitious new system will be adopted as the new worldwide standard for television broadcasting. Over the last 10 years the major technological problems have been solved, and Sony, Matsushita and Ikegami have already built HDTV prototypes.

But the gamble may backfire. Despite its technological dazzle, NHK's 1,125-line system has one gigantic handicap: it is incompatible with all existing American and Japanese 525-line sets and broadcasting stations and with Europe's 625-line system. "Thousands of millions of television sets all over the world would be rendered useless if the new system were adopted," says Kuroda of Sony.

'Economics': To avoid the cost of replacing all existing television equipment, CBS and Philips are developing HDTV based on a compromise: the systems would combine two satellite-broadcast channels to deliver a high-definition image. Conventional sets could pick up one channel for a 525-line image, the second channel would be received by HDTV sets and combined with the first to create cinema quality. With the technology within its grasp, the television industry has formed a committee—the Advanced Television System Committee—to hammer out an HDTV standard for a proposal to the Federal Communications Commission. But with many vested interests at stake, the wrangling is far from over. "It's not a matter of technology," says Fuminori Shiga, deputy chief of research at NHK's laboratories in Tokyo, "but of politics and economics."

WILLIAM D. MARBACH with JENNET CONANT
in New York and NANCY UKAI in Tokyo

HOW TELETEXT AND VIDEOTEX WILL SHAPE SOCIETY

Any technology that achieves widespread penetration will bring with it direct and indirect changes in the ways people relate to one another, to institutions, and to the technology. The direct changes usually show up quickly; in general, they are extrapolations of the existing social order. Indirect changes, on the other hand, tend to appear more slowly. They are often not extrapolations of the past but second-order consequences of direct effects. They challenge some basic foundations of organizations and institutions.

Second-order consequences are also somewhat less predictable than direct, extrapolative changes. There is an element of the unintended and unanticipated in these effects. They often reveal themselves only after the technology has been adopted and adapted by the users. In short, they may be considered *transformative effects*. Television, for example, was developed to provide entertainment for mass audiences but the extent of its social and psychological side effects on children and adults was never planned for. The mass-produced automobile has impacted city design, allocation of recreation time, environmental policy, and the design of hospital emergency room facilities.

So far, we have focused on direct policy issues likely to arise as a result of introducing videotex and teletext (developmental policy issues), together with the extrapolative policy issues that may also arise as a result of widespread penetration (consequential issues). In this chapter, our aim is to consider the indirect long-term transformative effects of this technology. In some sense we are now hypothesizing not only widespread penetration but societal adoption and integration of the technology. The question being addressed is: what happens to the present organization of society?

The more direct developmental and consequential effects can be targeted with the help of the types of methodologies used in this study. Transformative effects are less easily identified. They are also less easily tied to direct public policy intervention. Yet they are important for policymakers to understand because they provide a backdrop for the more direct policy choices; they will influence how such choices will interleave with other social changes in the coming decades. It is also important to look at transformative effects to devise, where possible, early warning signs that call attention to likely serious negative side effects of the new technology.

To identify transformative effects of teletext and videotex we have taken a building block approach. Within a general scenario of widespread penetration of teletext/videotex, we identify four key areas of societal impact. Each key area is then described against a backdrop of general societal trends and indicators, and a number of general themes comprising societal impacts and transformative effects are discussed. A workshop setting, with participants who are familiar with the long-term effects of technological innovation—especially communication or information technology—was used to generate much of the following information.

Reprinted by permission from J. Tydeman, et al, *Teletext and Videotex in the United States*, Data Communications, McGraw-Hill, Inc., New York, New York. 1982.

TELETEXT/VIDEOTEX SCENARIO: THE TECHNOLOGY

In considering transformative effects, we first of all need to make some basic assumptions for a "high-penetration" scenario. Whether or not the technology will develop in exact accord with the scenario is not important; what is important is *to identify the major changes that might occur, given the assumption that teletext/videotex has become almost as common as television or the telephone.* Assume the following scenario for 1998:

. . . It (teletext/videotex) has achieved relatively widespread penetration. It may not be in every home, but it is probably in a neighbor's home, and you might be considering getting the service yourself. It is used for all five classes of applications: information retrieval, messaging, transactions, computing, and telemonitoring. How it developed is not important for considering transformative effects. What is important is that the technology did develop and that it is being widely used. The service is paid for by information service providers, users, advertisers, and nonprofit/public organizations.

Networking capabilities are widely developed. Through packet-switched networks and satellite and terrestrial communication links, data and broadband networks have vastly increased in numbers and in services offered. Low-cost terminals are accepted and available much as cheap pocket calculators and digital watches were in the early 1980s.

Teletext and videotex exist in a world where digital communications have markedly altered the ways in which all electronic media—stand-alone or electronically linked—operate. Digital sound recording has not only upgraded the quality of sound reproduction but has also created an on-demand music delivery service for music and sound recordings. Video technology is comparable. Users are able to request particular programs from service suppliers when they want them. The dominant medium of the '60s and '70s—television—has become modular, with a variety of purposes, including program watching, terminal display, home movie projector, and more. The television set has also become interactive for both interconnect services (through telephone and cable) and for stand-alone uses (interactive videodiscs).

Microprocessors have become commonplace, not only in communications technology but in scores of other home and business products as well. Security and protection services, for example, have built-in microprocessors, allowing for multiple home, security, and emergency functions to be monitored simultaneously. Similarly, it has become more economical for utility companies to monitor and read home and office energy and water usage remotely.

For our analysis, then, the key features of the 1998 videotex and teletext environment are:

- widespread penetration
- growth of electronic networks
- interactive capabilities
- old media take new forms
- prevalence of microprocessors

KEY AREAS OF SOCIETAL IMPACT

For two broad groups of users—consumers and business—it is possible to identify four key areas where teletext and videotex technologies may make an impact. These are:

- the home and family life
- the consumer marketplace
- the business office
- the political arena

For each area we now examine some of the longer-term implications of teletext and videotex.

As stated in the scenario, these are not the only electronic technologies that will transform society. The effects we discuss, of necessity, include some of the impacts of associated technologies.

THE HOME AND FAMILY LIFE

Context By 1998, the post-Second World War baby-boom age group that has dominated society is between 45 and 55 years old. Lower death rates, higher income, and longer labor-force participation are prevalent for the elderly.

Rapid population growth continues in the south and the west, with most of the growth in "small big cities"—cities located in semirural areas with pleasant climates and willing workers. The rising cost of housing and house financing results in more shared living space—consumer units (the number of unrelated people living in the same household) continue to grow at a greater rate than household formation. The upturn in the birthrate that began in the mid-1980s puts further pressure on housing and begins to increase household size. There are still, however, in excess of 20 percent of the population living in single households (Institute for the Future, 1981).

In addition to TV, low-cost modular videotex terminals have given households another communication resource for everything from store-and-forward messaging to directory assistance and instant news updates. Middle- and upper-income families have several terminals available for different family members. New networks of interest and professional groups are linked via videotex systems. Much of the routine shopping is done from a home terminal by browsing through electronic catalogs. Not only does the videotex-equipped home have access to vast amounts of information, but the providers of information have some knowledge of the home and can tailor their information to the needs and interests of that home. Many videotex and teletext options are available, so consumers can choose from a range that extends from no-frills teletext to super-equipped videotex.

Transformative Effects All of the following effects were evoked by asking the question "What's going on in the American home in 1998?" They portend some big changes in the American home in the coming decades.

Electronic Home Family life is not limited to meals, weekend outings, and once-a-year vacations. Instead of being the glue that holds things together so that family members can do all those other things they're expected to do—such as work, school, and community gatherings—the family is the unit *that does those other things*, and the home is the place where they get done. Like the term "cottage industry," this view might seem to reflect a previous era when family trades were passed down from generation to generation and children were apprenticed to their parents. In the "electronic cottage," however, one electronic "tool kit" can support many information production trades.

Interdependence In the electronic home familial ties of interdependence may be based on new skills. Spouses may be drawn to each other as much for their ability to manipulate databases as for their ability to prepare gourmet meals or to play racquetball. But even more significant, particularly for the transition period, will be the skills of children. While even computer-literate adults are somewhat awed by digital technology, children are not, and they are learning to make good use of electronic information systems. Are child labor laws enforceable in this environment?

Men, Women, and Child Rearing The electronic cottage is the perfect technological solution to the problem of how women can have traditional careers and rear children at the same time, e.g., use the electronic technology to participate in information-related tasks from secretarial services to real estate management. It is also possible to use electronic communication to coordinate home-based tasks ranging from meal planning to electronic component production. The problem with this solution is that the problem is not simply a technological one. Nevertheless, knowledge workers in the 1990s may be more productive because they are working at home, and perhaps this increased productivity will allow both parents to be part-time parents and part-time workers, which in teletext/videotex math adds up to one full-time parent and two full-time incomes.

The Electronically Extended Family   If widespread use of in-home information and communication systems can recreate cottage industries, they might also recreate the extended family. In-home knowledge-related work seems a most suitable form of employment for the elderly. This possibility might conjure a view of self-sufficiency, independence, and isolation for the elderly. However, if the elderly are gainfully employed and fully occupied with productive work, it may be more desirable to have them around. This opens the whole question of government payment of retirement benefits and social security payments to a population that is employable. Mechanisms for enforcing retirement, or at least identifying bonafide retirees, are sought. Without IRS scrutiny of all electronic transactions, moonlighting and tax avoidance may become serious problems. We suspect that desirability may not be the key issue with respect to the elderly, but capital might be, as the next theme suggests.

Buying the Electronic Home   The electronic home is capital intensive, and someone has to capitalize it. But who? and how? One possibility is a kind of localized travel-communication trade-off: the family's second car might be traded for elaborate videotex and other electronic equipment. Alternatively the government might issue "information stamps," just as they now issue food stamps, if it became obvious that a lack of access to electronic information systems was creating a class of disadvantaged. That takes care of the cost of the electronics, but what about the home? It is costly and has been so for two decades. Consumer unit formation now significantly exceeds household formations. The elderly may hold a trump card here. It may be easier to add on rooms to existing homes and extend the family. Of course, the extended family need not be blood relatives. The house-holding elderly could "adopt" a younger family. Whether they are blood relatives or not, though, this extended family may wish to incorporate. Since a lot of work is going on in this home, there may be real tax advantages to this strategy. But what would be the impact on the tax base of communities and of the country as a whole? Are residential property taxes replaced by commercial taxes for home industries? What happens to zoning laws in such an environment? And finally, if families are corporations, are family relationships more subject to public scrutiny and legal sanctions than they are now?

The changes in work styles and family relationships described in these relations suggest other changes not directly related to work. Changes in the quality of interpersonal interaction in the family might include:

More Conflict   The family has often been seen as the institution that insulates family members from the competitive, conflict-prone world outside. But if the home is also the workplace, and family members are sharing business resources and swapping "knowledge" skills, the struggles with the outside world may increasingly become struggles in the home. This scenario raises questions about the stability of the already somewhat shaky family. It suggests that some other institution will need to evolve to fill the safe-haven role. It also foretells a steady stream of clients for marriage and family counselors who may grow to become a privileged—and powerful—profession comparable to today's physicians.

Peers Redefined   In contemporary society, peer groups are usually defined by age, thanks to an educational system that segregates students by age. Electronic home information systems such as teletext and videotex are blind to age. But they create classes of people based on interests, skills, and even specialized languages. As it becomes easier for individuals to link with various others of these classes, to establish relationships with members of these classes, to *identify* with them, ties with traditional peer group members may break down. And as these ties break down, so may the rules for appropriate behavior of one age group or another. Although the traditional rules for societal stratification are changing, it is not clear whether the new alliances result in a more or less socially stratified society.

The redefinition of peer relationships may *begin* with the establishment of personal electronic networks, but it probably won't get far so long as the educational system remains more or less intact. Some possible changes in the area of education are:

Retraining the Trainers In the information- and data-rich environment of 1998, there are numerous electronic resources available to the student and teacher for the learning process. As a result, the traditional role of the teacher has been transformed. Rote learning is greatly facilitated by numerous interactive systems accessible at school, home, and work. The teacher's role in this environment is to help young learners synthesize data and develop creative problem-solving skills. The best teachers have always seen themselves in this role, but the ''best'' are far from ''all.'' Retraining is a possibility, but the bureaucracy of education is big enough and powerful enough that many may resist. This resistance is likely to be politicized. In fact, the back-to-basics movement may be the first stage of this resistance.

Let There Be Generalists Just as the pocket calculator has changed the way students approach mathematics, videotex will change the way they approach education. In 1998, information technology is so widespread that job requirements have undergone a major shift. Rather than increasing specialization, there is, at the end of the century, a much greater demand for generalists with multispecialties. Since so much of information technology is devoted to relieving tasks that have, in the past, required highly specialized skills, it becomes advantageous to hire a knowledgeable generalist—in other words, a person who knows enough about the job area to function in it and who knows how to use information tools. However, generalists have traditionally been free-lancers; there are not a lot of corporate generalists.

FUTURE ENERGY TECHNOLOGIES

The search must continue for commercially attractive, clean sources of energy for generating the electricity our nation needs. There are several long-range programs underway to research new technologies with still unpredictable futures.

Are the nuclear energy technologies of the fast breeder reactor and fusion promising alternatives?

• Breeder reactors are designed to produce more fissionable material than they consume and to generate electric power simultaneously. In this way, they have the potential for extending the world's uranium reserves for centuries while providing much-needed electrical power. In fact, the uranium already mined and in storage, using breeder reactors, could generate as much electricity as 580 billion tons of coal—one and one-third times the nation's demonstrated coal reserve.

The breeder reactor can produce 50 times more energy from a pound of uranium than can be produced now in a current nuclear reactor. In fact, the neutrons produced in present nuclear power reactor systems are being wasted and could be used productively to breed new fuel. Once the present abundant source of neutrons, that is, the fissionable U-235, has been depleted (the U-235 resource is limited), no similar neutron source is available. Every day of present design power reactor operation loses forever the neutrons that could create valuable fuel.

Development of breeder reactors in other countries continues at an increasing pace. Large-scale demonstration breeder reactors presently are producing electricity in the Soviet Union (2 reactors) France (1), Great Britain (2), and Japan (1).

• Scientists have been working for over 25 years to control fusion as a power source. It may well be the most difficult technical task ever attempted, but the potential of fusion energy is enormous. There is enough deuterium—the fuel for fusion—in the world's oceans to supply current energy needs for billions of years, and the cost of extracting that deuterium is likely to be small.

For fusion reactions to take place, the high temperature gases must be held at certain minimum temperatures and densities. These conditions have been described as plasma confinement for at least one second at 100 million degrees Celsius at a density of about 100–1000 trillion (10^{12}) nuclei per cubic centimeter. Under these conditions, fusion can take place, releasing new helium nuclei, some free neutrons, and heat, which could be extracted for power generation.

Fusion power plants are inherently safe against "runaway reactions" since they contain only as much fuel as they can burn. Although the internal structure would become radioactive through neutron bombardment, the waste products of the fusion reaction itself are nonradioactive.

Work on fusion is continuing since the possible payoff of virtually unlimited energy supply is enormous. Fundamental research is still necessary, however, and in the absence of additional evidence the fusion reactor should not be considered a contributor to the national energy budget much before the middle of the next century. Electric utilities have allocated funds already to assure the availability of fusion reactors for maximum usefulness as quickly as possible.

What is magnetohydrodynamics?

The phenomenon of magnetohydrodynamics (MHD) produces electricity directly from heated gases, rather than by the mechanical spinning of a generator. The idea is to pass high temperature ionized gases through a powerful magnetic field. This produces a flow of electrons in the gases. This flow of electrons, when collected and transferred to an outside circuit, constitutes an electric current.

High efficiencies are in prospect for this process. It can be used in combination with existing turbogenerators, since the heat

Reprinted from *Alternative Energy Sources and Technologies: Answers to Your Questions.* Edison Electric Institute. 1983.

remaining in the superheated gases is still enough to make steam to power the existing turbines.

Magnetohydrodynamics (MHD) has been studied since the early 1940s. Two types of MHD generators are being considered. In one, the open cycle, the combustion gases form the conducting plasma, which is seeded with potassium carbonate or similar substances to promote ionization. Ionizing temperatures of from 3,400 to 4,700 degrees Fahrenheit are required, so the inlet air to the combustor must be preheated. The heat remaining in the expended combustion gas is used to provide heat for a conventional steam generating plant.

The second type of MHD generator maintains the plasma material separately from the combustion gases and uses heat exchangers to transfer the heat to the plasma. Typically, the plasma would be an inert gas such as argon seeded with cesium vapor. The ionization temperatures for the closed cycle MHD are around 3,000 degrees Fahrenheit.

After more than 30 years of investigation, however, there still are no clear-cut figures on the contribution MHD would make to the national energy budget. In combination with existing technology, MHD is expected to raise the efficiency of a steam plant by more than 15 percent. An investment of several billion dollars will have to be made to bring the technology up to a commercial stage.

While the technology is feasible, many problems remain. There are serious questions, for example, about recovery of the expensive seeding material, durability of some equipment, reliability of the electrodes, and performance of the superconducting magnet. Plant capital costs, durability, and emission controls are also major questions to be resolved.

Is the thermal energy in the ocean useful?

The idea of extracting useful work from the thermal energy in the world's oceans has been an attraction for over 100 years. Ocean thermal energy conversion (OTEC) is entering the engineering feasibility phase of the development process. Unlike other forms of solar energy, OTEC is most attractive for baseload—that is, full-time—generation of electricity.

The OTEC concept involves utilizing the temperature difference between warm surface waters and cold deep water to vaporize a fluid such as ammonia or propane. This vapor would then be used to drive a turbine generator to produce electricity.

Because of the small temperature difference involved, 35 degrees Fahrenheit or less, an OTEC plant would be very inefficient and would therefore require enormous equipment for relatively small amounts of power. One proposed design for an ocean thermal plant has an upper module 790 feet in diameter and 100 feet deep, with a cold water intake pipe 1,500 feet deep and 100 feet in diameter. The warm and cold ocean water would be pumped at about 6 billion gallons per hour (about one-third the flow of the Mississippi). The plant would have to be located 20 to 150 miles offshore to obtain the necessary water depth. This would necessitate a long and costly underwater transmission line.

In addition to the great expense associated with such a large plant, the engineering task of designing a structure to operate in a corrosive marine environment is formidable. The environmental impacts of an ocean thermal power plant are not known, but several can be identified. Mixing deep ocean water with surface water, for example, would vary the oxygen concentration of the ocean. The impact upon marine life is not known.

The French have been the most active in this technology, having installed several small systems. The direction most advocates recommend is to use OTEC installations to offset energy use in the continental U.S. For example, aluminum could be produced at sea and save electrical energy presently consumed in the United States. There is also the option of industrializing islands in the tropics and sub-tropics using off-shore power plants as a source of electricity.

The OTEC concept still requires a thorough investigation of the hardware requirements and the economics of installation and operation. In view of the obstacles and cost estimates to date, ocean thermal power is not expected to make a significant contribution to national electricity generation.

Can ocean motion—the tides—generate power?

Those who have had the experience of swimming in the ocean know waves pack a wallop and tides exert a strong pull. These forms of energy, too, are under study for possible use. So are the "rivers" in the oceans, such as the Gulf Stream and the Arctic Current.

A tidal power system operates in much the same way as a hydroelectric dam. A dam is constructed across a coastal inlet. The incoming tide runs through turbines in the dam, turning a generator to produce electricity. As the tide drops, the water runs out of the reservoir through the turbines, again generating electricity.

There are several advantages to tidal power. The energy of moving ocean water is free. Because tides depend on the unchanging cycles of the moon, tidal power would be intermittent but possibly more reliable than some other hydropower forms that can be affected by drought.

Unfortunately, there are only a limited number of places in the world where the tidal range—the difference in elevation between low and high tide—is great enough to justify construction. In the United States, the only possible sites are Passamaquoddy Bay in Northern Maine, Puget Sound in the Northwest, and the South coast of Alaska. Even these sites have problems—they have more desirable uses and are too far from places where the power is needed.

There are only two operating tidal plants. One is a 400-kilowatt unit at Kislaya Guba in the Soviet Union; the other is a 240,000-kilowatt unit at La Rance, France. There are no statistics on the Soviet plant, but the cost of electricity from the French plant is not competitive with costs from other methods of generating electricity.

Can energy be extracted from waves?

Concepts for extracting energy from waves fall into three categories: using the vertical rise and fall of waves to power either water or air turbines; using to-and-fro motion to turn turbines or to apply pressure intermittently against various oscillating devices; and converging waves into a trough or channel to maintain a "head" of water to drive turbines (i.e. to use the weight of falling water).

The Japanese utilize the up-and-down motion of waves to compress air to drive a small generator in a lighthouse. England has a modest research program for developing the contoured rocking vane or "Salter cam" and other wave energy conversion technology. Very little work is being done in the United States.

Studies indicate that producing the equivalent of the 2,000-megawatt power generated by the Columbia River dams would require collecting all the wave power from about 62 miles of the Oregon Coast at the rate of 32 megawatts a mile of coastline.

Using the swift currents in ocean waters, expecially those off Florida, to produce work has been proposed for many years. The intent is to translate the current movement to rotating motion by water wheel, Kaplan turbines, propeller turbines, and vertical axis turbines.

To date, very little has been done to bring this concept closer to reality. Very large equipment would be required, and it would have to be placed close to the water surface. There will have to be substantial mooring to withstand higher currents and storms. No studies have been conducted on salt water effects on machinery, fouling of the equipment by marine life, equipment reliability, or interference with navigation.

THE NEXT STEP INTO SPACE

Eleven years after the last moon walk and nearly three years after the space shuttle began flying, it began to seem as if NASA's days of glory and bold visions were alive only in movie theaters showing "The Right Stuff." The space agency needed a megaproject to galvanize its scientists and engineers—not to mention congressional appropriations committees—and decided that a permanently manned space station was the answer. Now, after years of lobbying, NASA has finally brought President Reagan on board. In his State of the Union address last week, Reagan made the expected pitch for just such a project. With it, he said, "we can follow our dreams to distant stars, living and working in space for peaceful, economic and scientific gain."

The dreams won't come cheap. A space station carries an estimated price tag of $8 billion just to develop and launch the first platform in 1992, and at least another $12 billion over the following eight years, if more platforms are added, Tinkertoy-style, to the original. Although it will be 1985 before any contracts are let, Rockwell International, Boeing, McDonnell Douglas and others are already experimenting with designs. The most likely plan calls for a modular station, with canisterlike components ferried up by the space shuttle and then assembled in orbit. (The station itself would also be able to maneuver within its orbit.) One module would provide living quarters for six to eight crew members, who would stay aloft for up to six months before the shuttle delivered the next shift (drawing). A "utility module" might house equipment to generate the station's supplies of air and water; electric power would be generated by huge solar panels. There would be a docking port for the shuttle, perhaps a "garage" where technicians could service satellites, and modules for experiments and commercial space factories. In size and in the permanence of the human presence, the station would totally eclipse such modest space facilities as Skylab, orbited in 1973, or the Soviets' current Salyut.

Stronger Alloys: The station's fortunes are tied to commerce. The military has shown little interest and the scientific community is lukewarm at best. Based on NASA's survey of more than 100 firms, prospective space products include exceptionally pure drugs in quantity, lighter yet stronger alloys than can be manufactured on Earth and purer optical fibers for communications. Similar projects have proved feasible in experiments aboard the shuttle—but they will have to be workable on a much larger scale to justify the space station.

Many researchers see less science than they would like emanating from the space station. They worry, too, that the project will siphon off funds and divert attention from other, more worthy missions. As Von Eshleman of Stanford University points out, "An $8 billion project can wipe out lots of $100 million projects." Researchers give more than 40 missions higher priority than the space station. Among the more compelling of these are retrieving a sample of Martian soil, photographing the Martian canyons from a drone airplane, radar-mapping the topography of Venus and probing asteroids and comets. Such missions would increase our knowledge of how the planets formed and of the geological processes that cause earthquakes and volcanoes on Earth.

NASA points out that many such missions will be able to take advantage of the space station, either as a launching or servicing platform. But that is just what some scientists fear: that in order to give the space station enough to do, other projects will be designed around it—which means that they won't fly until the station is built, sometime in the next decade. Moreover, satellites with different functions—such as earth-imaging and infrared astronomy—may need very different orbits to be most effective, but a space station can be in only one; scientists worry that they will surrender a lot of flexibility once their experiments are tied to the space station. "Space science in this nation is atrophying because of similar things done during the shuttle program," says planetary scientist Thomas M. Donahue, chairman of the Space Sciences Board of the National Academy of Sciences. "If the decision to build a space station is political and social, we have no problem with that. But don't call it a scientific program."

In particular, many space scientists doubt the need for a manned presence in space; they argue that robots and automation are safer, cheaper and a greater technological challenge. America could better prove its technological prowess by self-repairing unmanned factories, stations and probes, says Eshleman. If NASA is open to the idea of an unmanned station, a group of Stanford scientists have a plan for one. They are working on the "Pleiades Project," an unmanned flotilla of space platforms that would carry out the same scientific and commercial tasks planned for the manned station but at a fraction of the cost. A central platform for ground communications and docking would be surrounded by more platforms and "free fliers" carrying a single instrument, such as the "space telescope." Astronauts and technicians could visit periodically to check on the automated manufacturing and research facilities.

Pleiades has attracted some interest from NASA and the space industry. But the choice of a manned station seems to be based less on scientific grounds than on the belief that the next frontier will not be conquered until Homo sapiens himself occupies it. The allure of a human presence in orbit remains powerful, and may be especially so in the year the station is scheduled to reach orbit: 1992 is the 500th anniversary of Columbus's discovery of the New World.

SHARON BEGLEY with MARY HAGER
in Washington and JOHN CAREY in New York

ROBOTS ARE PLAYING NEW ROLES AS THEY TAKE A HAND IN OUR AFFAIRS

By Jeanne McDermott

You find Emilio Bizzi's office past the monkey experiments on the top floor of the psychology building at the Massachusetts Institute of Technology (MIT). An aura of continental ease surrounds the neuroscientist as he describes his work. "I am concerned with how the brain controls movement." He lifts his arm off the table to demonstrate, following its trajectory with a marveling but critical eye. "Robots clearly spell out the problem."

At Carnegie-Mellon University in Pittsburgh, Hans Moravec leans over a barrel-high contraption that rolls on wheels, scans the world with a camera and navigates by computer. He describes himself as a science-fiction fan who once wanted to build a time machine. Now a computer scientist, he pursues work that is equally delightful and futuristic. "Mobile robots," he grins, "are test-beds for intelligent machines."

The rehabilitation center at the Veterans Administration Hospital in Palo Alto, California, radiates cheer, especially when a quadriplegic client rolls in to meet the new electronic aide. An angular metal arm, no bigger than a human one, rests inconspicuously in one corner. Within an hour, it fetches and carries, responding to commands like a well-trained pet. The client drinks from the machine's hand. Explains Larry Leifer, the Stanford engineer who directs the center and conceived the project, "With robots, I want to replace function, not anatomy."

Times change fast, especially in the technological landscape. Twenty years ago, Bizzi, Moravec and Leifer would have been laughed out of their laboratories for consorting with robots. Science fiction, not serious science, vouched for the humanlike machines. But within the space of a generation, robots crossed over. The development of microcomputers bolstered the belief that intelligent machines, able to work and act as well as ponder, could be built.

Today they are with us, and in the future, whether they bring prosperity or unemployment, they promise to be omnipresent. In Japan, where more than a half of the world's robot population resides, the government plans to employ them in nearly every field from fire fighting to guiding the blind. The Japanese are calling it a "robolution," a revolution that extends from factory spot welders to devices that slice sushi

for overworked chefs to piano-playing home robots (available, with many other talents and a price tag of $42,000, from a leading Toyko department store).

Americans expect nothing less. "There is hardly an area that robotics will leave untouched," says Tom Binford, director of the robotics division of the Artificial Intelligence Laboratory at Stanford University. He cautions, "People talk about robotics as if the machines were here. Much of it remains to be developed." No one really knows when the machines will cluster on factory assembly lines or nurse the sick, build houses, mine planets and eventually do household chores. But optimism is a hallmark of the field. "We are coming full circle from the days of Rome," says Charles Rosen, chief scientist at Machine Intelligence Corporation in Sunnyvale, California. "Only it won't be human slaves."

Such speculation, however, is a poor guide to today's robots. "Let's face it," Rosen says benignly, "today's robots are stupid." About 6,000 robots work in the United States, most of them lugging parts in factories. They are metal arms that lunge and grab, pivot and relinquish, repeating the motion as perfectly as a replayed film. Some jerk like oil derricks and others bend over backwards like gymnasts. But whether they pick up transistors or engine housings, they are precise and obedient, going only where told to go. Their trump is a glimmer of flexibility; they can do more than one task.

Even these relatively rigid robots are perceived as posing a threat of unemployment for human workers. In Japan, where the workers at first welcomed robots, there are warnings that the honeymoon is over. But Soichiro Honda, whose cars are built by a joint human-robot workforce, points out that this problem lies in the hands of managers, not scientists or technicians. Any businessman incapable of taking advantage of robotics, he believes, cannot be called an able businessman. But one who fires employees because of robotics cannot be called able, either. Labor and robotics should "prosper and grow together," he says.

Managers will soon need all the wisdom they can muster, for scientists are already at work on basic questions. How do you give metal parts and silicon chips dexterity, mobility, intelligence or any other quality that humans possess? How do you make machines that cope with slivers of life's chaos? How do you control them? Feats that come naturally to living creatures evolved over millions of years. Roboticists hope to work faster.

Despite the breadth of the field, the core group of researchers behind the new generation of robots would scarcely fill a high-school auditorium. They train in computer science, physics, engineering and neuroscience, but cross disciplines in pursuit of big questions and the prospect of new frontiers. As David Nitzan, director of robotics at SRI International in Menlo Park, California, explains, "For another 20 years, robotics will remain a young field where anything goes." "Anything" is a license to take even the wildest ideas seriously.

It is only 20 years since the birth of the field of artificial intelligence (AI). Initially, AI focused on duplicating decision making and reasoning with a computer. Victor Scheinman, now a vice president of the Massachusetts robot firm Automatix, was a student working in Stanford University's AI Lab. "We wanted to give the computer a useful physical tool, a mechanical manipulator that could do more than just display data," he says. Scheinman and his cohorts played with arm designs. They linked a prosthetic arm to a computer, constructed a snakelike arm with air bags and finally settled on a slender all-electric manipulator. It was a breakthrough that put Scheinman's expertise in demand. In the early 1970s he traveled to MIT, where he designed a pint-size manipulator that at one point was envisioned as a medical drone. With such a device a surgeon in, say, New York could conduct an operation in the Arctic. But the idea took a back seat when General Motors placed its first large order for Scheinman's robot arm, a move that signaled major new industrial interest in robots of many kinds.

Scheinman, who recently returned to Stanford to complete his PhD, describes himself as a dreamer fascinated by the assembly process. According to friends, he hangs around factories the way others hang around ballparks. "We have been locked into a traditional approach to robotics," he says. Something in Scheinman's smile, as he sits in an office surrounded by robot arms that already qualify as antiques, assures you that the approach has been changing.

New robots confirm it. Microbot of Mountain View, California, makes a knee-high robot whose tendonlike wire cables, rather than motors at each joint, account for its diminutive stature. The company sold more than 1,000 to universities and firms as teaching devices. Now the Microbots are elbowing their way into the laboratory, pouring radioactive pharmaceuticals and inspecting soap flakes.

No matter how dexterous arms get, Ken Salisbury believes that robots literally deserve a hand. "Current robots are just not dexterous," says the impish-looking mechanical engineer, pointing to a three-fingered gripper he designed. "Try putting together a car with pliers. That is about the analogy." When Salisbury began his thesis handiwork at Stanford University, his major concern was practicality. He also built his gripper to satisfy curiosity, and for fun. Now he works at MIT's Artificial Intelligence Laboratory, an enclave with the feel of a think tank and the frenzy of a bus terminal, where the distinction between people and machines fall away. Nothing seems so prosaic here as a disembodied hand, made from bright-blue aluminum, with no palm and three fingers that sway haphazardly. Even in this stylized state, the device satisfies that vague longing to see the human body reflected in a machine, to see a living function translated into mechanical parts. As Salisbury explains that the robot hand has three fingers because three are the minimum necessary to pick up and reorient an object, he gestures with his own. A smile creeps across his face. Even he cannot view the device with detachment.

Arms and hands go only so far. Legs might someday carry robots into the more than 50 percent of the world's land mass that happens to be too rough and rocky for anything with wheels or tracks. At Carnegie-Mellon University (CMU), Marc Raibert and Ivan Sutherland are chasing down fundamental knowledge about legged machines with pogo sticks, you might say. Raibert, a robotics engineer who keeps a balance board in his office, explains with a wry smile, "They are springy, they interact with the ground. There seemed to be something fundamentally similar with the way pogo sticks behave and the way legs behave." Odd . . . until you think about it.

Ivan Sutherland was one of the few who took Raibert seriously. In his 40s, Sutherland is as terse and independent-minded as a prairie homesteader. The "father" of computer graphics and former head of computer science at the California Institute of Technology, he also knows a smart idea when he hears one. "It was the cleverest choice of building the simplest possible legged system," he says. The two teamed up, united by inquisitive minds and a maverick distaste for conventional wisdom. They beam with excitement about their recent findings but speak cautiously, fearing they will be misunderstood.

Raibert built a computer-controlled hopper. It is a springy metal pole, a little bit smaller than a two-year-old child, tethered on a stiff pipe like a horse on a lunge line. It hops in a circle, keeping its balance in one plane. Under computer control, the leg does an exquisite steeplechase. "Marc discovered that you can separate the control of the single-legged machine into three parts," Sutherland explains. The mathematical computations for balance in this case turn out to be unexpectedly simple. They depend on the height of the hopper, the position of its foot on landing and its upright attitude. What creates the undercurrent of excitement is that the simplicity may result in entirely new walking machines.

Underwriting his own research at CMU, Sutherland built a six-legged crawling machine. As most insects can tell you, six is a magical number in locomotion. It means that three legs always touch ground, providing a stabilizing tripod. Compared to Raibert's gleeful hopper, the crawler is a behemoth. A driver rides it through its paces. Sutherland worked out the control of its gait, center of gravity and other variables.

Today Sutherland is ready to tackle the problems of moving at a faster pace. "Have you ever watched a runner stop?" He pauses for an answer before giving his. "He leans back a lot. Now if he were standing still and learned back that far, he would fall over. The issue of locomotion is largely the issue of keeping upright. That is true with people. That is true of machines with many legs." Sutherland is now building a four-legged walker that won't fall over when it stops.

A small Anaheim, California, firm called Odetics has developed the only walking machine now adaptable to commercial uses, the Functionoid. With a cylindrical body and a fishbowl head that rest on six spindly legs, it is a lithe, compact powerhouse. It weighs 375 pounds and presses 1,800 pounds. Considering that strong-armed robots typically lift a fraction of their weight, the feat is impressive. Its delicate and elegant movements make it even more so. It tucks its legs up like an owl, and then stretches them like a cat. On radio command, it plants three legs on the ground and lifts the back end of a pickup truck. Odetics envisions the machine doing sentry duty, clambering around construction sites and mines— even defusing bombs.

With increasingly elaborate mechanical limbs, robotics circles back to where it began, to the search for artificial intelligence. Now the quest turns not to conscious reasoning, but to the unconscious processes that underlie behavior; the coupling of sense and response; the invisible strings that move the puppet.

The shift is bringing robots to their senses. And machines may have any senses imaginable. Robots sense electric fields as quickly as a shark and low-frequency sound waves as acutely as a pigeon, they map surfaces by showering an object with ultrasound or laser light, and feel with pressure-sensitive fingertips.

The problem is how to make sense of the torrent of information. Researchers at Stanford's Artificial Intelligence Laboratory set their sights on solving that problem in relation to the most complicated sense—vision. When you enter the lab, you see a lineup of computers behind glass. The product of 20 years of research, some of them can crudely see.

Tom Binford, a physicist and director of the robotics lab, is modest about what it has accomplished and immodest about its goals. "We work on the high performance end, on stereo computer vision," he says. He treats words like numbers: precise symbols for an imprecise world. Humans, he says, use stereovision, seeing a slightly different image from left and right eyes. Cameras can duplicate this. Binford concentrates on the mathematical processes that transform patterns of light into meaningful perceptions. "My focus is not the machine but the real world and the mathematical structures that represent it."

In another vision project, the computer is programmed to interpret an image of, say, an airplane. First, it detects edges, constructing an outline. Because of inevitable shadows, the outline looks like a cartoon drawn by a drunk. The computer smooths it out as well as possible. Then it riffles through its memory, searching a library of general shapes. It fits the shapes to the outline, like pieces to a puzzle. Finally, research associate Harlyn Baker explains, "It knows how these generalized shapes are arranged in objects like airplanes." After a good long wait, it recognizes a plane.

Understanding how the brain handles information is closely linked to the design of smart robots; it is hard to contemplate one without the other. James Albus, chief of the industrial systems division at the National Bureau of Standards in Maryland, thinks about both. An engineer by training, Albus became fascinated by neuroscience in the mid-'60s. He wanted to participate in a research frontier that would stretch well into the next century. "I spent a lot of time watching insects, birds, dogs," he says laconically, gazing out of the window of his paper-cluttered office. He concluded that brains exist, not to do calculus, but to control behavior. "The brain of a mosquito can fly. It can land. It can drill holes in the skin. It can lay eggs and avoid getting swatted," he observes. Yet the mosquito buzzes through life with no more than a few thousand neurons, a pesky monument to what a little computing power can do.

The problem is that it is difficult to spy on neurons and catch them in the act of controlling behavior. Like heaven, the brain is best known by analogy. Albus saw that robots provided a useful one. "No one had ever built a brain before," he explains. "The microchip made it possible to approach the number of computations that go on in the brain." Albus set out to test his belief that the brain controls behavior in much the same way that a military unit or bureaucracy controls its employees, hierarchically. Information from the senses cascades up a chain of command and decisions cascade down. Knowledge of the world shapes the flow. Albus maps the mathematical processes along that chain, identifying the computing procedures that are shared by computers and neurons.

Ricardo Uribe, who runs the Advanced Digital Systems Laboratory at the University of Illinois, is on an even bolder quest. He integrates an understanding of life itself with the distant dream of bringing a machine to life: "My goal is to use the concepts of living systems to design and build new machines." Uribe, who fled Chile after the military coup, speaks with the clarity of one who had done a housecleaning on old ideas. Indeed, he has. He believes that living systems should not be viewed as static structures made up of unchanging parts, like clockworks. Instead, Uribe looks at a cell or an organism as a collection of processes rather than parts. "It is the organization of processes maintaining itself," he says, "that maintains the system's identity despite a constant change of constituents." (For example, the calcium in a child's bone is not the same as the calcium in an adult's bone, nonetheless it is the same bone.)

The advantage of this approach is that it allows the use of more complex concepts for modeling "life." Using a computer, Uribe has mathematically simulated a living organism as complicated as a paramecium. Now, he and his students are trying to embody his concepts in hardware as a first step toward a more lifelike robot. They are starting the construction of a complex network of microcomputers, arranged in a latticework of cubes. Each edge will have one computer, and the corners, or nodes, will contain memory chips. Thus, each node will hold data sent to it by six different computers.

What is important in this model is not the individual computers, but the network as a whole. Another key feature is that, unlike the Albus model, there is no hierarchy of from-the-top-down control: each computer is as important as any other. The different computers are not synchronized, but can add data or draw it out of a common memory bank whenever necessary. This type of system, Uribe believes, is a much closer model of the way a living nervous system functions than is available in current computers. It would exhibit a fundamental property of living systems—autonomy—in that the collection of computers would not respond to an instruction or request in a predetermined way, but would answer in its own way.

Even Uribe is not sure he will see robots act like living things in his lifetime. But we can count on a population explosion of somewhat simpler devices. If one word describes the robots that will be with us during the next decade, it is "responsive." That quality assumes many dimensions. In a windowless laboratory, the scientists at the Jet Propulsion Laboratory in Pasadena, California, experiment with a one-armed robot and its coach, who eventually might be separated by millions of miles of cold space. "Imagine removing a TV camera from a satellite in space and sending a robot out from the shuttle. The operator on board the shuttle 'talks' to the robot with his hands. But there must be an intelligence built into the machine to understand the hands' language," says JPL scientist Antal Bejczy. The intelligence is something as simple as force and torque sensors clasped around the robot wrist. Bejczy transmits the forces and torques sensed by the robot to the joy stick. The coach feels exactly what the robot feels. The process reverses and the robot feels what the operator wants it to feel. Communication is literally at the fingertips.

Communication between a handicapped person and a robot prosthesis is every bit as critical. Neville Hogan, a mechanical engineer at MIT, is building a mechanical simulator that mimics the human arm. "It only makes sense to sneak a peek at Mother Nature and learn from the smart things that *we* do," he says. He flexes and extends his own arm, watching the motion with the single-minded intensity of a bird dog. "The muscle is springlike. It can quickly adjust to changes." He demonstrates the principle with a prototype clamped to a lab bench. When Hogan bumps it, the tension changes and the arm appears almost to relax: a small but significant step that takes an artificial arm right into the realm of robotics.

As the repertory of robot responses grows, so do its roles. A robot may bow on Broadway in 1984. Broadway producer Lewis Allen cast a robot and a dog as the only actors in a 45-minute play. The robot is a life-size Andy Warhol look-alike, a tribute to the artist's comment that he thought he would enjoy being a robot. What makes the robot unusual is that it avoids a set routine, such as those performed by figures at Disney World, programmed to respond to lights and sounds and the director's changing mind. So far, no Equity card.

The ultimate performer is the personal robot which reached the market this spring. Androbot, the San Jose, California, company launched by Atari founder Nolan Bushnell, is spawning them in a faceless industrial park where a handful of workers assemble the robots by placing circuit boards and battery-powered motors inside a shell and setting the unit on two knock-kneed wheels.

Robotics is breeding a new generation of machines that we may soon meet as pets, if not slaves. Tom Frisina, the youthful, hard-sell president of Androbot, introduces BOB, short for Brains On Board, a robot still in gestation. BOB scuttles across the room, relying on ultrasonic detectors to avoid walls. When it senses a warm body with infrared detectors, it stops, swaying ever so slightly. BOB does get disoriented, a feature that makes it slightly human. A bop on the head and it speaks—20 words with a mild robot accent.

BOB is cute, a delightful gimmick, but even among those robotics engineers working on more serious problems, there is a singular awe and admiration for the human organism. "We underestimate the simplest things that we do," says Charles Rosen of Machine Intelligence Company. Gaunt as a stork, he lifts a pack of Winstons off the table, defying me to explain how his muscles, eyes and brain choreographed the task in less than a second without apparent effort. "The only ones who really appreciate how smart people are," he leans forward as if to share a secret, "are those who try to do some of these things with a robot."

PART TWO

WORKING IN THE FUTURE

FUTUREVISION 2

. . . Clifford arrived at his office on the third floor of the Applied Studies Department of the Mathematics & Computer Services Building. On the average, he spent probably no more than two days a week at ACRE, preferring to work at home and use his Infonet terminal which gave him access to the Establishment data bank and computers. On this occasion he hadn't been in for eight days, but when he checked the list of messages on his desk terminal, he found nothing that was especially pressing; all the urgent calls had already been routed on to his home number and dealt with from there.

—*James P. Hogan,* The Genesis Machine

MOVERS AND SHAKERS:
INFORMATION AGE ENTREPRENEURS

INTRODUCTION AND OVERVIEW

Luke Walton is not puffed up by his unexpected and remarkable success. He never fails to recognize kindly, and help, if there is a need, the old associates of his humbler days, and never tries to conceal the fact that he was once a Chicago newsboy.
        —Horatio Alger, *Luke Walton*, 1894

Like many, if not most, of Horatio Alger's heroes, Luke Walton rose from humble beginnings to high achievement through entrepreneurship. Entrepreneurs are highly esteemed in American society, which has long been considered their most congenial habitat.

An entrepreneur, says Webster, is "one who organizes, manages, and assumes the risks of a business or enterprise." In capitalist societies, the entrepreneur is an indispensable figure, for it is he or she who raises and risks the capital required to commercialize new technologies and products.

The introduction of new technologies always has offered entrepreneurs their greatest opportunities. By finding new commercial uses for the new technologies —and risking everything to produce and market them—they have their chance for fame and fortune.

Computers, electronics and the other electricity-based technologies have spawned what some describe as "a new breed of entrepreneur." And yet, reading about their lives, we feel a sense of *déja vu*. We read, for example, that Steve Jobs, founder of Apple Computers, "had decidedly modest beginnings, lasted only a semester in college, landed a job with a videogame outfit named Atari. . . . His pleasant home in Los Gatos is nothing that would interest *Architectural Digest:* freshly laundered shirts lie on the floor of an unfurnished second bedroom. . . . He is a work junky."

But if our reporter is to be believed, Jobs is also a man in the tradition of Horatio Alger—self-made, modest in taste, a risk-taker and workaholic. And perhaps there is a reason for the similarity of traits, for entrepreneurship requires special skills and a special kind of personality.

In the pages that follow, you'll meet a number of men and women who have succeeded as information age entrepreneurs. As you read, you might also submit yourself to an important task in career exploration—self analysis. What does it take to be an entrepreneur? Do you have what it takes?

If not, read on. In the chapter that follows this one, you'll meet men and women who enjoy far greater job security than entrepreneurs possibly can.

THE READINGS

"The New Entrepreneurs" documents the surge in American entrepreneurship, explaining the competitive edge it gives the United States in international competition.

"Software To Go" describes the high-tech cottage industry spawned by the microcomputer boom, introducing several men and women who are thriving on new opportunities.

"Nine Who Dare" consists of portraits of women who decided to seek their fortunes working for themselves instead of the safer route of working for others.

"Blacks Who Left Dead End Jobs To Go It Alone" traces the career paths of those who left jobs in middle management to become entrepreneurs.

"The Origins of Sony's Walkman" proves that the entrepreneurial spirit can flourish even at the top of a corporation.

"Sir Clive's Very Big Gamble on a Very Small TV" describes the challenge to Japan's consumer electronics industry soon to be mounted by Britain's best known living inventor.

REFERENCES

Edison: A Biography, by Matthew Josephson, is a rich, interesting biography of America's most renowned inventor-entrepreneur. McGraw-Hill paperback, originally published in 1959.

Silicon Valley Fever: Growth of High Technology Culture, by Everett M. Rogers and Judith K. Larsen, chronicles the rise of the California enclave and the people who work there— "a place where talent and energy can make you a millionaire overnight." Basic Books hardcover, 1984.

FUTUREVISION 3

We must not, however, commit the only too common mistake of equating mere physical expansion or even increasing knowledge with 'progress,' however that may be defined. Only little minds are impressed by sheer size and number. There would be no virtue in possessing the Universe if it brought neither wisdom nor happiness. Yet possess it we must, at least in spirit, if we are ever to answer the questions that men have asked in vain since history began.

—*Arthur C. Clarke*

THE NEW ENTREPRENEURS

How startup companies give America a competitive edge

Aryeh Finegold's thick spectacles, narrow face, and receding hairline give him the look of a mild-mannered junior accountant. But Finegold, 36, is a former commander of Israeli paratroopers, a crack electronics engineer—and an impassioned entrepreneur. Recruiting talent to develop engineering work stations for Daisy Systems Corp., the company he started in 1980, Finegold routinely extracts pledges to work a minimum of 55 hours per week—and then gets even greater effort from his work force of 130 with personal touches such as handing out ice cream bars at midnight.

Not surprisingly, Daisy Systems is off to a fast start. The Sunnyvale (Calif.) company shipped its first product just 13 months after putting an initial $1.5 million in venture financing in the bank. Sales hit $7 million last year and are headed for $25 million this year. "I always have the sense I'm in a race with somebody," Finegold allows.

With varying degrees of success, hundreds of fledgling companies these days are reenacting Daisy Systems' dash to glory. Seeded by at least $5.5 billion in new venture capital over the past five years, startups are sprouting new products at a rate far exceeding that of even the venture boom of the mid-1960s, when the minicomputer and semiconductor industries took off.

Making millions

And the pace is accelerating. A bountiful $3 billion in venture capital was disbursed to startup companies in 1981 and 1982, according to Jane Koloski Morris, managing editor of *Venture Capital Journal*, which sees no letup in the torrent of cash pouring into venture deals.

Perhaps half of their money, say top venture capitalists, goes to early-stage ventures where it is used primarily for product development. This is magnified by the growing use of research and development partnerships and by the surge in initial public offerings, which raised $4.6 billion for 670 companies in the last two years, according to *Going Public: The IPO Reporter.*

Spurring this shower of investment are tax-law changes starting in 1978 that cut the maximum capital gains tax bite to 20% from nearly 50% for individuals. The corporate rate was eased to around 28% from about 30%. At the same time, the surge of the new-issues market, which allows investors, founders, and key employees to cash in on their successes, provides huge incentives. At Tandem Computers Inc., one of the most successful startups of the mid-1970s, lavish stock-option and stock-purchase plans have made millionaires out of 25 employees and given 100 others stock worth about $500,000. In December, a $32 million public offering gave Quantum Corp.'s five top officers, who own 10% of the disk drive maker, a paper fortune of $21 million. Kleiner, Perkins, Caufield & Byers, the lead venture investor in Tandem and Quantum, gained a 100-to-1 return on the Tandem investment and a 20-to-1 payoff on Quantum.

Beyond the financial incentive is the bait of having an opportunity to make a major new-product contribution. Although executives concede that some of the investment money is funding doomed efforts, most believe that the startups are remarkably efficient as engines of product development. As such, they constitute a major advantage for the U. S. against foreign—particularly Japanese—competition.

"The threat from Japan is aimed at commodity products," says San Francisco venture capitalist Thomas J. Perkins, "and the counterbalance has to be new and innovative products from new companies." The startups, executives say, are accelerating the product development cycle of many industries at a pace faster than any international competition can match. Agrees E. David Crockett, a senior vice-president of market researcher Dataquest Inc.: "In all, it is a healthy stimulus to U. S. industry."

The time is ripe, because the U. S. still holds a wealth of untapped, post-World War II science and technology hungering for application in commercial products. "Many of the technologies of the 1960s and early 1970s were based on prewar science," says William F. Miller, president of SRI International, a Menlo Park (Calif.) think tank. "There is a big backlog of postwar science now maturing. We're seeing just the leading edge of its commercialization." And Terence E. McClary, head of General Electric Co.'s venture-investment arm, adds: "We are at the tip of the iceberg in the exploitation and application of technology."

Entrepreneurial companies, by recruiting highly motivated scientists and engineers, rewarding them with equity positions, and focusing their efforts on one challenging assignment, can perform virtual miracles of product development. Complex computer systems that might take five years of effort at large companies are cranked out in 18 months by such upstarts as Dialogic Systems Corp. and Stratus Computer Inc. Small computers and work stations such as those built by Apollo Computer, Daisy Systems, and Convergent Technologies are rammed through in little over a year.

Startup ventures have been concentrated in the information and communication industries because the microelectronic revolution of the last decade opened up vast new markets. But the fever is also raging in medicine, energy, robotics, and a host of other businesses. The binge of venture funding even touches low-technology startups. Midway Airlines Inc. and Home Health Care of America Inc., for instance, got started with venture funding. But the bulk of the money is flowing to high tech, where rewards are potentially far greater than for deals that depend on marketing breakthroughs. "Anybody can start a service business," says venture capitalist Perkins. "And the marketing risk is accordingly very high. On the other hand, a winning bet on a technology risk can lock in an exclusive market—and even create an entirely new industry."

Not all of the big bets on innovation will pay off. Historically, as many as 2 out of every 10 venture-backed startups have failed outright, and only a few achieve the dramatic success of a Xerox, Intel, or Apple, whose products created new industries. Some observers say an oversupply of venture capital is funding development of products that are either imitative or aimed at market niches too limited to offer much return. "There are a lot of business plans now where it's difficult to see the product contribution," says Crockett of Dataquest.

Indeed, established companies in some industries are losing sales, staff, and technology to upstart competitors at a pace that has prompted lawsuits (page 81)—and raised questions about the ultimate value to the U.S. "It's clear that big companies play a key role in U.S. product development," concedes entrepreneur James L. Patterson, founder of Quantum Corp. "It's fair to ask if we are bleeding them to the point where it hurts the national technology effort."

For one thing, startups typically do not invent anything but rather develop commercial products from basic technology. Biotech companies such as Cetus Corp. and Genentech Inc., for instance, use gene-splicing techniques developed at universities as the basis of product development efforts. Many of the 100 or more companies launched to make microcomputers, notes Douglas C. Chance, general manager of Hewlett-Packard Co.'s computer products group, are using concepts originated by Xerox Corp. and Western Electric Co. and by university theorists. Some of these companies, he says, "are taking other people's technology and $10 million and claiming they have made a contribution."

Yet even as they grumble, large companies increasingly are recognizing the startup as a valuable resource, and they are trying to tap into it through licensing deals and equipment purchases, investments, spinoffs, and even internal changes designed to instill entrepreneurial values in their own companies. In each case, they are trying to tap, or replicate, the unique forces that can be rallied in an entrepreneurial setting and targeted at the task of applying technology to a specific market need.

"What we do," says Finis Conner, executive vice-president of Seagate Technology in Scotts Valley, Calif., "is to take proven technology and put it into a package that can be manufactured in high volume." Seagate, sprinting to an annual sales rate of $100 million in three years, demonstrated its first miniaturized disk-memory units just six months after setting up shop in a 4,000-sq.-ft. garage. Once a product is defined, pressure mounts to get it to market before others can react. "When you are creating a market," says Finegold of Daisy Systems, "the name of the game is to get out with something fast."

Selecting, as Seagate did, a product concept or market niche that established companies either have not yet spotted or see as unrewarding is a prerequisite for success in a startup. "What drives it is a willingness to take risks that large companies aren't willing to take," says L. William Krause, president of 3Com Corp., of Mountain View, Calif., a startup making local-area-network equipment. Avoiding lengthy reviews that often derail innovation in big companies is an advantage for most startups. Says a former Intel Corp. manager who now runs his own startup: "If I wanted to do a new product at Intel, I had to visit all those committees, and that made it extremely awkward to do things."

A single-minded focus

Executives of Intel and other established companies point out that such reviews are essential to prevent overlap and competition with other products—problems that today's startups will face once they have successful products in the field. Still, the single-minded focus of a startup is a key advantage in product development. "There are absolutely no distractions," says Philippe Villers, who founded robot maker Automatix Inc., in Burlington, Mass., in 1980 and chalked up revenues of $8 million last year.

Product ideas for startups are most often formed while the entrepreneurs are still employed by established companies. Frequently, the idea was rejected or sidelined by the bigger company. Villers, for example, was a co-founder of Computervision Corp. and had proposed that the company move into robotics. "I could convince only one member of senior management—me—to spread the company," Villers recalls. Czech immigrant Kornel Spiro got his idea for Dialogic Systems—an attachment designed to make International Business Machines Corp. mainframe computers perform better in time-sharing applications—while working as director for

The surge in venture funding

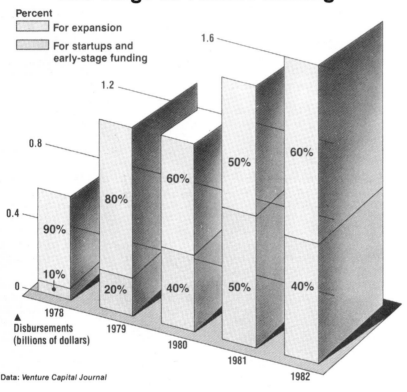

Percent
☐ For expansion
☐ For startups and early-stage funding

Disbursements (billions of dollars)

1978: 90% / 10%
1979: 80% / 20%
1980: 60% / 40%
1981: 50% / 50%
1982: 60% / 40%

Data: *Venture Capital Journal*

Arlene Cassidy—BW

Some bitter fruit from the crop of startups

President Canion with Compaq's portable computers: His former employer, Texas Instruments, charges that he pirated trade secrets.

One of the bitter side effects of the startup boom has been the surge in lawsuits between entrepreneurs and the established companies they left. Typically, such suits center on claims of harm done when a company's employees—carrying talent, technology, and ideas nurtured within the company—walk out the door and join a new venture that soon will be competing against the former employer.

In the case of Compaq Computer Corp., a year-old company based in Houston, Joseph R. Canion, co-founder and president, claims he did not come up with the idea for a portable computer able to handle software designed for International Business Machines Corp.'s Personal Computer until three weeks after leaving Texas Instruments Inc., where he was manager of terminal systems. But to staff his new company, TI charges, Canion recruited at TI's Data Systems Group, which also was working on an IBM-compatible personal computer. TI sued Compaq and its 10 ex-TI employees, charging them with pirating trade secrets. Compaq countersued, demanding a jury trial for its claim that TI tried to put the new company out of business.

'No choice.' Some startups succumb without a fight. Two telephone switching-equipment spinoffs of Northern Telecom Inc. drew legal action, for instance. But both companies, InteCom Inc. and Digital Switch Corp., agreed out of court to make payments to NTI. Says Richard L. Scroggins, chief financial officer of Dallas-based Digital Switch, which even without a suit being filed agreed to give up 1.25% of its revenues for five years: "In today's environment, a little company has no choice but to give in."

Executives at some established companies are reluctant to employ legal procedures to stem losses of people and technology. They say the best approach is to beat the startups at their own game. Legal recourse "grinds very slowly and is perhaps the least fruitful [approach]," says Gordon E. Moore, chairman of Intel Corp. "Where there are real trade-secret problems, we certainly won't hesitate to use legal weapons. On the other hand, our best defense is to keep this an exciting place to work and to move things to the market as rapidly as we can."

product planning at Amdahl Corp. "Something like this would be fifth or sixth on Amdahl's priority list," he says.

The distinction between the would-be entrepreneur's ideas and the employer's product plans sometimes becomes a court matter. And occasionally the effort to segregate the two can lead to bewildering mental gymnastics. After building a semiconductor laser-based device at an Exxon Enterprises subsidiary, Michael H. Coden and Frederick W. Scholl wanted to start planning a second-generation product. But they also were thinking about launching their own company, Codenoll Technology Corp. "We decided we shouldn't think about [the second-generation device] while at Exxon," Coden recalls. "As soon as we start thinking about it, it belongs to whoever we are working for at that time."

The cleanest deals involve products unrelated to a former employer's business. Often the startups get ideas mainly from staying close to the market and picking out niches that respond to customers' needs. Daniel Sinnott, for example, started Syntrex Inc., of Eatontown, N. J., in February, 1979, with only a general idea of entering the office-automation market. But in visits to banks, law firms, and other potential customers, Sinnott discovered that next to every word processor was a typewriter to handle simple tasks—addressing envelopes, for instance—that were awkward for the word processor. "Why not tie the typewriter into the work station?" he asked. Last year, Syntrex sold $31 million worth of typewriters and work stations that not only interconnect but also hook into a central computer. Syntrex's success, Sinnott explains, stems from having a "detailed understanding of the needs of the marketplace."

Staffing up for the product development effort is a crucial step that can determine the fate of a new venture. "Getting talent is as important as raising money," says one entrepreneur, "and you have to pay equity for both." In most high-tech startups these days, engineers, technicians, and even secretaries can count on substantial chunks of stock if they are among the early recruits. When 3Com, for example, was getting started, managers got a 1% stake in the company, engineers a quarter to a third of that, and production workers about 0.1%. "Ownership creates a special feeling it's hard to create otherwise," Krause points out.

But besides the chance to get rich,

startups must offer a real technical challenge to get the best people. Franklin Pass and Anthony J. Faras, two University of Minnesota professors who launched Molecular Genetics Inc. to make animal health care products in mid-1979, kept a low profile for the first 18 months while they assembled a team of 28 researchers. "You don't get good people if they suspect you're doing a lot of hyping," Faras says.

Recruiting was not easy for Gaymond W. Schultz and William R. Stensrud, who left middle-management jobs at Rolm Corp. early last year to set up Sydis Inc. in a guest cottage—dubbed the bunkhouse—at Schultz's home in Los Altos, Calif. To develop an office work station with telephone, computer, and local-network capabilities, Schultz and Stensrud needed experts in 10 specialties to head development projects—

Villers with his robot: A single focus with "no distractions" speeds product development.

plus a businessman to take the role of president. "It took us seven months to get the people we needed," Schultz recalls, "but in waiting for good people, we still were able to keep to our schedule." Sydis expects to announce its first product in mid-April.

First-rate talent is especially important for writing software, now as much as three-quarters of the job in computer and communications product-development efforts. "There is a quantitative difference in people's ability to write software," says Allen L. Ambler, software development chief for Dialogic Systems. "You have to avoid mediocrity." And getting software written fast is not enough, says Ram Banin, head of research and development for Daisy Systems. He recalls that one of his programmers sat thinking about a problem for three months, then in one month wrote 20,000 lines of code that solved a difficult problem. "Speed is less important than the robustness and elegance of the solution," says Banin.

Perhaps the most important ingredient in a startup's magic is the intensity

that comes from focusing a small band of talented people on a product idea that is slightly ahead of its time. "There is an atmosphere of one-upmanship in this industry," says J. William Poduska, founder of Apollo Computer Inc. "If you stroke these guys enough, they'll believe they can solve anything." Finegold, an Israeli-trained engineer who came to the U. S. for graduate work and stayed to work for Intel, draws analogies between commanding an army unit and starting a small company. Like the unit of paratroopers he once led, Finegold says, "Daisy Systems is an elite group of people who volunteered for a tough job." Managing such a group, he adds, is a matter of "training the guy and trusting him to make the right decision."

In addition, startups typically break projects into the smallest possible units to avoid creating unwieldy teams that require too much coordination. "If you assign five people to a task," says Ambler of Dialogic Systems, "they'll spend most of their time deciding how to break it up." Because of the coordination required, notes Krause of 3Com, big companies typically spell out their product development cycles in a fat volume of procedures and cross-checks. "Ours is on one sheet of paper," Krause boasts.

Many entrepreneurs also see an advantage in working with other entrepreneurs—rather than with corporate divisions—for components and support services. For example, Schultz of Sydis says his suppliers can design a new printed circuit board in 2 to 4 weeks instead of the 6 to 12 that might be required in a large company. "We work with people who are motivated to make a lot of money," Schultz explains, "so they work fast." Krause attributes 3Com's speedy work on a new local-area network system for personal computers to a three-way effort with Seeq Technology and Microsoft Inc., startups in semiconductors and software, respectively. "Confederated entrepreneurship is very

powerful," Krause says, "because . . . you have the profit motive working for you."

Except for the most lavishly funded startups, most entrepreneurs are also driven at least in part by an incessant shortage of funds. "Cash is more important than your mother"—an adage attributed to Alan F. Shugart, founder of both Shugart Associate's and Seagate Technology—is dogma in many new companies. At Gigabit Logic Inc., which so far has raised only $8 million toward its effort to make the fastest semiconductor chips on the market, the cash squeeze turned Research Director Richard C. Eden into a bargain hunter. Once a top scientist at Rockwell International Corp.'s solid-state electronics laboratory, Eden now takes pride in trimming the cost of a $75,000 computer-aided design system by getting the supplier to substitute used parts.

Partly because of the need for cash, startups may ship their products long before an established company would judge them ready for sale. Microbot Inc., for example, paused in development of a low-cost robot arm to sell 60 crude versions to such pioneering customers as Procter & Gamble, Siemens, and Teradyne. "We generated enough revenues to keep going," says President G. W. "Dusty" Rhodes, "and we learned that users wanted more features, which we incorporated into the final version." Bugs in a mass-produced item often appear after manufacturing is under way, notes Patterson of Quantum. "We decided to ship early and respond to problems so well that it wouldn't hurt us in the market," he says.

'A high incentive'

Many executives in established companies continue to question such measures, and wonder whether the surge in start-up activity is a net contributor to U. S. innovation. But the entrepreneurs counter that only by forcing the pace of innovation can the U. S. capitalize on its big lead in basic research. Says Miller of SRI International: "The best course is to outrun the Japanese." And the odds are that a startup company will turn ideas into products and get them to market faster and cheaper than most of its established competitors.

"When you have extremely driven people with a high incentive to get something out the door, a product can be brought to market three to five times more efficiently than in a big company," says James C. Anderson, a former Hewlett-Packard engineer who is now a partner in Merrill, Pickard, Anderson & Eyre, a San Francisco-based venture firm. "There is nothing like a startup for productivity." ∎

SOFTWARE TO GO

The microcomputer boom has spawned a high-tech cottage industry. The margins can be as incredible as the growth rate.

**By Harold Seneker
and Jayne A. Pearl**

CONSIDER Fred Beyer, a pleasant fellow just turned 40, who lives in blue jeans and once ran a stock-car racetrack in British Columbia. And his friend, Joe Ming, a New Yorker with a law degree and a yen to be in business. Undistinguished, if unordinary, men, but more typical than you may think in their ambitions.

Their fledgling company, Quick Brown Fox, is what the computer industry calls an "ISV"—Individual Software Vendor. Fred's yet-to-be commercially proved talents at programming are its principal asset. At the present time, they have 12 employees and a word processing program designed by Fred for personal computers that retails for $65 (the main competing program, the popular Wordstar, has a list price of $495 and sells, discounted, at $310), and the company hopes to sell over 100,000 copies at a $6 to $12 profit each.

The reason such high hopes cannot simply be dismissed out of hand is the microcomputer. Suddenly there are about 4 million personal computers around, with 5 million more expected to be sold this year. And most of the new owners have discovered the crying need for good software, which is to computers what blades are to razors. So a grass-roots industry has sprung up, writing, packaging and distributing millions of software diskettes (which cost $2 blank, wholesale) at up to $495 each, retail.

It has been too fast to get much of a fix on it, but the dimensions are surely big. "We figure $865 million," says Janice Antonellis, senior market analyst for International Data Corp., the Framingham, Mass.-based computer market research firm. "Of that, $500 million came from individual vending companies. But we only count the firms that do over $1 million a year. Also, that's at wholesale. At the retail level, it might be two to three times that much."

Senior research analyst Robert Freeman of Mountain View, Calif.-based Input, another well-known computer research firm, thinks microsoftware is growing 43% a year, that is, doubling in two years; IDC says 57% compounded, which would mean its multiplying an even more astounding 2½ times every two years.

Either way, who makes the programs? Not big corporations. It turns out they are a golden, if nonguaranteed, opportunity for the Fred Beyers and Joe Mings of the world. Much of such programming really can be done more competitively working solo at a personal computer, even on one's kitchen table, than it can be done for a

Joseph Ming of Quick Brown Fox with friend
A business that does best in an unstructured atmosphere.

big corporation.

"Some guy working by himself may be willing to gamble a man-year of his time developing a product that may eventually net him anywhere from $200,000 to $1 million, if he's successful," explains Edward Currie, president of Lifeboat Associates, a publisher of personal software in New York City. "But a large corporation would have to put in $500,000 to $1 million to do the same work, using several people with perhaps less motivation than the guy working alone, paying assorted corporate overhead— and after all that, it doesn't know a priori if it will have a success or not."

A lot of people—no one knows how many—have leaped into the opening that's available when you have almost no capital costs except your own spare time: *PC Clearinghouse Software Directory*, a publication of PC Telemart, Inc. of Fairfax, Va. that makes an effort to be as comprehensive as possible, has identified over 21,000 microsoftware packages for sale from 2,912 different sources.

For many, of course, it turns out to be a leap into the void. Currie estimates that perhaps 1 program in 100 is a clear-cut commercial success.

Nevertheless, there is now an entire industry to take these would-be software millionaires to market.

Some of those 2,912 are publishers, such as Lifeboat Associates, which edit, package and sell individuals' programs. They pay their authors royalties, consciously imitating book publishers or record companies.

Some are distributors who serve as outlets for self-publishers like Joe and Fred, who hope to build a company around their programs. The distributors sell their wares to computer stores and others.

God alone knows how many are direct mail distributors, whose ads speckle the dozens of computer magazines that now exist.

And a handful are "establishment" software companies like Management Science America or, recently, Visicorp, that will buy outright or pay advances ($10,000 to $50,000 against royalties, according to CEO of Management Science John Imlay) on programs for their own label and for established markets.

There is even at least one literary agent offering his services to budding software authors.

Of the retail price paid by the customer out there shopping for something to run on his newly uncrated PC, IDC figures that 35% to 40% stays with the retailer, 15% to 20% will go to the distributor, 35% to 45%

to the publisher, if there is one, and then 5% to 20% to the original author. People in the industry expect the spread in royalties to narrow down to something like the 8% to 15% common in the book publishing business. On the other hand, notes IDC's Antonellis, "one person, like the author, may capture more than one of these four levels of revenue."

Who are these people who are seeking fame and fortune?

"With mainframes, it used to be like a member of an orchestra, each working on his little piece of a very large program," remarks Trip Hawkins. He is the 29-year-old president of Electronic Arts, a startup in San Mateo, Calif. partly backed by Steve Wozniak of Apple Computer fame, to groom and publish a new breed Hawkins thinks he sees emerging.

"Now that each author can do the whole program himself, he is more like a novelist or a rock star. So the microcomputer changes the kind of person involved. They don't really fit well in a corporate environment."

An understatement. Fred and Joe, for instance, who rent the back of a floor in an aged loft building in Manhattan's SoHo district, maintain—in the center of one of the two large rooms— a coop of four or five pigeons passed along by a neighboring tenant. Try that in the offices of IBM sometime. But even this is too constraining, says Fred. "Eventually, I'd like to tour the country in my own bus, and have my office and computer terminal in the bus."

Once a program is in distribution, it faces a fickle market. "No one knows why one program is really successful," says Currie. Its commercial life might be as little as a few months for a hot video game, or it might extend for years for a business application. But sooner or later most will get shoved aside by a new package, one that's better, or cheaper, or simpler to use or simply more gaudily packaged and advertised.

At the moment, reports Currie, a lot of the work being done on microsoftware is "cosmetic, like putting manuals into IBM format and putting four-color on the package." Or it is imitative, "like recasting an old 8-bit program to 16-bit." That should change because there's so much room for improvement in existing software. "A lot of what's out there today is just junk," he complains.

Nevertheless, as competing programs appear, the cost of surviving in the marketplace naturally goes up. "One company, Lotus, is doing a promotion for its program called 1,2,3, a

hot-selling business package, that must be costing them $1 million a month," says Dennis Vohs, executive vice president of Management Science. "That'll raise the ante a little. And pretty soon we're going to start advertising on television. That'll raise it a bit more."

But meanwhile, whole new product categories or unthought-of specialties inevitably appear, limited only by the imaginations of people with PCs. Horoscope programs, veterinarians' accounts receivable programs, a sewing pattern resizer, genealogy programs, dairy herd records, all these already exist.

Says John Imlay, of MSA, "What you look for is a repetitive application that is a bother to people and that you can put on a machine and make 10 times easier. It can be anything, anything at all: handicapping golf, scheduling bowling lanes or johns in a bordello, you name it."

"We won't remain a one-product company," Joe hastens to tell a visitor. "It's too dangerous." Their next venture will be a program to teach kids touch-typing, dubbed Quick-Finger. Fred brightens. "It will play like an arcade video game, see, and you'll have to type faster and faster, and eventually keep your eyes off the keyboard to keep winning."

Time will tell how things go for Joe and Fred. Meanwhile, on the following pages FORBES looks at seven other new entrepreneurs—some who already have made it big in this space age cottage industry, some who clearly seem about to.

Software Rx

It is an adventure sidestepping through the sawdust and buzzing drills at Health Information Systems' expanding Brooklyn quarters to President George Weinberger's spartan but comfortable office. Once there, Weinberger, 35, is quick to relate how HIS, which leases hardware and sells software to the health care industry, grew from a $50,000 investment in 1978, went public in 1980 and now has a market value of $100 million despite sales of only $7 million.

Not bad for an ex-Brooklyn College computer professor who quit six years ago to become a consultant. One of Weinberger's early assignments was a rush job to help a health care facility deal with a last-minute revision in a New York State billing law. Working

80 to 100 hours a week for three weeks (sending someone to his home for a change of clothes), he finished his program on time—only to fall asleep at his client's terminal during installation.

But Weinberger awoke to an idea to market his brainchild to others in the industry. One surgical supplier client, Barry Septimus, was so enthusiastic about the potential that he joined Weinberger to start HIS and is now chairman.

At the time most nursing homes, hospitals and clinics still relied on outside service bureaus like Shared Medical Systems or McDonnell Douglas' McAuto to process their billings. Weinberger's approach made in-house computers more cost-efficient and more accessible to personnel with no computer skills. By offering to lease (mostly) Qantel minicomputer hardware along with his software, Weinberger saved his clients a step and could guarantee clients would keep up with the state of the art.

That's capital intensive—"Barry and I pooled our funds and borrowed from friends and family," Weinberger recalls. "At one point we were in debt to the tune of $800,000." But it worked. When Weinberger brought HIS public in November 1980, it was not cash he needed anymore, but visibility. Says he, "How can hospitals with budgets many times larger than ours have confidence in HIS' small revenue base? Going public gave us an aura that we weren't just a little storefront partnership." Of course, Weinberger didn't mind the $2.7 million raised from the initial 350,000 shares sold at 7¾.

But Weinberger had big things in mind, among them adapting his minicomputer program to take advantage of big, powerful IBM mainframes in the larger hospitals. HIS programmers "thought I was crazy," he recalls. "They thought it would be impossible to translate the program from a minicomputer, designed to run with maybe 20 terminals, to the completely different structure of a mainframe that can support some 2,000." Nonetheless, the company announced its new product in May 1982. The stock market reacted ecstatically, boosting HIS from 8 (adjusted for a 1981 2-for-1 split) to about 21 by year-end. HIS—unusual in its industry—met its Jan. 1 deadline for completion. Weinberger hopes to install 12 to 18 systems over the next 18 months. At over $1 million each, that could mean revenues of $20 million. After yet another 3-for-2 split and a 50% stock dividend,

the stock is back up, trading at about 32, making Weinberger's 31.6% stake worth a cushy $33.4 million.

Accounting for the millions

When Ronnie Green applied for a loan in 1977 to buy one of ComputerLand's first franchises, his banker simply laughed. Green, a data processing manager for 11 years who had originally hoped to be a research biochemist, lacked experience running a business. But he managed to get a $50,000 Small Business loan to set up shop in San Jose, Calif., and within two months he turned a profit.

Green found his sales job tough in those days, with virtually no software on the market for home computers. He also saw an untapped market in "mom-and-pop stores that were doing shoe-box accounting" and realized that "for the cost of one extra clerk, they could have a computer system"—if he could find supporting software.

Green didn't look far. He buckled down to write a program of his own. His first effort was an "editor," a programming tool for Apple customers. That sold for $40 and helped support his longer-term project: a general accounting system that would retail at $4,000 for control program machines (CP/Ms) like the Altos and IBM PC. It took over two years to finish, and by 1979, Green was ready to start Software Dimensions with about $4,000 from his store's profits. All the tools he needed were at his disposal: He put his wife in charge of running the store and had two of his ComputerLand employees help program some of the machines on display in his shop. "I was sneaky," he admits, giving himself $10,000 credit to purchase his first two computers.

From the beginning, Green's products—the accounting packages for the CP/M and later a program adapted for the Apple that sells for $1,000—were packaged and marketed outside, through publisher Systems Plus. "Back then packaging consisted of a diskette with photocopied instructions in a baggie," says Green. But as the industry quickly evolved, Green itched for more control over the process. And that required capital.

By late 1981 Software Dimensions was yielding 22% pretax on its $500,000 revenues, which he plowed back into product development. So Green again went knocking at bankers' doors.

This time they didn't laugh. He walked away with a $500,000 line of credit, from which he drew $200,000 to pay taxes and hire a small marketing and sales staff.

Meanwhile, getting the money turned out to have been easier than luring experienced help. "We were a small development house in the big valley and couldn't compete with large companies for people," Green explains. So Green moved his outfit to Citrus Heights, a suburb of Sacramento, where he could pay his employees up to 10% less, since the cost of living was lower.

By the next fiscal year, ended June 1982, sales hit $2.2 million, with profits of about $480,000, which were also reinvested. "There are a lot of teenage millionaires in the Valley," muses Green. "But if you intend to be around next year, you have to dump a lot of that into R&D."

Green figured he would need an additional $2 million. Before he could decide between going public or seeking venture capital, Green was approached by ASK Computer Systems, a minicomputer software outfit looking for quick entry into the micro market. A deal valued at about $12 million is in the works.

Now it is Green who is laughing. "No more hassles getting capital or going public," he says.

Odd job

Ensconced alone in his spacious Menlo Park, Calif. offices, R. Alan Carl, 37, contemplates his tiny software company, Automation Consultants. "One reason I started my own business is that I felt there is never a bad job market for an entrepreneur," he says.

After receiving a University of Chicago M.B.A., Carl worked his way up to assistant vice president at Wells Fargo's economics department doing statistical and economic work involving computers. Learning the equipment required developing some expertise in computers, so when Carl grew bored with banking, he and a partner each put up $1,000 for office supplies, and in 1976 started subcontracting as freelance programmers.

Carl and his partner soon had to bring in a staff of local college undergraduates to help keep up. The problem with that, he says, was that "it became difficult to control the quality when we weren't there ourselves. And profits kept eroding because installation required so much hand-holding." So the two decided to package (standardize) programs—also tough. Besides marketing and documentation, there was the problem of "getting businessmen spending $30,000 for a minicomputer to accept a packaged solution."

Carl also had difficulty convincing his partner not to take in venture capital. Amid the dispute, he bought out his partner in 1979. "That was the worst decision I've made yet," moans Carl. "We should have dissolved the partnership and split the assets."

Meanwhile, Carl had learned of a large gap in the software market: job costing systems for contractors—not just builders or programmers-for-rent like Carl but architects, landscapers, ad agencies and many others. He assigned development of a job-cost system on the Durango minicomputer to his cadre of programmers. By the time he was able to turn his attention to the program, he found it in serious trouble. "I yanked my staff off and finished the program myself in a month," he says. But that, in turn, hurt the neglected consulting side of his business. It wasn't long before Carl got behind in his payments to his ex-partner and had to sign over the rights to his job-costing package.

But Carl was saved by the new wave of microcomputers. He buckled down to adapt his original program—which ran only on larger minicomputers—for the new micros. It took nearly nine months of struggle, but in late 1981 he was ready—in time for a major computer trade show, where he met up with Peachtree publishers. "They liked it because our program was written in the same language as most of their other packages, because it was flexible enough to be used by so many different types of end-users without major modifications, and because it was deceptively simple."

Since Peachtree brought his program to market last November, they have been selling about 50 packages a month, for $1,000 each. Now that Peachtree has closed down its publishing, though, Carl will find other publishers. It's the only way to go, he says: "It's much better to have them market up to 1,000 copies a year and get my small cut. On my own I'd be lucky to sell 50 a year. They're going to earn their 80%."

Hail, Columbia

Wayne Erickson's MicroRIM Inc. may finally be on the brink of commercial success.

Erickson, 36, first developed his RIM (Relational Information Management) software for mainframes in 1977, while he was a programmer at Boeing's Computer Services division. It was later used by NASA to track the first space shuttle's errant ceramic tiles. But not without some false starts.

After Erickson and a Boeing colleague created their first prototype, their supervisors "smiled, but put it on a shelf somewhere." Other database software was available for large business applications, but, Erickson points out, nothing for the scientific field. RIM, he says, was programmed to "think like an engineer: to collect, organize and rearrange data in a more structured and flexible way." But Boeing, he says, didn't care.

Frustrated, Erickson left in 1979 to work at the University of Washington's computer center and enhance RIM on his own. Soon NASA, a Boeing client, approached Erickson. It needed RIM for its shuttle project. Erickson spent evenings and weekends over the next three months on the task. He was on to something.

He began to think about how to transpose RIM onto the new Heathkit personal computer he was building in his spare time. If that were possible, Erickson could endow a small computer with flexibility, speed and organizational power available then only with large systems.

Oddly, commercial possibilities didn't occur to Erickson until his older brother, Ron, an attorney whom the younger Erickson describes as "a wheeler-dealer type," convinced him that together they could take such a product to market.

So Erickson went back to the drawing board evenings and weekends, while Ron and an investment banker friend worked out the financial nitty-gritty. They formed MicroRIM in November 1981 with a $200,000 line of credit, which they and another board member they brought in had to personally guarantee. Erickson pared down his work at the university and quit the following year.

The first year brought in $360,000 revenues, with a loss of $200,000. But that did little to dampen some new investors' appetite for MicroRIM; they snapped up a $500,000 private stock offering last November.

MicroRIM is still not out of the woods. It has yet to break even, and as the offering prospectus cautions: "The company is dependent on one software product. . . . The absence of adequate financing could have an adverse effect. . . . New products may

render the company's product obsolete . . ." and, perhaps most ominous, "Computer software systems cannot be patented, and any copyright laws may not be meaningful." Meanwhile, though, in addition to the 1,500 copies of RIM that have been sold so far (it retails for $595 to $1,035, depending on which options are bought with it), the Coast Guard announced that it intends to buy 1,000 more to help track people and equipment. That should bring sales of $2 million to $3 million and propel MicroRIM into the black by this fall. And Wayne owns 40%.

Computer scholastics

Computers are dumb," says James Schuyler. True. Yet he started DesignWare in San Francisco three years ago to "teach" computers how to teach people.

Schuyler, 37, spent a lot of time in school himself. He worked his way through math and computer science degrees at Northwestern University as a computer consultant to some of his professors, mostly in programming, keypunching and writing for $3 an hour. By the time he had earned his Ph.D., Schuyler had started Sky Enterprises and employed six students to help him.

After graduation, Schuyler taught at Northwestern's school of education for a few years, "But once I got bitten by the entrepreneurial bug it was hard to shake," he says. By 1980 he had scrounged up $20,000 to get DesignWare's first computer courseware program off the ground. He bought about $10,000 worth of computers and split the rest of the money between office supplies and travel. By May he negotiated his first deal, to develop Computer Discovery, an electronic course on the history, programming and social impact of computers. It became part of Apple's Appleseed program, a giveaway to schools that purchased its computers. It has since been republished for over half a dozen other machines.

DesignWare was immediately profitable, generating 10% aftertax on $200,000 revenues its first year, which Schuyler plowed back into the company. Since then he and his now dozen or so programmers have continued to write educational software, mostly for schools. He depends on the likes of Harcourt Brace Jovanovich, Harper & Row and textbook publisher D.C. Heath to publish, market and distribute his dozen or so programs.

Most classroom packages, retailing for about $175, include several diskettes and 20 or 30 workbooks.

Last November Schuyler turned over about a third of his company to venture capitalists for $300,000 in order to develop a new line of consumer educational/game programs, which he plans to publish, market and distribute himself. Among them: Spellicopter, a spelling game geared to ages 5 to 12, where kids "fly" helicopters to pick up scrambled letters in order to spell a word.

While Schuyler still owns about a third of his company (outside investors own another third and other insiders the rest), he foresees further diluting of his share with a second round of venture capital. Another entrepreneur bites the dust? "That's what you have to do to cash in on your investment," shrugs Schuyler, shirtsleeves rolled up. "By the time I cash out on this I expect the company to be doing $20 million revenues, and my percentage will still be 15% to 20%. By 1986 or 1987 I expect to either go public or be acquired." Then what? "I plan to start a new company, something in the computer field but completely different. Now I have no idea what," he muses. "By then the industry will be completely changed."

Back to the dice table

When Adora Ku and Gary Duesterberg first met in 1975 while both were working in separate divisions of a university data processing department, they would send each other notes and arrange dates via their computer terminals. A year later they got married and in 1978 started Business Software House, Inc., which cleared almost 30% profits on $150,000 last year, up 50% from 1981.

Ku, 32, has the presidential post, while her husband, 34, takes second billing and does most of the software design and development. "I'm the one with the administrative background," Ku explains. The two still use their computers to set up social and business schedules, but now they use Personal Calendar, their first packaged software program.

Personal Calendar communicates schedules between people, schedules meetings or use of office space and equipment and analyzes employees' time. It can also track clients or patients who repeatedly cancel appointments and helps an executive break down billable time and "remember" appointments or important events.

As newlyweds, Ku and Duesterberg moved to Atlanta and a year later started consulting and designing custom application software for a minicomputer manufacturer, a local government agency and a construction company, among others. As business grew, they began to realize that "as a service-oriented business, we were limited by the number of hours in the day," says Duesterberg. With all the

Business Software's Duesterberg, Ku
Easy to get in, but hard to stay.

handholding that clients required, "when a customer called two times to learn how to operate his program, we lost money," adds Ku.

The idea of packaging or even reapplying custom programs was appealing but obstacle-ridden. For one thing, they lacked funds and experience for marketing and were unwilling to give up a major piece of the company to venture capitalists. Computer owners preferred custom-designed software. But the road was already being paved by early publishers of lower-cost, general-purpose packages.

One publisher, Peachtree Software, retained Ku and Duesterberg in 1979 to help develop inventory, general ledger and mailing list programs. "Then Peachtree tossed us some ideas it had for automating executive tasks and asked if we were interested in

designing one," explains Ku. The calendar scheduling idea impressed them, and they went to work.

It took a year to design and develop Personal Calendar. Peachtree did the documentation (essentially, the instruction manual) and packaging and brought the software program to market last December. The package originally retailed for $375, but competitive pressures forced Peachtree to slash the price to $195. So far it has been selling about 1,000 copies a month. "It could even outsell VisiCalc," exults Duesterberg. Peachtree started selling it in April for the 16-bit IBM PC and is repackaging Personal Calendar for home use.

"It's easy to get into this business, but hard to stay in," notes Ku. "You can hit it with one product like a pet rock, but then you have to go back to the dice table."

That's where she and Duesterberg are now.

Off the A train

Edward Brayman has been writing software for microcomputers out of his small Manhattan apartment for about a year. Its furniture: several file cabinets that support a long tabletop on which is set up about $25,000 worth of personal computers—Apple II, Apple III, IBM PC, printer and Rolodexes of diskettes. No couch, a few cushions stashed beneath a corner card table and showing little wear. A spiral staircase rises to a loft bedroom whose terrace overlooks the rear of several city tenements.

It's quite a leap, though, from the straitened circumstances in which he wrote his first program, BisiGraph, a business graphics package just sold to USA Software. Before last year Brayman claims he spent eight months working by day on a computer at a friend's apartment and by night "sleeping around."

"I was so broke, I had no place to stay except the streets or subway. Mostly the A train. That was the cleanest."

In 1976 New Yorker Brayman dropped out of college six credits away from a joint B.A./M.A. degree in math. He got his first job as a programmer in Salt Lake City. "I told the guy I had experience that I didn't have." After a year he returned to New York, where he landed another programming job on Wall Street. In two years he had worked his way up to data processing manager by spending most of his spare time in the firm's library, teaching himself.

It wasn't long before Brayman got the itch to strike off on his own. "I saw the software out there, and I knew I could do a lot better," he says. At the time there was virtually none available for the then-new Apple III. Sacrificing a place to sleep, he quit to work full time on his business graphics program, using a friend's Apple computer. "Originally the package was done as a quickie, to make a couple dollars so I could get off the streets," he says. He let a computer store use it as a demo, where an Apple executive was impressed enough to put him in touch with the presidents of several software publishers, and he was on his way.

Brayman negotiated the USA Software contract for BisiGraph with the aid of a tax attorney with whom he had been bartering computer consulting services in exchange for legal advice. This was for a fee, though, which took up most of the development costs. Since he had access to his friend's Apple, Brayman's only other cost was disks, which run about $2 each in quantity. The final package fits on one disk, but Brayman used about 50 along the way.

The BisiGraph package will be released in a month or so and retail near $150. "It's hopefully one of the best business graphics packages out there," Brayman boasts. "It's the simplest to use. All my programs have the entire reference manual built into them. At any point in the program, you hit one key and it goes to the right page in the manual and tells you what to do."

He is now holed up in his office/apartment, working on an equipment tax-leasing program that he plans to market solo through his own new company, Useable Software, which Brayman says is backed by a partner who just left a $100,000-a-year Wall Street job to join him full time.

"We already have more than 20 companies interested in buying the leasing package," he gloats. "But to sell 1,000 disks will cost close to $100,000 in advertising and packaging. For now I'm pretty well set. I know where the money is coming from. In fact, by early next year, between the proceeds from BisiGraph and the leasing programs, I hope to be joining the millionaires' club." ∎

NINE WHO DARE

On these pages are portraits of women who decided to seek their fortunes working for themselves instead of the safer route of working for others.

Inner strength

I have the character of an entrepreneur," says Diana Guetzkow, 36, which is why she is president and CEO of Netword Inc. of Riverdale, Md., outside Washington, while husband Daniel is executive vice president.

Netword is one of the carrier companies with Postal Service certification to tie into its electronic mail system. Netword is like an electronic Western Union office, transmitting other people's messages for a fee. The company transmitted about 270,000 letters so far this year, taking in about 60 cents a letter.

Guetzkow was born in West Germany of Polish refugee parents in 1947. "I'm the classic story of someone who had to fight adversity at a young age and find an inner strength. I was never a child," she says about growing up in America. "I never felt like I was one of the gang." But if it was lonely, she hasn't forgotten the opportunity offered. "There are not many countries where someone can do what I did here." She earned a degree in physics, then a Ph.D. in foreign policy. She finds her doctorate enormously handy, not because she tête-à-têtes with Henry Kissinger, but, she says, because "there are times I feel I have to use Dr. Guetzkow to get people to return my phone calls."

To start Netword she scraped together $100,000 from 40 investors. "I made that money last for two years of development time." It's not yet in the black. Nevertheless, in April she went public and sold all 3 million shares in one week, at $1 each, netting $2.7 million, which gives the company some running room. Why electronic mail? Guetzkow, who was working for the Energy Department, wanted out of government and into her own business—any business. "Daniel provided the technical brilliance to do what I wanted to do," she says.

Man or woman, makes no difference when starting up. "It's been equally tough," she says. "I don't know that we're going to succeed. But we work hard, we're honest and we have a good product."—**Jeff Bloch**

Diana Guetzkow, president of Netword, an electronic mail carrier
"I'm the classic story of someone who had to fight adversity at a young age and find an inner strength."

Naomi Friedman, plumbing contractor
"I dispel the myth of the big, tough male plumber."

Discovery Toy's founder and president, Lane Nemeth
"Nice story, but we're not interested," they said.

Pipe dream

Naomi Friedman is a philosopher-plumber. "Sewers are very important, the basis of our civilization," she says with a smile, emptying her bib overalls of tools. Then the 31-year-old Oakland, Calif. contractor gets down to business. "There's a lot of money in them. Most people don't argue over a bill when you're fixing their sewer."

Why did she want to be a plumber? Because she once called one and was impressed by the ease of the job and the size of the bill. But there's a king-size wrench between wanting and getting. The local union wasn't interested in lady plumbers. She looked for someone to teach her the trade. "Most of the time I'd go into plumbing companies and the receptionist would laugh at me. I'd never get beyond her, which was very frustrating."

She finally found an independent plumber willing to teach her if she worked nine months without pay. She did, then started her own business, earning a contracting license four years later in 1979. "You're supposed to have four years of journey-level experience. I just told [the state] that I had four years' self-employment experience and they bought it."

The run-in with the union has left her bitter. Friedman says: "I haven't heard any really good stories from women involved in unions as far as the way they're treated on the job site or within their unions." But then she concedes: "I know I couldn't charge $35 an hour if it wasn't for the unions."

Remembering her own hard start, Friedman helps others along. She gave up four months' work to help coordinate the first national conference for women in the trades and has spent time teaching plumbing to young blacks.

And there's a certain revenge. "When I go to a client's home, I dispel the myth of the big tough male plumber, just by being 5-foot-2 and slim."—**Roger Neal**

Knock on any door

Lane Nemeth couldn't find an educational toy for a friend's one-year-old son. There's nothing new about that, of course. But while most people simply grumble, Nemeth turned a few wasted mornings into a $25 million (annual sales) business, Discovery Toys. Her idea: Sell quality educational toys through home demonstrations. An old idea, you say? It has worked well enough for Tupperware, Amway and Avon.

"If you wanted to buy something for your eight-year-old child, you'd go into Toys "R" Us and you'd pull something off the shelf that you liked as a kid such as Monopoly," Nemeth says. "You'd never pick out Enchanted Forest, which is our very best eight-year-old's-game. So I go to your house and show you how it's played—it will appeal to the child in you immediately—and I explain what skill it is developing, and you buy it."

As director of a day-care center for three years in Concord, Calif., Nemeth knew something about toys to begin with. And she did some market research—she tried selling toys to her friends. "I sold tons of toys," she recalls. In 1977 she started the company in her garage in Martinez, near San Francisco, gathering $25,000 from friends and relatives. First-year sales were $280,000, last year $11 million. She figures on better than doubling that this year.

Like her predecessors, she has built a big, pyramiding sales force—7,000 at last count, mostly women—by paying off more in dreams than in salary or benefits. The salesperson gets 26% of her gross sales and a smaller cut on the sales of her own recruits. She can also get cars, fur coats, vacations and jewelry, like the diamond-encircled pin Nemeth invariably wears on her lapel.

Married for 15 years and with an eight-year-old daughter, Tara, Nemeth made some typical beginner's mistakes. After under-ordering her first year, she over-ordered the next. Christmas came and went, leaving Discovery Toys with $100,000 of unsold inventory and no cash. "Nice story, but we're not interested" was a common reply from bankers. One suggested her husband ought not to let her work. So Nemeth borrowed from loan sharks at 27.5%.

Luckily, some venture capitalists stumbled on one of her toy parties, liked what they saw and rode to the rescue. Today there are the typical postentrepreneurial growing pains. Structure must be built, more capital raised. "Right now we're in adolescence. Letting go is painful. But I've shown that you can be a business person and still be the best mother and a good wife. It's doable."—**R.N.**

Barbara Gardner Proctor of Proctor & Gardner Advertising
Pretend there's a man in the back room.

The best collateral

Barbara Gardner Proctor recalls the day she was fired back in February 1970. The advertising agency she worked for came up with a concept for a TV commercial. "A mass demonstration of housewives running down the street waving a can demanding that hairdressers foam their hair." Proctor thought it tasteless and offensive. She would work on campaigns she liked or get out of advertising. She decided to start her own company.

Today, Chicago's Proctor & Gardner Advertising is small but respected. It will do an estimated $12 million in billings this year. It specializes in advertising targeted to the black community and counts Alberto-Culver, Kraft Foods and Sears among the clients.

Born to a poor North Carolina family, Proctor says she spent part of her childhood living in a shack with no running water. She went on to earn an English degree from a small Alabama college. She settled in Chicago and landed a job as an advertising copywriter.

After getting fired, she went to the Small Business Administration looking for a loan to start her own agency. What was the collateral? "I am," she said, and got $80,000. Proctor & Gardner opened in spring 1970. She was divorced but added her former married name to the business to give the impression a man was in the back room keeping an eye on things.

Chicago's big Jewel Food Stores chain credits her with helping make its generic foods campaign a success in 1978. "I didn't want it to appear there was cheap stuff being put into black stores," she said. Her message was, "Generic foods are perfectly good foods. If apples aren't from Michigan, they're not grade A, but so what. They're still good apples."

Proctor, now 51, refuses liquor or cigarette accounts, opting for family products, and knows part of her success came from good timing. "There was a national hysteria about blacks burning down buildings. But black women have never had the same difficulty dealing with white men. We're not considered a threat."

Chicago's other advertising agencies do not think so.—**Barry Stavro**

Joan Helpern of Joan & David Helpern Inc.
"Shoes are used to categorize women as sex objects."

If the shoe fits

The bride complained to her new husband that she had a hard time finding shoes she liked. He was a logical one to hear the complaint. After all, he was in the shoe business. Her gripe: "All the shoes were being used to categorize women as sex objects. They had nothing to do with the way women lived their lives." So Joan Helpern, academic, started to learn the business, designing shoes at night. Then husband David sold his shoe and specialty stores, and they set up operations near Harvard Square in the mid-Sixties. Her first creation: a lady's oxford.

That oxford, now modified, is still a Joan and David selection, but after almost 20 years the company offers more than 600 designs a season, with sales expected to top 700,000 pairs, or more than $50 million, this year, and a new ready-to-wear line of apparel is being introduced. The Joan and David shoes are known for quality leather, low-key colors, lack of frills, and longevity. Joan Helpern, the president and CEO of Joan & David Helpern Inc., spends six months every year in Italy, arranging contracts with the 18 factories that make and ship her shoes to upper-crust department stores like Bloomingdale's as well as her own chain of 45 boutiques situated in other stores. Retail prices range from $88 to $250 a pair. Not cheap, but Helpern understands that people will pay through the nose if you offer something that appeals to them. "Today, people are smarter about spending."

Helpern, 57 and the mother of two, spent half her working life in academia. With a master's in social psychology from Columbia, she was one of the first to specialize in child development programs for public schools. Then she met and married David Helpern, owner of his own chain of stores in New England.

Helpern's luxurious New York showroom overlooks Central Park. Bijou, her white Bichon Frise, chews placidly on a leather glove as the business grows. Any advice to other aspiring women entrepreneurs? Yes. "Don't lock yourself up away from new ideas. And do what you're best at."—**Christopher Power**

Mary Farrar, owner of two construction companies
The answer to everything: Start a new company.

Iron lady

My résumé doesn't make any sense at all," says Mary Farrar, 43, referring to nearly 20 years spent as a housewife in Kansas City, Kans. Nothing else? Well, then there was that job as a part-time accountant, and there was that $500 she had saved. Five years later she owns two construction companies with 1983 sales of $6 million. "I didn't set out to storm the world," Farrar says, but in the male-dominated construction business in Kansas City, she has. "They think of me as just one of the fellas."

In the mid-1970s, with her five children off in school, she took a job as a bookkeeper with a new steel construction firm. The owner was mostly absent, so Farrar went from payroll chores to proofing blueprints and writing job estimates. She liked the responsibility, but when the boss turned down her offer to buy into the company, Farrar's husband, Jim, a sheet metal journeyman, urged her to start her own business.

A contractor friend offered a start with two jobs worth $250,000 erecting steel frames for warehouses. "It was a real shoestring operation." She used the $500 as a down payment to buy used hand tools and ladders and recruited laid-off workers. With suppliers offering 30 days' credit and her contractor friend doling out cash advances, she managed to juggle her weekly payroll. Farrar's plucky reputation led to more referrals, and System Erectors Inc. reached $2 million in sales in two years.

When the latest recession hit, though, manufacturers cut back on inventory, and the market for 150,000-square-foot warehouses dried up. What then? Says Farrar: "I started a new company. That's an entrepreneur's answer to everything."

Now Farrar's Hallmark Construction is a one-stop construction center, putting up buildings for the inexperienced, which means it finds sites, handles zoning, hires architects and does the general contracting. It has turned into a $5 million company.

Business is so good, Farrar says, her husband will soon head up her field operations. So her husband will work for her? Farrar handles that deftly: "Maybe that's not a good way to put it. He'll be working with us."**—Barry Stavro**

Linda Richardson, who sells marketing advice to banks
"It cost me three years, a lot of lost opportunities."

A second chance

I believed them when they told me I was green," says Linda Richardson, 38. She had started a small but successful business of teaching marketing to bank employees, but became persuaded that she didn't have the knowledge or experience to run her own business. So, in 1980 she sold her Philadelphia sales training firm to Hay Associates, a consulting firm.

"They promised me autonomy, but I didn't have it." Eleven months ago she took back the business and was again on her own with The Richardson Group.

With just a trace of bitterness she recalls the events that led her to sell out: "A little company can feel such pressure when somebody says things are going well for you now, but what if? Women are especially vulnerable. Where are the role models? There was no one for me to point at and say, she did it. It cost me three years, a lot of lost opportunities. It won't happen again," she vows.

Still, her $1,200-a-day fees will bring in about $1 million this year, and about 15% of that is profit. Richardson is in a real growth field: Banks, never strong on marketing, are finding that marketing is now essential to their survival. Says she: "I said this doesn't make sense; bankers were being taught to sell bulldozers, yet knowledge of bank products was one of their biggest problems."

Heady stuff for the former principal of a New York City alternative high school aimed at dropouts. "The kids and the drugs just got to be too much," she says of her academic career. In 1974 she went to work for Manufacturers Hanover. Charged with buying a sales training package, she designed her own. She taught the program she put together for a year. Then she decided to try it on her own.

She married a radiologist and moved to Philadelphia, taking the business with her. Then came the pain of selling out and finding she disliked working for others. "I was a little scared about opening up on my own again. But I was lucky to get a second chance."

Business is good. "We don't have to prospect anymore. Clients come to us." And she has shed her doubts about being able to manage it all. "I've found being on my own is far better. I can take the risks, call the shots, make the decisions."**—Jill Bettner**

Sandra Hunt, founder of BioSearch Inc.
"They scream at you, 'Diversify, diversify!' "

Don't just get married

Sandra Hunt remembers her father saying that. "He kept saying, 'You can't just grow up and get married. You have to make something of yourself.' " She started saving for college at 15 and worked at two jobs to pay for her B.S. in biology from the University of Texas at Arlington, outside Dallas. "Whenever I got tired I kept reminding myself that J.C. Penney made and lost three fortunes before he made one he kept. I hadn't even lost one yet."

Eleven years ago, at 27, she bought the equipment of the failing biological testing laboratory she worked for and was in business, pledging accounts receivable for loans. Business grew from $54,000 that first year to $1 million in 1982, and this year is running 10% ahead of that, she says. What's her secret? Lots of outfits could do what she was doing: making sanitation checks for food outfits and testing makeup for bacterial resistance. But Hunt tried to give better service.

When a local restaurant had sanitation problems, she helped devise an employee bonus system for cleanliness. "I heard clients say, 'Boy, it sure is hard breaking someone away to take you that sample,' " she says in her soft country accent. "So I started a courier service. It was common sense." And customers thought it was cute to find a woman in the business.

Hunt allowed herself a few heady moments when sales hit $400,000 in 1978 and she started M.B.A. work at Southern Methodist University. "They scream at you, 'Diversify, diversify, diversify.' So I started." She lost $50,000 investing in such dicey projects as electric cars and silver mines before she learned her lesson: "It was my biggest mistake because I was depending on someone else to do it right, not on myself. I'll never get into something I can't control again."

In March Hunt merged BioSearch into Professional Service Industries Inc., a Chicago-based company with $25 million in sales. BioSearch had three labs and 500 customers. Now a major PSI shareholder, she has taken over three more labs and two archeological surveying offices for PSI and spends 14-hour days learning the new businesses. Why work so hard when she seems to have it made? Hunt laughs. "Giving me more markets to handle is like giving an alcoholic the key to a liquor store."—**Toni Mack**

Donna Jeanloz, cofounder, The Renovator's Supply
If there is no business, work on the résumés.

This old house

Give some credit to the separatists of Quebec. Husband Claude was a manufacturing consultant there, and it got uncomfortable. They had been booted out of Africa earlier when a new dictator turned against the Peace Corps. Enough's enough. "We didn't feel we were directing our own lives," Donna Jeanloz says. "We were sitting on the couch, kicking ideas around about what else we could do, and the idea of a mail-order company to supply renovation products hit me."

Claude and Donna Jeanloz moved back to their renovated home in Millers Falls, Mass., took the $50,000 from selling the house in Montreal and started The Renovator's Supply five years ago. Today they are the largest sellers of reproduction hardware by mail in the U.S., with 125 employees and about $10 million a year in orders, enough to support a growing string of retail stores and a fledgling quarterly magazine, *Victorian Homes*. There is money, it turns out, in Victorian faucets, cupolas and weathervanes, gaslights and old-fashioned latches and locksets.

"We put out our first catalog in 1978, in black and white, 500 items. We did all the photography, wrote the blurbs ourselves, laid it all out, sent it to the printer and printed 50,000 copies," says Donna Jeanloz, 36, who had trained as a landscape architect. They bought lists from *The Old House Journal* and *Early American Life* magazines and made their first mailing.

Then they waited. "Claude started working on his résumé, and so did I. In January, suddenly, the orders came flooding in. We had no idea January was the best month for mail-order sales. But the results of that January 1979 elated us. We got going on another round with the catalog and really buckled down. Success came, and troubles too.

"We had stuff under the bed. The cellar was full. The attic was full. It was really getting awful. When we got up to 13 employees and we were working on three shifts, we really had to move out of the house."

She has no housekeeper. "I bring my children into the office when I don't have anywhere else to park them. But I don't think that's a good example. If I had any spare time, I should clean my house.

"We've always felt that one of our strong points was that since most of us here are young and have no prior experience, we don't have any preconceived ideas about how things should be done or what will or won't work. Sometimes having no idea it won't work is an asset."—**J.B.**

BLACKS WHO LEFT DEAD-END JOBS TO GO IT ALONE

MORE AND MORE BLACKS STUCK IN MIDDLE MANAGEMENT ARE BECOMING ENTREPRENEURS

Electrical engineer Jerry Lawson worked at large corporations for almost 20 years—the last 10 at Fairchild Camera and Instrument Corp., where in 1975 he became engineering director of the video game unit. Not until Fairchild's 1980 buyout by oil-services giant Schlumberger Ltd. did Lawson assess his future and conclude: "As a black man, I was not going to get anywhere in the corporation."

So Lawson decided to start his own video game design company. Lacking the operating experience to attract venture capitalists, he financed the business by using his Fairchild reputation to get contracts in advance from large vendors. Today Video-Soft Inc., of Santa Clara, Calif., has 11 employees and deals with such well-known toymakers as Milton Bradley, Mattel, and Hasbro Industries.

'MIRRORS AND BUBBLE GUM.' Although the drop in video game sales held the company short of its $1.2 million revenue goal for 1983—after it had grossed $400,000 in its first eight months in 1982—Lawson refuses to be discouraged. With two years of operations behind him, he hopes to raise the $500,000 to $1 million in venture capital needed to develop a new line of computer-enhancement devices such as touch-sensitive screens. "If I failed tomorrow," he says, "I'd say it was worth it."

Like Lawson, many black executives who find themselves stuck in middle management are quitting corporate life to become entrepreneurs. They want to call their own shots in businesses where color will not limit how high they rise or how much they earn.

"Capability and performance were important in corporate promotion, but equally important was the old-boy network—and race plays a significant part in limiting access to the network," says Charles K. Portis of Pittsburgh, who left Mellon Bank's trust department to found a financial consulting firm. Adds Don H. Barden, former special assistant to the president of American Ship Building Co. and now president of his own Lorain (Ohio) cable television company: "I wanted a company in the mainstream of American business, and you can't get that working for another company."

This impatience with the pace of corporate advancement seems to be increasing as black business school graduates become more confident of their skills. "A lot of blacks are deciding they're not going to make vice-president, and if they stay much longer, they'll get locked in financially," says Clarence Curry, director of the University of Pittsburgh's Small Business Development Center.

Like most new entrepreneurs, the black corporate escapee has problems securing capital. John Douglas, formerly director of investor and public relations at Castle & Cooke Inc. in Honolulu, notes that arranging financing for his startup UHF television station in San Jose, Calif., was "very creative—smoke, mirrors, and bubble gum." Douglas got $1 million from a group of Minority Enterprise Small Business Investment Corporations and $2 million from a Canadian equipment-leasing company, arranged for vendor financing by buying additional equipment with a 20% downpayment, and used bank loans for operating funds.

60-HOUR WEEK. Even when the business is under way, some blacks encounter the same obstacles they tried to avoid by leaving the corporation. "We've had to convince companies not to think of us as a minority-owned business," says Eddie L. Sampson, a former General Mills Inc. manager who heads Merit Electronics Corp. in Minneapolis. "When they think of minority concerns, they think of problems they've had or heard about."

To "alleviate the credibility issue" of being a black company, Sampson scrapped plans to make his own computer components and distributes those of established companies instead. Kibbie Pillette, a former corporate petroleum engineer and founder of Kibbie Corp. in Abbeville, La., found he had to use white salespeople to sell the well leak-detection and control system that he developed. Buyers of offshore drilling equipment resisted "buying anything from a black man," he says.

Almost all the entrepreneurs have found that success comes hard for small businesses. Portis took two years to equal his Mellon salary. And William L. Spearman Jr., a former International Business Machines Corp. systems engineer who founded Infodyn International Inc., rejoices that he no longer works a 7-day week of 12-hour days at the Denver software company. He is down to a 6-day week, 10 hours a day.

RUNNING THE SHOW. Still, most black former corporate managers feel that the freedom of running their own shows and the chance of a financial killing outweigh the hardships. Says Ardis Graham, formerly coordinator for computer auditing at the Dallas office of Big Eight accountant Arthur Young & Co. and now president of his own Dallas data processing company: "We grossed $250,000 that first year, and I have never wanted to go back." And Barden, already a millionaire from real estate ventures, recently won the cable television franchise for Detroit. He estimates that his cable company will have revenues of $100 million by 1990.

But for most, entrepreneurship remains a matter of working, waiting, and hoping. Notes Spearman, whose company barely kept operating through the recession: "It's been rewarding, though rough. When I was with IBM, I was very secure. Now I don't have any security, but I see the potential of greater financial and personal gratification." ∎

THE ORIGINS OF SONY'S WALKMAN

Asia
by Akio Morita

TOKYO—One day in the spring of 1979, Masaru Ibuka, honorary chairman of Sony, walked into my office with a portable stereo tape player and a pair of standard headphones. I must have looked surprised, for he quickly explained, "I like to listen to music, but I don't want to disturb others. I can't sit there by my stereo all day. This is my solution—I take the music with me. But the headphones are too heavy!"

I put them on and took a few turns around the office with the tape player. It was nice, having a peripatetic musical accompaniment, yet the set was cumbersome. You wouldn't want to carry it very long. This was the origin of Walkman.

As I thought about Mr. Ibuka's contraption, I realized that many young people live in a world of music. My sons and daughter are typical, I think. Good sound is as natural to them as the air they breathe, and their stereo is always on. Younger people have expensive stereo equipment at home and in their cars, and would listen all day if they could. But, I thought, what happens when a young couple goes for a drive?

As long as they're in the car, the music is with them. But if they go to the country or the seaside and get out of the car, off goes the quality sound. An ordinary tape unit played outdoors doesn't produce half the sound they're used to. I realized they needed a miniature stereo and light, comfortable headphones.

I immediately directed my staff to build an experimental cassette player with small headphones. They came up with a model that I could put in one pocket and with headphones I hardly felt. The sound was surprisingly impressive and clear. As I strolled I wasn't even aware of carrying anything.

Later I was listening to my new player at home and noticed my wife was annoyed. The look on her face seemed to say, "What is he listening to by himself?" Then it dawned on me that the set would need two pairs of headphones. Otherwise there would be trouble when either the boy or girl cut out the other. We added another headphone.

By the following week our production people had made another experimental machine with two jacks and a pair of headphones, and I invited my golf buddy Kaoru Shoji, the novelist, for a game. I handed him a set of headphones as we drove to the course. I had brought a tape of an Edvard Grieg piano concerto played by Mr. Shoji's wife, Hiroko Nakamura, an internationally known pianist.

We put on the headphones and I switched on the tape. A broad smile came over his face. But there was one drawback: We couldn't talk because of the headphones. We had to take them off each time we said something, and it was a nuisance.

So I had my staff attach a button-activated microphone to the player. Two people can converse while listening to the music without removing the phones. We call this the "hot-line."

I was confident we had a viable product, and I suggested to our manufacturing and sales people that we market it commercially. Much to my surprise, with a few exceptions they were unenthusiastic. They said it wouldn't sell. I was quite embarrassed, but the only way I could find out whether my idea was any good was to take personal responsibility for the machine. I volunteered to be manager of the project.

One of the staff dubbed the set Walkman, which is a little odd in English. The fellow in charge of Sony sales in English-speaking areas refused to market anything with that name. We hit upon the name Stow Away for England, and Sound About for the United States and other English-speaking countries.

The Walkman was an immediate sales success in Japan. It quickly became so popular that people around the world were soon asking about it by its Japanese-English name of Walkman.

My confidence in the appeal of the machine was borne out. When King Juan Carlos of Spain visited Japan this spring, he told me that he had a Walkman. I have received phone calls from conductors such as Herbert von Karajan, Zubin Mehta and Lorin Maazel asking me to get them more Walkmans.

Music lovers around the world use Walkman to listen to their favorite tapes without disturbing other people. I gather that students take Walkmans along to the library when they study.

Some fear that headphones can create hearing problems, but there is no danger if the volume is not too high. An ordinary stereo record player turned up high can annoy one's family and neighbors, especially in the cramped living conditions of Japan. Walkman avoids this noise pollution.

With a standard stereo, almost all the energy used to produce the sound is wasted because only a fraction of the sound goes to the listener's ears. The rest shakes the walls, floors and adjoining apartments. But since Walkman requires only enough volume for one or two listeners, it is also an energy-saving stereo.

Radios and television sets today are personal possessions. There are several in every family. Now the stereo has become personal as well, thanks to Walkman.

Mr. Morita is chairman of the board, Sony Corp. This article was translated from the Japanese literary magazine Bungei Shunju by The Asia Foundation's Translation Service Center.

SIR CLIVE'S VERY BIG GAMBLE ON A VERY SMALL TV

Sir Clive Sinclair, probably Britain's best-known living inventor, unveiled his pocket-size television last month with characteristic cockiness. Declaring that his 2-in. TV was lighter, cheaper, and brighter than anything on the market, he predicted it would do for television what the transistor had done for radio.

Bravura is Sinclair's stock in trade—even when facing rivals that dwarf his $82 million company, as he does in the promising market for take-it-with-you TV sets. This time, though, Sinclair—who says that he watches TV only "once in a blue moon"—has more than usual at stake, and he faces an uphill fight (BW—Apr. 18).

Although the company has already received more than 1,000 orders, its TV, which initially will sell for $120, is currently available only by mail order in Britain. By contrast, Sony's $167 Watchman, Seiko's $500 TV-wristwatch, and Casio's $200 pocket version will be in U. S. stores in time for the Christmas shopping season. Sinclair is planning to introduce a $99 version in the U. S., but not until late 1984.

MARATHONS. Sinclair has had his share of disasters in the past, including failures with digital watches, portable calculators, and even an earlier version of a pocket TV. In most instances, he was outpaced by either faster-moving or lower-cost producers.

Today, however, Sinclair is riding high on the phenomenal success of his midget computers. The under-$100 units brought computers to the British masses and made four-year-old Sinclair Research Ltd. a household name. Sales of the privately held company doubled last year, while its pretax profits rose 64% to $21 million.

For inventing computers that thousands of Britons could at last afford, Sinclair won knighthood as well as hero status in a nation committed to reviving entrepreneurial spirit. "He has given enormous confidence to everyone," says Kenneth Baker, Britain's Information Technology Minister. "He has proved that we don't have to lie back and let the Japanese roll over us."

Over the years, Sinclair, 43, has evolved an approach to product development that is surprisingly aggressive for such a small company. And that process stems from the company's unique culture. Sinclair, who is chairman of the British chapter of Mensa, the high IQ society, sets a curiously mixed tone for his company, which is housed in a converted Victorian mineral water bottling plant in Cambridge. A company bike substitutes for a company car, and marathon running in an annual company sponsored race is nearly *de rigueur* for the mostly under-40 staff. (He himself has twice raced in the New York City marathon.)

But at the same time, he pays top salaries and "is not frightened of spending money" on research, says an insider. In two years, Sinclair Research has nearly tripled in size to 70 employees, and its projects now range from a professional computer, slated for introduction next year, to ambitious long-term ventures into telecommunications and robotics.

Despite his love of the limelight, Sinclair has built an organization that relies heavily on teamwork. While he claims credit for all basic ideas, once a new product is conceived, he brings together a handful of people who lay out a development plan and divide the tasks among themselves. "We have our own brainstorming session, then we fill in the details," says Jim Westwood, a Sinclair director. Westwood helped develop the proprietary design that made it possible to put the little TV's circuitry onto a single silicon chip.

And unlike large companies, where products under development typically are passed from one group to the next, Sinclair Research allows the same team to take an idea all the way from planning to design to marketing. To Sinclair, continuity is critical to maintaining momentum. When different people are involved in different phases, he points out, there is unnecessary overlap because each group must document why the last one did what it did. At the same time, teams that work from scratch to completion tend to have "enormous dedication," he says. "The trick is to have small groups, reasonably isolated."

PRODUCTION DELAYS. Westwood, who has been with Sinclair for 20 years, says that this autonomy—along with the cachet of working for one of Britain's premier high-tech companies—is a key element in attracting top people. And because the company does not have a massive structure, he adds, "it moves quickly." Minister Baker claims that the technique has inspired other companies. Sinclair has had "a stimulative effect" on British business, he says. "The small-team approach is the way forward for lots of young companies."

One such team at Sinclair developed the flat tube that gives the new mini-TV its svelte 1¼-in. thickness. The tubes could not be manufactured with conventional technology, so the same team developed a new process.

The need to invent such manufacturing techniques contributed to production delays at a tube plant that Sinclair designed in Dundee, Scotland. Learning from past mistakes, he decided not to have his own company run the facility and contracted it out to Timex Corp., which builds Sinclair's computers. But then a six-week strike at Dundee further pushed back the debut for the 5½x3½-in. television, originally scheduled for introduction in the fall of 1982.

Sinclair Research relies on outside design collaboration, as well as outright purchase, for its success. For instance, the design for the TV's single-chip circuitry was developed over two years by engineers at Sinclair working with digitalization specialists at Ferranti Electronics Ltd. Finding the right battery for the TV came by fluke. Sinclair happened to be visiting Polaroid Corp.'s Boston laboratory just at the time when a powerful new film-pack battery cell was under development. Sinclair snapped up early rights to the wafer-thin lithium cell because its 15-hour life expectancy is several times that of the cells in rival mini-TVs.

'BLUE SKY' PROJECTS. With the TV now on the market, Sinclair, characteristically, is preoccupied with ideas for other products—among them, an electric car. Unlike some inventors-turned-businessmen, he still spends only a few hours a day on business matters. "The office routine is an interruption to what I see as my real work," he says, "which is thinking."

Meanwhile, Sinclair continues to build for the future. Nearly all of last year's profits are going into research and development. One of the company's three laboratories will be replaced by a brand-new facility, called Metalab, built in an 18th century house in Milton. It will contain $150,000 worth of equipment and material per researcher. This lab, which Sinclair says is for such "blue sky" projects as a fifth-generation computer, will have computer-aided design machines and a pilot semiconductor fabrication line for building proprietary chips from scratch. ∎

MORE REAL PEOPLE:
JOBS AND CAREERS WITH PROMISE

INTRODUCTION AND OVERVIEW

Do you love the idea of saying good-bye to freeway traffic jams or crowded commuter cars and doing your work at home? Maybe you do, but maybe you really don't.
> —"A Job with a View," *Forbes* Magazine

If you've read Chapter 4, "Movers and Shakers," you may have decided that not everyone is cut out for a life of entrepreneurship. If risk-taking is not for you, read on. In the following pages you'll meet men and women whose skills in the new technologies give them exceptionally high job security.

The fields emphasized in the readings are engineering, science, and technology. These fields will grow faster than average and offer better opportunities than most other fields in the decades to come.

A recent survey of the electronics industry shows a projected demand of nearly 200,000 new electrical and computer science engineers by 1985. But projections through 1985 reveal that there will be only 70,000 new graduates in those two fields. The opportunities are tremendous!

THE READINGS

"Joe Jaramillo: Programmer/Systems Analyst"

"Jackie Cunningham: Computer Services Technician"

"Garnet Hizzey: Manufacturing Engineer"

"Linda Cunningham: Environmental Science Engineer"

"Gloria Blue: Electrical Engineer"

"On the Leading Edge: Communicators and Information Managers for EEI"

"A Job with a View: Seven Who Telecommute"

REFERENCES

Exploring Careers, published by the U.S. Department of Labor's Bureau of Labor Statistics in 1979, is a publication intended primarily for youngsters of junior high school age, but others will find it useful as well. It emphasizes what people do on the job and how they feel about it and stresses the importance of "knowing yourself" when considering a career. It contains evaluative questions, activities and career games presented in 14 occupational clusters, as well as occupational narratives of real men and women. If your library does not have a copy, you may order one from the Superintendent of Documents, Washington, DC 20402.

Guide for Occupational Exploration, published by the Employment and Training Administration of the U.S. Department of Labor in 1980, provides information about the interests, aptitudes, adaptabilities, and other requisites of occupational groups, enabling the reader to compare these requirements with what he or she knows about himself or herself.

The language of the text is simple and nontechnical, intended for any reader's use, with or without counseling help: the youth who is planning a career; the person who must, or wishes to, change jobs; the partially qualified or unqualified jobseeker; and the counselor or vocational adviser who assists others with career exploration and planning and occupational choices or changes. If you cannot locate a copy, you may obtain one from the Superintendent of Documents, Washington, DC 20402.

"The Miracle Force." A 29-minute color film narrated by Orson Welles presents profiles of 5 contemporary engineers and shows some of their current activities in electric power, communication, aerospace, computers, and advanced biomedical systems. Each engineer works in a different region of the country and for a different type of organization—a public utility, a large corporation, a government agency, a small business, and an academic institution. For further information please contact the Institute of Electrical & Electronics Engineers, Inc., Public Information Department, 345 East 47th Street, New York, NY 10017, 212/705-7866.

Additional career resources are available from Modern Talking Pictures, 5000 Park Street North, St. Petersburg, FL 33709.

FUTUREVISION 4

But what'd finally got me awake wasn't just the ringing in my ears: the viewphone was starting into "Starlight Serenade" for about the tenth time. Finally remembering where I was, sort of, I crawled back across the bed's two meters of jelly to the phone on the other side. I took a look at myself in the mirrored screen. And then I hit BLANK SCREEN, before I pressed the VOICE button.

—*Joan D. Vinge,* Fireship

JOE JARAMILLO: PROGRAMMER/SYSTEMS ANALYST

Joe worked his way up in the computer field. "I feel that I've done rather well for someone with no college."

Joe Jaramillo grumbled and rubbed his eyes. The clock on his nightstand read 4:08 ... *4:08 on a Sunday morning*. A phone call had awakened him moments before, and a faraway voice had told him to come down to the bank right away.

Bracing himself for the violent assault on his eyes, Joe turned on the light. "Those are the breaks," he thought. "You have to expect this sort of thing when you're a systems analyst. All my work involves computers, and computers can't be kept waiting. It's no big deal to be awakened in the middle of the night. I have to be available 24 hours a day. All part of the job."

But these thoughts made it no easier for Joe to get up at 4:08 a.m.

Shaking one foot loose from the tangle of covers, Joe planted it firmly on the floor next to the bed. The other foot followed not far behind. As he reluctantly sat up, random thoughts about his job went through the fog of his mind.

"Almost 6 years," he remembered, "6 years next week since I was promoted from programmer to programmer/systems analyst. What a change! Back then I handled the computer all the time. Writing programs, running them, finding the "bugs". And all I saw was my own little slice of the bank. Now I work with people from consumer lending, internal operations, all the different bank departments. I see the whole show. I help people understand what the computer can do for them—how it can help them do their work here. And I have lots of room to be creative.... After I find out exactly what people need, I think things through and design a new system.

Then I install it and test it. But I rarely touch the computer anymore; I leave that work to the two programmers under me. If I worked in a smaller bank, I'd probably do more of my own programming...."

Joe reached over and turned on the radio. The voice of his favorite country and western singer filled his ears.

"... I've done rather well for someone with no college education! I've always liked computers, even in high school. I would have liked to learn about them in college, but I couldn't afford to go. That 6-month technical school course was the best alternative for me. It got me a job here with Commerce National Bank. Then I worked my way up the ladder. Even so, I was lucky. I got in when the getting was good. Today I'd need a bachelor's degree to be hired here...."

By now Joe's eyes had begun to adjust to the light. With a great effort he lifted himself to a standing position. Picking up his bathrobe, he somehow managed to put his arms in the proper sleeves and tie the belt around the waist. Now if he could only find the bathroom!

"... I've been on this assignment a long time," Joe's brain reminded him. "I started it 9 months ago. The head of the check-processing department, Tom Arnold, wanted a new system for processing checks. So I went over there to speak with Tom. I had to give him ideas on the possibilities and find out just what he wanted. Some people think that systems analysts are magicians, that we have a "sixth sense" that tells us what kind of system would be best. But it doesn't work that way. Unless people tell us what they're trying to do, we can't advise them how to do it.

"Tom complained that his check-processing system relied too much on people and not enough on machinery. He was afraid that the present system would not be able to keep up as the volume of checks grew. While he was at it, Tom wanted a better way of tracking down errors. And he wanted a system that would tell him who the bank's biggest customers were, how much money they maintained on deposit, and how long they kept it there. So I looked at the system he was using at the time...."

Feeling their way along the wall, Joe's hands found a switch and turned it on. Instantly the bathroom appeared around him. His left hand twisted the faucet on the sink; his right hand sprang back from the icy touch of the water. He gave it a minute to warm up.

"... Tom showed me how his department processed checks every day. The checks and deposit slips arrived in bundles. The first step was proofing and encoding. This was done by machines that took each check and printed on it the amount it was written for. The numbers were printed in a special ink that other machines could "read." Tom had 30 of these proof encoding machines in his department, and each was run by a clerk. As the

Reprinted from *Exploring Careers*, U.S. Department of Labor, 1979.

checks were encoded, the operator and machine made certain that the amounts were the same as a teller's tally. This is known as "proving." Another machine, a reader-sorter, then read the specially printed number on each check and sorted and tallied the amounts of all the checks from the 30 proof encoders. It sorted the checks by the city they came from so they could be sent back to other banks and exchanged for credit. The faster this was done, the more money the banks would have available for use by their customers, loans, credit advances, and the like. Finally, the checks were photographed by a microfilm camera for future reference.

"The system was good at first, but I could see Tom's point. They'd run into problems as more and more checks came through. Tom knew what he needed and I knew what kind of equipment was available from different manufacturers, so together we created a new system. We looked at the latest equipment and considered different ways of setting it up. We had to think about how reliable each machine would be, not just how fast it could do the job. Every time something breaks down and the system stops running, the bank loses money. So reliability mattered a lot. The cost of new equipment was important, too...."

The water had gotten warm. Joe rubbed his face with a wet washcloth. No reason to shave at this hour, he decided.

"... I met with Tom every day to discuss this project, sometimes for an hour or more. With his help I finally designed the right system. We decided that the hardware produced by the National Computer Technology Company was the best for our needs. Other companies make faster equipment, but it isn't as reliable...."

Back in the bedroom, Joe pulled clothes out of the closet and climbed into them. The sounds of the Beatles on the radio gave him new energy: "Woke up, fell out of bed, dragged a comb across my head...."

"... With the new system, the checks will be proofed, encoded, and automatically sorted into several categories. With the new proof machine, Tom will easily be able to get that information that he wants about certain accounts—whenever he wants it. The checks will be microfilmed while they're sorted on a high speed reader-sorter, so we will have a film record of them as the bank

"After I find out exactly what people need, I think things through and design a new computer system," says Joe.

received them. That will make it easier to track them down to find errors. And the new reader-sorter equipment will sort checks faster and will allow the bank to forward them to other banks faster than is possible now.

"When the new equipment was installed and tested, we linked it to the bank's computer. Since the two systems use different coded languages, we had to design an "interface" so that they could communicate with each other. My programmers did a great job on that.

"I'm happy with the new system. Simple, reliable, not too expensive. It was more of a challenge than that payroll system I designed last year, and I met the challenge...."

Joe was dressed and ready to go. "At the tone the time will be 4:30," said the radio just before he switched it off. Grabbing his coat, he dashed out the door and prayed that his car would start.

"... So all we have to do now is switch over to the new system. It has to be ready to process checks by tomorrow morning, when the bank opens. I thought the technicians would be able to handle the job, but obviously they've run into a problem if they need me at this hour. Well, fortunately, I don't have to make many of these night calls. If I did, I'd be a nervous wreck. It's a good thing I didn't become a firefighter...."

Exploring

Programmers and systems analysts spend much of their time solving problems.

- Do you enjoy doing math problems?
- Do you like puzzles and brain teasers?
- Do you read mystery stories?

Programmers and systems analysts work with problems that are long and detailed. Solving them takes a great deal of patience.

- Do you enjoy long, detailed projects, such as doing jigsaw puzzles, painting by numbers, or building and rigging a model ship?
- Do you like to read long books?
- Do you check over your homework and tests before handing them in?

Programmers and analysts look for creative solutions to the problems given them.

- Do you enjoy solving puzzles?
- Do you play games of strategy, such as checkers or chess?
- Do you like to think of new ways of doing things around the house?
- Do you occasionally rearrange your bedroom furniture?

Programmers and systems analysts often run into very stubborn problems. If at first they don't succeed in solving a problem, they must try, try again.

- Do you keep trying when you can't solve a problem right away?
- If you play a sport or musical instrument, do you practice faithfully?
- Are you willing to rewrite an essay or redo a math problem until you get it right?

Programmers and systems analysts work with information, called data, that usually is in the form of lists of numbers.

- Are you good at remembering historical dates, batting averages, telephone numbers, bus schedules, or other numerical information?
- Do you like to memorize the amounts of ingredients in a recipe?
- Do you find it easy to use a phonebook or dictionary?

Programmers and systems analysts work closely with others. They must be able to speak and write clearly.

- Do you talk about complicated subjects with your parents, teachers, or friends?
- Can you listen to or give a detailed explanation?
- Can you give clear instructions to do a task?
- Do you find it easy to say what you mean?

JACKIE CUNNINGHAM: COMPUTER SERVICE TECHNICIAN

"Cunningham, call Mr. Arnold, Commerce National Bank," crackled the radio's speaker.

"Not again," groaned Jackie. She had left Commerce National only a half hour before. After she turned the car around, Jackie looked at her watch. Almost noon. Jackie wondered whether there would be time for lunch today. She already had worked through lunch twice this week.

At one of the busy intersections traffic slowed to a crawl.

"Why are there so many cars on the road on the busy days?" she thought. Jackie drummed her fingers on the steering wheel and looked about. She caught sight of the pile of papers, tools, and trash from fast food restaurants on the back seat of the car. "What a mess," she thought. "Almost time for the semiannual cleaning. I hate to use this car for anything but work, it's so sloppy."

A car horn blared. Another horn sounded impatiently behind her and Jackie stepped on the accelerator. Soon she was pulling into a parking lot near the Benton Building, where Commerce National had its offices.

Jackie grabbed her jacket and picked up the briefcase that held her tools, reports, and repair manuals. She didn't have to take much with her because supplies were stored right at the bank. Data Products, the company Jackie worked for, saw to that. The company also sent spare parts and repair instructions directly to the bank's computer center. That way Jackie and the other service technicians didn't have to carry a lot of supplies around or transport spare parts from Data Products' regional office.

In fact, Jackie sometimes worked for several weeks without going to the regional office at all. As she saw it, her job was taking care of the computer equipment at her three "accounts"—the Commerce National Bank, the County Hospital, and the Wilson Manufacturing Company. So naturally she spent most of her time in those places, not at the Data Products office.

As she rushed through the parking lot, Jackie put on her jacket. "It couldn't be much hotter," she thought as she hurried into the air-conditioned building. Data Products expected the service technicians to dress up for work and fortunately Jackie liked to. But a suit, even this cotton one, certainly could be uncomfortable during the summer.

Jackie pulled out her Data Products' identification card as she passed the bank's security guard and headed for the computer center. When she entered the center, Jackie quickly spotted Mr. Arnold, who ran the office.

"Is it the sorter again, Tom?" she called from across the room.

"Right," replied Mr. Arnold.

"I wish you could have arranged to have it break down when I was here a little while ago instead of making me drive back."

"That would be too easy," joked Mr. Arnold.

Jackie went to the side room where the sorter was located. The room also was used to store supplies and it was cramped. However, Jackie did not have to move the machine as she did in some offices.

The sorter was used to group bank documents in several ways. Checking accounts, for example, could be grouped by the amount of money in them. Twice during the past 5 days the sorter had failed to separate the papers correctly. From Mr. Arnold's description of what had happened, Jackie got an idea of what the problem might be. By listening to the machine she decided that the rubber belts and metal rollers that moved papers through the sorter needed adjustment. Although she already had fixed several of the belts, Jackie was sure that they were the cause of the trouble. She knew that it was not unusual for complex equipment to require several adjustments. She was used to visiting an office several times to fix a machine.

Jackie raised the metal cover on the front of the sorter and turned on the machine. She listened to the hum from the rollers and belts. In a few seconds she located a belt that seemed to need adjustment.

From a cabinet in the room Jackie took a can of oil and a rag. After pouring some lubricant on the rag, she held it against the moving belt for a few minutes. She turned off the machine and tightened a screw at the end of the roller that the belt wound around. This made the belt tighter. Jackie then let the sorter run while she watched and listened to the belt.

"I've got you this time," she murmured to the machine. She had begun to think the sorter had a grudge against her. From the very first time she had worked with electrical equipment—as a hobby when she was a junior high school student—Jackie had noticed that some machines seemed to have personalities. She'd had a lot of experience with data processing equipment since then, and it only confirmed her impression that machines could be as different as people. Yes, quite a bit of experience, now that she thought about it. She'd taken electronics courses in high school. Then the training classes at basic school when she'd first started working at Data Products. And 2 years on the job.

Reprinted from *Exploring Careers,* U.S. Department of Labor, 1979.

In a way Jackie preferred mechanical problems to the electronic ones, because they were easier to explain to the customers. She could show them a worn or loose belt. Most electronic problems were caused by burnt-out circuit boards. Jackie could locate a bad board with a voltmeter and she could replace it with a new one. However, a burnt-out board looked exactly like a new one. It was sometimes hard to convince customers who knew little about computers that those innocent-looking boards caused their expensive computers to go haywire.

Jackie closed the machine cover and put away her tools. From her briefcase she took a repair report form. She filled in the date, the machine model, the account's name, and the code letters for the type of breakdown and repair.

She made out a repair report for every service call. Data Products used the information on the forms to determine what kinds of problems there were with the equipment the company made. Engineers used the information to design machines that broke down less often and could be serviced more easily.

Returning to the main computer room, Jackie wrote the date and a brief description of the work she had done in the record book that was kept with the equipment itself. The information in the book would be used by other computer technicians who might work on the machine. Jackie also used the records to keep track of the maintenance that she had done on the machines.

After putting the record book away, Jackie walked to Mr. Arnold's office.

"I think I've fixed it for good this time. But I'd like to be here the next time you use it, just to make sure that everything's okay. Will you be using it soon?"

"Not until tomorrow," said Mr. Arnold.

"Hmm, I'm scheduled for training the rest of the week—well, my backup can handle any problem."

"Training again! I thought you'd already learned everything you needed to know in Data Products' basic school. And aren't you going to night school now?" said Mr. Arnold.

"At basic school I learned how to keep wise guys like you happy and machines like your sorter working," replied Jackie. "The training this week is for your new 360 printer, and night school is part of my plan for the future. I want to be an engineer one day. Then I'll be designing these computers instead of fixing them.

"Well, I'd better run," Jackie continued as she picked up her briefcase. "We've been really busy the last 2 days and I'm supposed to do some maintenance at Wilson Manufacturing this afternoon. If I don't get it done Ken Marcus will have problems and he can be awfully disagreeable when his machines act up."

"Well, not everyone can be a nice guy like me," teased Mr. Arnold.

"True," replied Jackie. "See you next week."

"Take care," called Mr. Arnold, as Jackie rushed out the door.

Jackie called the office dispatcher from the security guard's desk to say that she had answered the Commerce National call. To her surprise there were no other repair calls. Jackie looked at her watch. There was plenty of time to get to the Wilson account. Suddenly she felt relaxed. "I guess I get to have lunch after all," she thought as she headed for her car.

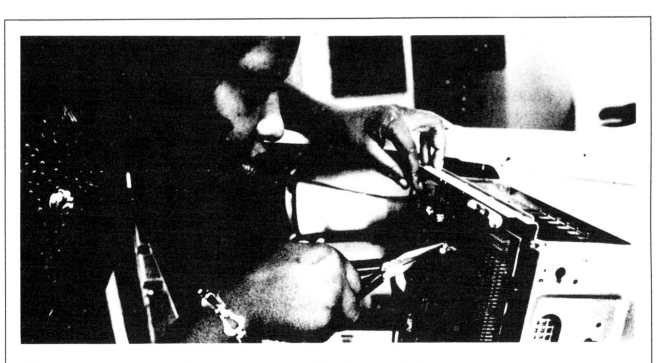

"It's amazing how some computers seem to be personalities," remarks Jackie. "Machines can be as different as people."

Exploring

Computer service technicians repair and service keypunch machines, computer terminals, and other computer equipment.

- Do you enjoy fixing things?
- Do you like to work with your hands?
- Are you interested in electronics and computers?
- Have you ever wondered how computers work? Have you ever tried to find out how other kinds of electronic equipment work—television sets, stereos, tape recorders, or calculators?
- Do you read the owner's manual for calculators, television sets, stereos, or radios? Are you interested in finding out about the machines' specifications?
- Have you ever tried to fix a radio or a pocket calculator?

Computer service technicians must find and correct the cause of computer breakdowns quickly. They work under pressure all the time.

- Do you like to solve problems? Do you like to do written mathematics problems?
- Do you like to do word puzzles or brain teasers?

- Can you usually understand instructions the first time?
- Can you do manual work quickly without making mistakes?
- How well do you work under pressure? Do you have trouble taking tests?

Computer service technicians must get along easily with their customers.

- Do you usually get along with people?
- Are you outgoing?
- Do you enjoy doing things with people?
- How good are you at calming someone down when he or she is angry with you?
- Can you talk your way out of trouble?
- How well can you explain things? Can you give directions?

Computer service technicians spend a lot of time in their clients' offices. They must dress neatly and act professionally.

- Do you like to dress well?
- Do you try to make a good appearance?

GARNET HIZZEY: MANUFACTURING ENGINEER

by Gail M. Martin

photo courtesy General Electric

Manufacturing engineer Garnet Hizzey is heading up a team that's working on an engine support for a new version of the Boeing 737. The support must be short, dense, and strong. The size will present problems in assembly; the strength requirements demand that it be made of composite materials that meet rigid specifications.

To overcome design and production problems, engineers from the design, tooling, materials, quality control, and fabrication departments of the company work cooperatively under Hizzey's direction. The multifaceted nature of this task, typical of those in industry today, demands an interdisciplinary approach that makes the manufacturing engineer the logical leader of this design engineering team.

Manufacturing engineers develop and coordinate production methods to transform conceptual designs into manufactured products in the most efficient manner. They have worked in industry for a long time. Some are known by the specialties in which they trained—mechanical, industrial, or environmental engineers—but others are now recognized and called manufacturing engineers. According to Mark Stratton, education director for the Society of Manufacturing Engineers, "By definition, manufacturing engineering is a multidisciplinary field that covers mechanical, industrial, and even environmental engineering."

The job of the manufacturing engineer has grown by leaps and bounds with the introduction of industrial robots, computer-aided manufacturing (CAM), and computer-aided design (CAD). In addition, the manufacturing engineering profession has taken on greater importance as manufacturing firms seek solutions to problems of spiraling energy costs, competition from foreign manufacturers, and lagging pro-

Gail M. Martin is an OOQ staffwriter.

Reprinted from *Occupational Outlook Quarterly/Fall 1982*, U.S. Department of Labor.

ductivity. Increasingly, manufacturing companies are turning to manufacturing engineers for some solutions to these difficulties.

Manufacturing Engineers on the Job

No two manufacturing engineering jobs are exactly alike. For this reason, manufacturing engineers must be practical "can-do" specialists who are more concerned with applications than with theoretical engineering. There are about 140 basic manufacturing processes and about 40,000 materials used in manufacturing industries today. The challenge of the manufacturing engineer is to work with these combinations, deciding what equipment might be used for making particular products and the materials that are best suited for each application.

In deciding what process to use, the manufacturing engineer develops the work standards. If two parts are to be welded together, for example, the time required to perform the welding operation must be standardized in order to compute the labor requirements and production costs.

Besides work standards, manufacturing engineers develop many other standards, including machine tooling standards. Machine tools include radial drill presses, lathes, milling machines, shapers, and grinders. These machine tools must be both designed and produced to certain standards. Tooling also must be technically sound and priced right. The manufacturing engineer decides whether the company will do its own tooling or buy it. In certain cases, it's always advisable to buy. For example, manufacturing cutting tools is highly specialized technology that is beyond the ability of most companies. The manufacturing engineer, then, must be well-versed in all of the options when specifying tooling standards in order to choose the most economical and practical alternative.

In process engineering, the manufacturing engineer plans the step-by-step sequence of production. This plan, called a process sheet, assures that the overall product is subdivided into individual components and subassemblies for production. The manufacturing engineer completes the production plan by deciding on a sequence of manufacturing steps that are expedient and economical.

Besides developing and implementing standards, the manufacturing engineer becomes involved with plant engineering. Planning the way to handle material is a part of this function. The difference between efficient or inefficient movement of parts and materials through the plant is often the difference between profit and loss. In some cases, the manufacturing engineer solves material handling problems by suggesting changes in the product's design.

Plant enginering also entails facilities engineering. In this capacity, the manufacturing engineer supervises the installation of new equipment, such as machine tools, production equipment, or spray paint booths, to insure that all are properly positioned and that the "startup" date will be met. The cost of failing to meet this date can often be measured in thousands of dollars per hour.

Even before the energy shortage, manufacturing engineers often developed cost trends of energy consumption. This aspect of plant engineering involves investigating potential savings in energy use and pinpointing waste. The manufacturing engineer analyzes utility bills that extend over long periods of time for clues regarding energy consumption as it relates to the production processes used.

The administrative and financial control duties of the manufacturing engineer have become as important as the engineering duties.

The manufacturing engineer develops and coordinates a comprehensive pro-

duction schedule and ensures that it is met. A missed production schedule could mean a missed opportunity in the marketplace for the company.

The manufacturing engineer also coordinates an overall cost reduction program throughout the plant. To do this, the manufacturing engineer studies trend charts and develops a budget. Sometimes, reducing costs requires equipment or facility modification.

At times, the manufacturing engineer becomes involved with research that

photo courtesy General Electric

photo courtesy General Electric

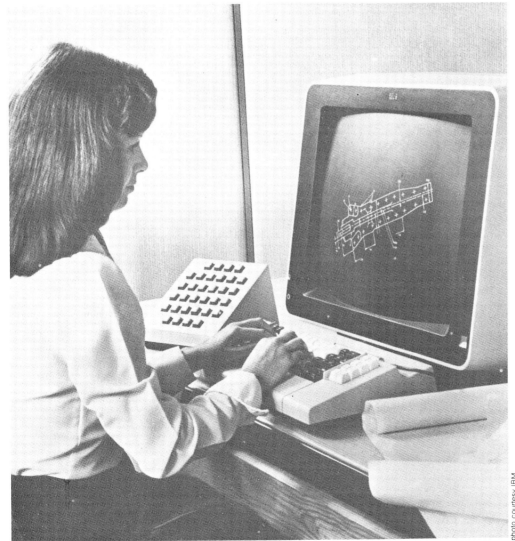

photo courtesy IBM

culminates in new products or processes. Research is an essential activity for all manufacturing companies that are interested in maintaining a competitive edge. For this reason also, it is crucial that the manufacturing engineer keep up with developments in the field as well as work on developing new applications.

Increasingly, manufacturing engineers are introducing changes to improve the work environment. At some establishments, they are designing factory jobs that provide greater worker satisfaction. In some cases, this means employing robots to do jobs that are boringly mechanical to humans. Using robots may also serve to remove people from extremely hazardous work environments, thus meeting another responsibility of the manufacturing engineer: Making the workplace safe from mechanical and health hazards.

Finally, product liability has become an area of prime concern for manufacturing companies, so manufacturing engineers have added meeting legal requirements to their list of job responsibilities. Sometimes new procedures must be adopted to change or improve a product. Some manufacturing engineers not only become involved in redesigning engineering processes but also participate in litigation and testify before investigative bodies.

Manufacturing Engineers Up Close
If the duties of the manufacturing engineer sound similar to those of other engineers it may be because many of the duties of the manufacturing engineer parallel or overlap those of the industrial, mechanical, or environmental engineer. For this reason, engineers educated in these disciplines often work as manufacturing engineers but don't always call themselves by this title.

The Society of Manufacturing Engineers (SME) surveyed 6,600 of its members to obtain information on the manufacturing engineering profession. "The Manufacturing Engineer: Past, Present, and Future" was completed in 1979 by Battelle/Columbus Laboratories. According to the report, nearly all manufacturing engineers surveyed work for private employers, although a small number are employed by the Federal Government, educational institutions, or organizations engaged in research. The principal industrial sectors in which respondents worked included manufacturing of fabricated metal products (21 percent), machinery (14 percent), transportation equipment (12 percent), and miscellaneous manufactured products (10 percent).

By far, the great majority of manufacturing engineers in the work force today have been trained in other disciplines or on the job. In the past, the typical manufacturing engineer was a machinist or mechanic who rose through the ranks to a management job at the plant. But, as technology became more sophisticated, manufacturing engineers needed more specialized, formal education. According to the SME report, the trend toward more formal education for manufacturing engineers will accelerate, and the value of apprenticeship programs for obtaining technical training will diminish in the years ahead. Nearly half of the manufacturing engineers who responded to the survey cited above had bachelor's or higher degrees as compared to only one-third in a similar study 10 years earlier.

Even though more manufacturing engineers in the survey were college educated, the need for manufacturing engineers has not been met by new graduates in this field. The demand for manufacturing engineers, at least during the 1990's, will have to continue to be met by graduates of related engineering disciplines and upgraded technicians because the number of degrees awarded in this field is quite small. According to the Engineering Manpower Commission's

1980 annual survey of enrollments in engineering, only 88 students were enrolled full time in manufacturing engineering or technology programs, and only 22 were full-time graduate students. This number is low partly because only a few schools offer degree programs in the field. For information on these schools, see the box that accompanies this article.

There is definitely more than one way to enter the manufacturing engineering profession; manufacturing engineers have entered through a variety of routes. Since the trend is toward more formal education for manufacturing engineers, the best route for someone interested in entering the field may be to graduate with a bachelor's degree in an engineering discipline. Employers have recruited engineers trained in several engineering disciplines.

All engineers, including those educated in manufacturing engineering or manufacturing engineering technology, undergo a learning period when first employed. While graduates of manufacturing engineering programs take coursework on topics specifically addressed to manufacturing processes, materials, or technology, they, as well as all other new manufacturing engineers, suffer from a lack of experience in the world of manufacturing. Areas that present challenges to the new manufacturing engineer include understanding modern manufacturing processes, knowing precisely what are the materials most suitable for production, being familiar with basic hardware and technology, and being adept at using computer programming languages.

Industry executives themselves recognize the limitations of academic training for the field of manufacturing engineering. In most cases, highly experienced manufacturing engineers must be recruited away from other companies. Companies are willing to hire newly

photo courtesy General Electric

photo courtesy General Electric

College Programs in Manufacturing Engineering or Manufacturing Engineering Technology

More than 225 U.S. colleges and universities offer accredited baccalaureate degrees in engineering. Here's a list of the schools offering programs accredited by the Engineers' Council for Professional Development/Accrediting Board for Engineering and Technology (name change as of Jan. 1, 1980) that lead to B.S. degrees in manufacturing engineering or manufacturing engineering technology:

Arizona State University
Tempe, Ariz. 85281

Boston University
Boston, Mass. 02215

Bradley University
Peoria, Ill. 61625

Brigham Young University
Provo, Utah 84602

California Polytechnic State University
San Luis Obispo, Calif. 93407

Houston, University of —
College of Technology
Houston, Tex. 77004

Memphis State University
Memphis, Tenn. 38152

Murray State University
Murray, Ky. 42071

New Jersey Institute of Technology
Newark, N.J. 07102

Pittsburg State University
Pittsburg, Kans. 66762

Southern Colorado University
Pueblo, Colo. 81001

Utah State University
Logan, Utah 84322

Weber State College
Ogden, Utah 84408

Source: Education Department, Society of Manufacturing Engineers (SME).

graduated engineers to work for them; however, some report having difficulty in doing so. Apparently, manufacturing engineering does not present a very glamorous image to engineering students who are unaware of new technological developments—such as CAD and CAM—that make manufacturing engineering an intriguing field.

According to the College Placement Council's survey of 1981-82 beginning salary offers, an average yearly salary offer of $24,833 was made to bachelor's degree holders with majors in industrial or mechanical engineering by automotive equipment, electrical machinery, and metal product manufacturers. The offers made to these new engineers ranged from $20,004 to $27,600 per year. Since most manufacturing engineers are employed in these industries, it is likely that beginning manufacturing engineers would receive similar offers.

Conclusion

Manufacturing engineering is a field that is constantly changing. It is definitely for the engineer who wants to be challenged. Energy costs, lagging productivity, and worldwide economic conditions have all increased demand for manufacturing engineers in industry as companies reindustrialize using the newest and most efficient technologies available. It is clear that the manufacturing world today is not what it was yesterday or 10 years ago, and chances are it will be even more different tomorrow and 10 years from now.

For a directory of colleges, universities, and technical institutes with programs in manufacturing engineering or manufacturing engineering technology, write to:

Society of Manufacturing Engineers
Education Department
1 SME Drive
P.O. Box 930
Dearborn, Michigan 48128.

LINDA CUNNINGHAM: ENVIRONMENTAL SCIENCE ENGINEER

Television, the unblinking eye that is the center of almost everyone's living room, has been decried as a bad influence on American youth. But influences come in different flavors, bad and good. Sometimes the set can turn *you* on, and that's what happened one day years ago when Linda Cunningham tuned in a Jacques Cousteau special. Thirteen year old Linda was entranced.

"I've always been interested in the outdoors and in sports," she recalls, "but when I first saw a Jacques Cousteau special on TV, I realized that the ocean held the greatest fascination for me. I decided then that I wanted to be one of Cousteau's divers or a member of his crew."

Even in Michigan, Linda could feel the "tidal pull." During high school, she still dreamed of working on—and in—the ocean. She saw, though, that she'd need more than a high school diploma to realize her ambition. Still, by the time she was 18, she had decided she didn't want to attend a conventional, four-year college.

"I felt it wouldn't prepare me for an outdoors, get-your-hands-dirty type of job," she says. So she researched technical schools with programs in ocean studies and eventually chose the Cape Fear Technical Institute in North Carolina. The Institute's program, called Marine Laboratory Technology, prepares students to do field work, lab work, and data analysis for scientists.

"We took classes in such things as small boat handling, welding, and fishnet making and repair," Linda says. "There was also a class called 'Practical Experience' that covered whatever jobs needed to be done: chipping off rust from the boats, painting, repairing equipment, etc. Because I had taken a SCUBA-diving course in high school, I was able to participate in underwater projects as well.

"What I liked about technical school was that I only took classes in the things I was interested in; if I had taken a liberal arts program at a four-year institution, I would have had to spend too much time in classes that didn't have much to do with my interest in the ocean."

She found two drawbacks to the Cape Fear program: no dorms and no sports program. These were minor problems for a woman who wanted to wrestle squid for a living.

"For the two years I attended CFTI, I lived in the home of an elderly woman who became like a grandmother to me. As for the sports—which I sorely missed—I introduced myself to the coaches at the local branch of the University of North Carolina and was eventually allowed to participate in team prac-

tices, although I couldn't actually compete with them."

Linda's program was small, about 100 students, half of whom were women. But the presence of women is a relatively recent phenomenon at many technical schools, and Linda ran into a few students and teachers who wished they could turn back the clock to the all-male days.

"In dealing with these people, I found that it was best to use a great deal of tact and to have a good sense of humor," she says. "I was thankful for the fighting spirit athletics has given me, which helped me to be firm in demanding challenging responsibilities and projects. But I also cooperated willingly if involved in anyone else's projects.

"Although I was teasingly called 'that Libber,' people treated me with respect and I had a great many friends. The skills I developed for dealing with people at CFTI have helped me through similar situations since."

While still enrolled at Cape Fear, Linda heard about a twelve-week ocean research program—Sea Semester, at Woods Hole, Massachusetts.

"I felt this was just what I needed to test myself, to see if I could take life at sea with Cousteau," she recalls. "I still had those romantic visions!" She convinced the Cape Fear admissions committee to substitute Sea Semester, plus two additional classes, for her last semester at CFTI.

The Woods Hole program began with six weeks of intensive classwork, including biology, navigation, and ecology. Then came the exciting part: six weeks at sea aboard the 100-foot schooner R/V Westward. On ship, the 22 students worked in the engine room, on deck, and in the galley, and also performed scientific tasks.

"We had about an even mix of men and women," she recalls, "and were all treated equally. On a ship, everyone has to pull their own weight. We were all frequently pushed to our limits. As the cruise progressed, we were given increasing responsibility until finally we each served as watch officer, reporting directly to the captain. It was truly a terrific experience."

Then, armed with her Associate in Applied Science degree, it was time to see how well she could paddle her own canoe. She landed a job at a public aquarium in Mystic, Connecticut. It wasn't exactly a cruise with Jacques Cousteau, but for a year she busied herself with lab work, monitoring water quality and growing live algae, rotifer, and brine shrimp cultures to feed the fish.

"I liked that part of my job very much," Linda says. "After I'd worked there about a year, though, I began to sour on the idea of aquariums or zoos as a means of educating—or, more realistically, *entertaining*—the public. I didn't feel this justified the waste of aquatic life that I saw every day behind the scenes. For this reason, I decided to go back to school for further education in what was becoming a new interest of mine: aquaculture." (Sometimes known by the more descriptive term "fish farming," aquaculture involves using a natural or artificial body of water for the growing of fish, mollusks, and seaweed for food.)

The four-year degree that didn't seem to make sense when she was in high school had become sensible. At age 22, Linda enrolled at the University of Michigan, in her home state, because, besides being a very good school, it was less expensive and had a volleyball coach she liked. Believing that an engineering degree is more marketable than one in science, Linda eventually transferred from the university's School of Natural Resources to the environmental science engineering program.

"In this program," she explains, "the science part of your degree determines which engineering courses you take. I am specializing in water quality; other people in the program are studying things as varied as air pollution and urban planning."

She's found no prejudice against women engineering students.

"Here at the University of Michigan, women in engineering programs are not an uncommon sight. Although most are in programs like environmental science, computer science, civil engineering, and chemical engineering, there are growing numbers studying mechanical engineering, electrical engineering, and naval architecture. From my own experience with counselors, teachers, and other students, women in engineering are no big deal."

She's realistic about her job options after graduation. "In looking for a job, I have been stressing my background in water and waste-water treatments, hydrology, and environmental analysis more than in aquaculture, although that's my primary interest.

"There's not much research being done in this country in the area of aquaculture yet," she says, "but I think it is an up-and-coming field. I hope that when I have enough seniority and experience on my job, I will be able to propose projects in aquaculture to the company I work for."

Jacques Cousteau would be proud.

GLORIA BLUE: ELECTRICAL ENGINEER

Gloria Blue pulled into her parking space and turned off the engine. Climbing out of the car, she noticed how warm the morning was. Although she had moved to Los Angeles from Chicago over 6 years ago and should have been used to the weather by now, spring-like days in November still seemed odd.

Gloria entered the modern brick building with the sign above the double glass doors that read "Auto Fidelity Inc." After greeting the receptionist, she stopped to chat with another co-worker before climbing the stairs to her own office, the one marked "Vice-President of Engineering."

Laying her briefcase on the table, Gloria ran over the day's work in her mind. Normally Friday was the easiest workday, but there'd be plenty to do today before going home for the weekend.

Auto Fidelity Inc., known as AFI, is one of the nation's leading distributors of sound equipment for cars and other vehicles. AFI manufactures radios, tape players, speakers, and other products and distributes them to stores and dealers across the country. As Vice-President of Engineering, Gloria Blue uses her electrical engineering skills to develop new products that meet the needs of customers. She is the bridge between the technical side and the sales side of AFI's business.

Armed with a cup of coffee, she sat down to the first task of the day—completing a technical bulletin she had begun earlier in the week. Since many car owners install two pairs of speakers in their cars instead of just one, Gloria and her staff had designed a new connector plug that allows the customer to connect all four speakers to the radio without splicing wires. But AFI couldn't get its sales campaign underway until the sales staff understood what the new connector could do, and what advantages it offered. Gloria's bulletin would explain all this to the sales people.

She had nearly finished writing it when Bob Cohen, chief design engineer, called. "Come on down to the lab when you have a chance," he said. "I've finished the model of the equalizer."

"I'll be right down," answered Gloria, anxious to see Bob's results.

Bob was leaning over a table, changing a few details on a drawing, when Gloria walked into the room. "It's over here," said Bob, turning to one of the metal workbenches littered with electronic devices, handtools, wires, half-dismantled radios, and loose parts. He picked up a small metal box with several knobs on one side and handed it to his boss. Removing the top and examining the box closely, Gloria commented, "I think we have a winner."

The equalizer was one of her better ideas. She had followed trends in the home stereo equipment market as well as in the automobile products sold by AFI's competitors. From all she had seen, Gloria felt that the public would buy a combination power booster and equalizer. The booster would increase the loudness of a radio or tape player, while the equalizer would allow the listener to adjust the volume of the treble, middle, and bass tones individually, thus "equalizing" the sound. No other company offered such a product for automobiles.

After creating the general concept, Gloria had handed the idea to Bob and his staff, who actually designed the device. They figured out what parts to use, arranged them in a package, and tested it. But they worked under the guidance of Gloria, whose job it was to make sure the product would be attractive, reliable, and inexpensive.

Gloria and Bob, both electrical engineers, performed quite different engineering jobs at AFI. Bob's position was purely technical, while Gloria had moved into a management job. The work was a far cry from what she had dreamed about as a teenager.

When she was in junior high, Gloria was sure she'd be a nurse one day. Her favorite aunt was a head nurse at one of Chicago's largest hospitals, and Gloria enjoyed talking with her about the job. By her senior year in high school, she had changed her mind. A long talk with her guidance counselor encouraged her to think about a career that involved mathematics; Gloria always had made excellent grades in math. So she started college with plans to become a math teacher.

That fall she met her husband-to-be, Larry, who was a junior at the engineering school. They frequently studied together and discussed their courses. Gloria grew more and more interested in Larry's engineering problems, and liked trying her hand at solving them. Before the school year was over, Gloria had decided to switch to electrical engineering. It took all summer to sell her parents on the idea but they finally agreed that the decision was hers to make. Gloria recalls how proud they were when she received her bachelor's degree in engineering.

Gloria started out in the research and development division of a large manufacturer of electrical products in Chicago, and spent the next 10 years there. She developed a solid reputation in the area of product development. At the same time, she was attending evening classes in business and management to earn a master's degree in business administration. This combination of technical and nontechnical skills made her just the right person for the California job advertised by AFI.

Gloria and Bob discussed the equalizer for almost an hour. Once the company's designer developed the cosmetics, or outer appearance, for the product, the factory could begin producing it. Then, after testing, it would

Reprinted from *Exploring Careers*, U.S. Department of Labor, 1979.

appear in the stores. Gloria looked forward to that day; of all the things she did for AFI, she most enjoyed seeing an idea grow into a successful product.

On her way back to her office, she bumped into Jim Leviton, the company president. "By the way, Jim," said Gloria, "I've looked at that new spectrum analyzer that California Instruments makes and read the literature on it. It can test a radio in about 2 seconds, much faster and better than we can now. And even though it costs $6,000, we need it badly for our laboratory."

"Let's get together with Al and decide if we can afford it," answered Jim. "How about this afternoon?"

"Fine," replied Gloria, "as long as we don't talk too long. I'll have that sales bulletin on the connector done before lunch, but I still have some preparing to do for Monday's meeting with Toshiro."

"That meeting will be a long one," thought Gloria. Hero Toshiro is an engineer who works with the manufacturing division of AFI. Gloria gives him her ideas in the form of a drawing or, as with the equalizer, a model. He and his staff then complete the design and put it into production. Gloria was encouraging the development of thinner and thinner radio and cassette mechanisms for the new year. She felt that the latest trends were leading in that direction, and she hoped that Toshiro and his staff could develop them in time for the new product year. At their Monday meeting they would discuss problems and progress of the new design.

After the conversation with Jim, Gloria continued on her way back to her office. "You'd never know how much work I have by looking at my desk," she thought as she sat down. The desk top was large but fairly empty. Between the "In" box on one side and a stack of trade journals on the other lay the bulletin she was working on. Everything else was put away. Gloria felt that you couldn't get ahead unless you were organized. And she was proud of her talent for organization.

Gloria glanced at her watch. It was 11:30, and she had an appointment for lunch at noon. With quick strokes of her pen she continued writing, changing a word here and adding a sentence there, until the bulletin was finished. Then, after checking the diagrams once more, she gave it to her secretary to be typed.

Gloria and Bob discuss plans for a new product. "A career in engineering has given me the opportunity to express myself creatively," says Gloria.

Exploring

Electrical engineers must deal with complex devices and understand how they work.

- Do you enjoy taking things apart to see how they work?
- Do you like to repair your bicycle?
- Do you fix your younger brothers' and sisters' toys?
- Are you good at repairing things around the house?
- Do you like to read about new inventions?

Electrical engineers apply what they know to solve practical problems.

- Do you like word problems in math?
- Do you like to solve engineering problems around the house, such as the best way of putting up a shelf?
- Do you wonder what relation your school subjects have to the real world?
- Are you more likely to study if you think a subject has practical value?

Electrical engineers deal with many ideas and objects that cannot be seen or felt. They must be able to think abstractly.

- Can you look at a pattern for a model or for clothing and picture the finished product?
- Can you look at a machine such as an automobile and picture its inner workings?

Electrical engineers look for creative answers to problems.

- Do you play games of strategy such as checkers, chess, or bridge?
- Do you enjoy solving puzzles?
- Do you like to think of new ways of doing things around the house?

Electrical engineers must pay attention to detail.

- Do you enjoy projects that involve precise, detailed handwork?
- Do you enjoy doing needlepoint? Painting by numbers? Building and rigging model ships? Building a radio from a kit?
- Do you go over your homework carefully before you hand it in?

Electrical engineers must continually read and learn, because new discoveries and inventions are made all the time.

- Do you like to read for pleasure?
- When you are curious about something, do you go to an encyclopedia or library to learn more about it?
- Do you like to read any popular scientific or technical magazines?
- Do you look up words you don't know in a dictionary?

Electrical engineers must be able to write clearly.

- Can you write street directions or other instructions?
- Can you write a recipe?
- Do you write your math or science homework clearly enough for others to follow it?

Electrical engineers must be able to discuss technical subjects.

- Can you express yourself well?
- If a teacher doesn't answer your question exactly, do you ask it again in a different way?
- Can you help your brothers, sisters, or friends with their homework?

ON THE LEADING EDGE: COMMUNICATORS AND INFORMATION MANAGERS AT EEI

Take one accomplished musician, one student of the Middle East, one former English instructor, and one entrepreneur, and you have—not the characters in a novel of mystery or intrigue—but four specialists in information management and communication.

All four are young—two in their twenties, two in their thirties—and all have followed unconventional paths to find themselves where they are today, working on the leading edge of technology, performing duties requiring unusual combinations of skills and a talent for improvisation.

Together they work in or for the Information and Publishing Services Department of Edison Electric Institute, the trade association of the investor-owned electric utilities.

Through various activities, programs, and products, EEI aims to enhance the exchange of useful information among its member companies, and to increase public understanding of the importance of electric power and of the industry's positions on vital issues.

To accomplish these aims, the Institute conducts publishing programs, producing books, magazines, trade publications, and pamphlets. It has developed educational grant programs for libraries, schools, and churches. And more recently, it has developed computerized data bases and electronic services for its member companies.

The Information and Publishing Services Department is charged with developing and producing many of these products and services. The development of data bases and electronic information services have placed the men and women who work in the department on the leading edge of change.

Their stories are a mirror, reflecting the great changes taking place in our society and the world of work.

Edison Electric Institute, 1983.

NORMAN RUBENSTEIN

From now on, the U.S. Department of Labor tells us, everyone entering the labor force can expect to change careers at least three times. Norman Rubenstein's work history confirms this trend. In his late twenties Norm was forced to choose between remaining in the career he had chosen—one whose outlook suddenly became clouded—or beginning a new career.

As a high school student in New Orleans, Norm loved to read, enjoyed writing and public speaking, and thought of becoming a writer. In college—first at Boston University, then at Tulane, in New Orleans—he majored in English literature and art history. After receiving his bachelor of arts degree from Tulane, he stayed on for an M.A. in English lit. By then he had decided on a career in teaching.

He entered the University of Virginia's graduate English department, teaching college composition and English literature courses as he worked for his Ph.D.

A New Situation

Then, like thousands of other young teachers in the early 1970s, Norm was confronted with a new and threatening reality. College enrollments were declining and the trend appeared irreversible as U.S. population growth approached zero. As enrollments declined, the prospects for college teachers declined as well.

It was a choice between hanging in—despite fierce competition and di-minishing rewards—or beginning anew. The revolution in information management and telecommunications ultimately enabled Norm to use his teaching and writing skills in new ways.

Norm's first instinct was to make the most of his writing. Moving to Washington, D.C., he found work as a free-lance writer. His first assignments included technical writing for the electric utility industry. Technical writing entails expressing technical subjects in language the general public can understand.

Through those first assignments, Norm acquired first-hand information about the electric utility industry. He also made the personal contacts that led to a staff position—first as a writer and then as manager of editorial services—with Edison Electric Institute.

Managing Information and People

Two years later, Norm was promoted to director of EEI's newly restructured Information and Publishing Services Department. Today his duties include managing both people and information. He is responsible for establishing assignments and schedules for the production of all the department's products and projects. He coordinates the production of publications generated by other departments of the Institute, and oversees the writing, design, and production of all printed materials.

He manages eight full-time staff members, as well as a network of vendors—the outside consultants, printers, publishers, and others who provide support services to the department. In addition to his management duties, he also plays an important role in marketing electronic information services to EEI's member companies.

Norm's duties involve five main clusters of skills—organizing and following through on all departmental activities; managing people; supervising such technical processes as design and production; marketing; and, of course, writing and editing. Obviously, the research, writing, and speaking skills he acquired as a teacher stand him in good stead. So, too, do the skills in organizing that teachers must possess. All of these skills were transferable skills that eased Norm's transition to a second career.

But his technical skills—a familiarity with computers and their applications in electronic information services—were acquired, for the most part, on the job. "If someone had told me ten years ago that I'd be working in computers," he says, "my reaction would have been incredulity." Analyzing his successful transition from the academic to the corporate world, Norm credits one basic trait—"a quality of open-mindedness and receptiveness to new technology."

Number-Crunching and New Discoveries

What Norm likes least about his duties is "the painful process of budgeting." But curiosity and the satisfaction of learning new skills is a strong incentive and motivator. "What's most exciting about the work," he says, "is discovering new uses for information technology that make the department, and all of us in it, more efficient and productive."

As far as Norm Rubenstein is concerned, electronic information services are where the action is in publishing. "As more and more people have personal computers, they'll have access to on-line products. And the publishing industry must respond to their desire for improved data bases and electronically transmitted text. We're seeing the beginnings of a publishing revolution right here in our department—today."

ALAIN CARR

Here's as graphic an illustration of the information explosion as any you'll find, taken from the *Harvard Business Review*:

"By the mid-eighteenth century, mankind's total knowledge had doubled from what it was at the birth of Christ. It doubled again by 1900 and again by 1950.

"That's 1750 years for the first doubling to take place, 150 years for the next and only 50 years for the next. But what's really mind-boggling is that the next *two* doublings of human knowledge took place in 1960 and 1968."

The passage was written in 1969, and no one has ventured an estimate of how many times our total fund of information has doubled since then. What's certain, however, is that our knowledge will suffer if we can't keep pace with the information at our disposal.

That's where Alain Carr, and other information age entrepreneurs, come in. The entrepreneurs of the first industrial revolution made new technologies useful by filling in the gaps or joining existing technologies to create new systems. Edison's great achievement was not the first incandescent light, which others would have soon invented, or the generator, which had been invented long before. His triumph was filling in the gap between the generator and the bulb, creating a system that made it possible to distribute and sell electricity.

So it is with the entrepreneurs of the second industrial revolution. Like their predecessors, they're filling in the gaps, picking up the pieces of the future that lie all around us, assembling them into new systems, and making them serve practical needs.

Information for Decision Makers

As Alain Carr sees it, the main result of the information explosion has been the creation of a completely new environment for decision makers. "In the 1950s," he says, "corporate decision makers had weeks to respond to an issue, but today they have to respond in days. Back then, their main concern was maximizing productivity. Today issues and decisions are more complicated, and worst of all, decision makers usually don't have all the information they need. They face a gigantic information gap that can be filled only through the innovative use of existing technologies."

But corporate decision makers aren't generally versed in the latest technologies. That's where consultants and entrepreneurs like Alain enter the picture. "The object," says Alain, "is to analyze people's needs, identify what's missing, and then, working backwards, provide a product or service to meet it—to fill the information gap." The product or service should be "far enough ahead to outdistance competitors, but not too far ahead—not so far ahead that it's threatening."

A Stock-Market Killing

A New Yorker, Alain Carr left high school determined to become an industrial designer. He began a program in industrial design at New York City's Pratt Institute. But in his first year at Pratt, he discovered a strong interest in business. Alain began reading such publications as *The Wall Street Journal*, educating himself in business and finance in the process. As his knowledge grew, so did his judgment and confidence. He invested his savings of $750 in 1000 shares of a 75¢ stock, and the stock soared to $56 a share, netting the young investor a $55 thousand profit, and convincing him that his future was not in industrial design.

From Pratt Institute Alain entered Columbia University's School of Business, and two years later received his master's degree in business administration.

An Entrepreneur's Path

He first worked as an acquisitions specialist for a major food corporation, evaluating the potential of companies that his corporation considered taking over. From the very beginning, he was fascinated by the creative opportunities in business.

"There are people in business," he says, "and business people. People in business strive to live up to the demands of their jobs—to fulfill minimal expectations. Business *people* are different. They're people who understand the dynamics of assembling resources creatively to move ahead of the pack."

After two and half years, Alain went off on his own, becoming a consultant. First he assisted owners of small businesses in grooming their companies for sale. Then he used his skills as a trouble shooter, helping companies in distress. Briefly, he was chairman of one of those companies, before selling it and returning to consulting. In 1980 he formed Information, Inc., capitalizing on his broad experience and analytical approach to business to devise products and services to fill the information gap.

One of Information, Inc's main goals is to respond to the needs of decision makers overtaken by the information explosion. Alain's company achieves this end through a three-step procedure. First, information is gathered in its original form, and irrelevant or tangential information is discarded. Second, the remaining information is condensed for easier and faster use by customers. Finally—and most importantly—the information is put on a

computer. There, it can be transmitted instantly, and individual pieces of information can be located quickly and easily. Computerization is especially important in dealing with very large quantities of information, since, in Alain's words, "Information has an inherent resistance to discovery."

A Strategy for EEI

As a vendor to Edison Electric Institute, Alain Carr's Information, Inc., has assisted the Institute in reorganizing its information and publishing services, developing data bases and data-based products and services aimed at filling the information gap for decision makers in the electric power industry.

Several data bases already have been created, each consisting of information vital to decision makers in electric power, each focused on one key topic such as industrial relations, the environment, regulatory decisions, and marketing programs.

Developing a data base involves hundreds of decisions along the way—devising the most efficient ways of collecting information, the best ways to abstract it, store it, and make it accessible to those who need it. In each of these decisions, Alain Carr and Information, Inc., have advised and assisted, drawing on experience and knowledge uniquely appropriate to the needs of corporations.

Initially, the strategy centered on what is called long shelf-life information. The data bases first developed by EEI contain information that will be as useful to its member companies two or more years from now as it is today.

The second phase of the strategy has been to deal with short shelf-life information—information whose value lies primarily in its currency. Alain's most recent project for EEI was to assist in creating a two-part service called Electronic Mail and Industry News.

Electronic Mail allows system users to send written messages via computer over telephone lines. This type of communication offers two principal advantages over traditional telephone conversations: first, the written word is more accurate than our memory of the spoken word; second, and more importantly, busy executives need not be in their respective offices at exactly the same time in order to communicate, since their message is filed electronically and available as soon as they check their electronic mailbox. Furthermore, because communication is virtually instantaneous, electronic mail loses none of the speed of telephone conversation.

Industry News, a service that uses the computer to transmit current information and news to desktop terminals around the nation, focuses specifically on the electric utility industry. Information, Inc. correlates information from a wide variety of sources and presents it in one, coherent package, a tremendous task carried out on a daily basis by Alain's team of information experts.

Advice to Would-Be Entrepreneurs

What skill or skills are most valuable to would-be enterpreneurs? Alain refers to a study which concluded that they share only one common skill—a strong vocabulary. In Alain's view, what's most important is "a strong belief in yourself, because you face incredible odds early on. You need a strong sense of self in order to persist."

Interpersonal skills may be the most important, he says: "You have to be enormously sensitive to people and their needs, because success depends on the quality of the people you assemble." The lack of certain basic skills needn't deter you. "You can team up with others who have complementary skills if you lack important skills yourself."

The most important training for entrepreneurship, according to Alain, may be joining a small company. "There you rub shoulders with decision makers." As far as formal education is concerned, an MBA is not a necessity. "It gives you valuable skills in accounting and finance—skills that are indispensable if you're not to be intimidated by bankers and investors. But you can acquire these skills taking evening courses in local colleges."

One character trait may be indispensable to entrepreneurs, Alain believes. And that's a willingness to accept risk. "Take risks while you're young," he says; "There's no debtor's prison in this country. Failing at 25 may be a nuisance, but at 55, it's a disaster."

SUSAN RANDELL

"Sweet are the uses of adversity." Shakespeare said it, meaning that hard luck or unexpected reverses can be good for us. It's a lesson that everyone learns sooner or later, and one that Susan Randell learned when she left college and took a job involving tasks she had never enjoyed.

Born in Swampscott, Massachusetts, Susan worked as an intern in the Massachusetts legislature for two summers when she was in high school. She finished high school a semester early and spent six months at Richmond College in Richmond, England, taking courses for college credit. There she became interested in the Middle East and began studying its cultures.

Returning to the United States, Susan entered George Washington University in Washington, D.C., where she began a major in international relations. At the same time, she took intensive courses in Farsi, the language of Iran and Afghanistan. Then, two and a half years into her bachelor's program, Susan chose to leave school temporarily and find a job.

Working Nine to Five

Susan was hired by EEI as a clerk typist, and later promoted to secretary of the Information and Publishing Services Department. But formal job descriptions lost much of their meaning as the department moved into the information age. Overcoming a long-standing math anxiety, she became familiar with the computer and its uses.

More than that, she became fascinated with the new technology and its implications.

Susan returned to George Washington University on a part-time basis, with EEI paying 75 percent of her tuition and book costs. She took courses in higher-level programming and business software applications. She learned how to use filing and spread-sheet systems. Using an electronic filing system, she designed formats for record-keeping in her department.

Today Susan's duties include keeping departmental accounts, tracking expenditures, coordinating with the accounting department on payments, recording orders for publications, following through to see that orders are fulfilled, and responding to the problems of customers. Her job also includes such standard secretarial chores as answering phones, typing, and filing.

Her secretarial chores, she says, are the least interesting to her. But at the same time, working in an office and dealing with co-workers and customers have enabled her, as she puts it, "to overcome a painful shyness, to manage time better—to grow in many ways, both personal and professional."

What she likes most about her job is finding ways to use new technologies to perform her duties more effectively. "This is the most challenging part," she says, "and the most satisfying." The skills that have proven most valuable to her in an office environment—and an

environment of change, as well—are catching on quickly without too much help from others, and such interpersonal skills as being diplomatic and patient with others and their problems. While she seems to have been endowed with these skills, she developed them further on the job.

Computers or the Middle East?

Working has added two and a half years to Susan's degree program. At the same time, it has given her new skills and opened up broader perspectives. "I wouldn't advise people to interrupt their college programs," she says, "but the truth is, I enjoy work more than school."

When she receives her BA this year, she faces difficult decisions. Information management and telecommunications offer growing opportunities that she's tempted to explore. All the same, she can't give up her dream of living in the Middle East, studying its cultures first hand, and perhaps writing about them. Whatever her choice, familiarity with new technologies, and skills in their use, should serve her well. "Whatever I decide," Susan says, "the skills I gained on the job will be an asset."

DON MACLEAN

The number of young men and women whose career paths have led from music to computers may be great, though no one knows for sure. The path is logical enough if one considers that both activities involve moving comfortably in a world of symbols—notes, bits, bytes—and that both are ruled by logic. And logic is logic, after all, whether it's sung, spoken, or printed out.

In high school Don MacLean thought of becoming a lawyer. He enjoyed writing and learned to write well. From the seventh grade through high school, he studied and excelled in languages—Latin, French, Spanish, and Russian. And all along, in the background, was a passion for music. He was an accomplished violist.

When he completed high school in Boston, Don faced a painfully difficult decision. He had dreamed of becoming a musician but never had made the final commitment. He says he should have done so at the age of twelve or so. Was it now too late? Don decided to take the risk and entered Oberlin Conservatory in Oberlin, Ohio. After three

years he received his bachelor of arts degree in music.

Then he was an unemployed musician.

From Music to Computers

Returning to Boston, Don worked for a year as a bank teller. Then he moved to Washington, D.C., where he found temporary work at EEI on a project requiring research skills, as well as skills in public relations, dealing with member companies. Working on this project, he acquired information about the electric power industry, and he was there, on the ground floor, as the department was reshaped. He was offered a staff position, which he accepted, and since then, he has helped define a job involving information management and communication.

When the department installed a microcomputer, Don was staggered by its possibilities. "Now," he says, "we could search 20,000 documents in minutes." His duties have evolved from those possibilities—from the application of the new technologies to the products and programs of EEI.

Using skills in word processing and on-line transmission that he developed on the job, Don administers the Institute's high school grant program, oversees the production of the *Utility Information Digest*, and helps implement the department's electronic information services.

Using his skills in technical writing, he develops and updates manuals that teach people how to use the services of

the department. With the marketing skills he's also developed on the job, he helps present the department's services to member companies.

A Future Entrepreneur

As Don sees it, he's developing skills that one day will enable him to go into business on his own, perhaps consulting or developing software. Those skills are not merely technical, but administrative and interpersonal as well. "While programming is a good skill," Don says, "a more valuable skill is the ability to motivate others to write good programs."

One skill that stands out in Don's education and brief work history is decisiveness, the skill of making decisions. "If you don't know what you want," he says, "just do something and do it well. It almost doesn't matter what it is, as long as you excel. It gives you confidence, it broadens your competence. Commitment is what counts."

GENERALIZATIONS: WHAT'S TO BE LEARNED FROM THESE FOUR?

You won't find the jobs described in this article in the U.S. Department of Labor's *Dictionary of Occupational Titles (DOT)*, which is sadly behind the times. Even after 2100 new titles were added to the 1977 edition, and 3500 classifications dropped, many new professions have been ignored. Nowhere is this more apparent than in computers. The *DOT* lists only eight categories of computer-related occupations, but if you count all the occupations that have grown up to serve the computer industry, the total would be much greater.

Forbes magazine recently described eight computer-related occupations neglected by the *DOT*. These include computer rental services, computer psychologist, computer camp counselor, computer sales trainer, computer fair organizer, software talent agent, software club director, and computer lawyer.

The jobs that Norm, Alain, Susan, and Don perform involve unique combinations of skills that overlap two or more occupations as described in the *DOT*. The conclusion: to learn about the world of work today, you'll have to do more than read the *DOT* or the *Occupational Outlook Handbook*. Keep your eyes and ears open, and talk to people. People enjoy talking about their work.

Transferable Skills and Open-Mindedness

Beyond that, keep in mind that transferable skills are vital to developing a successful career in a time of great change. Norm, Don, Alain, and Susan all made the most of transferable skills such as communication skills, organizing, supervising, managing time, accounting, and budgeting.

Remember, too, that a thoughtful, analytical approach to career development—best exemplified by Alain's approach to defining the information gap and devising services to fill it—is a valuable talent that may help you avoid mistakes.

Finally, the open-mindedness to technology that Norm describes—a trait that we can see in all four of our information managers and communicators—is not merely valuable, but essential as we move from industrial to post-industrial society. Be prepared for change. Be prepared to make the most of it.

A JOB WITH A VIEW: SEVEN WHO TELECOMMUTE

Do you love the idea of saying good-bye to freeway traffic jams or crowded commuter cars and doing your work at home? Maybe you do, but maybe you really don't.

Chris Rutkowski and son, Lars, 2 years old
While Rutkowski's wife finishes her book, Rutkowski runs his computer software business far from the smog and heat. Most of his 42 employees telecommute from their homes, too.

By Kathleen K. Wiegner and Ellen Paris

WE ARE WRITING this article in a stuffy Los Angeles office. It's 100 degrees outside. Thick smog. The air conditioner is broken, again. To get to and from this oven we drive endless miles over hot concrete, doing our bit for OPEC and the inner-city property speculators.

Wouldn't it be nice to work like Chris Rutkowski? Rutkowski is president of Rising Star, a fast-growing computer software company. Rising Star's offices are in gritty Torrance, Calif. A mere 3 miles away is Rutkowski's imposing Spanish-style home in lush Rolling Hills Estates, on the Palos Verdes peninsula. Rolling Hills is green, cool. While the baby-sitter herds his two small children and his wife word-processes another chapter of her book on infants, is Rutkowski drudging in his office? Not at all. He generally stays at home and manages Rising Star's 42 employees with the help of his Epson QX-10 computer. Of his employees, all but 6 do likewise.

"I'd never work anyplace without a view," chortles Rutkowski, really rubbing it in, as he looks out on the Pacific.

Up that same coast, Ronda Davé gazes out on sparkling San Francisco Bay from the ninth-floor condominium apartment that she shares with over $15,000 worth of home computer gadgetry. Davé, who holds a doctorate in educational psychology, runs a business providing consulting, technical editing and word processing for Bay Area graduate students who need a high degree of statistical data in their papers and theses.

As she talks, her computer whirs through statistical models while her printer clicks efficiently away in the background. Davé's programmer, working several miles away and also out of her home, is hooked into a Stanford University mainframe and may soon communicate directly with Davé's computer.

Welcome, then, to the wonderful phenomenon of telecommuting, which promises to change the daily lives of millions of Americans as radically as the automobile did beginning a half century or so ago. As with cottage industry of old, with telecommuting the job is coming to the worker rather than the worker to the job. It's early in the trend, but quite clearly something big is afoot. Further north of Davé's pad, at his home in tiny Reardan, Wash., Bruce Johnson does computer graphics design on his Apple II. Johnson says working at home like this is about the only way he can work: As the result of a high school football injury, he is confined to a wheelchair and finds conventional commuting virtually impossible.

Out in Minnesota, George Chamberlain taps computer programming instructions into the personal computer in his cell in Minnesota State Prison, where Chamberlain (who is part of a Control Data Corp.-sponsored rehabilitation program) has served 4 years of a 35-year sentence for sex offenses.

Telecommuting is as yet hardly a tidal wave. No one knows with any precision how many telecommuters there now are. But Jack Nilles estimates the telecommuter ranks at 10,000 to 20,000, mostly part-timers. Nilles is a senior research associate at the University of Southern California, and the person who claims to have coined "telecommuter" in 1973. He predicts that number could swell to 10 million by 1990. The trend has grown important enough that the National Research Council, an arm of the National Academy of Sciences, will, for the first time, hold a two-day seminar on the working-at-home phenomenon in November in Washington, D.C.

What's so attractive about telecommuting? Ask one practitioner and you'll get one answer, ask another and you'll get a different answer. Some like it for the view. Others, like 60-year-old Marjorie Whitecross, like it because it keeps them mentally active (and earning some money) in retirement. Still others telecommute to spend more time with children and spouses.

Telecommuting can even bring a degree of family togetherness. "Last night," reports Jim Anderson, a telecommuting general partner in a venture capital firm in San Francisco, "my wife and I had a discussion about whether to standardize the format for our home computers. I can't believe we were having that discussion."

Lawrence Lerner says telecommuting has greatly augmented his productivity. Lerner, 59, runs his 200-employee architectural firm with the help of Altos computers installed in his homes in Manhattan and Beverly Hills. From his at-home screens, Lerner communicates with his office staff at their screens about everything from equipment purchases to zoning permits. The relevant data for all decisions flow effortlessly between screens. And, thanks to telex line connections, Lerner can hold similar on-screen conversations with his associates in Tokyo and Sydney.

"My work is more concentrated when I'm home," says Lerner. "When I'm in an office, I am too much at the mercy of silly conversations to be really productive."

San Francisco's Ronda Davé and graduate student-client Tom Glodek
Her $15,000 system finally works, but only after seven months of lugging her equipment back and forth between home and suppliers. The servicemen, she says, "were novices."

Making steel in backyards is not feasible, as China's Mao learned. Nor, environmentalist fanatics to the contrary, can power be generated efficiently from little windmills and solar panels on roofs. But the U.S. economy is changing, depending less on heavy industry and more on information. John Naisbitt, author of the bestselling *Megatrends*, estimates that around 60% of American jobs now involve handling information. And where information is the product, telecommuting comes into its own.

The real father of telecommuting is the microcomputer. The microcomputer and the intelligent terminal are both growing smarter and cheaper. With a decent micro or terminal, or both, any moderately intelligent, curious person can retrieve data, process it on site and send it to another computer without leaving his home—a portion of which the IRS probably allows him to deduct. Hardly a day now passes without the introduction of some new and usually useful computer gadget—from new software for investors to new autodialers so your computer can call other computers in the middle of the night.

Another important boost for telecommuting has been the rapid proliferation of intelligently organized, easy-to-access databases, which are, in effect, the semifinished materials against which many telecommuters apply their computers and energy.

Take Darcy Bolton. Bolton, a 46-year-old former lab technician, runs his real estate businesses from his home in Irvine, Calif. with the aid of his Vector Graphic 3 computer. Two years ago Bolton added a new business line: patent searches for local lawyers.

It works like this: Through his Vector Graphic, Bolton is able to tap into McLean, Va.-located Pergamon International Information Corp.'s database, which contains filings with the U.S. Patent Office as well as references to domestic and international patent law cases. Bolton pays Pergamon $90 for each hour he is on line, tapping Pergamon's information. Bolton then charges his clients $100 for a routine patent search—which Bolton says he can do in about 40 minutes or sometimes less. Sixty dollars' worth of raw material upgraded into an end product worth $100, with the aid of relatively inexpensive equipment. Bolton says the patent searches easily gross him $4,000 to $5,000 a month, much of which is pure profit. Total cost of all his hardware: around $13,000.

Operating on a more modest scale is Katherine Ackerman, who may exploit more databases than anyone. Ackerman, 27, is a former *Chicago Tribune* research librarian who left the paper to have a baby last October. Rather than fob off her baby on relatives or hired help, she set herself up at home as an all-around expert on databases. Ackerman is in effect a rent-a-researcher. She is like a Japanese samurai of old, with a computer for a sword. She hires herself and her IBM Personal Computer out to clients too small to fight through the growing thicket of electronic information. Thus a smallish advertising agency trying to win a tiremaker's account hires Ackerman to dig up tire industry statistics. Ackerman accesses the Disclosure database and gives the agency the figures it needs for a presentation.

Tapping a base costs her anywhere from $35 to $95 an hour, plus another $6 to $10 an hour for telephone time. Ackerman bills these costs directly to her clients, adding her time at $35 an hour. She says she averages 15 hours ($525) a week and could work far more if she wanted.

"One of the best things about working at home like this," she explains, her voice rising over her baby's background screams, "is that if the baby does something cute I have the freedom to drop everything and take his picture, which I do a lot."

But not everyone loves the idea. The trade unions,

Irvine, Calif. patent searcher Darcy Bolton
By knowing how to massage the right database, Bolton can upgrade a $60 hour to a $100 hour with relatively inexpensive equipment.

already in decline in the U.S., see a new threat in telecommuting. Karen Nussbaum, 33, is the articulate founder of 9 to 5, National Association of Working Women, a membership organization for women office workers, which acts like a trade union but has no collective bargaining powers. Nussbaum claims that telecommuting can be a means of exploiting clerical workers—"like turn-of-the-century garment workers who ran sewing machines on their kitchen tables and were paid piece rates." As she speaks, Nussbaum grows indignant. "Even bathroom breaks can be on their own time," she huffs. Nussbaum says she wants home workers to be guaranteed the same rights and benefits office workers get.

"We think the opportunity for worker exploitation is rife with telecommuters," agrees Denise Mitchell, a spokeswoman for the Service Employees International Union, which represents 50,000 clerical workers, mostly women. "We think it [telecommuting] should be banned."

Trade unionists might not want to admit the fact, but telecommuting is opening up vast tracts of human potential. It allows many people, who have previously been doomed to lead unproductive lives, to blossom.

Old people, for example. Two years ago Eric Knudson, owner of a smallish software company called ACS America, was having trouble keeping his programmers. So he opened Wave III in Sarasota, Fla. Object: to train retirees to program computers for his own and other firms.

Knudson gave the retirees a free, three-month programming course and a job—at $90 a day for a preset programming quota—to those who successfully completed the course. Knudson says Wave III received over 6,000 applications; 100 people were accepted and finished the course. Knudson's original company, ACS America, has since run into cash problems, and Knudson has closed Wave III. But, says he, "That market is so ready for something challenging to do. . . ."

Or take the handicapped, another group well served by telecommuting. Northbrook, Ill.-based Lift, Inc. is a nonprofit, non-government-funded organization founded eight years ago. Lift trains severely disabled people—paraplegics, quadriplegics, men and women with polio, muscular dystrophy and spinal injuries—to become computer programmers. Lift gives the trainee an IBM model 3270-series terminal and six months' in-home training. When the six months are up, Lift hires the trainee for a year, contracting his services out to one of the 40-odd major corporations Lift works with. Generally the trainee becomes a regular employee of the company when the year is up. Allstate Insurance is working with its seventh disabled telecommuter from Lift, Standard Oil of Indiana its fourth. "It just revolutionizes their lives," says Lift cofounder William Woerner of his graduates. "[Programming] becomes their whole world."

For all its charms, telecommuting is obviously not for everyone. It is not, for example, for those who need the discipline of the central office to keep them from pruning the fruit trees or painting the shed.

A more pressing problem is this: The electronic workplace does not always come in—or stay in—sound working order. San Francisco's Ronda Davé, for example, shares her condominium with the tools of her trade: an Altos computer, an NEC printer, two Televideo terminals and sundry software programs, all of which she purchased separately. Because she bought them separately, the pieces had to be assembled.

That's where Davé's troubles began. First, she had to wait three weeks for Altos' technicians to arrive. "They were novices," says Davé contemptuously. "They installed the system improperly. Then, starting in May, we began having funny problems with the word processing software. Then the printer wouldn't function properly. Then, after two or three months, it [the printer] started jamming."

Worse than the jammed printer, manuscripts that were being laboriously word-processed would simply disappear from her system, wiping out costly hours of work.

So Davé and her two assistants lugged the printer to ComputerLand. Then she called in an NEC repairman to fix the printer, all to no avail. Finally, seven months after she purchased her equipment, ComputerLand discovered (and eventually fixed) a fault in the software.

Moral: Before you buy, make clear, in writing, your suppliers' obligations to install, start up and service your equipment. Like most serious telecommuters, Davé strongly recommends protecting oneself with a service contract. These can usually be purchased for around $1,000 for a reasonably sophisticated system.

To put it bluntly, then, telecommuting is not without its drawbacks.

With few exceptions, today's telecommuters are highly innovative and motivated owner-operators like Darcy Bolton and Kathy Ackerman. They are entrepreneurs essentially, people who might have gone into business for themselves even without computers. But for telecommuting to swell to the 10 million presaged by USC's Jack Nilles, America's big corporations will have to climb on the trend. Will they? The answer is: probably, but slowly and unevenly.

For one thing, there are still many technical bugs to be sorted out. In 1978 Chicago's Continental Illinois National Bank began a small experimental program of farming out secretarial work—dictation and letter writing, that sort of thing—to women in their homes. The women would call in, receive their assignments from tape recordings, complete the work and send it via computer to the bank. The bank was flooded with applications for the program; workers loved it. But the bank closed it in August 1982. The problem: Much of the equipment didn't mesh, requiring supervisors to step in. "So many people were getting involved," says Elizabeth Carlson, who oversaw the program, "that it was not cost effective."

But Carlson says the bank believes the problems have been worked out and is currently looking at resuming the program this year.

Another hurdle to corporate use is the Internal Revenue Service. Like the trade unions, these Washington bureaucrats see telecommuting as a threat to their livelihood, which is supposed to be in protecting the public. Corporations would be more interested in telecommuting if they could reduce such employment costs as Social Security payments, which they could do if their telecommuters were independent contractors. But an Internal Revenue Service spokesman warns that if a "continuing employee-employer relation exists," and if the employer supplies the employee's tools, including at-home telecommuting equipment, then, for Social Security purposes, the telecommuter is considered a regular salaried worker and is taxed at the SSA's full whack, regardless of where he works. Companies might be able to avoid this problem by selling employees the equipment on easy terms, assuming the tax collector did not construe the favorable terms as taxable income to the workers.

Probably the greatest hurdles, however, have to do more with industrial culture and psychology than economics. In 1981 Xerox hired APECS, a Dallas-based research outfit, to study telecommuting. What did the survey find? "I don't see a large number of people going to work at home full time for all their working lives," researcher Joanne Pratt told us, reflecting on her findings. "But I do see a large number of people taking advantage of this [telecommuting] for shorter periods of time—half a year, perhaps, or a couple days a week."

Don't expect to find middle and upper-middle managers among the telecommuters. Why not? Probably because they are either insecure in their jobs or still clawing their way up the corporate hierarchy (or both). The corporation—with its complex reward system of carpeted offices, secretaries and the like—is their culture. The fear of leaving it probably outweighs the advantages.

Put another way, most people are more comfortable in crowds. They crave and require peer approval. Constantly.

Margrethe Olson, a New York University business school professor, puts it this way: "Culture changes more slowly than technology."

In a pioneering 1976 book on telecommuting's potential influence on decentralizing American industry, USC's Nilles presented research showing that corporate managers feel far less confident about decisions reached using telecommunications (the phone, say) than they feel about decisions made in the course of face-to-face meetings with

colleagues—*despite the fact that the decisions are almost always identical.* They prefer eyeball-to-eyeball to voice-to-voice. As a result, corporate telecommuting will probably come in the form of a compromise, as it has already on a small scale at Rockwell International. Last year Rockwell's Semiconductor Device Division, based in Newport Beach, Calif., hired 18 semiconductor designers in San Diego. Rather than drive the 80 miles up to Newport Beach, or move there, the designers commute to a small facility near their San Diego homes. From this convenient outpost they telecommute to Newport Beach. Rockwell was thus able to hire on new workers without all the associated relocation costs and the workers have been content to remain in their San Diego environment. "We are all very happy with this arrangement," says the San Diego operations project manager, Dan Pearson.

In this way the new technological possibilities will begin to combine with the deep-seated psychological realities. Or, as telecommuting architect Larry Lerner puts it: "Lunch with other executives or people from your com-

Clerical workers' group 9 to 5 founder Karen Nussbaum
With labor unionists, Nussbaum argues that telecommuting will exploit women working at home. She compares it to the garment workers of the early 1900s, who were paid piece rates.

pany is still an important ritual. You cannot isolate yourself totally.''

Lerner thinks telecommuting will grow and that small businessmen will be the leading edge: ''Cutting myself out of the daily office routine was a real advantage to my company. I wanted to train a new generation of executives, and I used this as an excuse to put them on their own while I was in close touch but out of sight. And it's worked beautifully. They now make more of the everyday decisions without saying, 'Gee, what would Larry think?'—which was my main motivation in the first place.''

If all this makes telecommuting sound marginal, remember this: Back at the turn of the century nobody—not sage, not simpleton—had any notion of how drastically the automobile would transform the economy and the society. Who could have predicted the effect of the automobile on the American landscape, on foreign policy or on the social mores of a newly mobile nation? Perhaps energy-efficient telecommuting, by making possible large-scale home work, will reverse many of these trends, bringing families closer together. The computer revolution is in its early stages. Where it will go, no man can say. But here are a few possibilities:

The University of Southern California's Nilles, estimates that the U.S. could eliminate 74 million barrels of gasoline imports annually if about 14% of the work force shifted to telecommuting. If those figures are right, the U.S. would eliminate its gasoline import requirement with about 13 million new telecommuters. Again, that won't happen soon. But obviously telecommuting is bad for energy producers, good for most everyone else.

Or think about urban land prices, which would probably fall relative to rural and suburban land prices should large numbers of workers telecommute. By the same token, the spread of the automobile enabled people to live farther from work, driving down the relative cost of urban land, driving up the relative cost of suburban land.

There is evidence this process is already under way as our society moves from a hard economy to a soft economy, from heavy industry to knowledge- and service-based industries. In a startling article in July's *Scientific American*, Larry Long and Diana DeAre, two U.S. Bureau of the Census demographers, presented their analysis of the 1980 census. They reported that for the first time since the decennial census was instituted, in 1790, America *ceased urbanizing* in the 1970s. Why? Certainly not because more people are taking up farming. The people who moved to the rural areas to take up new jobs there do not conform to the ordinary image of the rural population. Rather than being farm workers, they are in many instances either workers with the kind of technical training required in modern industry or professionals.'' For better or worse, the hick has become a sophisticate. In an oblique reference to telecommuters the demographers add:

''The new rural demographic concentrations appear to represent small centers of urban culture transplanted to the countryside and enabled to survive by recent advances in communications, transportation and methods of industrial production.''

When the BMWs and new-wave restaurants start invading your local farm villages, you will know the telecommuters are taking over. ■

Architect Larry Lerner, telecommuting coast to coast and to Japan
Working from homes in New York and Los Angeles has boosted his productivity. "When I'm in one of my offices, I am too much at the mercy of silly conversations to be really productive." But people still need to meet face to face. "Lunch with other executives or people from your office is still an important ritual."

DOWN TO BASICS:
JOB CHARACTERISTICS

INTRODUCTION AND OVERVIEW

The growing impact of robotization/computer-ization will increase the current figure of 6000 robots operating in plants and 2 million desk-top computers to 1 million robots and as many as 20 million desk-top computers by 1990, displacing many workers.

—AFL-CIO, *The Future of Work*

The demand for workers with specific technical skills is outstripping the supply. The American Electronics Association predicts a 40 percent increase in technical and non-technical workers by 1988.

—*The Trend Report*, 1983

Once you've found it—the career or job that you think is right for you—you'll want to go one step further by matching work characteristics to your personal characteristics. What skills and aptitudes does the job require? Do these correspond with your own skills and aptitudes? What are working conditions like, and do they suit your style? What are the rewards, and can they satisfy you?

The readings that follow will acquaint you with the required skills and aptitudes, working conditions, and rewards of a broad range of occupations. As in Chapter 5, the emphasis is on science, engineering, and technology, including computers, robotics and environmental careers. When exploring environmental careers, keep in mind that the electric power industry is one of the largest employers of professionals in land use planning, fisheries management, waste management, forestry, and scores of other occupations in the environmental field.

THE READINGS

"The Assorted Soldiers in the Computer Army"

"Systems Analysts"

"Programmers"

"Computer Operating Personnel"

"Computer Service Technicians"

"New Occupations in the Robotic Age"

"The Job Market for Engineers: Recent Conditions and Future Prospects"

"Environmental Careers"

REFERENCE

Occupational Projections and Training Data, 1984 Edition, published by the U.S. Department of Labor's Bureau of Labor Statistics, contains detailed statistics on current and projected occupational employment, as well as new estimates on occupational demand and supply. If you cannot locate a copy in your library, you may order one from the Superintendent of Documents, Washington, DC 20402.

There was only a short line and in a moment he was standing in front of the box office window. "Ring?" the window asked. He looked at the price list. "Second," he said and slid his Master Charge into the appropriate slot. "License, please," said the window, winking an arrow that pointed at another slot. He inserted his license into the other slot, a bell went ding and mira! He was inside Partyland, ascending the big blue escalator up to his first hand experience of direct, interactive personal communication. Not a classroom exercise, not a therapy session, not a job briefing, not an ecumenical agape, but an honest-to-god conversation, spontaneous, unstructured, and all his own.

—Thomas Disch, The Man Who Had No Idea

THE ASSORTED SOLDIERS IN THE COMPUTER ARMY

A new battery of computers has invaded the workplace. Armed with incredible speed and enormous memories, these machines have the power to perform innumerable tasks that were once accomplished by people. The new computers are smaller, cheaper, and smarter than any that have gone before them. But without the human touch, computers could do nothing. Without a computer workforce, not a nanosecond of the machine's time would ever be put to use. Computers have replaced some workers because the machines can perform some jobs, ranging from sorting data to performing complex mathematical calculations, faster than people. But at the same time, computers have brought into being a host of new occupations and created thousands of new jobs. Indeed, an army-sized computer work force has come into being.

This work force is devoted to the development, operation, and care of computers. It includes engineers who design new models; manufacturing workers who make the machines; sales and marketing workers who find users for the engineers' creations; systems analysts and computer programmers who translate business or scientific problems into terms the computer can work with; and computer service technicians, operating personnel, and data-entry clerks who keep the machines running.

Literally dozens of job titles exist for the various types of work people do throughout the industry, as a quick look at the "Job Description Guide" accompanying this article shows. Specific titles vary from company to company, but most can be grouped in these five categories: Systems analysts, programmers, other professionals, service technicians, and operating personnel. These categories differ from those used in the previous article because occupations are discussed here for which the Census Bureau does not collect data.

Systems Analysts

Systems analysts are the problem solvers for the computer user. Suppose, for example, that a company wanted to computerize its personnel operations, a task that was actually done long ago by most large corporations. The analyst would begin by discussing the jobs to be performed with managers and personnel specialists. In these discussions, the analyst would want to learn exactly what kind of information was needed, what was to be done with it, how quickly it had to be processed, and how it was currently being collected and recorded. The analyst would also evaluate the computer equipment already owned by the company in order to determine if it could carry the additional load of the personnel data or if new equipment was needed. Next, the analyst would develop the system, that is, decide how the data would be collected, prepared for the machines, processed, stored, and made available to users. At every step, both what was to be done and which machine was to do it would be specified. The proposed system would then be explained to company officials through charts and diagrams; an analysis of the costs and benefits of the new system compared with those of current procedures might also be prepared by the analyst for presentation at this stage. If the company decided to adopt the proposed system, the analyst would write the necessary programs—the topic of the next section of this article—or, more likely, prepare specifications for programmers to follow.

The problems systems analysts deal with range from monitoring nuclear fission in a powerplant to forecasting sales for an appliance manufacturer. Because the work is so varied and complex, analysts usually specialize in business, scientific, or engineering applications. Some employers, such as large engineering firms or defense agencies, employ all three kinds of systems analysts.

Systems analysts must be able to think logically and should enjoy working with ideas. The ability to concentrate and pay close attention to details is also important. Most analysts work independently, but whether working alone or as part of a team they must be able to work well with other people and communicate effectively. Leadership and managerial ability are important for analysts who wish to advance into supervisory positions.

According to surveys conducted by the Bureau of Labor Statistics and private firms engaged in research on computer occupations, beginning systems analysts earned about $330 a week in 1980. Experienced analysts earned from $420 to $460, and lead systems analysts earned from $470 to $495 weekly.

Computer Programmers

Most programmers are concerned with the final products of a computer operation. They are called applications programmers and, like systems analysts, they usually specialize in either business and commercial or scientific and engineering work. But before a computer can produce anything, the machine must be prepared by another kind of programmer, called a systems programmer or software systems engineer.

Programs written by systems program-

Reprinted from *Occupational Outlook Quarterly/Summer 1981*, U.S. Department of Labor.

mers give a particular computer the ability to perform a range of tasks, whereas the applications programmer prepares the instructions that make the computer perform a particular task. For example, the systems programmer's work enables the computer to understand specific computer languages and to control peripheral equipment such as card sorters and printers. This internal programming also allocates the computer's resources, controlling the flow of data in the way a traffic cop controls downtown traffic. A computer's memory, for example, can handle only so many pieces of information. Say the computer has to do three jobs—process some personnel records, update a plant inventory, and balance the budget. The program for each of these jobs would state how much of the computer's memory is needed to process that job. If all three programs together require more memory than the computer has, the machine's internal program will enable it to determine which job should be done first. More likely, the program will allow the computer to work on all three simultaneously, performing one function on one job at the same time that it performs some other function on another job.

Switching metaphors, the jobs of the systems programmer and the applications programmer are something like those of a football coach and a quarterback who calls his own plays. The coach, like the systems programmer, prepares the team so that it can make many different plays. During a game, the quarterback decides which play the team should execute. But the quarterback cannot make the team carry out a play unlike anything the coach has prepared the team for. For example, to be absurd about the whole thing, if the coach has prepared the team to make only running plays, the quarterback will not be able to call for a forward pass.

Applications programmers take over where systems analysts leave off. They write programs that tell the machines what to do and instructions for the computer operators who will run the programs through the machines. The programmer begins with the instructions given by the systems analyst. Next, the program is written, but it cannot be written like a memo in ordinary English. A computer cannot understand words that have more than one meaning, which most do. The program is therefore written in a

special computer language. Some of these languages, such as those used in scientific work, are unintelligible to anyone who has not studied them. Others are closer to everyday speech. For example, to return to the computerization of personnel records, one part of the system would keep track of the amount of time each employee worked each pay period and how much pay the employee had earned. One instruction in the program for this task might read, "If TOTAL no more than 40 hours, compute straight time; if TOTAL more than 40 hours, compute 40 hours straight time, compute additional hours straight time plus one half." The particular language used depends on the kind of program being written and the specific computer that will run the program. Some frequently used languages are BASIC, COBOL, PL/1, FORTRAN, and Assembly.

Computers not only cannot understand English, most of them cannot read ordinary print. So, once the program has been written, it is put into a form that the machine can read—punched cards, magnetic tapes, or disks. The programmer then tests it, looking

for errors or bugs, and corrects or debugs the program. Finally, the instructions for the operators are written.

Programs range from the relatively simple to the highly complex. Sometimes devising and debugging one takes only a day. Other times the programs are so intricate that they take a team of programmers more than a year to develop.

All programmers, like systems analysts, must be able to think logically and perform exacting, analytical work. They must also be patient, persistent, ingenious, and able to work accurately under pressure. Employers also prefer programmers who have some knowledge of the business, scientific, or engineering problems that the programs deal with. For example, a business programmer would benefit from a knowledge of accounting and an engineering programmer should be familiar with calculus.

Applications programmers often work as part of a team. Depending upon the project, there may be a programming manager or senior programmer assisted by a staff of programmers, junior programmers, and trainees.

In 1980, beginning applications programmers earned about $260 a week, and systems programmers without experience started at about $315 weekly. Experienced applications programmers averaged about $400 a week, compared to about $460 for systems programmers. Lead applications programmers earned about $445 and lead systems programmers received about $505 a week.

Other Professionals

As computer technology is developed and refined, shifts in demand for computer skills of all kinds also occur, creating the need for workers in new occupations. And so, even while battalions of computer programmers and systems analysts take their place in the army of professionals working with computers, they are joined by rank on rank of new specialists. Among these new workers in the computer field are data base specialists, data communications programmers and programmer analysts, documentation specialists, technical service managers and other managers, and sales and marketing workers.

Data base specialists design and control the use of an organization's information resources or data base. They may analyze the use of data in order to determine if the organization needs additional information or does not need some that it currently collects. They are also responsible for security procedures that protect the data base and for unsnarling backups and redundancies in the data base. They must be well-versed in programming and the uses of a data base.

Data communications programmers and programmer analysts are specialized programmers and analysts whose work results from one of the recent developments in the use of computers. Not so long ago, an organization's computer sat in a room to which material was brought for processing. Each computer was independent. Increasingly, however, computers are being linked together into networks. Data communications programmers and programmer analysts are specialists in the use of such networks and the electronic transmission of information by way of satellites or telephone lines. They evaluate an organization's computers, programs, and peripheral equipment, modify the internal programming of computers for an individual company's needs, and advise the applications programmers on technical matters.

Documentation specialists are experts in various computer systems, their user manuals, and marketing information. They advise users and buyers on the features of different systems. They must deal both with systems analysts and computer programmers who develop and refine the computer system and with the system's users. Documentation specialists also help design new systems.

The increasing number of people working with computers naturally calls for new managers. Technical services managers direct the technical staff that is responsible for maintaining the system, its software or programs, its telecommunications system, and its data base. They need substantial experience in systems programming and extensive, current knowledge of computer technology. Data-center-operations managers direct all computer and peripheral machine operations; data entry, data control, scheduling, quality control, and the distribution of the final product or output all come under their jurisdiction. Information systems directors are executives who are responsible for the management of the entire system and all the electronic data processing done by the organization.

Sales and marketing professionals in the computer industry are not usually computer scientists themselves, but they play an important role in the field. Without them, the new technology would never be put to use by so many organizations. They serve as liaisons between the computer industry and the users. Like programmers and systems analysts, they usually specialize in either business or scientific systems.

Sales representatives who market business systems must be familiar with all phases of company organizations and the details of modern management procedures. Since business is a vast and varied world itself, many sales representatives specialize in particular industries. Sales representatives specializing in scientific applications must have a technical background that affords an understanding of the customer's needs so that representatives can recommend specific combinations of equipment to meet those needs. Careers in sales are most available to college graduates who have experience in sales and an allied technical or managerial field.

Marketing technical support representatives provide technical support in the marketing of hardware and software. They visit and provide services to customers both before and after sales. They are also involved in system studies and feasibility studies, demonstrate equipment, and give technical presentations. They must be well-versed in the systems their company sells and, like other marketing workers, they must be able to assimilate new product specifications and capabilities and analyze customer requirements.

Computer Service Technicians

Computer service technicians, also known as field engineers or customer engineers, are responsible for installing and servicing the computer system. They also keep maintenance records on the machines they service, fill out time and expense reports, keep inventories of spare parts, and order parts as needed. Some specialize in a particular model or a certain type of repair.

In installing new equipment, service technicians lay cables, hook up electrical connections, test the machinery, and correct any problems before the customer starts to use the system.

At regular intervals, they perform preventive maintenance on the system and peripheral equipment. This includes making routine adjustments, oiling some parts, and cleaning mechanical and electromechanical parts. Technicians check the equipment for loose connections and defective components or circuits. They also run special programs to force the system to operate at peak capacity in order to detect weaknesses. This allows the technician to locate potential trouble before the system breaks down during normal operations. The technician is then able to do any necessary remedial work.

When computer equipment breaks down, technicians must find the cause of the failure and make repairs. Finding the problem is the most difficult part of the job because the systems are now so complex. The problem can be in the central processing unit, in one of the peripheral machines, or in the cables connecting one unit to another. As a result, the cause of a breakdown might take several hours to find and just a few minutes to fix.

Technicians use several kinds of tools to test equipment, including voltmeters, ohmmeters, and oscilloscopes. They also run special diagnostic programs that help pinpoint certain malfunctions. The employer supplies the tools and test equipment, but technicians are responsible for keeping them in good working order.

Besides knowing how to use specialized tools and equipment, computer service technicians must be familiar with technical and repair manuals for each piece of equipment. They must keep up with technical in-

formation and revised maintenance procedures issued periodically by computer manufacturers. And they must also have logical, analytical minds in order to apply their technical knowledge.

Although technicians spend most of their time working on machines, they must be skilled at working with people too. They must listen to customer complaints, answer questions, and give technical advice on ways to keep the system in good condition. In addition, some experienced technicians help train new workers or perform supervisory duties. Generally, computer service technicians must be independent, since they usually work alone. Those with leadership skills may become service managers.

Generally, computer service technicians must be available to work at all hours. Because computer installations generally operate around the clock, technicians are often on call to make emergency repairs. Although the normal workweek is 40 hours, overtime is standard for these workers.

Average weekly earnings of fully trained computer service technicians were about $380 a week in 1980, according to the limited data available. Senior technicians with several years' experience earned about $430 weekly. Highly skilled specialists earned even more.

Computer Operators

Computer operating personnel are concerned with entering data and instructions into the computer system (input), operating the computer, and retrieving the results (output). Operating personnel include keypunch operators, data-entry clerks, console operators, production control personnel, high-speed-printer operators, and card-tape-converter operators.

Information can enter today's computer systems in a variety of ways. For many years, information was punched into cards that were then read by the computer. But advances in technology have made many different kinds of equipment available. As a result, the title "keypunch operator" is giving way to more general titles, such as "key-entry clerk" and "data-entry clerk."

Most data-entry clerks operate machines that have a keyboard somewhat like a typewriter's no matter whether the machine puts the information on magnetic tapes, disks, or cards. Manual dexterity is, therefore, important in all these jobs. Data-

entry work can be stressful and monotonous. Clerks must maintain a proficient speed while enduring repetitive work and remaining seated at one machine all day. Also, since there can be anywhere from a few operators working in a room to several hundred, they should be able to tolerate noise. Data-entry clerks can move into supervisory positions, but these positions are relatively few. They are also sometimes promoted into production control.

In 1980, beginning data-entry personnel earned a little less than $200 a week. Experienced workers earned just over $200 weekly. Lead operators averaged between $215 and $245 weekly.

Production control clerks see that all the information needed for a data-entry job is together, schedule a due date, check the completed work, forward it for processing to the computer operating sections, and recheck it after it is processed. Production control clerks can advance to senior control clerk or to production control analyst. They can also enter training programs for operators and programmers.

Once the information is coded, that is, prepared in a form the computer can read, it is ready to be processed and stored or printed. Computer console operators are the workers who actually run the computer when it performs these operations. Following instructions for each job, they load the input; make sure that the output unit has the paper, tape, or other material it needs; clear the system; and start the machine. While the machine is running, they monitor it, watching the console and paying special attention to signals—such as error lights—that could indicate a malfunction. If the computer stops or an error is indicated, operators must locate the problem, solve it if possible, or terminate the program and notify a supervisor.

In large data processing operations, there may be a senior operator tending the central console, assisted by other operators who change tapes or disks and check out other peripheral equipment. In newer, more complex installations, computers may run many programs at once. In such an installation, when an error or equipment failure occurs, much more is demanded of the operator, whose actions may affect many programs.

Console operators must adapt the computer to the program. Therefore, operators must know the capability of the machine and how to change circuit boards or chips for each program. Operators must also know what to do if the equipment breaks down and which manuals to consult for each job. They also keep a log of the work done by the computer for each operation and prepare reports on the computer's use. The occupation thus demands a combination of mechanical skill and reasoning ability.

Keypunch and auxiliary equipment operators should be able to work under close supervision as part of a team. They must also feel comfortable working with machines and doing repetitive, organized tasks. Console operators, however, must use independent judgment, especially when working without supervision on second and third shifts.

Computer operators spend long periods of time on their feet as they set up, operate, and control equipment. They frequently experience pressure to meet deadlines. In some establishments, computer operators are required to lift and carry tapes, disks, cards, paper, and other supplies that may weigh up to 50 pounds.

Beginning console operators earned about $200 per week in 1980 according to the available data; experienced workers earned $265 to $330 per week. Lead operators averaged from $300 to $375 a week.

In some systems, devices directly connected to the computer provide the output in the form desired by the programmer. In others, high speed printers or card-tape converters run by auxiliary equipment operators—high-speed-printer operators and card-tape-converter operators—perform this function.

Frequently, data on punched cards, magnetic tape, or discs are kept for future use. Tape librarians classify and catalog this material and maintain files of current and previous versions of programs, listings, and tape data. In smaller organizations, tape librarians may do some data-entry work as well as coordinate activities between the programmer and the operations department. The average weekly earnings for tape librarians in 1980, according to the limited data available, were $225.

Conclusion

The computer field offers a growing number of interesting positions. The growing battery of computers has spawned an army of computer professionals and other workers ready to change and develop as new technology emerges. For an enterprising person, it may be a good army to be in.　∞

Career Resources for Computer Occupations

Comp Job, 3rd Edition, 1979, John H. Westlund, editor. Employment Services, P.O. Box 3265, Chico, Calif. 95927. $16.98. A directory of employment for software positions in the computer world. 75 pp. Includes counseling section and company listings.

A Look Into Computer Careers, American Federation of Information Processing Societies, 1815 North Lynn Street, Suite 800, Arlington, Va. 22209. 16 pp.

Facts on Computer Careers, jointly published by American Federation of Information Processing Societies (address noted above) and Council of Better Business Bureaus, Inc., 1150 17th Street NW., Washington, D.C. 20036.

Career Opportunity Index, P.O. Box 1878, Huntington Beach, Calif. 92647. Professional edition, $10.00; Western and Southwestern edition, $10.00; Vocational Technical edition, $7.50. Lists major employers of computer scientists.

Computer Career News, Connie Winkler, editor. P.O. Box 1001, Oradell, N.J. 07649. Career newspaper published every 2 weeks; features articles on developments in computers, salary news of computer professionals, and opportunities.

Graduate Assistantship Directory in the Computer Sciences, 1981-82 edition, Association for Computer Machinery A.C.M. Order Department, P.O. Box 64145, Baltimore, Md. 21264. $5.00. This directory lists both assistantships and fellowships available in university computer science departments and university computing centers for graduate studies.

Office Machine and Computer Occupations, Bulletin No. 2075-6. Reprinted from *Occupational Outlook Handbook, 1980-81 edition.* Available from any regional office of BLS, listed on the inside front cover of this magazine. $1.25. Make check payable to Superintendent of Documents.

Opportunities in Data Processing for Positions as Peripheral Equipment Operators Grades GS-2 through 4, Computer Systems Operators Grades GS-4 through 7. U.S. Office of Personnel Management Announcement No. WA-5 06, revised October 1977. 8 pp.

Computer Specialist, Opportunities in the Federal Government GS-7 through GS-12. U.S. Office of Personnel Management Announcement No. 420, January 1979. 6 pp.

Peterson's Annual Guide to Careers and Employment for Engineers, Computer Scientists, and Physical Scientists, 1980 edition, Sandra Grundfest, editor. Peterson's Guides, 228 Alexander Street, Princeton, N.J. 08540.

Computers and Careers: A Suggested Curriculum for Grades 9-12. Contains 14 instructional units to introduce and prepare students for computer careers U.S. Department of Education, Bureau of Occupational and Adult Education, 1973. Available from ERIC.

Elements of Computer Careers. Textbook provides students with an awareness of basic elements in careers in the computer field: Educational requirements, salary levels, and opportunities for advancement. U.S. Department of Education, National Institute of Education, 1977. 34 pp.

SYSTEMS ANALYSTS

Nature of the Work

Many essential business functions and scientific research projects depend on systems analysts to plan efficient methods of processing data and handling the results. Analysts begin an assignment by discussing the data processing problem with managers or specialists to determine the exact nature of the problem and to break it down into its component parts. If a new inventory system is desired, for example, systems analysts must determine what new data must be collected, the equipment needed for computation, and the steps to be followed in processing the information.

Analysts use various techniques, such as cost accounting, sampling, and mathematical model building to analyze a problem and devise a new system. Once a system has been developed, they prepare charts and diagrams that describe its operation in terms that managers or customers can understand. They also may prepare a cost-benefit analysis to help the client decide whether the proposed system is satisfactory.

If the system is accepted, systems analysts translate the logical requirements of the system into the capabilities of the computer machinery or "hardware." They also prepare specifications for programmers to follow and work with them to "debug," or eliminate errors from the system. (The work of computer programmers is described elsewhere in the *Handbook.*)

The problems that systems analysts solve range from monitoring nuclear fission in a powerplant to forecasting sales for an appliance manufacturing firm. Because the work is so varied and complex, analysts usually specialize in either business or scientific and engineering applications.

Some analysts improve systems already in use by developing better procedures or adapting the system to handle additional types of data. Others do research, called advanced systems design, to devise new methods of systems analysis.

Working Conditions

Systems analysts usually work about 40 hours a week—the same as other professional and office workers. Unlike many computer operators, systems analysts are not assigned to evening or night shifts. Occasionally, however, evening or weekend work may be necessary to complete emergency projects.

Employment

About 205,000 persons worked as systems analysts in 1980. Employment of these workers is concentrated in two geographic regions—about one-third of the total are employed in the Midwest and one-fourth work in the northeastern portion of the United States. Most systems analysts worked in urban areas for manufacturing firms, government agencies, wholesale businesses, and data processing service organizations. In addition, large numbers worked for banks and insurance companies.

Training, Other Qualifications, and Advancement

There is no universally acceptable way of preparing for a job as a systems analyst because employers' preferences depend on the work being done. However, college graduates generally are sought for these jobs, and, for some of the more complex jobs, persons with graduate degrees are preferred. Employers usually want analysts with a background in accounting, business management, or economics for work in a business environment while a background in the physical sciences, mathematics, or engineering is preferred for work in scientifically oriented organizations. A growing number of employers seek applicants who have a degree in computer science, information science, information systems, or data processing. Regardless of college major, employers look for people who are familiar with programming languages. Courses in computer concepts, systems analysis, and data base management systems offer good preparation for a job in this field.

Prior work experience is important. Nearly half of all persons entering this occupation have transferred from other occupations, especially from computer programmer. In many industries, systems analysts begin as programmers and are promoted to analyst positions after gaining experience.

Systems analysts must be able to think logically and should like working with ideas. They often deal with a number of tasks simultaneously. The ability to concentrate and pay close attention to detail also is important. Although systems analysts often work independently, they also work in teams on large projects. They must be able to communicate effectively with technical personnel, such as programmers, as well as with clients who have no computer background.

In order to advance, systems analysts must continue their technical education. Technological advances come so rapidly in the computer field that continuous study is necessary to keep skills up to date. Training usually takes the form of 1- and 2-week courses offered by employers and "software" vendors. Additional training may come from professional development seminars offered by professional computing societies.

An indication of experience and professional competence is the Certificate in Data Processing (CDP). This designation is conferred by the Institute for Certification of Computer Professionals upon candidates who have completed 5 years' experience and passed a five-part examination.

In large data processing departments, persons who begin as junior systems analysts may be promoted to senior or lead systems analysts after several years of experience. Systems analysts who show leadership ability also can advance to jobs as managers of systems analysis or data processing departments.

Job Outlook

Employment of systems analysts is expected to grow much faster than the average for all occupations through the 1980's as computer usage expands, particularly in computer service firms, accounting firms, and organizations engaged in research and development. Many systems analysts also will be needed by computer manufacturers to design software packages. In addition to jobs that will be created by increased computer usage, some openings will occur as systems analysts advance to managerial positions, become consultants, or enter other occupations. Because many of these workers are relatively young, few positions will result from retirement or death.

The demand for systems analysts is expected to rise as computer capabilities are increased and as new applications are found for computer technology. Sophisticated accounting systems, telecommunications networks, and scientific research are just a few areas where use of computer systems has resulted in new approaches to problem solving. Over the next decade, systems analysts also will be developing ways to use the com-

Reprinted from *Occupational Outlook Handbook,* 1982-83, U.S. Department of Labor.

puter's resources to solve problems in areas that have not yet been recognized.

Advances in technology that have drastically reduced the size and cost of computer hardware will have differing effects on employment of systems analysts. Employment in data processing firms may not grow quite as rapidly as in recent years as more small businesses install their own computers rather than rely on a data processing service. This will be offset, however, by a rising demand for analysts to design systems for small computers that are specifically adapted to meet problem-solving needs of small firms.

Graduates of computer-related curriculums should enjoy the best prospects for employment. College graduates who have had courses in computer programming, systems analysis, and other data processing areas should also find many opportunities. Persons without a college degree and college graduates unfamiliar with data processing will face competition from the large number of experienced workers seeking jobs as systems analysts.

Earnings

Earnings for beginning systems analysts in private industry averaged about $330 a week in 1980, according to surveys conducted in urban areas by the Bureau of Labor Statistics and private firms engaged in research on computer occupations. Experienced workers earned from $390 to $460, and lead systems analysts earned about $490 weekly. Overall, systems analysts earn well over twice as much as the average for all nonsupervisory workers in private industry, except farming. In the Federal Government, the entrance salary for recent college graduates with a bachelor's degree was about $200 a week in early 1981.

Systems analysts working in the North and West earned somewhat more than those in the South, and generally their earnings were greater in data processing service firms or in heavy manufacturing than in insurance companies or educational institutions.

The shortage of trained computer personnel has resulted in an upward pay spiral that is expected to continue.

Related Occupations

Other workers in mathematics, business, and science who use logic and reasoning ability to solve problems are programmers, financial analysts, urban planners, engineers, mathematicians, operations research analysts, and actuaries.

Sources of Additional Information

Further information about the occupation of systems analyst is available from:

American Federation of Information Processing Societies, 1815 North Lynn St., Arlington, Va. 22209.

Association for Systems Management, 24587 Bagley Rd., Cleveland, Ohio 44138.

Information about the Certificate in Data Processing is available from:

The Institute for Certification of Computer Professionals, 35 E. Wacker Dr., Suite 2828, Chicago, Ill. 60601.

PROGRAMMERS

Nature of the Work

Computers can process vast quantities of information rapidly and accurately, but only if they are given step-by-step instructions to follow. Because the machines cannot think for themselves, computer programmers must write detailed instructions called programs that list in a logical order the steps the machine must follow to organize data, solve a problem, or do some other task.

Programmers usually work from descriptions prepared by systems analysts who have carefully studied the task that the computer system is going to perform—perhaps organizing data collected in a survey or estimating the stress on portions of a building during a hurricane. These descriptions contain a detailed list of the steps the computer must follow, such as retrieving data stored in another computer, organizing it in a certain way, and performing the necessary calculations. (A more detailed description of the work of systems analysts is contained elsewhere in the *Handbook*.) An applications programmer then writes the specific program for the problem, by breaking down each step into a series of coded instructions using one of the languages developed especially for computers.

Some organizations, particularly smaller ones, do not employ systems analysts. Instead, workers called programmer-analysts are responsible for both systems analysis and programming.

Programs vary with the type of problem to be solved. For example, the mathematical calculations involved in payroll accounting procedures are different from those required to determine the flight path of a space probe. A business applications programmer developing instructions for billing customers would first take the company records the computer would need and then specify a solution by showing the steps the computer must follow to obtain old balances, add new charges, calculate finance charges, and deduct payments before determining a customer's bill. The programmer then codes the actual instructions the computer will follow in a high-level programming language, such as COBOL.

Next, the programmer tests the operation of the program to be sure the instructions are correct and will produce the desired information. The programmer tries a sample of the data with the program and reviews the results to see if any errors were made. If errors did occur, the program must be changed and rechecked until it produces the correct results. This is called "debugging" the program.

Finally, an instruction sheet is prepared for the computer operator who will run the program. (The work of computer operators is described in the statement on computer operating personnel.)

Although simple programs can be written in a few hours, programs that use complex mathematical formulas or many data files may require more than a year of work. In some cases, several programmers may work together in teams under a senior programmer's supervision.

Applications programmers are usually business oriented, engineering oriented, or science oriented. A different type of specialist, the systems programmer, maintains the general instructions (called software) that control the operation of the entire computer system. These workers make changes in the sets of instructions that determine the allocation of the computer's resources among the various jobs it has been given. Because of their knowledge of operating systems, systems programmers often help applications programmers determine the source of problems that may occur with their programs.

Working Conditions

Programmers work about 40 hours a week, but their hours are not always from 9 to 5. Once or twice a week programmers may report early or work late to use the computer when it is available; occasionally, they work on weekends. When a new program is being tested, programmers may get calls from computer operators asking for advice at all hours of the day or night.

Employment

In 1980, about 228,000 persons worked as computer programmers. Most were employed by manufacturing firms, data processing service organizations, government agencies, and insurance companies.

Many programmers work in large firms that need and can afford expensive computer systems. Small firms, which generally require computers only for payroll or billing purposes, often pay data processing service organizations to do this work. Small firms may maintain their own low-cost, small business computers. Systems programmers usually work in research organizations, computer manufacturing firms, and large computer centers.

Training, Other Qualifications, and Advancement

There are no universal training requirements for programmers because employers' needs vary. Most programmers are college graduates; others have taken special courses in computer programming to supplement their experience in fields such as accounting or inventory control.

Employers using computers for scientific or engineering applications prefer college graduates who have degrees in computer or information science, mathematics, engineering, or the physical sciences. Graduate degrees are required for some jobs. Very few scientific organizations are interested in applicants who have no college training.

Although some employers who use computers for business applications do not require college degrees, they prefer applicants who have had college courses in data processing, who are experienced in computer operation or payroll accounting but who have no college training are promoted to programming jobs; however, they need additional data processing courses to become fully qualified programmers. Although it may be preferred, prior work experience is not essential for a job as a programmer; in fact, about half of all entrants to the occupation have little or no work experience.

Computer programming is taught at public and private vocational schools, community and junior colleges, and universities. Instruction ranges from introductory home study courses to advanced courses at the graduate level. High schools in many parts of the country also offer courses in computer programming.

An indication of experience and professional competence at the senior programmer level is the Certificate in Computer Programming (CCP). This designation is conferred by the Institute for Certification of Computer Professionals upon candidates who have passed a basic five-part examination. In addition, individuals may take another section of the exam in order to specialize in business, science, or systems applications.

In hiring programmers, employers look for people who can think logically and are capable of exacting analytical work. The job calls for patience, persistence, and the ability to work with extreme accuracy even under pressure. Ingenuity and imagination are particularly important when programmers must find new ways to solve a problem.

Beginning applications programmers usually spend their first weeks on the job attending training classes. After this initial instruction, they work on simple assignments while completing further specialized training programs. Programmers generally must spend at least several months working under close supervision before they can handle all aspects of their job. Because of rapidly changing technology, programmers must continue their training by taking courses offered by their

Reprinted from *Occupational Outlook Handbook*, 1982-83, U.S. Department of Labor.

employer and software vendors. For skilled workers, the prospects for advancement are good. In large organizations, they may be promoted to lead programmers and be given supervisory responsibilities. Some applications programmers may become systems programmers. Both applications programmers and systems programmers often become systems analysts or are promoted to managerial positions.

Job Outlook

Employment of programmers is expected to grow faster than the average for all occupations through the 1980's as computer usage expands, particularly in firms providing accounting, business management, and computer programming services, and in organizations involved in research and development. In addition to jobs resulting from increased demand for programmers, many openings will arise each year from the need to replace workers who leave the occupation. Because many programmers are relatively young, few openings will result from retirements or deaths. However, many vacancies will be created as experienced workers transfer into jobs as systems analysts or managers.

The demand for applications programmers will increase as many more processes once done by hand are automated, but employment is not expected to grow as rapidly as in the past. Improved software, such as utility programs that can be used by other than data processing personnel, will simplify or eliminate some programming tasks. More systems programmers will be needed to develop and maintain the complex operating programs made necessary by higher level computer languages, as well as to link or coordinate the output of different computer systems.

Job prospects should be excellent for college graduates who have had computer-related courses, particularly for those with a major in computer science or a related field. The number of persons with computer skills is not expected to keep pace with rising demand. Graduates of 2-year programs in data processing technologies also should have good prospects, primarily in business applications.

Programmers debug programs before they are run.

Earnings

Average weekly earnings of programmer trainees in private industry ranged from $250 to $330 in 1980, according to surveys conducted in urban areas by the Bureau of Labor Statistics and firms engaged in research on data processing occupations. In general, programmers earn about twice as much as the average earnings of all nonsupervisory workers in private industry, except farming. Systems programmers generally earn more than applications programmers, and lead programmers earn more than either systems or applications programmers. For example, experienced systems programmers averaged about $470 a week compared to $400 for applications programmers. Average weekly salaries for lead systems programmers were $505, compared to $430 for lead applications programmers. In the Federal civil service, the entrance salary for programmers with a college degree was about $200 a week in early 1981.

Programmers working in the North and West earned somewhat more than those working in the South. Those working for data processing services and public utilities had higher earnings than programmers employed in banks, advertising, or educational institutions.

Related Occupations

Other workers in mathematics, business, and science who solve detailed problems include systems analysts, mathematicians, statisticians, engineers, financial analysts, actuaries, mathematical technicians, and operations research analysts.

Sources of Additional Information

Additional information about the occupation of programmer is available from:

American Federation of Information Processing Societies, 1815 North Lynn St., Arlington, Va. 22209. Information about the Certificate in Computer Programming is available from:

The Institute for Certification of Computer Professionals, 35 E. Wacker Dr., Suite 2828, Chicago, Ill. 60601.

COMPUTER OPERATING PERSONNEL

Nature of the Work

All data systems require specialized workers to enter data and instructions, operate the computer, and retrieve the results. The data to be processed and the instructions for the computer are called "input;" the results are called "output."

Information is entered into a computer system by data entry personnel in a variety of ways. In some systems, *keypunch operators* prepare input by punching patterns of holes in computer cards to represent specific letters, numbers, and special characters, using a machine similar to a typewriter. In others, *data typists* use special machines that convert the information they type to holes in cards or magnetic impulses on tapes or disks. Most newer systems are capable of remote data entry. The user sits at a machine equipped with a typewriter keyboard and an electronic screen that displays the data as they are entered directly into the computer. In some newer systems, data enter the computer at the source of the transaction being recorded, for example, at the loading dock or at a supermarket checkout line.

Once the input is coded—prepared in a form the computer can read—it is ready to be processed. *Console operators*, who monitor and control the computer, decide what equipment should be set up for each job by examining the special instructions that the programmer has written out. To process the input, they make sure the computer has been loaded with the correct cards, magnetic tapes, or disks, and then start the computer. While it is running, they watch the computer console, paying special attention to signals, such as error lights, that could indicate a malfunction. If the computer stops or an error is signalled, operators must locate the problem and solve it or terminate the program.

In some systems, devices directly connected to the computer provide output in the form desired by the programmer. In others, high-speed printers or card-tape-converters run by auxiliary equipment operators—*high-speed printer operators* and *card-tape-converter operators*—perform this function.

Frequently, data on punched cards, magnetic tape, or disks are kept for future use. *Tape librarians* classify and catalog this material and maintain files of current and previous versions of programs, listings, and test data. In smaller organizations, librarians may do some data entry as well as coordinate the activities of the programmer and the operations department.

Working Conditions

Because electronic computers must be operated at carefully controlled temperatures, operators work in well-ventilated rooms; air-conditioning counteracts the heat generated by machine operations. When the equipment is operating, however, the computer room can be noisy.

Some console and auxiliary equipment operators work evening or night shifts because many organizations use their computers 24 hours a day. Tape librarians usually work only day shifts.

Employment

About 558,000 persons worked as console, auxiliary equipment, and keypunch operators in 1980.

Although workers in these occupations are employed in almost every industry, most work in manufacturing firms, wholesale and retail trade establishments, and firms that provide data processing services for a fee. Many additional computer and peripheral equipment operators work for insurance companies, banks, and government agencies.

Training, Other Qualifications, and Advancement

In firms that have just installed a new computer system, tabulating and bookkeeping machine operators may be transferred to jobs as keypunch or auxiliary equipment operators, or console operators. Most often, however, employers recruit workers who already have the necessary skills to operate the equipment.

Many high schools, public and private vocational schools, private computer schools, business schools, and community or junior colleges offer training in computer operating skills. The military services also offer valuable training in a number of computer skills. In addition, a growing number of business firms across the country hold weekend seminars on data processing for high school students. Similarly, computer professional associations encourage student participation in professional conferences.

Employers in private industry usually require a high school education, and many prefer to hire console operators who have some community or junior college training, especially in data processing. The Federal Government requires a high school diploma, unless applicants have had specialized training or experience. Many employers test applicants to determine their aptitude for computer work, particularly their ability to reason logically. Keypunch operators and other data entry personnel often are tested for their ability to work quickly and accurately.

Beginners usually are trained on the job. The length of training needed varies—auxiliary equipment operators can learn their jobs in a few weeks, but console operators require several months of training because they must become sufficiently familiar with the computer equipment to be able to identify the causes of equipment failures.

Keypunch and auxiliary equipment operators should be able to work under close supervision as part of a team. They also must feel comfortable working with machines and doing repetitive, organized tasks. Console operators, however, must use independent judgment, especially when working without supervision on second and third shifts.

Advancement opportunities for keypunch and auxiliary equipment operators are limited because data entry techniques are becoming more specialized. However, promotion to a supervisory position is possible after several years on the job. With additional training, often including community or junior college study, a few operators advance to jobs as console operators.

Console operators also may be promoted to supervisory positions, or to jobs that combine supervision and console operation. Through on-the-job experience and additional training, some console operators advance to jobs as programmers.

Job Outlook

Changes in data processing technology will have differing effects on computer operating occupations. Employment of console and peripheral equipment operators, for example, is expected to rise much faster than the average for all occupations through the 1980's. Employment of keypunch operators, on the other hand, should continue to decline.

Recent advances in miniaturizing circuits have enabled manufacturers to reduce both the size and the cost of computer components. As this technology develops, a continued expansion in the use of computers is expected, especially by small businesses. Employment of console and peripheral equipment operators in data processing service firms may grow less rapidly than in the past

Reprinted from *Occupational Outlook Handbook*, 1982-83, U.S. Department of Labor.

as more small firms install their own computer systems, but overall demand for these workers should remain fairly strong.

This same technology will further reduce demand for keypunch operators. The primary reason for this decline is the increased use of computer terminals and storage of data on disks and cassettes. As direct data entry techniques continue to become more efficient, the importance of punched cards as a form of input will diminish. Despite the anticipated decline in employment, many openings will occur each year as workers transfer to other occupations, retire, or die.

Earnings

Weekly earnings of keypunch operator trainees in private industry averaged around $200 in 1980, according to surveys conducted in urban areas by the Bureau of Labor Statistics and firms engaged in research on data processing occupations. Lead operators earned from $220 to $250 weekly.

Weekly earnings of beginning console operators averaged about $205. Experienced workers earned from $240 to $300, and lead operators earned from $300 to $375 weekly. Average weekly earnings for tape librarians in 1980 were $230.

In the Federal Government, console operators and keypunch operators without work experience started at about $140 a week in

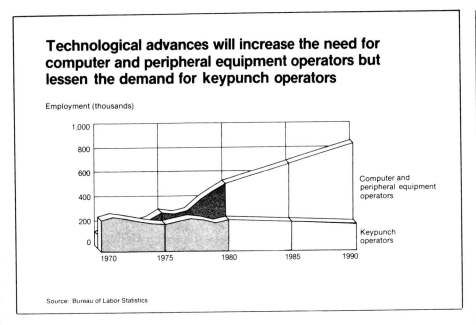

Technological advances will increase the need for computer and peripheral equipment operators but lessen the demand for keypunch operators

Source: Bureau of Labor Statistics

early 1981. Throughout the economy in 1980, console operators earned slightly more and keypunch operators earned slightly less than average earnings for all nonsupervisory workers in private industry, except farming.

Related Occupations

Other occupations in which workers organize data and process information on electronic equipment include secretaries and typists, printing typesetters and compositors, transcribing machine operators, and file clerks.

Sources of Additional Information

Further information on data processing careers is available from:

American Federation of Information Processing Societies, 1815 North Lynn St., Arlington, Va. 22209.

COMPUTER SERVICE TECHNICIANS

Nature of the Work

Computer systems play a vital role in our lives. They help us make telephone calls, receive paychecks on time, and reserve tickets for travel, hotels, and entertainment. In business and industry, computer systems perform countless tasks—from maintaining business records to controlling manufacturing processes.

A computer system consists of a central processing unit and additional equipment such as remote terminals and high-speed printers. Keeping this intricate equipment in good working order is the job of the computer service technician.

At regular intervals, computer service technicians (often called field engineers or customer engineers) service machines or systems to keep them operating efficiently. They routinely adjust, oil, and clean mechanical and electromechanical parts. They also check electronic equipment for loose connections and defective components or circuits.

When computer equipment breaks down, technicians must quickly find the cause of the failure and make repairs. Determining where in the system the malfunction has occurred is the most difficult part of the technician's job, and requires a logical, analytical mind as well as technical knowledge. As computer systems have grown more complex and networks of minicomputers (mini's) have developed, the potential for malfunctions also has grown.

Breakdowns can occur in the central processing unit itself, in one of the peripheral machines, such as a reader or a printer, in the remote mini's that are connected to the central unit, or in the cables or datacommunications hookups that connect these machines. To locate the cause of electronic failures, technicians use several kinds of tools, including voltmeters, ohmmeters, and oscilloscopes. They run special diagnostic programs that help pinpoint certain malfunctions. Although it may take several hours to locate a problem, fixing the equipment may take just a few minutes. To replace a faulty circuit board, solder a broken connection, or repair a mechanical part, technicians use a variety of handtools, including needle-nosed pliers, wirestrippers, and soldering equipment. The employer supplies tools and test equipment, but technicians are responsible for keeping them in good working order.

Computer technicians often help install new equipment. They lay cables, hook up electrical connections between machines, thoroughly test the new equipment, and correct any problems before the customer uses the machine.

Some technicians specialize in maintaining a particular computer model or system, or in doing a certain type of repair. For example, some technicians are experts in correcting problems caused by errors in the computer's internal programming.

Besides knowing how to use specialized tools and test equipment, computer technicians must be familiar with technical and repair manuals for each piece of equipment. They also must keep up with the technical information and revised maintenance procedures issued periodically by computer manufacturers.

Technicians keep a record of preventive maintenance and repairs on each machine they service. In addition, they fill out time and expense reports, keep parts inventories, and order parts.

Although technicians spend most of their time working on machines, they work with people also. They listen to customers' complaints, answer questions, and sometimes offer technical advice on ways to keep equipment in good condition. Experienced technicians often help train new technicians and sometimes have limited supervisory duties.

Working Conditions

Computer installations generally run around the clock and working time lost because of a breakdown can be very expensive. For this reason, technicians must be available to make emergency repairs at any time, day or night. Although the normal workweek is 40 hours, overtime is commonplace. The method of assigning overtime varies by employer. Some technicians are on call 24 hours a day. Others work rotating shifts—days one week, nights the next.

For most technicians, travel is local; they usually are not away from home overnight. Employers pay for travel, including reimbursement for job-related uses of the technician's car, as well as work-related education expenses.

Although some bending and lifting are necessary, the job is not strenuous. Work hazards are limited mainly to minor burns and electric shock, but these can be avoided if safety practices are followed.

Employment

In 1980, about 83,000 persons worked as computer service technicians. Most were employed by firms that provide maintenance services for a fee and by manufacturers of computer equipment. A small number were employed directly by organizations that have large computer installations.

Computer technicians generally work out of regional offices located in large cities, where computer equipment is concentrated.

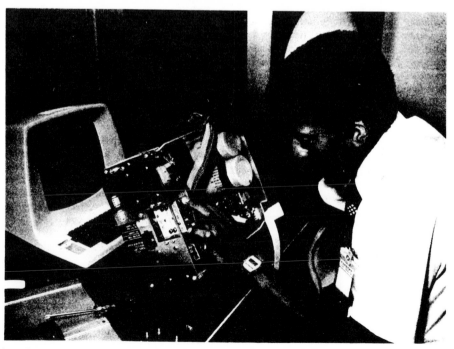

Locating the problem often is more difficult than making the repair.

Reprinted from *Occupational Outlook Handbook,* 1982-83, U.S. Department of Labor.

Most are assigned to several clients, depending on the technician's specialty and the type of equipment the user has. Workers with several accounts must travel from place to place to maintain these systems and to make emergency repairs. In some cases, more than one technician will share an account and service different parts of a system. In other cases, an experienced technician may be assigned to work full time at a client's installation in order to maintain all phases of that operation. Technicians who work for a nationwide organization must sometimes transfer to another city or State.

Training, Other Qualifications, and Advancement

Most employers require applicants for technician trainee jobs to have 1 to 2 years' post-high school training in basic electronics or electrical engineering. This training may be from a public or private vocational school, a college, or a junior college. Basic electronics training offered by the Armed Forces is excellent preparation for technician trainees.

A high school student interested in becoming a computer service technician should take courses in mathematics and physics. High school courses in electronics and computer programming also are helpful. Hobbies that involve electronics, such as operating ham radios or building stereo equipment, also provide valuable experience.

Besides technical training, applicants for trainee jobs must have good vision and normal color perception to work with small parts and color-coded wiring. Normal hearing is needed since some breakdowns are diagnosed by sound. Because technicians usually handle jobs alone, they must have the initiative to work without close supervision. Also important are a pleasant personality and neat appearance, since the work involves frequent contact with customers. Patience is an asset, because some malfunctions occur infrequently and are very difficult to pinpoint. In some companies, applicants must pass a physical examination. A security clearance may be required in cases where technicians regularly service machines located in restricted buildings, such as Federal Government installations engaged in classified activities.

Trainees usually attend company training centers for 3 to 6 months to learn elementary computer theory, computer math, and circuitry theory and to further their study of electronics. Classroom work is accompanied by practical training in operating computer equipment, doing basic maintenance, and using test equipment to locate malfunctions.

In addition to formal instruction, trainees must complete 6 months to 2 years of on-the-job training. At first, they work closely with experienced technicians, learning to maintain card readers, printers, and other machines that are relatively simple, but that have the basic mechanical and electronic features of a large computer system. As trainees gain experience, they work on more complex equipment.

Because manufacturers continually redesign equipment and develop new uses for computers, experienced technicians frequently must attend training sessions to keep up with these changes and to broaden their technical skills. Many technicians take advanced training to specialize in a particular computer system or type of repair. Instruction also may include programming, systems analysis, and other subjects that improve the technician's general knowledge of the computer field.

Experienced technicians with advanced training may become specialists or "troubleshooters" who help technicians throughout their territory diagnose difficult problems. They also may work with engineers in designing equipment and developing maintenance procedures. Technicians with leadership ability may become supervisors or service managers.

Most computer equipment operates on the same basic principles, but machines built by different companies may be unique in design and construction. For this reason, technicians may find it difficult to transfer between companies that maintain different brands of equipment. However, because of the pressing need for experienced technicians, many opportunities exist for well-qualified workers to transfer to other firms that handle the same type of computer hardware.

Training and experience in computer maintenance may also help qualify a technician for a job in equipment sales, programming, or management. (See the statements on programmers and manufacturers' salesworkers elsewhere in the *Handbook*.)

Job Outlook

Employment of computer technicians is expected to grow much faster than the average for all occupations through the 1980's. As the Nation's economy expands, more computer equipment will be used and many more technicians will be needed to install and maintain it. Business, government, and other organizations will buy, lease, or rent additional equipment to manage vast amounts of information, control manufacturing processes, and aid in scientific research. The development of new uses for computers in

fields such as education, medicine, and traffic control also will spur demand.

The very strong demand for computer technicians is related to the growing number of computers in operation and the geographic distribution of these computers. Continued reductions in the size and cost of computer hardware will bring the computer within reach of a rapidly increasing number of small organizations. As more and more of these small systems are installed, the amount of time technicians must spend traveling between clients will increase.

Employment of computer service technicians is much less likely to be affected by downturns in business activity than is the case in other fields. Because computer operations are rarely curtailed during economic slumps, employment of computer service technicians should remain relatively stable.

Earnings

Earnings of computer service technician trainees were about $270 a week in 1980, according to the limited information available. Fully trained workers earned about $385 a week, while senior level technicians with several years' experience earned between $430 and $575 a week.

Related Occupations

Workers in other occupations who repair and maintain the circuits and mechanical parts of electronic equipment include appliance repairers, automotive electricians, business machine repairers, electronic organ technicians, instrument repairers, radio repairers, radar mechanics, and television service technicians.

Sources of Additional Information

For general information on careers in computer maintenance, contact the personnel department of computer manufacturers and computer maintenance firms in your area. The State department of education in your State capital can furnish information about approved technical institutes, junior colleges, and other institutions offering postsecondary training in basic electronics. Additional information about these schools is available from:

U.S. Office of Education, Division of Vocational/ Technical Education, Washington, D.C. 20202.

Computer and Business Equipment Manufacturer's Association, 1828 L St. NW., Washington, D.C. 20036.

The State employment service office in your area may also be able to provide information about local job opportunities.

NEW OCCUPATIONS IN THE ROBOTIC AGE

New jobs and new occupations might emerge as a result of the new technology. Analysts generally agree that new jobs will be created with the coming of robots; but, as with potential worker displacement, estimates on what type of jobs and how many will be created is a subject of debate.

The introduction of robots into the workplace will create jobs in the programming, maintenance, and operation of robots. According to Peter Blake, "These will definitely be jobs not previously found on shop floors." Also, the increased use of robotic technology is creating demand for robotics engineers and manufacturing engineers experienced in robotic applications. Engineers with related specialties will also be in demand for research and development of robots by users as well as by robot manufacturers. In addition, successful use of robots in industry will require computer specialists to develop the proper software for applications.

According to Don Smith, Director of the Industrial Development Division of the Institute of Science and Technology at the University of Michigan, robotic maintenance workers will represent the largest number of new jobs. According to the Carnegie Mellon University study, different skills are required for operation and maintenance. While maintenance duties require more extensive retraining, operation or monitoring duties are essentially unskilled and are more easily picked up. The levels and skills required also differ according to the type and complexity of robots.

For persons involved in the operation of robots, elaborate retraining is unnecessary. Almost anyone can be taught to operate a robot with very minimal training. Typically, experienced maintenance people require a week of formal training to adapt their skills to routine servicing and monitoring of robots. Frequently, the robot manufacturers or vendors provide the training programs that give participants the necessary skills to maintain and operate robots. Workers are also often given on-the-job training of several weeks following the training programs. Some of the large robot users, such as General Motors, employ their own training specialists within the plant to insure that their workers have the skills to maintain robots and other types of electronic systems.

More extensive instruction is necessary to learn the skills associated with robot maintenance. Skill requirements in the primary stages of robot maintenance include knowledge of hydraulic valves, basic electricity, numerical controls, and other areas of general plant and machine maintenance. Although some of the courses needed to learn to maintain a robot are very technical, they do not require skills very different from those involved in maintaining other pieces of complex machinery, according to the Carnegie Mellon University study. Researchers of the study concluded that anyone who has experience in machine maintenance can be easily retrained to maintain robots.

Besides maintenance workers, programmers are also needed for developing software for robotic applications, and it is expected that computer software specialists for manufacturing systems will be much in demand. "It is in the software instructions that robots represent a state-of-the art development," says David Babson, publisher of the *Babson Weekly Staff Letter*.

In the engineering profession, a new manufacturing engineer will be in demand—the robotics specialist. This engineer must be capable of planning the robot installation of programmable machines, including robots, and the specifications for their capability and work environment and designing the production line around the capabilities of programmable automation.

Besides working on applications for industrial users, manufacturing engineers will be especially in demand at computer companies that enter the robot manufacturing market. According to David Babson, most computer firms, especially those in the mainframe business, have years of experience in software development, but they lack an intimate knowledge of machinery and how factory procedures differ from industry to industry.

New employment opportunities will be found not only in businesses that purchase and use robots but also in robot manufacturing companies. The robot manufacturing industry will employ between 60,000 and 100,000 persons by 1990, based on estimates done for the Society of Manufacturing Engineers. If the robot business expands, businesses that supply products to robot manufacturers will also grow. Robot manufacturers will employ persons chiefly in three areas—machine construction, computers, and software. Engineers will be needed, as well, to design and direct the assembly of robots, as mentioned above. In addition, personnel will be needed to market robots and provide customer services.

Retraining Workers

Probably a more controversial aspect of wide-scale adoption of robotic technology in industry, than even the potential number of workers affected, is worker retraining. Some see worker retraining as a natural and inevitable outcome of the robots' takeover of dull and dirty jobs on the production line. They describe the change in terms of transition rather than disruption. Others aren't so sure it will be that easy for workers. "There will be jobs taken over by the new robots, for that is their very nature. But perhaps the question is whether the robot is displacing or replacing," says Joseph Jablonowski the editor of *American Machinist*, in the November 1981 issue. Calling them "displaced" seems to imply these workers will still have jobs. When workers are displaced, the employer could reassign them to other, similar jobs, or retrain them for new jobs. When they are replaced, they are put out of work with no promises of retraining from anyone.

Reprinted from *Occupational Outlook Quarterly/Fall 1982*, U.S. Department of Labor.

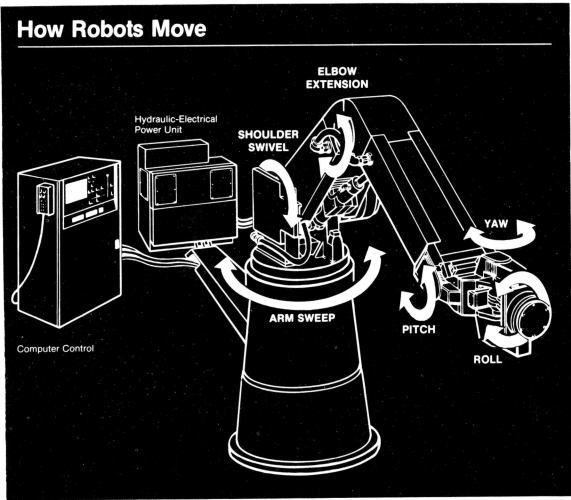

How Robots Move

ELBOW
EXTENSION

Hydraulic-Electrical
Power Unit

SHOULDER
SWIVEL

YAW

ARM SWEEP

PITCH

ROLL

Computer Control

courtesy Cincinnati Milacron

For those who see the robot coming in to replace workers, the question of who will retrain affected workers looms large. That this is an area of interest to labor is evidenced in the increasing interest of unions in issues concerning new technology. Indeed, Harley Shaiken sees this trend continuing and predicts that new technology will be "one of the central issues in collective bargaining in the 1980's." A comparative survey done by the industrial union department of the AFL-CIO of major collective bargaining agreements in manufacturing and nonmanufacturing in March 1980 shows that 14.1 percent of agreements they surveyed included provisions for worker retraining after the introduction of new technology.

The problem of retraining workers is complicated by the fact that generally the first workers to be displaced will be the most unskilled in the labor force. Dr. William Spurgeon, program manager of production research at the National Science Foundation articulates this dilemma: "Robots are here to stay and their number in factories will increase. People will be displaced. They can be retrained, but for what? Robots displace unskilled or semiskilled persons who don't have much training. What if these people cannot be trained for more skilled jobs? Just to say retraining is much too simple an answer. We need to look deeper than that."

The Carnegie Mellon University study notes that, for the most part, industry is not equipped to deal with the structur-

ally unemployed segment of the work force whose skills will no longer be needed. Workers in this section of the work force include people who have been trained but never hired and unskilled entry-level employees who have been displaced. Says the study, "...Although industry is assuming some of the responsibility for dealing with worker retraining, it cannot be held responsible for dealing with the entire problem of unemployability, especially where basic educational background is inadequate."

Although some companies who are adopting robots are making efforts to retrain displaced workers for new jobs, there have been no surveys done on how widespread these efforts are in industry. So far, most programs to retrain workers to work with robots have been provided by employers in conjunction with robot manufacturers or vendors.

Community colleges and vocational schools are also developing programs to train workers to operate and maintain robots. "Meeting the Demand for Robotics Technicians," published in the Summer 1981 issue of *Robotics Today*, describes a program established at Macomb County Community College in Warren, Michigan, to train robotics technicians. The Macomb program, now 3 years old, was the first of its kind in the country. Similar programs at other educational institutions for retraining of workers could prove useful to both the community colleges and workers.

The Carnegie Mellon University study does suggest one

avenue of retraining that can help—vocational education. "Vocational education is another mechanism which has been used to generate the needed training and education to adapt to advanced technology," says the report. This suggestion raises the question of what role, if any, the government should play in recommending or taking action for worker retraining.

Even the business press has become conscious of the potential problems of worker displacement and worker retraining. *Business Week* of June 9, 1980, featured an editorial, "When the Robots Move In," that pointed out that while managers of U.S. industry have begun to realize that robots will take over an increasing number of jobs in the coming decade, they still think of it as a technological challenge rather than as a problem also of retraining and reemploying of workers. "It would be pure wishful thinking," the editorial said, "to assume that the conversion can be made painlessly and that the problem of displaced workers will solve itself. As the robots move in, human workers will have to be retrained and shifted to jobs that do not represent demotions. This is fairly easy to arrange when the robots are taking over only the most dangerous and distasteful jobs in industry. It will be far harder when automation starts replacing workers in light assembly operations."

And to the editors, the solution does not lie solely with government programs or public education. They suggest that "U.S. companies should decide what sort of retraining they can offer and how they can break down and restructure jobs to provide work for those who cannot be reeducated."

Obviously, there are no simple answers to these questions. But, when the business press starts posing such questions, one has to believe there may be real problems behind the concerns. An appropriate observation was made by Hesh Weiner in his review of *Automatic Unemployment* in the *Business and Society Review*. He conjectured: "It appears, for the moment, that the computer, built to answer questions posed by people, has raised some tough questions that people themselves will have to answer." This is undoubtedly true; and perhaps the time to start is now.

THE JOB MARKET FOR ENGINEERS: RECENT CONDITIONS AND FUTURE PROSPECTS

by Douglas Braddock

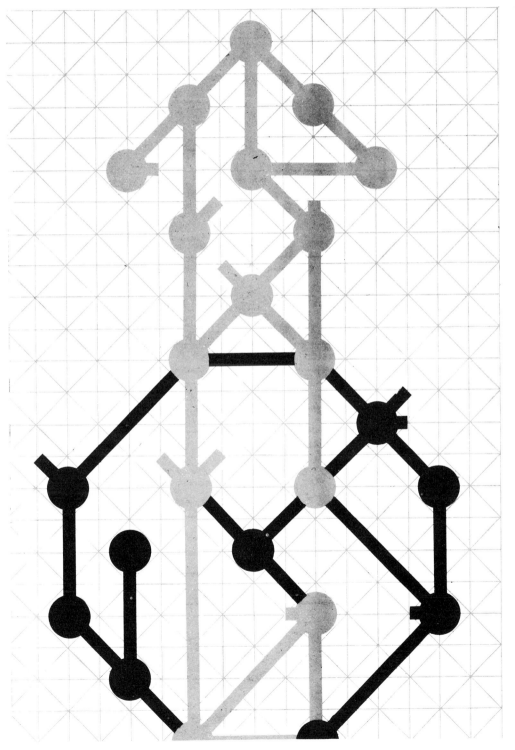

During the last few years, reports about shortages of engineers have been frequent, and many observers have expressed concern that the shortages may intensify. Employers complain that they cannot find the engineers they need; the Defense Department doubts that enough engineers will be available in the future to meet defense needs, and others fear that the United States will be unable to compete economically with other countries unless we produce more engineers. Even though the 1981–82 recession dampened the demand for engineers in most specialties, many observers continue to believe that future shortages will endanger national defense and hinder the technological and economic competitiveness of the United States. Contrary to these expressions of anxiety, however, actual shortages in the past few years appear to have been limited to certain specialties; and the latest BLS projections indicate an overall balance between supply and requirements for the rest of the 1980's. In examining current and potential shortages, several distinct points must be dealt with: What a shortage is, the evidence for a current shortage, the evidence for an adequate supply, and the assumptions that lead to a projected shortage.

What Is a Shortage?

Employers, workers, professional associations, education planners, training officials and other observers use various definitions when they claim that a shortage exists in a particular occupation. In traditional economic terms, however, a shortage means that sufficient workers are not available and willing to work at the existing wage. Raising wages should, therefore, eliminate the shortage because higher wages

Douglas Braddock is a labor economist in the Division of Occupational Outlook, BLS.

Reprinted from *Occupational Outlook Quarterly/Summer 1983*. U.S. Department of Labor.

"Services of engineers are vital to meeting national goals such as maintaining a strong economy, increasing economic productivity, maintaining technological leadership, and providing a strong national defense."

would attract more people into the occupation. However, some conditions may cause shortages to persist even when wages rise. For example, a lengthy training period—such as that needed for engineers—may cause delays in supply adjustments.

An increase in relative salaries naturally annoys and inconveniences employers and the increase itself is what many employers characterize as a shortage. Employers who do not raise salaries cannot fill all their vacancies. For those who do, the use of engineers in some marginal activities is no longer profitable. Certain employers, however, may have constraints on their ability to raise engineers' salaries—for example, universities with uniform salary scales for all disciplines or government agencies with rigid civil service pay scales. For these employers, a rise in relative salaries results in a genuine shortage because they do not pay the new prevailing wage.

The term shortage is used in several ways other than the inability to find enough workers at the prevailing wage. One is a policy goal shortage; that is, a situation in which simultaneously meeting the goals of numerous national policies requires or will require more engineers than are currently employed or are likely to be produced in the future. Services of engineers are vital to meeting national goals such as maintaining a strong economy, increasing economic productivity, maintaining technological leadership, and providing a strong national defense.

The Recent Job Market for Engineers
It is difficult to determine whether or not there has been a shortage of engineers in recent years because data collection programs do not gather information about job vacancies that would quantify shortages in specific occupations. However, information on sala-

ries, unemployment, and transfers out of the occupation and surveys of employers and working engineers can assist in an evaluation of the market for engineers.

The best available indicator of market conditions is salaries. Although an increase in salaries relative to other occupations is not in itself proof of a shortage, one is unlikely to occur without some bidding up of salaries. Therefore, one question to ask when trying to determine if a shortage exists is "Are wages of engineers increasing

more rapidly than those of other workers?" This question in turn can be asked several ways:

• How do starting salaries for engineers compare with starting salaries for selected occupations that require a college degree and for all men college graduates?

• And how do salaries for experienced engineers compare with salaries for experienced workers in selected occupations that require a college degree and for all men college graduates?

The chart and tables 1 and 2 provide

Photo by General Dynamics

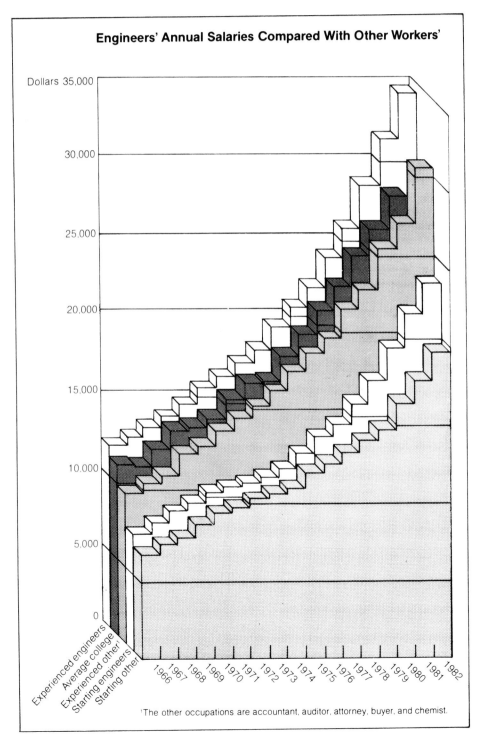

Engineers' Annual Salaries Compared With Other Workers'

¹The other occupations are accountant, auditor, attorney, buyer, and chemist.

an answer to all these questions. Note that only men's salaries are given for college graduates because until recently almost all engineers were men.

As the chart and table 1 show, the starting salary of engineers relative to the average starting salaries of five other professional occupations—accountants, auditors, attorneys, buyers, and chemists—covered by the Bureau's annual survey of professional, administrative, technical, and clerical pay has increased substantially since the early- and mid-1970's, a period of modest demand. In fact, the relative advantage of beginning engineers is greater now than in the late 1960's, a period of high demand for engineers.

Experienced engineers, however, have not seen their salaries change noticeably compared to the other groups since the mid-1970's (see table 2), or even since the early 1960's.

These differing trends for starting salaries and for salaries of experienced engineers are consistent with a market for new graduates that has seen them in short supply since the late 1970's while experienced engineers have not been.

Another possible measure of shortage is the unemployment rate. A decrease in the rate would be consistent with a shortage, as employers expand recruiting effort and lower hiring standards. Table 3 shows that the unemployment rate for engineers in recent years has been between 1.2 and 2.4 percent, higher than the 0.7-percent rate in 1966–68, when there also was much concern about engineering shortages, but below the high of 2.9 percent in 1971. It is, thus, consistent with a slight shortage but not a severe one.

The frequency with which people leave an occupation can also indicate a shortage. For example, if engineers are in short supply, one would expect employers to take steps necessary to keep engineers from transferring to other

". . . the relative advantage of beginning engineers is greater now than in the late 1960's, a period of high demand for engineers."

occupations, thus reducing the rate at which engineers leave the field. During 1980, 4.4 percent of all engineers left engineering to enter another occupation. This rate is much lower than the 8.9-percent rate for all occupations, but only slightly lower than the 5.1-percent rate for all professional and technical workers. Such a transfer rate may be consistent with modest shortages, but not with critical shortages. Comparable BLS data are not available for earlier periods. However, National Science Foundation data for engineers with the BS degree show that 3.7 percent left engineering annually, on average, during 1972–78, and 4.3 percent during 1968–72, periods when few shortages were reported. These

rates, while not strictly comparable, indicate that separations in 1980 were not substantially lower than in non-shortage periods.

Another way to study labor market conditions for engineers is simply to ask employers whether or not there is a shortage. The National Science Foundation asked 225 firms in October 1981 about labor market conditions for new entrants to scientific and engineering occupations. This survey found probable shortages in computer, electrical, electronic, and petroleum engineering; a rough balance in industrial, chemical, and mechanical engineering; and a probable surplus in civil engineering. One byproduct of the survey was confirmation of the lack of agreement on

what constitutes an adequate supply. Some employers who had met all their hiring goals still reported a shortage if they had to offer higher salaries than they had planned, or had to hire graduates with a lower class rank than desired. Only 3 percent of those reporting a shortage of scientists and engineers said they had reduced production or research and development (R&D) as a result of shortages.

In August 1982, the National Science Foundation repeated this survey. It found that employers reported fewer shortages of engineers than in the previous year. Over 50 percent of the firms that answered both the October 1981 and August 1982 surveys said that hiring new entrants had become easier.

Table 1. Starting salaries of engineers relative to starting salaries of other professional occupations and average salaries of all college-educated men, 1963-82

| | Ratio of engineers' starting salaries to: | |
| | Average starting salaries of 5 professional occupations | Men 18 years and over with 4 or more years of college |
Year		
1963	—	.751
1964	—	.747
1965	—	—
1966	1.128	.696
1967	1.124	.753
1968	1.132	.738
1969	1.098	.728
1970	1.088	.753
1971	1.073	.758
1972	1.062	.718
1973	1.060	.695
1974	1.081	.737
1975	1.075	.716
1976	1.107	.717
1977	1.107	.693
1978	1.136	.703
1979	1.167	.702
1980	1.184	.740
1981	1.211	.771
1982	1.193	—

Source: Bureau of Labor Statistics.

Table 2. Salaries of experienced engineers relative to salaries of experienced professionals and college-educated men, 1963-82

| | Ratio of experienced engineers' salaries to: | |
| | Experienced workers in 5 professional occupations | Men 18 years and over with 4 or more years of college |
Year		
1963	—	1.141
1964	—	1.120
1965	—	—
1966	1.205	1.056
1967	1.194	1.115
1968	1.191	1.072
1969	1.140	1.046
1970	1.132	1.084
1971	1.130	1.103
1972	1.123	1.063
1973	1.127	1.056
1974	1.112	1.111
1975	1.110	1.077
1976	1.113	1.069
1977	1.117	1.047
1978	1.112	1.059
1979	1.139	1.051
1980	1.122	1.085
1981	1.117	1.113
1982	1.123	—

Source: Bureau of Labor Statistics.

Table 3. Engineers' unemployment rates, 1962-83

Year	Rate
1963	1.2%
1964	1.5
1965	1.1
1966	0.7
1967	0.7
1968	0.7
1969	0.8
1970	2.2
1971	2.9
1972	1.9
1973	1.0
1974	1.4
1975	2.6
1976	2.0
1977	1.3
1978	1.2
1979	1.2
1980	1.3
1981	1.5
1982	2.4

Note: The standard error of the 1982 rate is 4.4%. Other years' standard errors may vary slightly.
Source: Bureau of Labor Statistics.

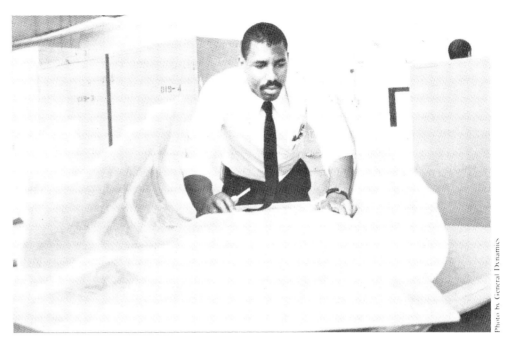

Photo by General Dynamics

Overall, the available data—ranging from salary information to reports of dissatisfaction—indicate that there probably have been shortages of some types of engineers in recent years, but the shortages have not been severe. Substantial evidence exists for shortages of recent engineering graduates in certain fields. Newly graduated electronics, computer design, and petroleum engineers have been in much higher demand than other engineers and probably have been in short supply. Little evidence exists, however, for shortages of experienced engineers.

The Job Outlook for Engineers

Two separate sets of projections are needed in order to forecast a future labor market: Projections of demand and projections of supply. Numerous recent articles, public statements, and reports about future shortages of engineers from business associations and from Defense Department officials and other sources deal primarily with projected demand. One report in particular—Technical Employment Projections of Professionals and Paraprofessionals by the American Electronics Association—has often been cited as projecting a very large increase in requirements and has been the basis for much alarm over future shortages. The American Electronics Association conducted a survey of companies in the electronics industry in late 1980. The survey requested respondents to project the number of engineers and those in other technical occupations that they would require in 1981, 1983, and 1985 based on their judgment in December 1980. Overall, very high growth was projected for engineering and other technical occupations. For example, requirements for electronics/electrical engineers were projected to increase 78 percent from 1980 to 1985. Some observers incorrectly applied these pro-

jections to employment of engineers in all industries and concluded that very large numbers of engineers and other technical personnel would be needed by 1985. Furthermore, the numbers needed were much larger than the educational system could produce.

This report probably overstated future requirements because of biases inherent in the methodology. Projections based on company plans are generally upwardly biased because companies plan for and expect growth in sales and, therefore, in employment. Not only may the companies overstate industry growth, but many companies plan to increase their market share, even though one company can only increase its share at another's expense. Such overly optimistic estimates of future needs are particularly striking in defense-related fields because, while only one firm can be awarded each major defense contract, each firm is likely to assume that it will get the contract when responding to a survey. Another drawback of this survey is that most people tend to see the future as very much like the present. These projections of rapid growth may, therefore, be extrapolations of the rapid growth of the past few years rather than a realistic assessment of long-term trends.

In contrast to many predictions of shortages, BLS projects that require-

ments for engineers will be in rough balance with the supply, on average, for the rest of the 1980's. This projection was developed as part of the Bureau's regular occupational outlook projections that are prepared every 2 years for vocational guidance, education planning, and other purposes. The general assumptions contained in the Bureau's projections include growth in the economy sufficient to reduce unemployment, increased productivity, and increased defense expenditures.

Between 120,000 and 136,000 openings for engineers are projected annually over the 1980's depending on the rate of growth of the gross national product and changes in its composition. Replacement needs are expected to account for about three-fourths of the openings as employers replace engineers who transfer to other occupations or stop working. Growth will account for about one-fourth of the projected openings. Actual growth is projected to be 2.5 to 3.2 percent a year, because of increasing investment in industrial plants and sharply rising defense spending. The projected rate of growth is faster than the average projected for all occupations. It is actually lower than the 4.7-percent annual growth achieved over the 1976–81 period.

The National Center for Education

"During the 1980's, the United States will be turning out twice as many bachelor's degree graduates in engineering as in the 1960's, a decade of rapid economic growth . . ."

Statistics projects that an average of 74,000 bachelor's degrees in engineering and engineering technology will be awarded annually over the 1980–90 period. (There were 75,000 in the 1980–81 academic year.) If entry rates observed during the 1970's—averaging about 80 percent—continue, roughly 60,000 new engineering graduates can be expected to seek engineering jobs annually. In the past, almost all recent engineering graduates who sought jobs received offers because they are preferred by employers for many engineering jobs. This preference is not likely to change during the 1980's, so all available recent engineering graduates, about 60,000 annually, are expected to find engineering jobs. As a result, between 44 and 50 percent of the projected 120,000 to 136,000 job openings during the 1980's could be filled by those graduates.

This might indicate a potential shortage; however, during 1980, only about 44 percent of those who entered engineering were recent engineering graduates. Most of the other entrants were transfers from other occupations—most likely people with previous experience or training in engineering or a related occupation. Some entrants were recent science and mathematics graduates, immigrant engineers, and persons over 55 who had not worked the previous year. Therefore, if the supply of new engineering graduates maintains current levels and if roughly the same percentage seek engineering jobs as was the case in the 1970's, no major imbalances will occur.

Potential Problems

Even though the BLS projections indicate a rough overall balance between requirements and supply, there are still some potential problems related to future engineering employment and education.

• Foremost among these problems are concerns over shortages of engineering faculty. About 10 percent of engineering faculty jobs were vacant in the fall of 1980, according to the National Science Foundation. Because employment conditions for new BS engineering graduates have been so good recently, while salaries in academia have reportedly not kept pace, the number of Ph.D. candidates in engineering has declined. Further, high demand for engineering Ph.D.'s in industry has induced many new Ph.D.'s in engineering to work there rather than in an academic setting. Many people conclude that if the number of new Ph.D.'s remains low and industry continues to outbid engineering schools for them, faculty shortages could seriously curtail the number of new engineers. However, according to the Bureau's projections, future bachelor's degree recipients in engineering need only remain at the 1981 level of 75,000 for supply and demand to be in rough balance.

• Related to the fear of a faculty shortage are concerns over the quality of engineering education, in part because of the large proportion of foreign nationals—some of whom are not proficient in English—hired as new faculty in recent years. In addition, laboratory equipment is scarce and obsolete at many universities.

• While the Bureau projects an overall balance, on average, over the decade, imbalances over short periods of time and among specialties are inevitable, given the nature of the engineers' labor market. Most engineers are directly or indirectly involved in producing goods such as industrial machinery and other producer durables, and buildings, factories, and other structures—products for which demand fluctuates widely over the business cycle. Another large group of engineers is involved with producing military hardware or doing related R&D. Defense spending has fluctuated widely, directly affecting the demand for engineers, and may continue to fluctuate over the longer run, even though in the short run it is expected to increase.

• The lead time to turn high school graduates (assuming they have the appropriate high school courses) into engineering graduates is 4 years. Alternative sources of supply, such as transfers from other fields, make adjustments possible, but there are limits to how rapidly supply can be increased or decreased. Engineering has a great many subdivisions and specializations. An engineer's experience is often limited to one or a few specializations, and employers, when seeking experienced engineers, often have narrow hiring specifications. Therefore, mobility between specializations to bring about adjustments in supply and demand is impeded.

• Many areas of engineering are characterized by rapidly changing technologies. In these areas, there clearly will not be sufficient engineers with formal training or experience. It is unrealistic to expect that the educational system or government planners will anticipate needs in a technology that may not yet exist or is only in the early stages of development. Therefore, needs have to be met by training engineers from related specializations.

Despite these destabilizing conditions, employers have generally been able to accomplish engineering goals. It seems probable that this will also be the case in the future. During the 1980's, the United States will be turning out about twice as many bachelor's degree graduates in engineering as in the 1960's, a decade of rapid economic growth, high defense spending, and a space program that put an astronaut on the moon. **ထ**

ENVIRONMENTAL CAREERS

Chemist, Wastewater Treatment

The chemist in a wastewater treatment plant analyzes samples of streams, raw and treated wastewater, sludge and other byproducts of the wastewater treatment process to determine the efficiency of the plant processes and to insure that plant effluents meet local, State, and Federal requirements. The chemist decides what tests are needed and develops workable testing procedures to obtain the information in a minimum amount of time.

The chemist conducts highly specialized and complex chemical, bacteriological, and physical analyses of wastewater and samples. Some of these samples are taken within the plant before, during, and following treatment. These chemists test samples taken from major users of the treatment plant in order to monitor and regulate waste discharges into the sewer and treatment systems and to make surcharge assessments.

Often the sample or test solution is a complex mixture of many compounds and elements and the identification of a specific element can require many hours of extensive separation work to remove interfering constituents. These procedures may involve many identification procedures and the use of sophisticated equipment.

Chemists may specialize in testing that requires special instruments such as the gas chromotograph, the atomic absorption spectrophotometer, or the infrared spectrophotometer. The chemist must be able to develop new techniques to use the equipment and also make adjustments and repairs on these complex electronic instruments.

Another important responsibility of the chemist is to identify problems in the wastewater treatment and to develop new procedures in the use of the equipment and the laboratory in order that they may be fully utilized.

Chemists also take part in special research and studies on plant operations and the treatment unit processes.

A chemist must be able to work independently and plan and organize the work efficiently. In most plants, the chemist also supervises one or more laboratory technicians.

Working in a laboratory may require standing for long periods and exposure to fumes, odors, and toxic substances.

Job Requirements

Most of these chemists have baccalaureate degrees with major work in chemistry, biochemistry, or a closely related field. Some employers also require 2 years of laboratory experience or an equivalent combination of experience and training. In some laboratories, additional course work in instrumentation is needed to operate the specialized equipment.

In smaller laboratories, high school gradution plus college-level courses in chemistry, biology, and bacteriology might be accepted as the minimum educational background.

Reprinted from *Environmental Protection Careers Guidebook*, U.S. Department of Labor and U.S. Environmental Protection Agency, 1980.

In addition to the academic preparation, the chemist needs a thorough knowledge of the treatment processes and the pertinent local, State, and Federal requirements and regulations. This knowledge is usually obtained on the job.

Certification is not always required. However, in larger plants chemists are encouraged to become certified and it is usually a requirement for advancement. With certification, a chemist could advance to the position of assistant superintendent or superintendent of a treatment plant.

Opportunities

Federal legislation requires that local governments control water pollution and safeguard public health and welfare. It is anticipated that chmists will continue to be in demand to analyze wastewater samples and insure that treatment processes and effluents meet current government requirements. Recent legislation requiring users to pay their fair share of the cost of wastewater treatment has increased monitoring of commercial and industrial establishments to see that they do not exceed the effluent limitations established. Increased sampling requirements have placed greater demands on laboratories to analyze these samples.

Laboratory Technician, Wastewater Treatment

The laboratory technician in a wastewater treatment plant performs routine chemical, biochemical, and physical analyses of samples taken from streams, raw and treated wastewater, sludge and other byproducts of the sewage treatment process, in order to monitor the characteristics of the wastewater and to measure how efficiently the treatment processes are working.

The technician collects the samples before, during, and following treatment and takes them to the laboratory for analysis. For routine tests, the technician sets up, adjusts, and operates the laboratory equipment and instrumentation such as microscopes, centrifuges, balances, scales, ovens, and other equipment in order to analyze the samples. The technician may assist the chemist in performing more difficult tests which use sophisticated equipment such as the infrared, ultraviolet, visible, and atomic absorption spectrophotometers; the gas chromatograph; and the total carbon analyzer.

In some areas, laboratory technicians also analyze samples of wastewater before it enters the collection system of the treatment plant. This is increasingly important to meet local and Federal pollution control requirements and to be sure that industry pays its fair share of treatment costs.

Today, technicians perform a variety of quantitative and qualitative analyses on wastewater for such characteristics as color, turbidity, pH, alkalinity, hardness, nitrogen, oxygen demand, chlorine residual, and other information. They also prepare the media and set up the equipment for other bacteriological tests to be performed by the chemist or microbiologist.

Careful, accurate records of test results are important to make precise determinations. An interest in and ability to do detailed exacting work are a must. Technicians must also be able to work well with other plant personnel; they often work under the close supervision of a chemist.

Technicians may be required to stand for long periods of time in the laboratory and are sometimes subject to unpleasant odors, fumes, and toxic and potential disease-producing substances.

Job Requirements

There are a number of community colleges that offer 2-year programs in pollution abatement control. A typical such program includes instruction in wastewater unit processes and waste management, as well as biology, chemistry, English, mathematics, and physics. A plant practicum is sometimes required, which gives the student additional training in program-related employment. This program prepares a student to perform all necessary analytical tests, both bacteriological and chemical, which are employed in a wastewater plant. With this training, the student receives an associate arts degree which could later be applied toward a bachelor's degree. This training also prepares the student for field work including inspections and collecting samples, or even responsibility for a complete wastewater treatment plant, or for some limited portion of the treatment.

Most employers consider graduation from high school, supplemented by 2 years of college-level courses in chemistry or the biological sciences, a good background for working in a treatment plant laboratory. In some cases, a portion of the educational requirement may be met with an equivalent combination of training and experience. On the other hand, it is not unusual for someone with a baccalaureate degree in chemistry or biology to work as a technician.

The technician should have a good knowledge of the unit processes used in the plant, industrial waste characterization and quantity evaluation, theory and techniques of qualitative and quantitative environmental chemistry, and instrumentation and analytical techniques. He/she should have practical experience in modern laboratory methods and techniques, and skill in the proper use of the various kinds of laboratory equipment.

Opportunities

The anticipated growth of new treatment plants and expansion of existing facilities should mean a continued need for laboratory technicians.

With additional education, a laboratory technician could become a chemist or move into a supervisory position. This laboratory experience would also be helpful for employment in other laboratories with local and Federal regulatory agencies or in private industry.

There will probably be some openings for laboratory technicians to staff new plants, and to replace technicians lost through normal attrition.

Engineering Technician

Engineering technicians assist professional engineers in a variety of office and field work related to pollution control projects. These technicians apply technical engineering skills to various projects, such as the preparation and review of plans and specifications for the construction of water distribution systems, swimming pools, purification plants, and wastewater treatment facilities. They work on projects dealing with large ecosystems, or they may specialize in one area such as air, noise, or water pollution control.

Beginning technicians perform limited measuring, computing, drafting, plan review, and inspection duties. For example, technicians review construction details such as sizes of units, capacities, length of pipelines, unit locations, and other information. They compute quantities of materials required and costs of repairs.

Other office duties include maintaining various records related to inspections and progress of projects, answering inquiries concerning technical details of the work, and filing construction plans, blueprints, and other documents.

In some positions, engineering technicians work outside much of the time. For example, they conduct stream surveys and collect water samples, record flow measurements, set up sampling equipment, and collect other water pollution control information. Sometimes they conduct field surveys and set stakes and monuments in preparation for construction projects. They may serve as surveyor helpers on a survey team or even perform manual labor in clearing brush or weeds.

Other duties include such activities as inspecting public water supplies, investigating complaints of pollution or environmental crises, like a fish kill, or testifying in court concerning pollution problems. In some positions, technicians assist in training water and wastewater-treatment-plant operators.

A person in this work should have an aptitude for mathematics and science and enjoy technical work. Attention to detail with a high degree of accuracy is also important. This work could require some travel.

Communication skills are essential in working with engineers, other professionals, and the public to explain pollution control requirements and to answer questions.

Job Requirements

Technician positions require varying combinations of education and experience. In some cases, 2 years specialized experience in basic engineering meets the minimum requirement. Other employers require the completion of as many as 2 years of college with basic courses in engineering and drafting and, in addition, 2 years of experience in drafting or engineering.

In high school, courses in mathematics, science, and mechanical drawing are important. In addition, specialized training in drafting or engineering technology is required. This can usually be obtained in vocational or technical schools or at the college level.

In general, technicians must have a working knowledge of drafting techniques, plan design, and layout procedures. Mathematics courses should include algebra, geometry, and trigonometry as well as mechanical drawing. Technicians must develop skill in the use of drafting instruments and be able to use calculators and scales.

Curricula in junior and community colleges prepare students for technician work and graduates of a 2-year training program can usually apply these credits toward a bachelor's degree. In order to advance above technician-level duties it would probably be necessary to complete requirements for a bachelor's degree in engineering.

Opportunities

With experience, technicians can advance to higher level duties or perhaps supervise subordinate technicians.

Construction and repair of water distribution systems, water purification plants, wastewater treatment facilities, and other pollution control projects should continue strong throughout the eighties. Some technicians will be needed to work with engineers in order to keep up with the increased construction. Some engineering firms hire temporary and part-time engineering technicians to meet production deadlines.

Engineering technicians are employed by Federal, State, and local water pollution control agencies. Others work for consulting engineering firms, architectural firms, municipal treatment plants, and some business and industrial firms concerned with pollution control.

Engineering Aide

An engineering aide performs simple technical tasks and manual work either with a field survey party or in a drafting room, office, or laboratory, under supervision of an engineer, drafter, or technician.

An aide may assist in determining elevations and laying out construction sites, measure distances between survey points, set stakes, and cut and clear brush from the line of survey. An aide often performs manual tasks such as carrying tools, stakes, and other equipment to the work site.

In the drafting room or office, the aide may trace maps and plans, copy notes, and make simple engineering computations. Aides also perform simple office duties such as filing plans and specifications, answering the telephone, and running errands.

A person in this work should be physically capable, have good eyesight, be able to follow instructions, and be dependable. Good eye-hand coordination and finger and manual dexterity are important to perform both drafting and field work.

Accuracy, attention to detail, and the temperament to perform routine, repetitive work are required.

Job Requirements

The aide is usually a high school graduate and receives on-the-job training in specific duties. In high school, mathematics, science, and drafting are valuable courses and provide a good foundation for a person interested in this type of work. Shop courses are also useful.

There are many technical courses available in vocational-technical schools and junior or community colleges that would be helpful to a person wanting to enter this field.

Usually, no experience is required. Workers can often learn these duties in a few months through on-the-job training.

Opportunities

A very limited number of engineering aides are employed by engineering firms, water purification plants, wastewater treatment plants, and government agencies.

With experience, an aide can sometimes advance to technician level duties. In most cases, however, additional technical training is required.

MORE BASICS:
EDUCATION AND TRAINING

INTRODUCTION AND OVERVIEW

*The most formidable challenge will be to train
people to work in the information society. Jobs
will become available, but who will possess the
high-tech skills to fill them? Not today's
graduates, who cannot manage simple arithmetic
or write basic English. And certainly not the
unskilled, unemployed dropouts who cannot even
find work in the old sunset industries.*
—John Naisbitt, *Magatrends*

Having decided on a job or career, you will next
want to acquire the necessary qualifications, usually
through formal education or training.

Chapter 7 contains several resources that will
acquaint you with the requirements of a variety of
occupations, and with several ways of meeting those
requirements. Included in these resources is an up-to-
date and authoritative listing of apprenticeship
programs, which are becoming increasingly
important. Shortages of skilled personnel in the
computer, cable television, and non-traditional
telephone industries are so great that the Communications Workers Union has begun the first
apprenticeship program in its history.

THE RESOURCES

"Math and Your Career"

"Science and Your Career"

"Input for Computer Workers: Education and
Training for Computer Occupations"

"How To Get Credit for What You Already Know"

"Apprenticeship"

REFERENCE

The *Occupational Outlook for College Graduates,
1983-84 Edition,* prepared by the U.S. Department of
Labor's Bureau of Labor Statistics, is a guide to career
opportunities in a broad range of occupations for
which a college degree is, or is becoming, the usual
background for employment. Each occupational
statement presents information on the nature of the
work; places of employment; education, skills, and
abilities required for entry; employment outlook;
related occupations; and earnings. If you cannot find a
copy in your library, you may obtain one by writing to
the Superintendent of Documents, Washington, DC
20402.

FUTUREVISION 6

His fordship Mustapha Mond! The eyes of the saluting students almost popped out of their heads. Mustapha Mond! The Resident Controller for Western Europe! One of the Ten World Controllers. One of the Ten . . . and he sat down on the bench with the D.H.C., he was going to stay, to stay, yes, and actually talk to them . . . straight from the horse's mouth. Straight from the mouth of Ford himself.

—*Aldous Huxley,* Brave New World

SCIENCE AND YOUR CAREER

by Gail M. Martin

The discoveries of science touch every area of our lives. Nearly every home has a central heating system, electric lights, a telephone, and a TV—all scientific discoveries put to everyday use. Many homes have electronic calculators, home computers and video games —products of our electronic age. Some of our hobbies and forms of recreation also involve science. Photography, gardening, biking, or sailing all use some scientific principles.

The scientific world is a vast one in which there are always as many questions remaining as there are answers found: What causes hurricanes and can we control them? How can we harness the great energy in ocean waves and tides? These are only two of the many questions that perplex oceanographers who study our oceans. Astronomers, who investigate the universe, probe similar complex and unanswered questions: Will the universe expand forever? How do stars form? Is there life on other planets? For every scientific discipline, there is a string of unanswered questions and unsolved problems. Hundreds of thousands of scientists are employed to unravel these mysteries.

Not everyone can be a scientist—and not everyone wants to be—but some understanding of science can be useful in other careers and for other reasons. A scientific background helps develop logical thinking and scientific investigation can be intriguing. Learning, for

Gail M. Martin is an OOQ staff writer.

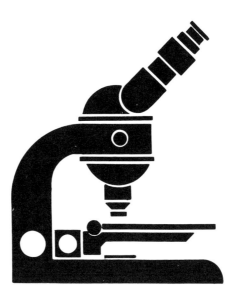

example, why days are shorter in winter than summer can be interesting and fun. A knowledge of science also helps us understand some of the forces affecting our lives. Voters, for instance, must make informed decisions about the worth of proposed scientific and technical projects that their tax dollars will support.

Finally, if all other reasons don't convince you, consider these facts: Most high schools require a minimum of 1 year of science to graduate, and most colleges mandate at least this much for entry into nonscience curriculums; scientific and technical courses require considerably more. Employers and college admissions officials look favorably upon students who have taken difficult courses, such as science.

Careers in the Scientific World

Science is related to many occupations. Workplaces that serve as scientist's laboratories range from the wheat fields of Kansas to capsules under the sea and in outer space. Branches of science overlap each other, and, sometimes, there are many subdivisions within one branch. Major branches of science include the life sciences, the study of living organisms and the physical sciences, the study of inorganic matter. All of these are interrelated, since all deal with nature or natural phenomena. All scientists study nature, then, seeking explanations for natural phenomena and ways to utilize their discoveries.

Life sciences. Since each living organism is part of a larger interacting system, biology is intertwined with other important fields of study. Knowledge of biology is central to understanding much of the world and life about us. Scientists working in the biological sciences work in many areas, including microbiology, the study of microorganisms; botany, the study of plant life; and zoology, the study of animal life. Each branch is subdivided even further. Specialists in zoology, for example, include ornithologists, who study birds; herpetologists, who study snakes and reptiles; and entomologists, who study insects.

Biology is also an integral part of many other careers. More than 200 oc-

Reprinted from *Occupational Outlook Quarterly/Summer 1983*, U.S. Department of Labor.

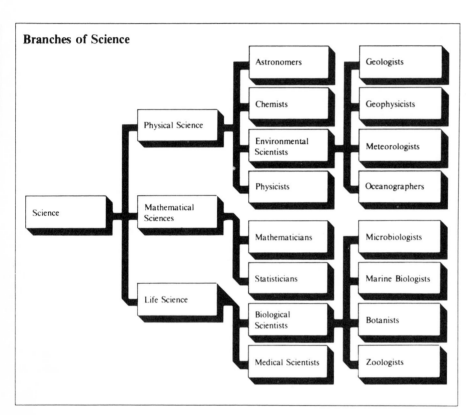

Branches of Science

Science → Physical Science → Astronomers, Chemists, Environmental Scientists, Physicists → Geologists, Geophysicists, Meteorologists, Oceanographers

Mathematical Sciences → Mathematicians, Statisticians

Life Science → Biological Scientists, Medical Scientists → Microbiologists, Marine Biologists, Botanists, Zoologists

cupations in the medical sciences require knowledge and study of biology. For example, physicians, dentists, and veterinarians rely on their knowledge of biology, as do physical therapists and emergency medical technicians.

A background in biology is important for many jobs in the field of agriculture. Agronomists develop practical applications for discoveries in plant and soil science to produce high quality food. Crop scientists study the genetics, breeding, and management of field crops, as well as ensure quality production of seed. Soil scientists use soil physics, soil chemistry, and soil microbiology to enhance soil fertility and the growth of plants.

Physical sciences. Scientists who work in the physical sciences work principally in the many branches of chemistry and

physics. Chemists, who make up one of the largest science occupations, study and work with the 103 known elements and look for new ones. Biochemists study and work with chemical reactions and processes of living organisms. Pharmacists prepare and dispense drugs by mixing precise formulas. In Europe, pharmacists are generally called "chemists," an indication of how important chemistry is to their work.

Many people use "applied chemistry" in their careers. The food prepared by chefs and cooks, for example, involves chemical reactions, since all cooking ingredients are chemicals. Some ingredients, like sugar and salt, are single compounds, but most are mixtures of different compounds. Dietitians, nutritionists, and medical writers may also have an interest in the chemical content

of foods. Both farmers and horticulturists make use of the products of chemistry, such as fertilizers. Besides supplying plants with minerals they need to grow, fertilizers also contain elements such as sulfur, magnesium, iron, manganese, zinc, copper, and chlorine.

Physicists investigate the relationship between matter and energy and study such phenomena as light, heat, electricity, magnetism, and gravity. Nuclear physicists specialize in delving into the forces, reactions, composition and structure of the positively charged center of the atom. Geophysicists concentrate on learning about the interior of the earth, the movement of continents, and the earth's magnetic and gravitational fields. Geologists study the history and composition of our planet, as well as movements such as earthquakes and volcanos. Oceanographers focus on the land beneath the oceans, as well as on the oceans and their movements.

Other physical scientists keep track of the atmosphere and beyond. Meteorologists study the atmosphere, and some make predictions about the weather. Astronomers study the universe beyond the earth and other planets and solar systems. Astrophysicists study specific stars or galaxies and the origin of the universe.

Although scientists specialize, most need a knowledge of more than one branch of science. For example, agronomists frequently combine their knowledge of several sciences, such as chemistry, biology, geology, and mathematics, in solving a problem. In addition, they may work closely with scientists in other disciplines, including microbiology, biochemistry, meteorology, entomology, genetics, and agricultural engineering. Likewise, the astronomer needs an extensive knowledge of other fields of science, particularly physics.

Engineering. Engineers put science to use and make it possible for society to benefit from many scientific discoveries. Engineers use chemistry, mathematics, and physics to solve practical problems, develop new products, and improve systems and processes. Like science, engineering is a very broad field with many branches; over 25 engineering specialties are recognized by professional societies, and there are over 85 subdivisions within the major branches.

Some major divisions of engineering include mechanical engineering, electrical engineering, civil engineering, chemical engineering, and industrial engineering.

Mechanical engineers strive to harness power resources by using machinery to accomplish tasks. Some

Some Occupations Related to the Life Sciences

High school graduation usually necessary or recommended

Animal breeder
Animal caretaker
Animal husbandry worker
Biological photographer
Cosmetologist
Dog trainer
Dog warden
Farmer
Fish farmer
Florist

Gamekeeper
Greenskeeper
Grounds keeper
Hunting and fishing guide
Kennel attendant
Lab assistant
Landscape gardener
Medical secretary
Museum worker

Nurse, aide
Nurse, practical
Nursery manager
Orchardist
Orderly
Recreation worker
Taxidermist
Tree surgeon
Veterinary assistant

Two years of college or specialized school usually necessary or recommended

Biomedical equipment technician
Cytotechnologist
Dental ceramist
Dental hygienist
Dental laboratory technician
EEG technician
Electrologist
Fingerprint classifier
Fish and game warden
Food service supervisor

Forestry technician
Histologic technician
Inhalation therapist
Medical laboratory worker

Medical records technician
Mortician
Occupational therapist assistant
Paramedic
Radiologic technologist
Respiratory therapy technician

Four or more years of college usually necessary or recommended

Agronomist
Anatomist
Animal cytologist
Animal ecologist
Animal husbandry specialist
Animal paleontologist
Animal physiologist
Animal taxonomist
Anthropologist
Athletic trainer

Audiologist
Audiometrist
Bacteriologist
Biochemist
Biogeographer
Biologist
Biophysicist
Biostatistician
Botanist
Cooperative extension worker

Coroner
County agricultural agent
Curator
Dairy technologist
Dentist
Dietitian
Entomologist
Fish culturist
Food and drug inspector
Forester

Geneticist
Health educator
Health services administrator
Horticulturist
Industrial hygienist
Industrial therapist
Landscape architect

Meat inspector
Medical illustrator
Medical librarian

Medical records administrator
Medical social worker
Microbiologist
Naturalist
Nurse, professional/RN
Occupational safety and health worker
Occupational therapist
Optometrist
Ornithologist

Parasitologist
Physical anthropologist
Physical therapist
Physician
Podiatrist
Psychologist
Public health officer
Range manager
Recreation director
Rehabilitation counselor

Respiratory therapy worker
Roentgenologist
Sanitarian
Soil scientist
Speech pathologist/clinician
Taxonomist
Teacher/professor, biology
Veterinarian
Virologist
Zoologist

Based upon material developed by Fairfax County Public Schools, Fairfax, Virginia.

mechanical engineers develop and design machines that produce power; others work on machines that use power. Electrical engineers may design, develop, and supervise the production of everything electrical. Many electrical engineers specialize in electronic engineering. Chemical engineers serve as "process" engineers by adapting laboratory research into mass-production methods for making medicines, plastics, and many other chemical products. They work on development and manufacture of new products. Civil engineers design and build roads, buildings, harbors, airfields, tunnels, bridges, and water-supply and flood-control systems. Industrial engineers work on the operating efficiency of the production cycle of manufacturing.

Specialists in the engineering field include biomedical engineers, who use engineering skills to improve health care. They may, for example, design artificial organs or adapt computers for use in diagnosis and treatment of patients. In the energy area, petroleum engineers work on the development, recovery, and field processing of petroleum. Geological engineers analyze the earth's structure and composition to determine the location, extent, and depth of ores, oil, or underground water. Mining engineers locate and extract minerals from the earth and prepare them for use by manufacturing industries. Nuclear engineers design nuclear reactors and help install and maintain them.

Technicians and technologists. Technicians and technologists also need a background in science. Technicians and technologists often use the ideas or carry out the technical plans of the engineers or scientists. They are the "doers" rather than the innovators or designers, although they may do some design or similar work. Nearly every industry employs some type of technologists and technicians.

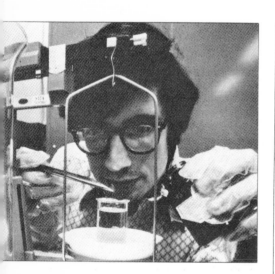

Some Occupations Related to the Physical Sciences

High school graduation usually necessary or recommended

Air conditioning technician
Computer service technician
Cook and chef
Electrician
Elevator constructor
Electroplater
Electrotyper and stereotyper
Instrument repairer
Pest controller
Photoengraver
Printing press operator and assistant

Two years of college or specialized school usually necessary or recommended

Engineering technician (various specialties)
Nuclear technician
Science technician (various specialties)

Four or more years of college usually necessary or recommended

Aerospace engineer
Acoustical engineer

Anesthesiologist
Anthropologist
Archaeologist
Astronomer
Astrophysicists
Biochemist

Biomedical engineer
Cartographer
Ceramic engineer
Chemical engineer
Chemist
Civil engineer
Clinical chemist
Computer engineer

Consumer protection specialist
Dentist
Electrical engineer
Environmental scientist
Food and drug analyst
Geographer
Geological engineer
Geologist

Geophysicist
Industrial engineer
Illuminating engineer
Mechanical engineer
Metallurgical engineer

Meteorologist
Mineralogist
Mining engineer
Nuclear engineer
Oceanographer
Patent examiner
Patent searcher
Petroleum engineer
Pharmacologist
Physicist

Quality control engineer
Radar technician
Safety engineer
Seismologist
Systems analyst
Toxicologist
Traffic engineer
Wood technologist

Based upon material developed by Fairfax County Public Schools, Fairfax, Virginia.

Scientific and engineering technicians have a sound understanding of testing and measuring devices and of other practical techniques. Some technician occupations include electrical and electronics technician, drafter, industrial engineering technician, broadcast technician, mechanical engineering technician, meteorological technician, geological technician, biological technician, and air-conditioning, refrigeration, and heating technician.

Qualifications

What does it take to be a scientist or engineer? Most jobs require an aptitude for science and a solid education.

Scientists, engineers, and technicians must be attentive to minute details, as well as the willingness to suspend judgment until the final results are in. Science-oriented careers also require orderly thinking, systematic work habits, and perseverance. Above all, the field requires an unquenchable thirst for knowledge.

Naturally, different amounts and kinds of science are needed for different occupations. For some jobs, high school science may be adequate. To be a photographic assistant or a nurse's aide, for example, may only require rudimentary science courses. For many other jobs, such as mortician or dental hygienist, however, additional training at a technical institute or junior college may be needed. A bachelor's degree from a 4-year college is often the minimum qualification for scientific and engineering jobs, and, increasingly, many science occupations require a doctorate.

Students should take as much science in high school as possible. Basic science courses such as biology, chemistry, physics, or earth science form a good background. Scientific and engineering careers, as well as science-related

careers, usually also require a good background in mathematics.

Science is an ever-growing field. But occupations related to science are so numerous that no simple statement about employment opportunities applies to all areas of science. Some scientific specialists are in great demand, while others are not. For example, astronomers are likely to face keen competition for jobs during the 1980's, but geophysicists should have good op-

portunities. For specific information on training required, earnings, and employment outlook in many careers, see the *Occupational Outlook Handbook*.

While looking into these occupations, students should try to speak to people who work in scientific, engineering, and science-related occupations. These workers can explain their jobs, how they qualified or trained for them, and what their working conditions are like.

∞

MATH AND YOUR CAREER

by Gail M. Martin

We use math every day of our lives—in balancing a checkbook, grocery shopping, cooking, playing cards, making up a personal budget, or working on a car, for example. This type of math is often referred to as "consumer math."

Math—usually of a higher level—is important in a great many occupations too. Auto mechanics, for example, must solve problems with gear ratios and know metric conversion. Surveyors measure length and angles and use the Pythagorean theory. Tax accountants, farmers, and real estate brokers are a few of the many professionals who must know how to calculate various types of interest rates.

Even if math were never used in personal life or on the job, it would still be a useful subject to study. In studying math we develop skills in problem-solving; we learn how to think through

a problem logically, break it down, and solve it step by step. We also learn how to pose questions, analyze situations, translate results, and make good estimates. That's why the study of math is an important part of a well-rounded education.

Recognizing the place of mathematics in the education process, most high schools require at least a year of math for graduation. Entry to most colleges also requires some years of math, regardless of major. And standardized nationwide achievement tests used to screen college applicants contain many mathematical problems. In short, wise students learn math whether they see a use for it or not.

How Much Is Enough?

Some students think that since computers and pocket calculators are so widely available, math is no longer as important to learn as it used to be. Actually, just the opposite is true. Instead of making math skills less important in the working world, computers have increased the number of jobs requiring math, as well as increased the level of math needed for many other occupations. Applications of mathematical skills are now being used in economics, the life sciences, and the social sciences, for example.

Naturally, varying amounts and kinds of mathematical training are needed for different occupations. For some jobs, such as secretary or cashier,

Photo by Gail M. Martin

a year or less of high school consumer math is enough. But more of these occupations will require at least some high school math in the future. And as technology increases, workers with only elementary training in mathematics may face a narrower range of career possibilities. Students interested in the skilled trades often need several years of "shop" math. Several years of regular high school mathematics are often needed for admittance to a technical or junior college, especially in technical or science programs.

The general rule for students planning on earning a bachelor's degree is, "Take as much math as possible." For

Reprinted from *Occupational Outlook Quarterly/Summer 1983,* U.S. Department of Labor.

science, engineering, and a few social science programs, courses must usually include algebra, advanced algebra, geometry, trigonometry, and advanced senior mathematics. Even students planning to pursue a liberal arts education would do well to carry a heavy load of mathematics during high school, since college admissions officials favor applicants who have good grades in difficult subjects, such as mathematics.

Deciding how much high school math to take is easier if career goals have been established. However, it is better to take what may seem to be too much math rather than too little. Career plans change, and one of the biggest roadblocks in undertaking new educational or training goals is poor preparation in mathematics.

There is another reason for taking as much high school math as possible, even if a college education is not anticipated. Students with a good math background qualify for more jobs than students with minimum math. For example, vocational students sometimes find that they lose job opportunities to other students who have higher levels of math and score higher on apprenticeship entrance examinations. Not only do people qualify for more jobs with more math, but the jobs they qualify for can be performed with added success. An economist, for instance, who also has a good background in statistics is more adept at using various forecasting methods than one who does not have the same math background.

The Next Move

Mathematics is more than just a collection of rules and formulas to memorize. Rather, it is a tool that can be used in school and out, at leisure and at work. It is not an easy subject for many people to learn. But it is a subject that is becoming increasingly important in the working world, a subject worth putting some extra effort into. For an idea of the math required for various occupations, see the following list. In addition, it would be useful to talk to people who work in these occupations.

∞

How Math Is Used in 100 Occupations*

Occupations (column headers): Accountant · Accounting Systems Analyst · Administrator: Shopping Mall · Advertising Agent · Airline Passenger Service Agent · Airplane Mechanic · Airplane Pilot · Air Traffic Controller · Appliance Store Manager · Appraiser (Real Estate) · Architect · Artist (Graphic) · Attorney · Auditor · Auto Mechanic · Bank Teller · Biologist (Environmental) · Carpenter · Carpet Cleaner · Cartographer · Chiropractor · Computer Programmer · Computer Systems Engineer · Contract Supplies Counter Clerk · Contractor (General) · Controller (Hospital) · Data Processor · Dentist · Dietician · Doctor (G.P.) · Draftsman · Economist · Electrician · Electronics Technician · (Civil) Engineer · (Electrical) Engineer · (Electronics) Engineer · (Industrial) Engineer · (Petroleum) Engineer · Environmental Analyst · Farm Advisor · Fire Prevention Officer · Fireman · Forestry Land Manager · Forestry Recreation Manager · Geologist (Environmental) · Highway Patrolman · Hydrologist · Income Tax Specialist · Insurance Agent

MATHEMATICS

GENERAL MATHEMATICS
- Whole Numbers
- Fractions
- Decimals
- Estimation
- Quick Computation
- Rounding
- Averaging
- Other Number Bases
- Ratio/Proportion
- Per Cent
- Statistics
- Statistical Graphing
- English Measurement
- Metric Measurement
- Area/Perimeter
- Volume
- Angle Measurement
- Geometric Concepts
- Pythagorean Theorem
- Square Root
- Exponents
- Scientific Notation
- Probability
- Negative Numbers
- Set Theory
- Ancient Numeration

ALGEBRA I
- Linear Equations
- Linear Inequalities
- Formulas
- Polynomials (Operations)
- Factoring Polynomials
- Rational Expressions
- Co-ordinate Graphing
- Systems of Equations
- Simplifying Radicals
- Quadratic Equations

GEOMETRY
- Induct'n, Deduct'n, Logic
- Angles/Perpendiculars
- Parallel Lines/Planes
- Congruent Triangles
- Similar Polygons
- Circles
- Constructions/Loci
- Distance in Plane
- Transformations

ALGEBRA II – TRIG.
- Linear/Quadratic Functions
- Trigonometric Functions
- Trig. Identities, etc.
- Complex Numbers
- 2nd Deg. Eq./2 Variables
- Systems in 3 Variables
- Exponents/Logarithms
- Polynomial Equations
- Sequences/Series
- Permutations/Combinations
- Vectors
- Matrices/Determinants

OTHER
- Use of the Calculator
- Computer Operations
- Computer Programming
- Higher Mathematics

*Reprinted from *When are We Ever Gonna Have To Use This?* by Hal Saunders, by permission of Dale Seymour Publications. Copyright 1981, 1980 by Hal Saunders.

MATHEMATICS

Occupation columns (left to right):

1. Insurance Claims Supervisor
2. Interior Decorator
3. Investment Counselor
4. Landscape Architect
5. Librarian
6. Machinist
7. Marketing Rep. (Computers)
8. Masonry Contractor
9. Medical Lab Technician
10. Meteorologist
11. Motorcycle Sales and Repair
12. Navigator
13. Newspaper: Circulation
14. Newspaper: Production
15. Newspaper: Reporter
16. Nurse
17. Oceanographer (Biological)
18. Optician
19. Orthopedic Surgeon
20. Painter
21. Payroll Supervisor
22. Personnel Administrator
23. Pharmacist
24. Photographer
25. Physical Therapist
26. Plumber (County Inspector)
27. Police Officer
28. Political Campaign Manager
29. Printer
30. Psychologist (Experimental)
31. Publisher: Order Manager
32. Production Manager
33. Purchasing Agent
34. Radio Technician
35. Real Estate Agent
36. Roofer
37. Savings and Loan Counselor
38. Sheet Metal/Heating/Air Cond.
39. Social Worker
40. Stock Broker
41. Surveyor
42. Technical Researcher
43. Temp. Employ. Agency Clerk
44. Title Insurance Officer
45. Travel Agent
46. T. V. Repair Technician
47. Urban Planner
48. Veterinary Practice
49. Waitress
50. Wastewater Treatment Operator

GENERAL MATHEMATICS

- Whole Numbers
- Fractions
- Decimals
- Estimation
- Quick Computation
- Rounding
- Averaging
- Other Number Bases
- Ratio/Proportion
- Per Cent
- Statistics
- Statistics Graphing
- English Measurement
- Metric Measurement
- Area/Perimeter
- Volume
- Angle Measurement
- Geometric Concepts
- Pythagorean Theorem
- Square Root
- Exponents
- Scientific Notation
- Probability
- Negative Numbers
- Set Theory
- Ancient Numeration

ALGEBRA I

- Linear Equations
- Linear Inequalities
- Formulas
- Polynomials (Operations)
- Factoring Polynomials
- Rational Expressions
- Co-ordinate Graphing
- Systems of Equations
- Simplifying Radicals
- Quadratic Equations

GEOMETRY

- Induct'n, Deduct'n, Logic
- Angles/Perpendiculars
- Parallel Lines/Planes
- Congruent Triangles
- Similar Polygons
- Circles
- Constructions/Loci
- Distance in Plane
- Transformations

ALGEBRA II — TRIG.

- Linear/Quadratic Functions
- Trigonometric Functions
- Trig. Identities, etc.
- Complex Numbers
- 2nd Deg. Eq./2 Variables
- Systems in 3 Variables
- Exponents/Logarithms
- Polynomial Equations
- Sequences/Series
- Permutations/Combinations
- Vectors
- Matrices/Determinants

OTHER

- Use of the Calculator
- Computer Operation
- Computer Programming
- Higher Mathematics

INPUT FOR COMPUTER WORKERS: EDUCATION AND TRAINING FOR COMPUTER OCCUPATIONS

The relative newness of the computer field and its rapidly changing technology have presented special problems in training qualified computer personnel. As a result, training programs have been forced to meet the requirements of this changing technology without the luxury of long-term planning.

Training the Company Way

The dramatic rise in computer use during the 1950's far outstripped the availability of personnel with data processing skills. Opportunities in the computer fields increased rapidly and the demand for skilled workers resulted in many people seeking training in this field. But schools were not yet providing courses in data processing. Computers were needed to provide practical experience for the student, and this equipment was pro-

hibitively expensive during the 1950's. Also, the relatively few people who were qualified to teach at that time could earn considerably more money in the business world.

As equipment costs gradually declined and more instructors became available, a growing number of public and private colleges, universities, and vocational schools began to include data processing in their curriculums. Nevertheless, the number of graduates with specific training for computer jobs continued to fall further behind the rapidly growing demand. To fill this widening gap, a large number of private vocational schools, many of them newly established, offered computer training. Some of these schools, however, were criticized for employing poorly qualified teachers and providing obsolete equipment. The computer manufacturers themselves,

therefore, became the major source of training in the 1950's and 1960's. Many people trained in this way acquired only limited skills because the instruction usually focused on the operating procedures for only one company's system. Employees trained in this manner found it difficult to transfer or advance to jobs requiring knowledge of different types of computers and related equipment.

Computer manufacturers continued to provide training until the early 1970's. Thereafter, manufacturers considered training a separate service that required a separate charge. The resulting awareness of the cost of computer education led many users to look for alternative training methods.

One alternative computer users began to pursue was that of training their own computer personnel. These in-house programs

Reprinted from *Occupational Outlook Quarterly/Summer 1981*, U.S. Department of Labor.

were generally run at the user's site and were usually administered by company personnel or an educational services firm. Naturally, they were tailored to meet the specific needs of the company.

Training Now

Although the education and training of computer workers have advanced markedly since 1950, an acute shortage of qualified teachers exists because salaries and research facilities at educational institutions are not competitive with those in other industries. Educational programs are hard pressed to keep up with changes in technology and applications. And the subject matter in apparently similar courses offered at different institutions is sometimes inconsistent. Because of these problems and other factors, colleges and universities are still not producing enough graduates to meet the demand for computer professionals. Graduates of programs in computer science are only filling 1 out of 6 jobs at the bachelor's level, 1 out of 11 jobs at the master's level and 1 out of 4 jobs at the doctor's level, according to John W. Hamblem's ''Computer Manpower—Supply and Demand—by States,'' published by Information Systems Consultants.

Despite the current shortcomings of computer education and training, a number of positive developments have occurred in the past few years. Many students at the college and university level now receive computer training even if they do not major in computer science. For example, most schools offer computer courses to their business and engineering students. One college administrator has estimated that 1 out of 3 undergraduates and 1 out of 2 graduate students currently use computers in their coursework. More high schools are now offering computer education that provides students with some programming knowledge as well as an understanding of the logic of computing. In an attempt to meet the needs of those already in the labor force,

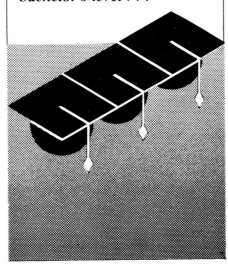

"... colleges and universities are still not producing enough graduates to meet the demand for computer professionals. Graduates of programs in computer science are only filling 1 out of 6 jobs at the bachelor's level ..."

many schools offer night courses in computer sciences. These programs are often tailored to meet specific requirements of the job market. Computer vendors and others have refined their training programs to cover a variety of computer concepts and practical applications. These programs are especially useful for occupations with high turnover, as they are self-paced and relatively inexpensive. And finally, in order to make programs more relevant and to encourage consistency among computer curriculums, the Association for Computing Machinery has issued revised recommendations for computer education programs. These guidelines include detailed course descriptions and recommendations on program organization and implementation.

To Each Occupation Its Own Training

Training requirements for computer workers range from a high school diploma to the doctoral degree. Regardless of educational level, however, employers desire computer personnel who have a background in computer science or data processing and a knowledge of the business served by the computer operations.

The most complicated computer work, which involves systems design and analysis and systems programming, is generally done by persons having 4 years or more of college

training. Equipment maintenance and the middle range of computer work involving scientific applications or complex business applications programming is typically performed by those with college, junior college, or computer vendor school backgrounds. The work requiring the least formal education involves basic applications programming, equipment operations, and putting information into a form that the computer can process. This work is usually carried out by high school graduates, many of whom have received either formal training from a public or private school or on-the-job training from a computer manufacturer or their employer.

The educational characteristics described here are typical of workers in the major computer occupations as classified by the Census Bureau: Systems analyst, programmer, service technician, keypunch operator, and equipment operator. The last two jobs are discussed together.

No single way of preparing for a job as a *systems analyst* exists because employers' preferences depend on the type of work done in the firm. Generally, however, a bachelor's degree is the minimum educational requirement. In addition to a bachelor's degree in a suitable field, some employers prefer applicants who have related work experience.

For a systems analyst job with a bank, insurance company, or business firm, a college degree in accounting, business, or economics is appropriate. For work in a scientific or technical organization, applicants need a degree in the physical sciences, mathematics, engineering, or computer science. A growing number of employers seek applicants who have a degree in computer science, information science, or data processing.

Regardless of college major, most employers look for people who are familiar with programming languages. Courses in computer concepts, systems analysis, and data base management offer good preparation.

Most employers of systems analysts also

"Unlike systems analysts, programmers often have no previous experience in programming when hired."

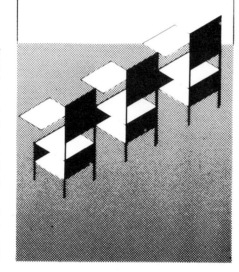

prefer applicants who have some experience in computer programming. Nearly half of all persons entering systems analysis transfer from other occupations. Because of the importance of combining programming experience with education, many workers begin as programmers and are later promoted to analyst trainees. Employers, computer manufacturers, and colleges and universities offer formal training in systems analysis.

Systems analysts can earn a Certificate in Data Processing from the Institute for Certification of Computer Professionals. Recipients must have 5 years of experience and pass a five-part examination.

Programmers, like systems analysts, are not the products of a single system of training because the needs of employers vary. Most programmers are college graduates. Employers who use computers for business purposes may not require applicants with college degrees, but they do prefer people who have taken at least some courses in data processing, accounting, and business administration. Organizations that use computers in scientific or engineering projects usually require programmers to have a bachelor's degree with a major in the physical sciences, mathematics, engineering, or computer science. Some of these jobs require advanced degrees. Unlike systems analysts, programmers often have no previous experience in programming when hired.

Public and private vocational schools, community and junior colleges and universities teach computer programming. Instruction ranges from introductory courses to advanced courses at the graduate level. High schools in many parts of the country also offer courses in computer programming.

Senior programmers who pass a five-part examination can earn a Certificate in Computer Programming from the Institute for Certification of Computer Professionals.

Computer service technicians usually work as trainees for 6 months to 2 years. New trainees generally have 1 to 2 years of posthigh school training in basic electronics or electrical engineering at a computer school, technical institute, junior college, or college. A few are trained through apprenticeship. The electronics training provided by the Armed Forces is also excellent preparation for this occupation. High school courses in electronics or hobbies that involve electronics, such as operating ham radios or building stereo equipment, may provide a useful introduction to the work involved in this occupation.

High school graduation is the minimum educational requirement for *computer equipment operators* such as keypunch operator, auxiliary equipment operator, and console operator. Many employers prefer console operators who have some community or junior college education. Beginners usually are trained on the job; the length of training varies. Auxiliary equipment operators can learn their jobs in a few weeks, but console operators require several months of training before they are sufficiently familiar with the equipment to be able to trace the causes of breakdowns.

Formal computer training is desirable for equipment operators because most employers look for applicants who already are skilled in operating data-entry equip-ment or computer consoles. High schools, vocational schools, computer and business schools, and community and junior colleges offer computer training. Computer vendors also offer structured training programs for many of these workers.

Working and Still Learning

With the rapid change in computer equipment and technology there is a great need for continuing education programs for computer personnel. The extent of job-related, supplementary training varies widely. Some employers have regularly scheduled programs in subjects such as computer languages or data processing operations. Others provide training only when changes are made in computer procedures or equipment. Many companies also maintain a tuition refund plan or pay their employees' fees for attendance at professional seminars. Regardless of the type or length of training, the employer usually pays for it if it is work related.

The most common types of supplementary training include computer vendors' course offerings, in-house training programs, on-the-job training, professional seminars, and reimbursement for college, correspondence, and vocational school courses. The length of post-employment training ranges from a few hours to more than 1 year, but the bulk of this training is usually completed in 1 to 12 weeks.

Among computer occupations, systems analysts frequently take computer science courses as well as systems, programming, and management training. Programmers usually train in programming languages and techniques and, to a lesser extent, systems analysis and design. The training of computer service technicians often involves computer electronics and related courses. Console, peripheral equipment, and keypunch operators train in data preparation, production control, and computer equipment operation techniques, and, occasionally, programming. ∞

HOW TO GET CREDIT FOR WHAT YOU KNOW: ALTERNATIVE ROUTES TO EDUCATIONAL CREDIT

This article is based on a leaflet prepared by the Women's Bureau of the U.S. Department of Labor. Special thanks to Shirley J. Gregory and the Consumer Information Center for help in researching the information used in it.

Not long ago, anyone who missed the opportunity to get a high school diploma when a teenager or a college degree when a young adult had to accept the fact that the opportunity for formal education had been lost. But those days of "last chance" education are over. Many programs now offer adults the opportunity not only to get the formal educational qualifications so necessary in today's competitive job market but also to acquire them without spending long hours in a classroom. Innovative programs allow students to study part time and at home, to work at their own pace and on their own schedule, and to earn credit for knowledge, experience, and noncollegiate courses.

High School Credit

Adults can earn high school equivalency certificates through the General Educational Development (GED) program, which is operated by the GED Testing Service in connection with State departments of education and local school systems. GED examinations test individual competencies in English, social studies, mathematics, natural science, and literature and are designed to measure ability to think clearly about ideas and concepts rather than knowledge of facts. They are available in English, Spanish, and French. Because GED programs are operated by local school systems, information about testing procedures and times and about preparatory courses should be obtained from the superintendent of schools in your community.

For general information about GED programs, write

GED Testing Service
One Dupont Circle NW.
Washington, D.C. 20036.

College Credit

Colleges now offer the nontraditional student a flexible range of alternatives for earning degrees through combinations of on- and off-campus study, correspondence courses, and credit for experience, knowledge, and other types of instruction. However, the kind and amount of credit colleges grant for alternatives to full-time on-campus study varies. Students should find out if the institution they plan to attend will accept credits earned in alternative programs.

Credit by Examination

The College-Level Examination Program (CLEP) consists of two types of tests that measure knowledge regardless of how it was acquired. Multiple-choice general examinations test knowledge in five broad areas: English composition, humanities, social science/history, mathematics, and natural science. Multiple-choice subject examinations measure ability in a wide variety of specialized subjects, such as general psychology, biology, English literature, and accounting. The College Entrance Examination Board administers the tests every month at more than 900 test centers in the United States and Canada and, at the request of individuals taking the tests, sends the scores to colleges and universities. Each educational institution makes its own decisions about acceptable scores and the amount of CLEP credit it will grant toward a degree. For more information, write

CLEP
College Board
Department C
888 7th Avenue
New York, N.Y. 10019.

The Proficiency Examination Program (PEP) is operated through the American College Testing Program (ACT) in connection with the New York Regents External Degree Program. The ACT-PEP exams are given in 47 subjects within the general categories of arts and sciences, education, nursing, business, criminal justice, health, and foreign languages. They are used to assess knowledge for credits in the Regents External Degree Program (see the section on degree programs below). In New York, the ACT-PEP tests are divided into two series—the College Proficiency Examinations Program (CPEP) and the Regents External Degree Examinations (REDE).

To obtain information about ACT-PEP, write

ACT-PEP
P.O. Box 168
Iowa City, Iowa 52243.

To obtain information about CPEP and REDE, write

University of the State of New York
Regents External Degree
   Exams/College Proficiency Exams
Cultural Education Center
Albany, N.Y. 12230.

Credit for noncollege learning. The Office on Educational Credit at the American Council on Education evaluates courses given by private employers, community organizations, labor unions, government agencies, and the military services and makes recommendations about the number of college semester hours they equal. The recommendations and course descriptions are published annually in *The National Guide to Educational Credit for Training Programs.* It is available from

American Council on Education
Office of Educational Credit
One Dupont Circle NW.
Washington, D.C. 20036.

It costs $25, plus $2 for postage and handling.

The Office on Educational Credit also publishes the *Guide to the Evaluation of Educational Experience in the*

Armed Forces. It can also be obtained from the above address; price: $36 per 3-volume set.

Credit for experience. The Task Force on Volunteer Accreditation of the Council of National Organizations for Adult Education has developed a series of "I Can" lists to help volunteers identify skills for which college credit might be given. The Council's book, *I Can: A Tool for Assessing Skills Acquired Through Volunteer Experience,* includes "I Can" lists for 12 volunteer job titles as well as other information about evaluating volunteer skills for educational credit. The publication may be purchased for $4.95, plus 50 cents for postage and handling, from

Ramco Associates
406 West 31st Street
New York, N.Y. 10001.

The Educational Testing Service worked with the Council of National Organizations for Adult Education on the "I Can" project and developed several additional lists for identifying and assessing volunteer and homemaker skills and a workbook to assist women seeking such credit. The workbook, *How to Get Credit for What You Have Learned as a Homemaker or Volunteer,* may be purchased for $5 from

Accrediting Women's Competencies
T–154
Educational Testing Service
Princeton, N.J. 08541.

Credit for correspondence and independent study. The Division of Independent Study of the National University Extension Association (NUEA) includes a wide variety of correspondence and independent study courses and programs among its membership institutions. Course materials are mailed to students from the individual college or university and completed assignments are returned to the school, where they are graded by the same standards used in classroom instruction. The Association publishes NUEA *Guide to Independent Study Through Correspondence Instruction, 1980–82 Edition.* It is available for $4.50, plus $1.25 postage and handling, from

Peterson's Guides
Book Order Department
P.O. Box 2123
Princeton, N.J. 08540.

An additional $2.50 for special handling or $3.25 for UPS shipment will speed delivery.

For general information about the NUEA program, contact

NUEA
Suite 360
One Dupont Circle NW.
Washington, D.C. 20036.

Many private correspondence schools also offer courses and programs for which some colleges give credit. It is important to find out if the school is accredited before paying for courses, and you should also check to see if your college or university will accept the credits you want to transfer toward a degree. The National Home Study Council, a nationally recognized accrediting agency for correspondence schools, publishes the *Directory of Home Study Schools.* Free copies of the directory, as well as other publications about home study programs, are available from

National Home Study Council
1601 18th St. NW.
Washington, D.C. 20009.

Degree programs. At least two national programs offer students an opportunity to earn degrees without ever spending time on campus attending formal classes—the New York Regents External Degree Program and Thomas A. Edison College. These programs give credit for all kinds of documented learning: Courses taken at other colleges, noncollegiate courses that have been evaluated and rated as comparable to college courses, military education, proficiency examinations, and individual assessments of knowledge and skills that cannot be measured adequately by testing. For more information, write

Regents External Degree Program
College Proficiency Examination
  Programs
Cultural Education Center
Albany, N.Y. 12230

Thomas A. Edison State College
CN 545
101 West State St.
Trenton, N.J. 08625.   ∞

APPRENTICESHIP

*"Oh, at home had I but stayed,
'Prenticed in my father's trade . . ."*

Back in the days when A. E. Housman wrote these lines, many boys became apprentices because tradition dictated that a trade be passed from father to son. Today, young men and women pursue the skilled trades through apprenticeship not because of tradition but because apprenticeship develops marketable skills and leads to satisfying, well-paying jobs. Unfortunately, those who aspire to the skilled trades today are not guaranteed apprenticeships as were the early craftworkers' sons. The carpenter's son in Housman's poem chose to forego an apprenticeship that was his for the asking. Today, hundreds of thousands of applicants are asking to enter apprenticeship programs that can accommodate only a fraction of their numbers. Nevertheless, the number of apprentices continues to grow, because enough well-qualified young people persist in applying, knowing they can earn the rewards the carpenter's son might have realized had he followed in his father's footsteps.

As desirable a career opportunity as it is, apprenticeship remains a serious and difficult period of study and on-the-job training that demands qualified, dedicated, and conscientious people riveted to the goal of becoming skilled craftworkers. Career seekers can decide whether they are such people by finding out what apprenticeship is, what the qualifications are for different trades, and what opportunities there are for qualified applicants in registered apprenticeship programs. With this knowledge, people choosing careers can better decide whether apprenticeship is right for them and, if it is, which trade and what program to enter.

What is Apprenticeship?

Apprenticeship is a prescribed learning experience during which an individual called an apprentice learns a trade through several years of on-the-job training and related instruction. On-the-job training covers all aspects of a trade. For example, apprentice auto mechanics learn not only how to repair automotive equipment but how the various systems are designed, how to diagnose malfunctions, how to use the principal tools and test equipment found in an automotive shop, pertinent safety precautions, and cleanup of tools and work areas.

Related instruction can take place in a classroom or through home-study courses. The teaching covers the techniques of the trade and also the theory behind the techniques. It includes detailed discussion of how typical tasks are performed and the safety precautions that must be taken. Classes are taught by experienced craftworkers and other skilled persons and require the study of various trade manuals and educational materials. Classes can be scheduled during the day or in the evening.

Apprenticeships usually last about 4 years, but may range from 1 to 6 years. During this time, apprentices work under journey workers—the status they too will attain after successfully completing their apprenticeships. Under the journey worker's guidance, the apprentice gradually learns the mechanics of the trade and performs the work under less and less supervision.

Apprentices are full-time employees. Generally, an apprentice's pay starts out at about half that of an experienced worker and increases periodically throughout the apprenticeship. Many programs are cosponsored by trade unions that offer apprentices union membership.

The sponsor of an apprenticeship program plans, administers, and pays for the program. Sponsors can be unions, employers, or a combination of the two. When an apprentice is accepted into a program, he or she and the sponsor sign an apprenticeship agreement. The apprentice agrees to perform the work faithfully and complete the related study, and the sponsor agrees to make every effort to keep the apprentice employed and to comply with standards established for the program.

Apprenticeship programs are commonly registered with the Federal Government or a federally approved State apprenticeship agency. Registered programs meet federally approved standards relating to job duties, related instruction (a minimum of 144 hours a year is recommended), wages, and safety and health conditions. Apprentices who successfully complete registered programs receive certificates of completion from the U.S. Department of Labor or a federally approved State apprenticeship agency.

Registered programs offer apprenticeships in over 700 occupations. The list accompanying this article—by no means all-inclusive—gives an indication of the range. In recent years, apprenticeships have even been initiated in public service occupations, such as firefighter, police officer, and emergency medical technician.

Most registered programs are sponsored jointly by employers and labor unions. The administrative body in such joint programs is called a Joint Apprenticeship Committee. Representing the union, management, and the public, the Joint Apprenticeship Committee reviews applications for apprenticeships and interviews applicants. It also consults with the State apprenticeship council (if there is one) and with regional representatives of the Bureau of Apprenticeship and Training—the administrative arm for apprenticeship in the U.S. Department of Labor's Employment and Training Administration—concerning Federal apprenticeship standards, equal employment opportunity, safety, and similar matters.

Given the chance, people often prefer to enter registered programs rather than unregistered programs because they can be sure of receiving training that meets standards approved by the U.S. Department of Labor. Also, graduates of registered programs may have an easier time getting jobs or changing employers because employers have greater

Reprinted from *Occupational Outlook Quarterly/Winter 1983*, U.S. Department of Labor.

Apprenticeable Occupations

aircraft mechanic, electrical and radio	carpenter	foundry metallurgist	optician	roofer
airframe and power plant mechanic	cement mason	furrier	optomechanical technician	rotogravure-press operator
airplane mechanic, armament	chemical laboratory technician	glazier	ornamental ironworker	sheet-metal worker
assembler, electro-mechanical	computer peripheral equipment operator	instrumentation technician	orthotist	shipwright
automobile body repairer	cook	jeweler	painter	sign writer
automobile mechanic	cosmetologist	laboratory technician	patternmaker	silversmith
baker	custom tailor	landscape gardener	photoengraver	stationary engineer
biomedical equipment technician	dairy equipment repairer	lead burner	plasterer	stereotyper
blacksmith	dental laboratory technician	leather stamper	plater	stonemason
bookbinder	drafter, mechanical	lithographic plate maker	plate finisher	stone setter
bricklayer	dry cleaner	locksmith	plumber	television and radio repairer
butcher, all-round	electrical repairer	machinist	pottery machine operator	terrazzo worker
cabinetmaker	electronics mechanic	maintenance mechanic	printer-slotter operator	tile setter
calibration laboratory technician	engraver	metal fabricator	private branch exchange installer	tool-and-die maker
car repairer	environmental control system installer-servicer	millwright	programmer, business	truck-body builder
	farm equipment mechanic	model maker	prosthetics technician	upholsterer, inside
	firefighter	monotype keyboard operator	pumper-gager	wallpaper printer
	floor layer	numerical control machine operator	quality control inspector	wastewater treatment plant operator
		operating engineer	radiographer	welding technician
			rigger	X-ray equipment tester

confidence in the quality of the training received in registered programs. Many employers offer excellent training opportunities but do not participate in a registered apprenticeship program, preferring to recruit only qualified skilled workers instead of training unskilled workers for their own particular needs.

Why Apprenticeship?

All the arguments for learning a skilled trade apply to apprenticeship: A skill sets craftworkers apart from other workers, is satisfying and rewarding, and is a marketable asset. But why learn a trade through apprenticeship instead of through some other method? Among other reasons, apprenticeship gives workers versatility by teaching them all aspects of a trade. It helps them learn to work with different kinds of people in an actual working situation. It familiarizes them with the overall picture of a company's operation and organization. Generally, an organized program of apprenticeship can earn graduates recognition as skilled workers and can ensure them good jobs with good pay.

A study of apprenticeship graduates and other craftworkers in six cities concluded that "apprenticeship training gives construction [craftworkers] considerable advantage over those trained by informal means." Apprenticeship graduates in the study were more educated, worked more steadily, learned their trades faster, and were more likely to be supervisors than nonapprenticed craftworkers. The same study showed that apprenticeship produced better skilled, more productive, and safer craftworkers. Apprenticeship graduates were also more likely to experience fewer and briefer periods of unemployment than craftworkers trained in informal ways, since employers retain better skilled workers and often specifically request them for a job.

But the apprenticeship picture is not all roses. The competition to "get in" is high. Apprentices face possible unemployment if the sponsoring employer runs out of work temporarily. The work can be technically hard and physically demanding. Apprentices must show they are learning the trade or be dropped during the probationary period. Beginning apprentices may feel their work is menial or boring. And more advanced apprentices may feel that their pay is less than what they could earn elsewhere with their skills.

Women face many unique obstacles to apprenticeship—traditionally a male domain. Although more women are entering apprenticeship programs and being accepted by their male peers, many feel they are breaking into a man's world—that they need much courage and self-confidence in addition to the abilities required of all apprentices. They have to contend with the stereotyped attitudes of many of their male coworkers. For example, men often try to protect women from heavy or dirty work, believing that women are too frail or delicate to handle it. On the other hand, some men make work even harder for women, because the men feel that women don't belong in the trade. A study of apprenticeship programs in Wisconsin concluded: "The barrier to women is not the difficult or dirty nature of some of the jobs, but the breaking of a taboo and the treading onto a territory that has remained the preserve of its male initiates." Additional enforcement of civil rights laws and greater numbers of women in apprenticeship may help to change these attitudes.

Selecting a Trade

When deciding what trade to enter, prospective apprentices should consider such factors as the vocational characteristics of the different trades, their qualifications as applicants, and the market for jobs in the geographic area in which they would serve an apprenticeship. Counselors can help applicants find out about the trades, give them tests to evaluate their abilities, and tell them something about the job market in their local area. But the applicants must decide for themselves not only what they would be best at, but what they would enjoy doing the most, and what they would stick with for the duration of an apprenticeship.

Although there are many apprenticeable occupations, not all are available in all areas of the country. Some areas offer only certain types of apprenticeship. For example, in the District of Columbia most apprenticeships are in the construction industry because there is little local industry to support the industrial trades. In fact, throughout the country, construction accounts for well over half of the registered apprentices.

When exploring occupations, one should consider the working conditions of each. Does the work require stamina, as in ironworking or sheet-metal work? Does it require moving from job to job, as in construction, or wearing special clothing, as in insulation work? Is it monotonous? Is it clean as in electrical work or dirty as in automotive maintenance? What are the special safety and health hazards?

The characteristics of the particular apprenticeship program should also be examined. What training facilities are available? What is the work environment? What kinds of related instruction are given? Does the program have mandatory classroom work, or does it require apprentices to complete home-study lessons and pass periodic examinations? What does it cost for books and tools? Most program sponsors provide study materials, but often appren-

tices must purchase standard manuals, such as those used by electricians. Also, apprentice mechanics are frequently required to supply their own set of basic tools. Is union membership required? If so, when is it offered to apprentices, and are they charged reduced union dues? Does the program offer dual enrollment in a community college through which an associate degree could be earned while completing an apprenticeship? Finally, is the apprenticeship program registered with the Federal or State government? This question is significant, as registration indicates that the program is likely to be of high quality.

After examining the trades, prospective apprentices should examine themselves. What do they like to do? Where do they like to work? Are they good at close work or would they rather work with less detail? What are their qualifications? Do they have a high school diploma? Are their reasons for wanting to enter an apprenticeship good enough to satisfy the committee that will interview them? Most importantly, are they willing to commit themselves to working, studying, and completing the term of an apprenticeship?

Qualifying for a Program

The process of qualifying for an apprenticeship program can be brief or long, depending on the individual's qualifications and the requirements and schedules of the different programs. Special programs, discussed in more detail below, provide tutoring and counseling to those who need help in qualifying.

Having a close relative in the trade used to be an advantage in competing for an apprenticeship. Not any more, say sponsors. Having a skilled craftworker in the family may help an applicant find out about openings. But, under law, all applicants must be qualified to enter registered programs and be treated equally during the selection process without regard to race, religion, color, sex, or national origin.

The requirements. Generally, program sponsors look for prospective apprentices who have the mechanical and mental abilities to master the techniques and technology of a trade. Therefore, sponsors set qualification standards that applicants must meet. Federal regulations require that apprentices be selected on the basis of objective and specific standards.

Requirements vary from trade to trade, program to program, and plan to plan. However, they usually cover four factors: Age, education, aptitude, and physical condition. For example, an applicant may have to pass an aptitude test, have a high school diploma, meet an age requirement,

pass occupationally essential physical requirements, have acceptable school grades, have work experience in a similar field, and be interviewed. A particular program may require a driver's license and experience working successfully as part of a group.

In accordance with child labor laws, the minimum allowable age for an apprentice is 16 years; however, most programs set the minimum age for entry at 18 because company insurance policies frequently cover only workers 18 and over. The maximum age varies among programs and is subject to provisions of individual State laws on age discrimination. For example, one program for carpenters sets the maximum at 28 years, another at 27. The maximum age for veterans is higher because at least part of their time in the service can be subtracted from their age.

The minimum level of education required also varies. Most programs require entrants to have a high school diploma or its equivalent. Regardless of the level of education required, apprentices need a firm grounding in reading, writing, and mathematics—all basic to the skilled trades. Courses in shop math, drafting, and physics and other courses related to the technical and mechanical trades are also highly recommended.

Educational attainment of apprentices has been climbing steadily. The number of apprentices with some college education has increased. Unable to find suitable jobs in their own fields, college graduates have turned increasingly to the skilled trades for work. This movement has put the high school graduate at somewhat of a disadvantage when competing for apprenticeship openings. College graduates are at times more sought after by program sponsors because of their potential for management responsibility. However, the high school graduate with a vocational education may have taken more relevant courses in high school and may show more sincere interest during an interview. Also, some employers prefer to hire high school graduates in the belief that these workers are more likely than college graduates to make a skilled trade their lifetime vocation.

Vocational schools can help people prepare for apprenticeship. Although they don't provide on-the-job experience, they do make students familiar with materials in the shop, techniques of the craft, and safety practices. Also, advanced standing is sometimes granted to entering apprentices who have attended vocational school. This training could result in a shortened apprenticeship and a higher starting wage.

Many apprenticeship programs require applicants to have certain aptitudes as demonstrated by passing appropriate validated tests. For example, the applicant may be required to pass a Specific Aptitude Test Battery (SATB) test administered by a State Job Service agency. The SATB tests two or more of the following nine general aptitudes: General learning ability (cognitive functioning), verbal aptitude, numerical aptitude, spatial aptitude, form perception (the ability to perceive small details in an object), clerical perception (the ability to distinguish pertinent detail), motor coordination, finger dexterity, and manual dexterity.

Each battery tests different combinations of these nine general aptitudes because each occupation requires different specific abilities. For example, the SATB for a machine operator measures only an applicant's finger dexterity,

PART III. SUMMARY OF FACTORS (To be filled in by the Committee member during the interview.)

Education: Survey of high school and college courses beyond those directly applicable to the trade.

Poor background. Took minimum academic courses. Poor grades.	Fair background. Some academic electives. Grades below average.	Medium background. Average course electives with fair grades.	Good background. College prep or some college work.	Excellent background. Extra subjects, college or post-high school with good grades.

Remarks: _____

Physical Factors: An assessment of physical ability to perform the requirements of the classification, lost time, health history, stamina and family health.

Unsatisfactory because:	Doubtful—Verification needed:	Satisfactory

Interest: Desire to be a craftsman, reasons for choosing this trade, knowledge of the trade, etc., interest in hobbies that would have a direct reflection on the trade.

Total lack of interest (just wants a job)	Little interest, past association shows very slight interest	Fair interest indicated by past associations and hobbies	Displays a real interest	Manifests strong desire to be craftsman

Remarks: _____

Attitude: Towards hard work: (Has he or she ever done any?) Towards school work: (How was his or her attendance in school?) Towards authority: (Will he or she work under supervision?) Towards teamwork: (Has he or she ever belonged to any organized groups, extra-curricular activities and sports?) Towards responsibility: (Past employment, school activities and military records.)

Unacceptable	Poor	Fair	Good	Excellent

Remarks: _____

Personal Traits: Appearance, aggressiveness, sincerity, dependability, character, and habits.

Unacceptable	Poor	Fair	Good	Excellent

Remarks: _____

After careful consideration of all factors, my grade for this applicant is:

0	10	20	30	40	50	60	70	80	90	100

In appropriate box, write in exact numerical grade such as 67, 83, or 95.

(Interviewer) _____ (Date) _____

while the one for a medical technician tests four aptitudes—general learning ability, verbal aptitude, form perception, and clerical perception.

The length of a SATB depends on the aptitudes it measures. Some questions are written, and some tests use pegboards and other apparatus for measuring manual aptitudes such as finger dexterity. "Low," "medium," and "high" scores are given. Some programs will accept only a "high" rating, others a "medium" rating.

All nine general aptitudes are tested by the General Aptitude Test Battery (GATB). This is frequently used by counselors to help people interested in apprenticeship decide which trade to pursue.

Some companies devise and administer their own tests. They report the scores to whoever is handling the apprenticeship application. Such tests often measure an applicant's familiarity with the tools and the terms of the trade.

People who get nervous or who have other problems taking tests can get a helpful booklet published by the Employment Service called "Doing Your Best on Aptitude Tests." Also available are special versions of the tests for people who speak Spanish.

Finally, most programs require good general health as proven and documented by an examination by a physician. General physical factors, such as health history, family health, and stamina, are discussed during the interview. Sometimes specific levels of physical abilities are required to do such things as close, detailed work. By law, physical size can no longer eliminate an applicant from consideration unless the sponsor can prove that size would prevent

---

APPRENTICESHIP AGREEMENT

This AGREEMENT may be terminated by either of the parties, citing cause(s), with notification to the registration agency in compliance with Title 29, CFR Part 29.6	**PRIVACY ACT STATEMENT** — The information requested herein is used for apprenticeship program statistical purposes and may not be otherwise disclosed without the express permission of the undersigned apprentice. **Privacy Act of 1974 - P.L. 93-579**

1. AGREEMENT BETWEEN APPRENTICE AND ("X" one)
   a. ☐ Employer
   b. ☐ Joint Committee
   c. ☐ Non-Joint Committee

2. DATE OF AGREEMENT (Month, Day, Year)

3. NAME OF APPRENTICESHIP STANDARDS (Name & Address of Sponsor)

The program sponsor and apprentice agree to the terms of apprenticeship standards as incorporated as part of this agreement. The sponsor will not discriminate in the selection and training of the apprentice in accordance with the Equal Opportunity Standards in Section 30.3, Title 29, Code of Federal Regulation, Part 30.

4. NAME OF APPRENTICE (Last, First, Middle)

5. DATE OF BIRTH (Mo.,Day,Year)

6. SEX ("X" one)
   a. ☐ Male
   b. ☐ Female

7. SOCIAL SECURITY NO.

8. APPRENTICE'S ADDRESS (No., Street, City, County, State, ZIP Code)

9. RACE/ETHNIC GROUP ("X" one)
   a. ☐ Am. Indian or Alaskan Nat.
   b. ☐ Asian or Pacific Islander
   c. ☐ Black (not Hispanic)
   d. ☐ Hispanic
   e. ☐ White (not Hispanic)
   f. ☐ Information Not Available
   g. ☐ Not Elsewhere Classified

10. VETERAN STATUS ("X" one)
    a. ☐ Non-Veteran
    b. ☐ Vietnam-Era Veteran (8/5/64 - 5/7/75)
    c. ☐ Other Veteran

    C #

11. HIGHEST EDUCATION LEVEL ("X" one)
    a. ☐ 8th grade or less
    b. ☐ 9th
    c. ☐ 10th
    d. ☐ 11th
    e. ☐ 12th grade or more

12. SIGNATURE OF APPRENTICE — DATE

13. SIGNATURE OF PARENT/GUARDIAN (if minor) — DATE

14a. TRADE — b. D.O.T. CODE (9 digits)

15. TERM (Hours, Months, Years)

16. PROBATIONARY PERIOD (Hours, Months, Years)

17. CREDIT FOR PREVIOUS EXPERIENCE (Hrs., Mos., Yrs.)

18. TERM REMAINING (Hrs., Mos., Yrs.)

19. DATE APPRENTICESHIP BEGINS (Indenture Date)

20. RELATED INSTRUCTION TRAINING (No. Hrs. per Yr.)

21. APPRENTICE WAGES FOR RELATED INSTRUCTION TRAINING ("X" one)
    a. ☐ will be paid
    b. ☐ will not be paid

22. PRESENT JOURNEYMAN'S WAGE RATE — $

23. EFFECTIVE DATE OF WAGE RATE (Mo., Day, Yr.)

24. APPRENTICE WAGES - The apprentice schedule of pay shall be listed for each advancement period. The work processes listed in the standards (item 3 above) are a part of this agreement.

PERIOD a.	TERM (Mo./Yr.) b.	% c.	DOLLAR AMOUNT (in dollars & cents) d.	PERIOD a.	TERM (Mo./Yr.) b.	% c.	DOLLAR AMOUNT (in dollars & cents) d.
1				6			
2				7			
3				8			
4				9			
5				10			

25. SIGNATURE OF COMMITTEE (if applicable) — DATE SIGNED
a.

26. SIGNATURE OF AUTHORIZED OFFICIAL (Employer/Sponsor) — DATE SIGNED

SIGNATURE OF COMMITTEE (if applicable) — DATE SIGNED
b.

28. REGISTRATION AGENCY

27. NAME AND ADDRESS OF DESIGNEE TO RECEIVE COMPLAINTS (if applicable)

29. SIGNATURE (Registration Agency) — DATE REGISTERED

ETA 671 (Mar. 1979)

the applicant from learning the trade or being able to do the work. For example, some apprenticeship programs for law enforcement officers have a minimum height requirement. Also, some tasks, such as railroad work, require great physical strength and stamina. Physical handicaps that would not interfere with a person's performance on the job would not be grounds for disqualifying an applicant.

The interview. All applications are reviewed by the sponsor—often the personnel office—to make sure applicants have fulfilled the general requirements. If they have, the Joint Apprenticeship Committee or the administrative body representing the sponsor will interview each applicant.

At the interview, a group of about four people will ask questions about the applicant's physical health, interest in the trade, and attitude toward the type of work that would be performed by the apprentice. Personal traits such as aggressiveness and sincerity also will be noted. Questions such as these may be asked: Do you like to work with your hands? What makes you think you'd be a good craftworker? Do you know that the work is hard? Interviewers want to know if applicants are qualified, but the oral examination also helps them to determine whether applicants would commit themselves to the work and whether they would be persistent enough to finish the program.

After the interview, the committee rates the applicant numerically, based on his or her qualifications and the interview (see sample evaluation sheets). This rating determines the applicant's place on the register, or waiting list, for apprenticeship openings. People who want to move up on a register may improve their rating by increasing the level of their qualifications, such as by taking courses. If applicants think they were unfairly rated, they can request another interview, or another review of their application by the committee.

Although there is no set of questions that interviewers must ask, records of interviews are kept, including brief summaries of specific factors covered, such as motivation, ambition, and willingness to accept direction. These records are required of registered programs and help the committee members review their notes and explain ratings to applicants.

If, after 2 years, an applicant has not been referred for an apprenticeship opening, the applicant must reactivate his or her file by reapplying. Although the process of reapplication does not require another interview, applicants should try to improve their ratings by making a better impression at a second interview.

Getting In

Getting on a register is a major step toward apprenticeship, but it's only halfway there. The other half is being placed in a program. The wait on a register can last months or even years, depending on the number of qualified applicants and the number of openings.

Openings for new apprentices occur usually only once or twice a year. Therefore, qualified applicants should be prepared for a long wait between referrals. However, usually more than one program per trade operates in an area, and different programs may recruit at different times during the year. Trades with seasonal needs for workers, such as construction, may recruit only during the warmer months. The service and manufacturing industries, on the other hand, can recruit any time during the year, as they are not usually affected by the weather.

Qualified Applicants. Recently, the number of qualified applicants seems to have reached flood level on many registers of local apprenticeship programs. Although about 60,000 openings for apprentices occur each year, in 1979, 367,647 people wanted to get into them. Of that number, 37,205 were women. In the construction trades alone, an estimated eight applicants are qualified for every opening.

The more populated areas have larger numbers of applications, but often have enough industry to support more apprentices. So, although the less populated areas may have less competition for openings, they may not support as many apprentices.

Openings. The availability of apprenticeships in an area depends on three major elements: (1) economic conditions, (2) the willingness of employers to train skilled craftworkers, and (3) new technology.

As economic conditions change, so does the demand for skilled workers. When employment is high and construction and industrial production are booming, more skilled workers are needed, and more apprentices must be trained to help fill the need. When economic conditions are bad, apprenticeships are scarce.

Where To Go for Help

Many organizations, such as labor unions and public agencies, can provide information about apprenticeship. Special programs are available to help people qualify for apprenticeship and to encourage special groups to apply.

Two agencies are designed primarily to help sponsors. These agencies are State and regional offices of the Bureau of Apprenticeship and Training (BAT) and State apprenticeship councils. Their addresses are listed at the end of this article.

People who live in areas not served by any of these sources can go directly to a Joint Apprenticeship Committee or other program sponsor for information about specific programs. For more general information, they can contact regional BAT offices in nearby areas by mail, or they may contact their school counselor or a local job service office.

Special Programs. Many special programs, funded by the Department of Labor, promote apprenticeship to disadvantaged groups and to other people previously not encouraged to apply for apprenticeship openings. These outreach programs are sponsored by concerned groups and labor organizations to provide information, tutoring, counseling, and other services that help prepare people for entry into apprenticeship programs. General programs are designed to help large groups, such as members of minority groups and women. Others pinpoint specific subgroups, such as Navajo Indians or women in a certain location or trade.

Outreach counselors give applicants such information as when programs are recruiting, what the eligibility requirements are, what information the applicant must have on file with the office, and where and when tutoring will begin for preparing to take qualifying examinations. Tutoring sessions last from 1 to 8 weeks, with the average applicant attending 2 weeks of sessions. Session leaders discuss how to take and pass examinations, and they counsel and prepare applicants for the interview. Special subjects such as

basic math, reading, or mechanical reasoning also may be offered.

In today's highly technical world, whether in industry, commerce, or public services, apprenticeship is still one of the best ways to acquire the occupational skills required for full qualification in an ever-increasing number of career fields.

This article provides some general information about apprenticeships. To find out about specific requirements of local programs, potential applicants should contact local sources of information. To find out about these programs, they should check local directories or contact their local Employment Service office. ◯◯◯

Regional Offices
Bureau of Apprenticeship and Training

States Served

Region I
JFK Federal Bldg.
Room E-432
Government Center
Boston, Massachusetts 02203
Telephone: 617/223-6740

Connecticut	New Hampshire
Maine	Rhode Island
Massachusetts	Vermont

Region II
1515 Broadway and 44th Street
Room 3731
New York, New York 10036
Telephone: 212/944-3060

New Jersey	Puerto Rico
New York	Virgin Islands

Region III
P.O. Box 8796
Philadelphia, Pennsylvania 19101
Telephone: 215/596-6417

Delaware	Virginia
Maryland	West Virginia
Pennsylvania	

Region IV
1371 Peachtree St. NE.
Room 700
Atlanta, Georgia 30367
Telephone: 404/881-4405

Alabama	Mississippi
Florida	North Carolina
Georgia	South Carolina
Kentucky	Tennessee

Region V
Federal Bldg.
Room 701
230 South Dearborn St.
Chicago, Illinois 60604
Telephone: 312/353-7205

Illinois	Minnesota
Indiana	Ohio
Michigan	Wisconsin

Region VI
555 Griffin Square Bldg.
Griffin and Young Sts.
Room 858
Dallas, Texas 75202
Telephone: 214/767-4993

Arkansas	Oklahoma
Louisiana	Texas
New Mexico	

Region VII
Federal Office Bldg.
Room 1100
911 Walnut St.
Kansas City, Missouri 64106
Telephone: 816/374-3856

Iowa	Missouri
Kansas	Nebraska

Region VIII
U.S. Custom House
Room 476
721 19th St.
Denver, Colorado 80202
Telephone: 303/837-4791

Colorado	South Dakota
Montana	Utah
North Dakota	Wyoming

Region IX
211 Main Street
Room 344
San Francisco, California
  94105-1978
Telephone: 415/974-0552

Arizona	Hawaii
California	Nevada

Region X
Federal Office Bldg.
Room 8014
909 First Avenue
Seattle, Washington 98174
Telephone: 206/442-5286

Alaska	Oregon
Idaho	Washington

State and Territorial Apprenticeship Agencies

Arizona
Apprenticeship Services
Department of Economic
  Security
207 East McDowell Road
Phoenix 85004

California
Division of Apprenticeship
  Standards
Department of Industrial
  Relations
455 Golden Gate Ave.,
  Room 3230
San Francisco 94102

Colorado
Apprenticeship Council
Division of Labor
323 Centennial Building
Denver 80203

Connecticut
Apprentice Training Division
Department of Labor
200 Folly Brook Boulevard
Wethersfield 06109

Delaware
Apprenticeship Officer
Delaware State Department of
  Labor
State Office Bldg., 6th Floor
820 North French Street
Wilmington 19801

District of Columbia
DC Apprenticeship Council
500 C Street NW., Room 241
Washington 20001

Florida
Bureau of Apprenticeship
Division of Labor
Dept. of Labor & Employment
  Security
1321 Executive Center Dr. East
Tallahassee 32301

Hawaii
Apprenticeship Division
Department of Labor and
  Industrial Relations
825 Mililani Street
Honolulu 96813

Kansas
Apprenticeship Section
Div. of Labor-Management
  Relations and Employment
  Standards
Department of Human
  Resources
512 West 6th Street
Topeka 66603-3178

Kentucky
Apprenticeship and Training
Kentucky State Apprenticeship
  Council
620 South Third Street,
  6th Floor
Louisville 40202

Louisiana
Division of Apprenticeship
Department of Labor
P.O. Box 44094
Baton Rouge 70804

Maine
Maine State Apprenticeship
  and Training Council—
  Department of Manpower
  Affairs
Bureau of Labor
State Office Building
Augusta 04333

Maryland
Apprenticeship and Training
Maryland Apprenticeship and
  Training Council
Division of Labor and Industry
1201 66th Street
Baltimore 21237

Massachusetts
Division of Apprentice
  Training
Department of Labor and
  Industries
Leverett Saltonstall Bldg.
100 Cambridge Street
Boston 02202

Minnesota
Division of Voluntary
  Apprenticeship
Department of Labor and
  Industry
Space Center Bldg., 5th Floor
444 Lafayette Road
St. Paul 55101

Montana
Apprenticeship Bureau
Division of Labor Standards
Department of Labor and
  Industry
Capitol Station
Helena 59620

Nevada
Department of Labor, Capitol
  Complex, Room 601
505 East King Street
Carson City 89710

New Hampshire
Commission of Labor
Department of Labor
19 Pillsbury Street
Concord 03301

New Mexico
N.M. State Apprenticeship
  Council
Labor and Industrial
  Commission
2340 Menaul NE., Suite 212
Albuquerque 87107

New York
Apprentice Training
Department of Labor
The Campus Bldg. #12,
  Room 428
Albany 12240

North Carolina
Apprenticeship Division
North Carolina Department of
  Labor
4 West Edenton Street
Raleigh 27601-1472

Ohio
State Apprenticeship Council
Department of Industrial
  Relations
2323 West Fifth Avenue,
  Room 2250
Columbus 43215

Oregon
Apprenticeship and Training
  Division
State Office Bldg., Room 466
1400 South West Fifth Avenue
Portland 97201

Pennsylvania
Pennsylvania Apprenticeship
  and Training Council
7th and Forster Streets
Department of Labor and
  Industry
Labor and Industry Bldg.,
  Room 1618
Harrisburg 17120

Puerto Rico
Apprenticeship Division
Department of Labor
Right to Employment Division
GPO Box 4452
San Juan 00936

Rhode Island
Apprenticeship Council
Department of Labor
220 Elmwood Avenue
Providence 02907

Vermont
Vermont Apprenticeship
  Council
Department of Labor and
  Industry
120 State Street
State Office Building
Montpelier 05602

Virgin Islands
Division of Apprenticeship
  and Training
Department of Labor
Christiansted, St. Croix 00820

Virginia
Division of Apprenticeship
  Training
Virginia Department of Labor
  and Industry
P.O. Box 12064
Richmond 23241

Washington
Apprenticeship and Training
  Division
Department of Labor and
  Industries
605 East 11th Avenue
Olympia 98504

Wisconsin
Division of Apprenticeship
  and Training
Department of Industry, Labor
  and Human Relations
P.O. Box 7946
Madison 53707

State Offices
Bureau of Apprenticeship and Training

Alabama
1931 9th Avenue, South
South Twentieth Building
Birmingham 35205
205/254-1308

Alaska
Room E-512
Federal Building and
Courthouse, Box 37
701 C Street
Anchorage 99513
907/271-5035

Arizona
2120 North Central
Suite G-110
Phoenix 85004
602/261-3401

Arkansas
Room 3014
Federal Building
700 West Capitol Street
Little Rock 72201
501/378-5415

California
Room 344
211 Main Street
San Francisco 94105-1978
415/974-0556

Colorado
Room 464
U.S. Custom House
721 19th Street
Denver 80202
303/837-4793

Connecticut
Room 367
Federal Building
135 High Street
Hartford 06103
203/244-3886

Delaware
Lock Box 36
Federal Bldg.
844 King Street
Wilmington 19801
302/573-6113

Florida
Room 3080
Hobbs Federal Building
227 North Bronough Street
Tallahassee 32301
904/681-7161

Georgia
Room 725
1371 Peachtree Street NE.
Atlanta 30367
404/881-4403

Hawaii
Room 5113
P.O. Box 50203
300 Ala Moana Boulevard
Honolulu 95850
808/546-7569

Idaho
Suite 250
Owyhee Plaza
1109 Main Street
Boise 83702
208/334-1013

Illinois
Room 505
7222 W. Cermak Road
North Riverside 60546
312/447-0382

Indiana
Room 414
Federal Building and U.S.
Courthouse
46 East Ohio Street
Indianapolis 46204
317/269-7592

Iowa
Room 367
Federal Building
210 Walnut Street
Des Moines 50309
515/284-4690

Kansas
Room 225
Federal Building
444 S.E. Quincy Street
Topeka 66683
913/295-2624 (Ext. 236)

Kentucky
Room 554-C
Federal Building
600 Federal Place
Louisville 40202
502/582-5223

Louisiana
Room 215-B
Hoover Bldg.
8312 Florida Boulevard
Baton Rouge 70806
504/923-3431

Maine
Room 101-B
Federal Building
P.O. Box 917
68 Sewall Street
Augusta 04330
207/622-8235

Maryland
Room 1028
Charles Center—Fed. Bldg.
31 Hopkins Plaza
Baltimore 21201
301/962-2676

Massachusetts
Room 1001
JFK Federal Building
Government Center
Boston 02203
617/223-6745

Michigan
Room 308
Corr Building
300 East Michigan Avenue
Lansing 48933
517/377-1746 or 1750

Minnesota
Room 134
Federal Building and U.S.
Courthouse
316 Robert Street
St. Paul 55101
612/725-7951

Mississippi
Suite 1003
Federal Building
100 West Capitol Street
Jackson 39269
601/960-4346 or 4349

Missouri
Room 547
210 North Tucker
St. Louis 63101
314/452-4522

Montana
Room 394—Drawer #10055
Federal Office Bldg.
301 South Park Avenue
Helena 59626-0055
406/449-5261

Nebraska
Room 700
106 South 15th Street
Omaha 68102
402/221-3281

Nevada
Room 316
Post Office Building
P.O. Box 1987
301 East Stewart Avenue
Las Vegas 89101
702/385-6396

New Hampshire
Room 311
Federal Building
55 Pleasant Street
Concord 03301
603/834-4736

New Jersey
Room 410
402 East State Street
Trenton 08607
609/989-2209

New Mexico
Room 1116
Western Bank Building
505 Marquette NW.
Albuquerque 87102
505/766-2398

New York
512 U.S. Post Office
and Courthouse
Albany 12207
518/472-4800

North Carolina
Room 376
Federal Building
310 New Bern Avenue
Raleigh 27601
919/755-4466

North Dakota
Room 344
New Federal Building
653 2nd Avenue North
Fargo 58102
701/237-5711 (Ext. 5415)

Ohio
Room 605
200 North High Street
Columbus 43215
614/469-7375

Oklahoma
Suite 1440
50 Penn Place
Oklahoma City 73118
405/231-4818

Oregon
840 Federal Building
1220 SW. 3rd Avenue
Portland 97204
503/221-3157 or 3177

Pennsylvania
Room 773
Federal Building
228 Walnut Street
Harrisburg 17108
717/782-3496

Rhode Island
100 Hartford Avenue
Providence 02909
401/838-4328

South Carolina
Room 838
Strom Thurmond Fed. Bldg.
1835 Assembly Street
Columbia 29201
803/765-5547

South Dakota
Room 104
Federal Building
400 South Phillips Avenue
Sioux Falls 57102
605/336-2980 (Ext. 326)

Tennessee
Suite 406
1720 West End Avenue
Nashville 37203
615/251-5408

Texas
Room 2102
VA Building
2320 LaBranch Street
Houston 77004
713/750-1696

Utah
Room 314
Post Office Building
350 South Main Street
Salt Lake City 84101
801/524-5700

Vermont
Suite 103
Burlington Square
96 College Street
Burlington 05401
802/951-6278

Virginia
Room 10-020
400 North 8th Street
Richmond 23240
804/771-2488

Washington
1009 Federal Office Building
909 First Avenue
Seattle 98174
206/442-4756

West Virginia
Room 305
550 Eagan Street
Charleston 25301
304/347-5141

Wisconsin
Room 303
Federal Center
212 East Washington
Avenue
Madison 53703
608/264-5377

Wyoming
Room 8017
J.C. O'Mahoney
Federal Center
P.O. Box 1126
2120 Capitol Avenue
Cheyenne 82001
307/772-2448

RESOURCES:
WHERE TO TURN FOR HELP

INTRODUCTION AND OVERVIEW

Chapter 8 includes information on a computer-based statewide career information delivery system available to individuals in 39 states. It also includes a state-by-state listing of sources of occupational information, excerpted from the most recent *Occupational Outlook Handbook* (1984-85 edition).

In addition to these resources, nearly every community offers many other resources for career planners. Most Y's, community colleges, and high schools offer career services, programs, and other aids to career development and job hunting.

THE RESOURCES

"CIDS: Statewide Career Information Delivery Systems"

"Where To Go for More Information"

REFERENCE

The *Occupational Outlook Handbook*, published biannually by the U.S. Department of Labor, is a basic resource for all career planners. It describes what workers do in each job; the training and education they need; their earnings, working conditions, and job prospects. It also includes information about the effects of the business cycle, defense spending, energy development, and other economic variables on employment. You may be able to find a copy in your counselor's office or school or public library. If not, you can purchase it from the Superintendent of Documents, Washington, DC 20402.

CIDS: STATEWIDE CAREER INFORMATION DELIVERY SYSTEMS

by
Wynonia L. Dunn

Statewide Career Information Delivery Systems (CIDS) provide national, State, and local information to individuals who are exploring careers or searching for jobs. State systems address a need that most people face at one time or another—the need for timely, accurate, and relevant occupational and educational information for making career-related decisions. The availability of such information helps individuals make smoother transitions at key points during their career life, such as the transition from school to work, a return to the labor force, the changing of careers, or the search for a new job.

One shared characteristic of all the State CIDS is that they are computer based. They also have several other traits in common:

• They deliver national, State, and local career information to users.

Wynonia L. Dunn is currently with American College Testing as the assistant director for DIS-COVER, a computer-based career guidance and information system. This article is based on *Status of Statewide Career Information Delivery Systems,* a report she prepared for the National Occupational Information Coordinating Committee while on an Intergovernmental Personnel Assignment from the Fairfax County, Virginia, Public Schools. For additional information, see *Technology for Career Information Delivery,* published by the National Center for Research in Vocational Education, National Center Publications, Box F, 1960 Kenny Road, Columbus, Ohio 43210. (Order No. SN 34; price: $7.25; payment should accompany order.) Information can also be provided by the Association of Computerized Systems from Career Information Clearing House, 247 Hendricks Hall, University of Oregon, Eugene, Oregon 97403.

• They use, to the maximum extent possible, the pertinent data available through the Occupational Information System (OIS).

• They sort and select occupations according to variables identified by the client.

• They serve users in a wide variety of settings—secondary schools, post-secondary institutions, libraries, CETA facilities, job service officers, vocational rehabilitation centers throughout the State.

The specific objectives of the CIDS include the following:

• Help students and clients learn about the range of career opportunities presently available and those that are likely to be available in the future;

• help entrants to the labor force become aware of occupations they would find satisfying;

• encourage people to seek out vocational information on their own;

• help people learn of educational and training opportunities available for the occupations that interest them;

• support related programs, including career education, career and employment counseling, employment and training and educational planning.

The Department of Labor (DOL) initiated the Statewide CIDS program in the 1970's by funding the development of 9 State systems. Oregon was the first State awarded a Federal grant. After Oregon successfully demonstrated the feasibility of developing a Statewide computer-based system to deliver career information, DOL funded 8 additional systems: Alabama, Colorado, Massachusetts, Michigan, Minnesota, Ohio, Washington, and Wisconsin. In November 1979, the National Occupational Information Coordinating Committee (NOICC) awarded CIDS developmental grants to 15 States: Alaska, Arizona, Connecticut, Delaware, Florida,

Georgia, Hawaii, Iowa, Kansas, Maine, Maryland, Nebraska, New York, North Carolina, and South Carolina. In May 1981, NOICC awarded CIDS developmental grants to an additional 6 States: Idaho, Montana, New Jersey, Vermont, Virginia, and Wyoming.

In addition to the States that developed CIDS with the assistance of Federal grants, 8 States and the District of Columbia have developed systems without Federal grants. These States are Arkansas, Illinois, Indiana, New Mexico, North Dakota, Oklahoma, South Dakota, and Texas.

Status

Of the 39 State CIDS, all but 3 offer State-specific occupational and educational information. Military files and national educational information are also provided in many systems. The accompanying box "Information Available Through CIDS," indicates the kinds of material available in each State; additional information—such as bibliographies or local area data—may also be available.

Most States use a combination of delivery modes for all this information. The primary delivery modes are the on-line computer, microcomputer, printed material, needlesort, microfiche, and a toll-free hotline. The trend appears to be to retain the on-line computer and expand market penetration by using microcomputers. The number of State CIDS sites—almost 10,000 at present—is expected to increase dramatically because of the proliferation of microcomputers within school systems and agencies. Fifteen State systems now offer microcomputer delivery; five States were scheduled to add microcomputer delivery to their systems by the fall of 1982; and two State CIDS will offer microcomputer delivery in 1982.

Microcomputers are being used in several ways: 1) storing the search

Information Available Through CIDS	Occupational information				Military	Educational information		Financial aid	Apprenticeships	Approximate number of user sites
	National	State	Job Bank	Employer	Military	National	State	Financial aid	Apprenticeships	
Alabama	●	●	●		●	●	●	●		150
Alaska	●	●			●	●	●	●	●	200
Arizona	●	●	●	●	●	●	●	●	●	200
Arkansas	●	●			●	●	●	●	●	330
Colorado	●	●		●		●	●	●	●	90
Connecticut	●	●	●		●	●	●	●	●	160
Delaware	●	●	●	●	●	●	●	●	●	80
Florida		●	●	●			●	●	●	1.000
Georgia		●					●	●	●	130
Hawaii		●	●				●	●	●	100
Idaho		●					●	●	●	100
Illinois	●	●	●	●	●	●	●		●	180
Indiana	●	●			●	●	●	●		180
Iowa	●	●			●		●	●	●	850
Kansas		●		●	●			●	●	130
Maine	●	●	●		●	●	●	●	●	100
Maryland	●	●			●	●	●	●	●	400
Michigan	●	●		●	●		●	●	●	2.000
Minnesota		●					●	●	●	300
Montana	●	●					●	●	●	50
Nebraska	●	●				●	●	●	●	270
New Jersey (all planned)	●	●		●	●	●	●			120
New Mexico	●	●			●	●	●	●	●	20
New York	●	●				●	●	●		300
North Carolina		●	●				●	●		130
North Dakota		●					●	●	●	15
Ohio	●	●			●	●	●	●	●	300
Oklahoma		●				●	●	●		520
Oregon	●	●			●	●	●	●	●	500
South Carolina	●	●	●		●	●	●		●	260
South Dakota	●	●		●	●	●	●	●		350
Vermont	●	●			●	●	●	●	●	20
Virginia	●	●					●	●	●	860
Washington		●			●		●	●	●	290
Washington, D.C.	●	●	●	●	●	●	●	●		30
Wisconsin	●	●					●	●	●	600
Wyoming	●	●				●	●		●	60
Puerto Rico	●	●				●	●	●	●	30

being used by one State or another. They share some characteristics while at the same time each possesses unique features.

The software usually consists of an accessing or search strategy along with standard information files. Each State adds local information and special needs files to the core software programs to build information systems that meet the needs of the client population.

Most States use only one of the various software packages available, but seven systems currently use at least two. A State usually uses more than one software package because one was already in operation before the inception of the State CIDS. More States might add new software packages in the future, however, because they are developing their own software and because they might be able to increase access to localized information by making it available through software packages already prevalent within the State.

Future
In view of the current status of the CIDS, the majority of State systems should not only survive but actually grow in the 1980's. Technology is making possible the delivery of career information in a highly efficient, cost-effective way to diverse population groups. Technological advances coupled with a rapidly increasing computer sophistication on the part of CIDS staffs and the public should foster growth. In particular, the increasing proliferation of microcomputers in the schools should enhance the growth of State systems.

Educators, State legislators, and the public currently see the need for accurate, relevant occupational information that can be disseminated in a timely, efficient manner. The State systems are meeting this need. ∞

strategy on a floppy diskette and using it in conjunction with the total data base through the on-line computer, needlesort, or microfiche; 2) using more than one floppy diskette to store the occupational data base as well as the search strategy; 3) using microcomputers as terminals for an on-line system; 4) incorporating the use of hard disc technology to expand storage capacity.

State CIDS use a variety of computer programs or software packages. More than 10 software packages are currently

WHERE TO GO FOR MORE INFORMATION

Whether you have questions about a particular job or are trying to compare various fields, the *Occupational Outlook Handbook* is a good place to begin. The *Handbook* will answer many of your initial questions. But remember that it is only one of many sources of information about jobs and careers. After reading a few *Handbook* statements, you may decide that you want more detailed information about a particular occupation. You may want to find out where you can go for training, or where you can find this kind of work in your community. If you are willing to make an effort, you will discover that a wealth of information is available.

Sources of Career Information

Professional societies, trade associations, labor unions, business firms, and educational institutions put out a great deal of free or low-cost career material. Many of these organizations are identified in the Sources of Additional Information section at the end of every *Handbook* statement.

If you want information for an occupation not covered in the *Handbook*, check the directories in your library's reference section for the names of organizations that may provide career materials. There are directories that list organizations, firms, and individuals in fields as diverse as publishing, advertising, banking, insurance, retailing, manufacturing, health care, energy, the environment, performing arts, social welfare, education, training and development, management consulting, and much more. Since there are thousands of directories covering a wide variety of fields, you may want to begin by looking in the *Guide to American Directories* or *The Directory of Directories*. Another good starting point is the *Encyclopedia of Associations*, a multivolume publication that lists thousands of trade associations, professional societies, labor unions, and fraternal and patriotic organizations.

The National Audiovisual Center, a central source for all audiovisual material produced by the U.S. Government, provides free lists of material available for rental or purchase. Subject areas include jobs and careers. Contact the National Audiovisual Center, General Services Administration, Information Services Section, Washington, D.C. 20409. Phone: (301) 763-1896.

Carefully assess any career materials you obtain. Keep in mind the date and source, in particular. Material that is too old may contain obsolete or even misleading information. Be especially cautious about accepting information on employment outlook, earnings, and training requirements if it is more than 5 years old. The source is important because it affects the content. Although some occupational materials are produced solely for the purpose of

objective vocational guidance, others are produced for recruitment purposes. You should be wary of biased information, which may tend to leave out important items, overglamorize the occupation, overstate the earnings, or exaggerate the demand for workers.

Libraries, career centers, and guidance offices are important sources of career information. Thousands of books, brochures, magazines, and audiovisual materials are available on such subjects as occupations, careers, self-assessment, and job hunting. Your school library or guidance office is likely to have some of this material; ask the staff for help. Collections of occupational material also can be found in public libraries, college libraries, learning resource centers, and career counseling centers.

Begin your library search by looking in an encyclopedia under "vocations" or "careers," and then look up specific fields. The card catalog will direct you to books on particular careers, such as architect or plumber. Be sure to check the periodical section, too. You'll find trade and professional magazines and journals in specific areas such as automotive mechanics or interior design. Many libraries and career centers have pamphlet files for specific occupations. Collections of occupational information may also include nonprint materials such as films, filmstrips, cassettes, tapes, and kits. Computerized occupational information systems enable users to obtain career information instantly. In addition to print and nonprint materials, most career centers and guidance offices offer individual counseling, group discussions, guest speakers, field trips, and career days.

Counselors play an important role in providing career information. Vocational testing and counseling are available in a number of places, including:

—guidance offices in high schools.

—career planning and placement offices in colleges.

—placement offices in vocational schools.

—vocational rehabilitation agencies.

—counseling services offered by community organizations, commercial firms, and professional consultants.

—Job Service offices affiliated with the U.S. Employment Service.

The reputation of a particular counseling agency should be checked with professionals in the field. As a rule, counselors will not tell you what to do. Instead, they are likely to administer interest inventories and aptitude tests, interpret the results, talk over various possibilities, and help you explore your options. Counselors are familiar with the job market and

also can discuss entry requirements and costs of the schools, colleges, or training programs that offer preparation for the kind of work in which you are interested. Most important of all, a counselor can help you consider occupational information in relation to your own abilities, aspirations, and goals.

Don't overlook the importance of **personal contacts.** Talking with people is one of the best ways of learning about an occupation. Most people are glad to talk about what they do and how well they like their jobs. Have specific questions lined up; you might question workers about their personal experiences and knowledge of their field. By asking the right questions, you will find out what kind of training is really important, how workers got their first jobs as well as the one they're in now, and what they like and dislike about the work. These interviews serve several purposes: You get out into the business world, you learn about an occupation, you become familiar with interviewing, and you meet people worth contacting when you start looking for a job.

Sources of State and Local Information

State occupational information coordinating committees can help you locate information about job prospects in your State or area. By contrast, the *Handbook* provides information for the Nation as a whole. The committee may provide the information directly, or refer you to other sources. In many States, it can tell you where you can go to use the State's career information delivery system (CIDS).

These systems, currently in place in most States, provide national, State, and local information to individuals who are exploring careers or searching for jobs. They serve users in a wide variety of settings—secondary schools, post-secondary institutions, libraries, job training sites, Job Service offices, and vocational rehabilitation centers.

Using a variety of delivery modes including on-line computer, microcomputer, printed material, needlesort, microfiche, and toll-free hotline, these systems provide information on occupations, educational opportunities, student financial aid, apprenticeships, and the military.

To find out what kinds of career materials have been developed for your State, contact the director of the State occupational information coordinating committee. Their addresses and telephone numbers are listed at the end of this section of the *Handbook*.

Employment security agencies in all 50 States, the District of Columbia, and Puerto Rico develop detailed information about the labor market. Typically, State agencies publish reports that deal with current and projected

Reprinted from *Occupational Outlook Handbook*, 1984-85, U.S. Department of Labor.

employment, characteristics of the work force, changes in State and area economic activities, and the employment structure of important industries. Major statistical indicators of labor market activity are released on a monthly, quarterly, and annual basis. To learn which studies, reports, and analyses are available for a particular State, contact the chief of research and analysis in the State employment security agency. Their addresses and telephone numbers are listed at the end of this section.

Sources of Education and Training Information

As a rule, professional or trade associations can provide lists of schools that offer career preparation in a particular field—operations research, publishing, or arts management, for example. Whenever possible, the Sources of Additional Information section at the end of every *Handbook* statement directs you to organizations that can provide training information.

For general information, a library, career center, or guidance office may be the best place to look; all of them ordinarily have collections of catalogs, directories, and guides to education and training opportunities. Computerized career information systems available in many schools, colleges, and Job Service offices generally provide information on education and training, student financial aid, and related matters.

A number of handbooks gives pertinent information on courses of study, admissions requirements, expenses, and student financial aid at the Nation's 2-year and 4-year colleges and universities. School and public libraries almost always have copies, as do large bookstores. Remember that these directories are updated and revised frequently; be sure to use the most recent edition. Libraries and guidance offices often have collections of college catalogs as well.

Postsecondary Schools with Occupational Programs, a publication of the U.S. Department of Education's National Center for Education Statistics, lists vocational-technical institutes, trade and technical schools, business schools, and other institutions—such as hospitals—that provide career training. Dozens of vocational areas are included—accounting, automotive mechanics, cosmetology, graphic arts, radio and television repair, truck driving, welding, and more. The 1982 edition may be available in counseling centers or large public libraries, or may be purchased for $9.50 from the Superintendent of Documents, U.S. Government Printing Office, Washington, D.C. 20402. Specify GPO stock number 065–000–00192–6.

Directory of Educational Institutions, an annual publication, lists schools accredited by the Association of Independent Colleges and Schools (AICS). Most AICS-accredited institutions are business schools. They offer programs in secretarial science, business administration, accounting, data processing, court reporting, paralegal studies, fashion merchandising, travel/tourism, culinary arts, drafting, electronics, and more. For a copy of the *Directory,* write:

Association of Independent Colleges and Schools, 1 Dupont Circle, NW., Suite 350, Washington, D.C. 20036. Phone: (202) 659–2460.

Allied Health Education Directory is published annually by the American Medical Association (AMA) and lists programs for health professions training that meet the standards of the AMA Committee on Allied Health Education and Accreditation (CAHEA). Currently, CAHEA accredits training programs for 26 occupations including diagnostic medical sonographer, physician assistant, medical record administrator, nuclear medicine technologist, perfusionist, and radiographer. Ordering information for the current edition of the *Directory* is available from: Department of Allied Health Education and Accreditation, 535 N. Dearborn St., Chicago, Illinois 60601.

Information on private trade and technical schools is available from the National Association of Trade and Technical Schools (NATTS). Among their many publications are *Handbook of Trade and Technical Careers and Training, How to Choose a Career and a Career School,* and *College Plus: Put Your Degree to Work with Trade and Technical Skills.* For a complete list, contact NATTS at 2021 K St. NW., Washington, D.C. 20006. Phone: (202) 296–8892.

The National Home Study Council supplies information about home study programs. They distribute *Directory of Accredited Home Study Schools* (free) and *There's a School in Your Mail Box* ($5.00, including postage). Requests for these publications should be directed to National Home Study Council, 1601 18th St. NW., Washington, D.C. 20009. Phone (202) 234–5100.

Labor unions and school guidance offices can provide information about apprenticeships. Local Job Service offices usually have at least one counselor familiar with apprenticeship programs in the area. In some cities, Apprenticeship Information Centers (AIC's) affiliated with the U.S. Employment Service furnish information, counseling, and aptitude testing, and direct people for more specific help to union hiring halls, Joint Apprenticeship Committees, and employer sponsors. The local Job Service can tell you whether there's an AIC in your community.

Sources of Financial Aid Information

If possible, consult a high school guidance counselor or college financial aid officer for advice on sources of financial aid. Don't neglect any possibility, for many organizations offer scholarships, fellowships, grants, loans, and work-study programs. Study the directories and guides to sources of student financial aid available in guidance offices and public libraries. Many career information systems provide information on financial aid.

Particularly useful is the American Legion's *Need a Lift?*, a booklet containing career and scholarship information for both undergraduate and graduate students. The 1983 edition costs $1.00 prepaid (includes postage) and can be obtained from: American Legion, Attn: Emblem Sales, P.O. Box 1055, Indianapolis, Ind. 46206.

Meeting College Costs, a College Board publication that is updated annually, explains how to apply for student financial aid. High school students should ask their guidance counselors for the current edition. A listing of College Board publications on student financial aid may be obtained from: College Board Publication Orders, Dept. A, Box 886, New York, N.Y. 10101.

The Federal Government provides several kinds of financial assistance to students: Grants, loans, work-study, and benefits. Information about programs administered by the U.S. Department of Education is presented in a pamphlet entitled, *Five Federal Financial Aid Programs, 1983–84: A Student Consumer's Guide.* This pamphlet is revised every year; request the current edition by calling (301) 984–4070, or by writing to: Pell Grants, P.O. Box 84, Washington, D.C. 20044.

Federal financial aid for students in the health professions is administered by the U.S. Department of Health and Human Services. Currently, major programs include Health Education Assistance Loans (HEAL), Health Profession Student Loans, Nursing Student Loans, and National Health Service Corps Scholarships. The financial aid office at the school in which you are enrolled, or plan to enroll, can provide information on eligibility requirements and application procedures. Information about National Health Service Corps Scholarships also can be obtained by calling (301) 443–1650 between 8:30 a.m. and 5:00 p.m. Eastern time, Monday through Friday, except Federal holidays, or by writing to: NHSC Scholarships, Parklawn Building, Room 17A–31, 5600 Fishers Lane, Rockville, Md. 20857.

Some student aid programs are designed to assist specific groups: Hispanics, blacks, native Americans, or women, for example. *Higher Education Opportunities for Minorities and Women: Annotated Selections,* published annually by the U.S. Department of Education, is a useful guide to organizations that offer loan, scholarship, and fellowship assistance, with special emphasis on aid for minorities and women. Opportunities for financial aid are listed by field of study, including architecture, arts and science, business, education, engineering and science, health, international affairs, journalism, law, political science and public administration, psychology, sociology, social work, speech pathology and audiology, and theology. Educational opportunities with the Armed Forces are also described. This publication can be found in many libraries and guidance offices, or may be purchased from the Superintendent of Documents, U.S. Government Printing Office, Washington, D.C. 20402. Price for the 1982 edition is $5.00 and the GPO stock number is 065–000–00175–6. The 1983 edition is forthcoming.

Career and Counseling Information for Special Groups

Certain groups of jobseekers face special difficulties in obtaining suitable and satisfying employment. All too often, veterans, youth, handicapped persons, minorities, and women experience difficulty in the labor market. The reasons for job market disadvantage vary, of course. People may have trouble setting career goals and looking for work for reasons as different as a limited command of English, a prison record, or lack of self-confidence. Some people are held back by their background—by growing up in a setting that provided only a few role models and little exposure to the wide range of opportunities in the world of work.

A growing number of communities have career counseling, training, and placement services for people with special needs. Programs are sponsored by a variety of organizations, including churches and synagogues, nonprofit organizations, social service agencies, the Job Service, and vocational rehabilitation agencies. Some of the most successful programs provide the extensive support that disadvantaged jobseekers require. They begin by helping clients resolve personal, family, or other fundamental problems that prevent them from finding or keeping a suitable job. Some agencies that serve special groups provide an array of supportive services designed to help people find and keep jobs.

Agencies that provide employment counseling as well as other kinds of assistance are identified in *Directory of Counseling Services*, a publication that lists accredited or provisional members of the International Association of Counseling Services, Inc. (IACS), an affiliate of the American Association for Counseling and Development. The 1981–82 edition is available for $6 (including postage) from IACS at 5999 Stevenson Ave., Suite 307, Alexandria, Va. 22304. Phone: (703) 823–9800.

Women's centers are an excellent resource for women seeking employment and counseling assistance. Many women's centers are located on college campuses. Some of these centers have a primarily academic orientation, sponsoring historical research and policy studies, for example. Others emphasize direct service to women in the community through outreach programs and counseling and job placement services. Still others offer vocational training. Women's centers are also operated by community organizations. Many of these centers emphasize nontraditional jobs for women, and almost all provide information and referral services.

Most States and many cities and counties have commissions or councils for women, many of which are actively engaged in improving employment opportunities for women in their area. A number of commissions have prepared resource directories for women, and a few operate employment or counseling programs.

Resource materials for women abound. Publications of the Women's Bureau of the U.S. Department of Labor, for example, include *Job Options for Women in the 80's* and *A Woman's Guide to Apprenticeship*. Single copies of each may be obtained, while the supply lasts, by sending a self-addressed mailing label to: Women's Bureau, U.S. Department of Labor, Room S–3005, 200 Constitution Ave., NW., Washington, D.C. 20210. Phone: (202) 523–6668.

Women's Handbook, a publication of the U.S. Small Business Administration (SBA), describes services available for women seeking to enter the ranks of small business owners. It is available from SBA offices nationwide. For addresses and telephone numbers of SBA field offices, look under "United States Government" in your local telephone directory. The publication may also be requested from: Consumer Information Center, Pueblo, Colo. 81009.

Professional Women's Groups Providing Employment Assistance to Women, a 1983 publication of the American Association of University Women (AAUW), is available for $2.00 (includes postage) from AAUW Sales, 2401 Virginia Ave., NW., Washington, D.C. 20037. Phone: (202) 785–7772. AAUW issues a number of other materials, including *A Job Hunter's Kit*, designed for women reentering the labor force, recent college graduates, and those interested in a mid-career change. Write for a current publications list.

Where the Jobs Are: Selected Careers for Women is published by the Business and Professional Women's Foundation (BPW). For information about the current edition, and a list of other BPW materials on women and work, send a stamped, self-addressed envelope to Publications List, BPW Foundation, 2012 Massachusetts Ave., NW., Washington, D.C. 20036. Phone: (202) 293–1200. Bibliographies and information sheets on women's employment issues are available free of charge from the Marguerite Rawalt Resource Center at the same address.

Other career resources include *Directory of Special Opportunities for Women*, published in 1981 by Garrett Park Press (Garrett Park, Md.). The *Directory* lists sources of career training, financial aid, and other assistance for women entering or reentering the labor force. The publication also identifies employment-oriented networks, programs, and organizations for women. Look for it in a library, guidance office, or counseling center.

Suit Yourself . . . Shopping for a Job is self-help publication, with tips, techniques, and self-assessment tools for organizing a job search. Published in 1980 by Wider Opportunities for Women (WOW), a national nonprofit women's employment organization, it can be purchased for $7.50 (includes postage) from WOW, 1325 G St. NW., Washington, D.C. 20005. WOW issues other materials as well; request a current publications list. Phone: (202) 783–5155.

Directory of Special Programs for Minority Group Members: Career Information Services, Employment Skills Banks, Financial Aid Sources (Garrett Park, Md.: Garrett Park Press), now in its third edition, lists thousands of educational, career, and other services and programs that help minority group members in their educational and career advancement

Career information for minority group members also appears in specialized magazines including *The Black Collegian* and *Minority Engineer*.

The Veterans Administration issues a wide variety of materials on career decisionmaking,

student financial aid, job search, and other employment-related topics. Contact: Department of Veterans Benefits (232A), Veterans Administration Central Office, 810 Vermont Ave., NW., Washington, D.C. 20420. Phone: (202) 389–2972.

The 1981–82 edition of *Directory of Organizations Interested in the Handicapped* lists more than 150 voluntary and public agencies in the rehabilitation field and briefly describes their purpose, programs, and publications. Copies of the *Directory*, and many other print and audiovisual materials on employment of people with disabilities, may be obtained from: President's Committee on Employment of the Handicapped, Washington, D.C. 20210. Phone: (202) 653–5044.

State vocational rehabilitation agencies are an important source of career and counseling information for people with disabilities; they are listed in the *Directory*.

Job Opportunities for the Blind, a project of the National Federation of the Blind in partnership with the U.S. Department of Labor, operates a nationwide toll-free number: 1–800–638–7518. Services offered by the organization include recorded materials, a listing of job openings, and seminars on employment-related topics for blind and deaf-blind applicants.

Employment counseling and placement services for older workers have been established in some communities. The area agency on aging can tell you whether there is a senior employment program in your community. Local offices of the State employment service should also be able to provide information about job placement services for older workers. Information about the small but growing network of nonprofit senior employment agencies can be obtained from the National Association of Older Worker Employment Services, 600 Maryland Ave., SW., West Wing 100, Washington, D.C. 20024. Phone: (202) 479–1200.

Federal laws, Executive Orders, and selected Federal grant programs bar discrimination in employment based on race, color, religion, sex, national origin, age, and handicap. Employers in the private and the public sectors, Federal contractors, and grantees are covered by these laws. The U.S. Equal Employment Opportunity Commission (EEOC) is responsible for administering many of the programs that prohibit discrimination in employment. Information about how to file a charge of discrimination is available from local EEOC offices around the country. Their addresses and telephone numbers are listed in telephone directories under U.S. Government, EEOC, or from: Equal Employment Opportunity Commission, 2401 E St. N.W., Washington, D.C. 20507. Phone: (202) 634–6922.

Information on Federal laws concerning fair labor standards—including the minimum wage law—and equal employment opportunity can be obtained from the Office of Information and Consumer Affairs, Employment Standards Administration, U.S. Department of Labor, Room C–4331, 200 Constitution Ave., NW., Washington, D.C. 20210.

Information on Finding a Job

These days, a well-planned job search is essential. For information on job openings, follow up as many leads as possible. Parents, neighbors, teachers, and counselors may know of jobs. Check the want ads. Investigate your local Job Service office and find out whether private or nonprofit employment agencies in your community can help you.

Where to Find Out About Job Openings

- Job Service offices
- Civil Service announcements (Federal, State, local)
- Classified ads
  - Local and out-of-town newspapers
  - Professional journals
  - Trade magazines
- Labor unions
- Professional associations (State and local chapters)
- Libraries and community centers
- Women's counseling and employment programs
- Youth programs
- School or college placement services
- Employment agencies and career consultants

Merchandising Your Job Talents, a 21-page pamphlet prepared by the U.S. Department of Labor, offers tips on organizing your job search, writing a resume, taking preemployment tests, and making the most of the interview. The pamphlet is available at most Job Service offices, or may be purchased from the Superintendent of Documents, U.S. Government Printing Office, Washington, D.C. 20402. Price of the 1983 edition is $2.75 and the stock number is 029–014–00212–7.

Informal job search methods. Informal methods of job search are the most popular, and also the most effective. Informal methods include direct application to employers with or without referral by friends or relatives. Jobseekers locate a potential employer and file an application, often without certain knowledge that an opening exists.

You can find targets for your informal search in several ways. The *Yellow Pages* and local chambers of commerce will give the names and addresses of appropriate firms in the community where you wish to work. You can also get listings of most firms in a specific industry—banking, insurance, and newspaper publishing, for example—by consulting one of the directories on the reference shelf of your public library. Friends, relatives, and people you meet during your job search are likely to give you ideas about places where you can apply for a job.

Want ads. The "Help Wanted" ads in a major newspaper contain hundreds of job listings. As a job search tool, they have two advantages: They are cheap and easy to acquire, and they often result in successful placement. There are disadvantages as well. Want ads give a distorted view of the local labor market, for they tend to underrepresent small firms. They also tend to overrepresent certain occupations, such as clerical and sales jobs. How helpful they are will depend largely on the kind of job you seek.

Bear in mind that want ads do not provide complete information; many give little or no description of the job, working conditions, and pay. Some omit the identity of the employer. In addition, firms often run multiple listings. Some ads offer jobs in other cities (which do not help the local worker); others advertise employment agencies rather than employment.

If you use want ads, keep the following suggestions in mind:

—Don't rely exclusively on want ads; follow up other leads, too.

—Answer ads promptly. The opening may be filled before the ad stops running.

—Follow the ads diligently. Checking them every day as early as possible gives you the best advantage over other applicants, which may mean the difference between a job and a rejection.

—Don't expect too much from "blind ads" that do not reveal the employer's identity. Employers use blind ads to avoid being swamped with applicants, or to fill a particular vacancy quietly and confidentially. The chances of finding a job through blind ads tend to be slim.

—Be cautious about answering "no experience necessary" ads. Most employers are able to fill job openings that do not require experience without advertising in the newspaper. This type of ad may mean that the job is hard to fill because of low wages or poor working conditions, or because it is straight commission work.

Public employment service. The public employment service, also called the Job Service, is often overlooked in finding out about local job openings. Run by the State employment security agencies under the direction of the Labor Department's U.S. Employment Service, the 1,700 local Job Service offices provide help without charge. Job Service staff help jobseekers find employment and help employers find qualified workers. To find the office nearest you, look in the State government telephone listings under "Job Service" or "Employment."

Job matching and referral. Upon entering a Job Service center, an applicant is interviewed to determine the type of work for which he or she indicates an interest and aptitude. The interviewer determines if the applicant is "job ready" or if counseling and testing services are needed. Applicants who know what kind of work they are qualified for may spend some time examining the Job Bank, a computerized listing of public and private sector job openings that is updated every day. The Job Bank is self-service; applicants examine a book or microfilm viewer and select openings that interest them. Afterwards, a Job Service staff member may describe a particular job opening in some detail and arrange for an interview with the prospective employer.

Counseling and testing. Job Service centers also help jobseekers who are uncertain about their qualifications and the kind of work they want. Most centers are staffed with a specialist who furnishes complete counseling and testing services. Counselors help jobseekers choose and prepare for an occupation based on their qualifications and interests. They aim to help individuals become aware of their job potential and then develop it. The testing program measures occupational aptitudes, clerical and literary skills, and occupational interests. Testing and counseling before job referral ensure a better match between applicant and job.

Services for special groups. By law, veterans are entitled to priority in interviewing, counseling, testing, job development, and job placement. Special counselors called veterans employment representatives are trained to deal with the particular problems of veterans, who

---

JOB INTERVIEW TIPS

Preparation:
- Learn something about the company
- Have specific job or jobs in mind
- Review in your mind your qualifications for the job
- Be prepared to answer broad questions about yourself

Personal Appearance:
- Well groomed
- Suitable dress
- No chewing gum
- Only smoke when invited

The Interview:
- Answer each question as well as you can
- Be prompt in giving responses
- Be well mannered
- Use good English and avoid the use of slang
- Be cooperative and enthusiastic
- Don't be afraid to ask questions

Test (if employer gives one):
- Listen carefully to instructions
- Read each question carefully
- Write legibly and clearly
- Budget your time wisely and don't stay on one question too long

Information to Take With you:
- Social Security number
- Driver's license number
- Education, which should include school name or number and address; curriculum; dates of attendance; highest grade completed or date of graduation
- Previous employment (summer, work-study, or part-time). Include the following for each job: name of employer; address of job; job title; dates of employment

- Hobbies or special interests
- Special skills
- References. Usually an employer requires three references. Get permission from people before using their names. If you can avoid it, do not use the names of relatives. For each reference, give the following information: name; address; telephone number; occupation

may find it difficult to readjust to civilian life. Although such veterans often face multiple problems, joblessness alone is a major barrier to resuming an ordinary life. Special help for disabled veterans begins with outreach units in each State, whose job it is to identify jobless disabled veterans and make them aware of the many kinds of assistance available.

A special effort is made to assist youth between the ages of 16 and 22—students, dropouts, and graduates entering the labor market. Youthful applicants are tested, counseled, and aided in choosing work that suits their abilities and interests. Each year, local Job Service centers conduct a Summer Youth Program to provide summer jobs in city, county, and State government agencies for low-income youth. In addition, the Job Corps, with more than 100 centers throughout the United States, provides an opportunity for young people to learn a skill or obtain the educational base needed to advance in society.

The Job Service also refers applicants to opportunities under the Job Training Partnership Act (JTPA) of 1982, which replaces the Comprehensive Employment and Training Act (CETA) as the principal Federal legislation in this field. JTPA focuses on preparing economically disadvantaged persons for jobs in the private sector.

Private employment agencies. In the appropriate section of the classified ads or the telephone book you can find numerous advertisements for private employment agencies. All are in business to make money, but some offer higher quality service and better chances of successful placement than others.

The three main places in which private agencies advertise are newspaper want ads, the *Yellow Pages,* and trade journals. Telephone listings give little more than the name, address, phone number, and specialty of the agency, while trade journals generally advertise openings for a particular occupation, such as accountant or computer programmer. Want ads, then, are the best source of general listings of agencies.

These listings fall into two categories—those offering specific openings and those offering a general promise of employment. You should concentrate on the former and use the latter only as a last resort. With a specific opening mentioned in the ad, you have greater assurance of the agency's desire to place qualified individuals in suitable jobs.

When responding to such an ad, you may learn more about the job over the phone. If you are interested, visit the agency, fill out an application, present a resume, and talk with an interviewer. The agency will then arrange an interview with the employer if you are qualified, and perhaps suggest alternative openings if you are not.

Most agencies operate on a commission basis, with the fee contingent upon a successful match. The employer pays agencies advertising "no fees, no contracts" and the applicant pays nothing. Many agencies, however, do charge applicants. You should find out the exact cost before using the service.

Community agencies. A growing number of nonprofit organizations throughout the Nation provide counseling, career development, and job placement services. These agencies generally concentrate on services for a particular labor force group—women, youth, minorities, ex-offenders, or older workers, for example. It's up to you to discover whether your community has such agencies and whether they can help you. The local Job Service center should be able to tell you whether such an agency has been established in your community. Your church, synagogue, or local library may have the information, too.

College career planning and placement offices. Career planning and placement offices at colleges and universities offer valuable services to students and alumni for a modest fee. Many services, in fact, are free. College placement offices operate as employment agencies, matching applicants with suitable jobs and lining up interviews. On large campuses, for example, they set up schedules and facilities for interviews with industry recruiters. And many offices maintain lists of local part-time, temporary, and summer jobs.

College career planning and placement offices also provide services related to counseling and job search techniques. They may, for example, maintain a career resource library; administer tests that enable students to identify and evaluate interests, work values, and skills; conduct workshops on such topics as job search strategy, resume writing, letterwriting, and effective interviewing; critique drafts of resumes and videotapes of mock interviews; maintain files of resumes and references; and conduct job fairs.

State and Local Information. For each State, the District of Columbia, and Puerto Rico, the following list provides the title, address, and telephone number of two principal sources of labor market and career information: The State employment security agency's chief of research and analysis, and the director of the State Occupational Information Coordinating Committee (SOICC).

Alabama

Chief, Research and Statistics, Department of Industrial Relations, Industrial Relations Bldg., Room 427, 649 Monroe St., Montgomery, Ala. 36130. Phone: (205) 832–5263.

Director, Alabama Occupational Information Coordinating Committee, First Southern Towers, Suite 402, 100 Commerce St., Montgomery Ala. 36130. Phone: (205) 832–5737.

Alaska

Chief, Research and Analysis, Employment Security Division, Department of Labor, P.O. Box 1149, Juneau, Alaska 99811. Phone: (907) 465–4502.

Coordinator, Alaska Occupational Information Coordinating Committee, Pouch F—State Office Bldg., Juneau, Alaska 99811. Phone: (907) 465–2980.

Arizona

Chief, Labor Market Information, Research and Analysis, Department of Economic Security, 733-A, P.O. Box 6123, Phoenix, Ariz. 85035. Phone: (602) 255–3616.

Executive Director, Arizona State Occupational Information Coordinating Committee, 1535 West Jefferson, Room 345, Phoenix, Ariz. 85007. Phone: (602) 255–3680.

Arkansas

Assistant Director, Research and Analysis, Employment Security Division, P.O. Box 2981, Little Rock, Ark. 72203. Phone: (501) 371–1541.

Director, Arkansas State Occupational Information Coordinating Committee, P.O. Box 2981, Little Rock, Ark. 72203. Phone: (501) 371–3551.

California

Chief, Employment Data and Research Division, Employment Development Department, P.O. Box 1679, Sacramento, Calif. 95814. Phone: (916) 445–4434.

Executive Director, California Occupational Information Coordinating Committee, 1027 10th Street, No. 302, Sacramento, Calif. 95814. Phone: (916) 323–6544.

Colorado

Chief, Research and Development, Division of Employment and Training, Department of Labor and Employment, 1728 Lincoln St., Denver, Colo. 80203. Phone: (303) 839–5833, Ext. 43.

Director, Office of Occupational Information, Colorado Occupational Information Coordinating Committee, 218 Centennial Bldg., 1313 Sherman St., Denver, Colo. 80203. Phone: (303) 866–4488.

Connecticut

Director, Research and Information, Employment Security Division, Department of Labor, 200 Folly Brook Blvd., Wethersfield, Conn. 06109. Phone: (203) 641–4280.

Executive Director, Connecticut State Occupational Information Coordinating Committee, 90 Washington St., First Floor, Hartford, Conn. 06115. Phone: (203) 566–2502, 2503, 5047, 5699.

Delaware

Chief, Office of Planning, Research and Evaluation, Department of Labor, University Plaza Complex Office, Chapman Rd., Route 273, Newark, Del. 19702. Phone: (302) 368–6921.

Director, Delaware Occupational Information Coordinating Committee, Drummond Office Plaza, Suite 3303, Building No. 3, Newark, Del. 19711. Phone: (302) 368–6772.

District of Columbia

Chief, Branch of Labor Market Information, Department of Employment Services, 500 C St., N.W., Room 411, Washington, D.C. 20001. Phone: (202) 724–2414.

Executive Director, D.C. Occupational Information Coordinating Committee, 500 C St. NW., Suite 621, Washington, D.C. 20001. Phone: (202) 639–1083.

Florida

Director, Research and Analysis, Division of Labor and Employment Security, Coldwell Bldg., Tallahassee, Fla. 32301. Phone: (904) 488–1048.

Director, Florida Occupational Information Coordinating Committee, 124 West Jefferson St., Tallahassee, Fla. 32301. Phone: (904) 224–3660.

Georgia

Director, Labor Information Systems, Department of Labor, 254 Washington St., SW., Atlanta, Ga. 30334. Phone: (404) 656–3177.

Executive Director, Georgia Occupational Information Coordinating Committee, 501 Pulliam St., SW., Room 339, Atlanta, Ga. 30312. Phone: (404) 656–3117.

Hawaii

Chief, Research and Statistics, Department of Labor and Industrial Relations, 830 Punchbowl St., Honolulu, Hawaii 96813. Phone: (808) 548–7639.

Executive Director, Hawaii State Occupational Information Cordinating Committee, 830 Punchbowl St., Room 205, Honolulu, Hawaii 96813. Phone: (808) 548–3496.

Idaho

Chief, Research and Analysis, Department of Employment, P.O. Box 35, Boise, Idaho 83735. Phone: (208) 384–2755.

Coordinator, Idaho Occupational Information Coordinating Committee, Len B. Jordan Bldg., Room 301, 650 W. State St., Boise, Idaho 83720. Phone: (208) 334–3705.

Illinois

Director, Research and Analysis Division, Bureau of Employment Security, Department of Labor, 910 S. Michigan Ave., Chicago, Ill. 60605. Phone: (312) 793–2317.

Executive Director, Illinois Occupational Information Coordinating Committee, 217 E. Monroe, Suite 203, Springfield, Ill. 62706. Phone: (217) 785–0789.

Indiana

Chief of Research and Statistics, Employment Security Division, 10 N. Senate Ave., Indianapolis, Ind. 46204. Phone: (317) 232–7701.

Director, Indiana Occupational Information Coordinating Committee, 17 W. Market St., 434 Illinois Bldg., Indianapolis, Ind. 46204. Phone: (317) 232–3625.

Iowa

Chief, Audit and Analysis, Department of Job Service, 1000 E. Grand Ave., Des Moines, Iowa 50319. Phone: (515) 281–5802.

Executive Director, Iowa State Occupational Information Coordinating Committee, 523 E. 12th St., Des Moines, Iowa 50319. Phone: (515) 281–8076.

Kansas

Chief, Research and Analysis, Department of Human Resources, Department of Labor, 401 Topeka Ave., Topeka, Kans. 66603. Phone: (913) 296–5058.

Director, Kansas Occupational Information Coordinating Committee, 512 W. 6th St., Topeka, Kans. 66603. Phone: (913) 296–5286.

Kentucky

Manager, Labor Market Research and Analysis, Department of Manpower Services, Cabinet for Human Resources, 275 E. Main St., Frankfort, Ky. 40621. Phone: (502) 564–7976.

Coordinator, Kentucky Occupational Information Coordinating Committee, 275 E. Main St., D.H.R. Bldg. 2nd Floor East, Frankfort, Ky. 40621. Phone: (502) 564–4258.

Louisiana

Chief, Research and Statistics, Department of Labor, P.O. Box 44094, Capital Station, Baton Rouge, La. 70804. Phone: (504) 342–3141.

Director, Louisiana State Occupational Information Coordinating Committee, 1000 Science Hwy., Baton Rouge, La. 70802. Phone: (504) 342–5149.

Maine

Director, Research and Analysis, Bureau of Employment Security, 20 Union St., Augusta, Maine 04330. Phone: (207) 289–2271.

Executive Director, Maine State Occupational Information Coordinating Committee, State House Station 71, Augusta, Maine 04333. Phone: (207) 289–2331.

Maryland

Director, Research and Analysis, Department of Human Resources, 1100 N. Eutaw St., Baltimore, Md. 21201. Phone: (301) 383–5000.

Executive Director, Maryland Occupational Information Coordinating Committee, Jackson Towers, Suite 304, 1123 N. Eutaw St., Baltimore, Md. 21201. Phone: (301) 383–6350.

Massachusetts

Director, Job Market Research, Division of Employment Security, Hurley Bldg., Government Center, Boston, Mass. 02114. Phone: (617) 727–6556.

Executive Director, Massachusetts Occupational Information Coordinating Committee, One Ashburton Place, Room 2110, McCormack Bldg., Boston, Mass. 02108. Phone: (617) 727–9740.

Michigan

Director, Research and Statistics, Employment Security Commission, 7310 Woodward Ave., Room 516, Detroit, Mich. 48202. Phone: (313) 876–5445.

Executive Coordinator, Michigan Occupational Information Coordinating Committee, P.O. Box 30015, Lansing, Mich. 48909. Phone: (517) 373–0363.

Minnesota

Director, Research and Statistical Services, Department of Economic Security, 390 N. Robert St., St. Paul, Minn. 55101. Phone: (612) 296–6545.

SOICC Director, Department of Economic Security, 690 American Center Bldg., 150 E. Kellogg Blvd., St. Paul, Minn. 55101. Phone: (612) 296–2072.

Mississippi

Chief, Research and Statistics, Employment Security Commission, P.O. Box 1699, Jackson, Miss. 39205. Phone: (601) 961–7424.

SOICC Director, Vocational Technical Education, P.O. Box 771, Jackson, Miss. 39205. Phone: (601) 359–3412.

Missouri

Chief, Research and Statistics, Division of Employment Security, P.O. Box 59, Jefferson City, Mo. 65104. Phone: (314) 751–3215.

Director, Missouri Occupational Information Coordinating Committee, 421 E. Dunklin St., Jefferson City, Mo. 65101. Phone: (314) 751–3215, 3323.

Montana

Chief, Research and Analysis, Employment Security Division, Department of Labor and Industry, P.O. Box 1728, Helena, Mont. 59601. Phone: (406) 449–2430.

Program Manager, Montana State Occupational Information Coordinating Committee, Room C317 Cosgrove Bldg., Capitol Complex, Helena, Mont. 59620. Phone: (406) 449–2741.

Nebraska

Chief, Research and Statistics, Division of Employment, Department of Labor, P.O. Box 94600, State House Station, Lincoln, Nebr. 68509. Phone: (402) 475–8451.

Executive Director, Nebraska Occupational Information Coordinating Committee, 538 Nebraska Hall, University of Nebraska, Lincoln, Nebr. 68588. Phone: (402) 472–2062.

Nevada

Chief, Employment Security Research, Employment Security Department, 500 E. Third St., Carson City, Nev. 89713. Phone: (702) 885–4550.

Director, Nevada Occupational Information Coordinating Committee, Capitol Complex, Kinkead Bldg., Room 601, 505 E. King St., Carson City, Nev. 89710. Phone: (702) 885–4577.

New Hampshire

Director, Economic Analysis and Reports, Department of Employment Security, 32 S. Main St., Concord, N.H. 03301. Phone: (603) 224–3311, Ext. 251.

SOICC Director, New Hampshire Occupational Information Coordinating Committee, c/o Department of Employment and Training, 155 Manchester St., Concord, N.H. 03301. Phone: (603) 271–3156.

New Jersey

Director, Division of Planning and Research, Department of Labor, P.O. Box 2765, Trenton, N.J. 08625. Phone: (609) 292–2643.

Acting Staff Director, New Jersey Occupational Information Coordinating Committee, P.O. Box CN056, Trenton, N.J. 08625. Phone: (609) 292–2682.

New Mexico

Chief, Research and Statistics, Employment Services Division, P.O. Box 1928, Albuquerque, N. Mex. 87103. Phone: (505) 841–8645.

Director, New Mexico State Occupational Information Coordinating Committee, 401 Broadway, N.E., Albuquerque, N. Mex. 87102. Phone: (505) 841-4496.

New York

Director, Research and Statistics, Department of Labor, State Campus, Bldg. 12, Albany, N.Y. 12240. Phone: (518) 457-6181.

SOICC Director, Department of Labor, State Campus Bldg. #12, Room 559A, Albany, N.Y. 12240. Phone: (518) 457-2930.

North Carolina

Director, Labor Market Information, Employment Security Commission, P.O. Box 25903, Raleigh, N.C. 27611. Phone: (919) 733-2936.

SOICC Director, Department of Administration, 112 W. Lane St., 218 Howard Bldg., Raleigh, N.C. 27611. Phone: (919) 733-6700.

North Dakota

Chief, Research and Statistics, Employment Security Bureau, P.O. Box 1537, Bismarck, N.Dak. 58505. Phone: (701) 224-2868.

Director, North Dakota Occupational Information Coordinating Committee, Pinehurst Building—P.O. Box 1537, Bismarck, N. Dak. 58505. Phone: (701) 224-2733.

Ohio

Director, Research and Statistics, Bureau of Employment Services, 145 S. Front St., Columbus, Ohio 43216. Phone: (614) 466-3240.

Director, Ohio Occupational Information Coordinating Committee, State Department Bldg., 65 S. Front St., Room 904, Columbus, Ohio 43215. Phone: (614) 466-2095.

Oklahoma

Chief, Research and Planning, Employment Security Commission, 310 Will Rogers Memorial Office Bldg., Oklahoma City, Okla. 73105. Phone: (405) 521-3735.

Executive Director, Oklahoma Occupational Information Coordinating Committee, School of Occupational and Adult Education, Oklahoma State University, 1515 W. 6th Ave., Stillwater, Okla. 74074. Phone: (405) 377-2000, ext. 311.

Oregon

Assistant Administrator, Research and Statistics, Employment Division, Department of Human Resources, 875 Union St., NE., Salem, Oreg. 97311. Phone: (503) 378-3220.

Coordinator, Oregon Occupational Information Coordinating Committee, 875 Union St., N.E., Salem, Oreg. 97311. Phone: (503) 378-8146.

Pennsylvania

Chief, Research and Statistics, Department of Labor and Industry, 7th and Foster Sts., Harrisburg, Pa. 17121. Phone: (717) 787-3265.

Director, Pennsylvania Occupational Information Coordinating Committee, Governor's Office of Policy Development, 506 Finance Bldg., Harrisburg, Pa. 17120. Phone: (717) 787-2086.

Puerto Rico

Chief, Department of Labor and Human Resources, Bureau of Employment Security, 505 Munoz Rivera Ave.—15th Floor, Hato Rey, P.R. 00917. Phone: (809) 751-3737.

Executive Director, Puerto Rico Occupational Information Coordinating Committee, Poudencio Rivera Martinez Bldg., 505 Munoz Rivera Ave., Hato Rey, P.R. 00918. Phone: (809) 753-7110.

Rhode Island

Supervisor, Employment Security Research, Department of Employment Security, 24 Mason St., Providence, R.I. 02903. Phone: (401) 277-3704.

Executive Director, Rhode Island Occupational Information Coordinating Committee, 22 Hayes St., Room 315, Providence, R.I. 02908. Phone: (401) 272-0830.

South Carolina

Director, Manpower Research and Analysis, Employment Security Commission, P.O. Box 995, Columbia, S.C. 29202. Phone: (803) 758-8983.

Director, South Carolina Occupational Information Coordinating Committee, 1550 Gadsden St., Columbia, S.C. 29202. Phone: (803) 758-3165.

South Dakota

Chief, Research and Statistics, Office of Administrative Services, Department of Labor, P.O. Box 730, Aberdeen, S. Dak. 57401. Phone: (605) 622-2314.

Executive Director, South Dakota Occupational Information Coordinating Committee, 108 E. Missouri, Pierre, S. Dak. 57501. Phone: (605) 773-3935.

Tennessee

Chief, Research and Statistics, Department of Employment Security, 519 Cordell Hull Bldg., 436 Sixth Ave. North, Nashville, Tenn. 37219. Phone: (615) 741-2284.

Director, Tennessee Occupational Information Coordinating Committee, 512 Cordell Hull Bldg., 436 Sixth Ave. North, Nashville, Tenn. 37219. Phone: (615) 741-6451.

Texas

Chief, Economic Research and Analysis, Employment Commission, 15th and Congress Ave., Austin, Texas 78778. Phone: (512) 397-4540.

Executive Director, Texas Occupational Information Coordinating Committee, 15th and Congress Ave., Room 526T, Austin, Tex. 78778. Phone: (512) 397-4970.

Utah

Director, Research and Analysis, Department of Employment Security, P.O. Box 11249, Salt Lake City, Utah 84147. Phone: (801) 533-2014.

Director, Utah Occupational Information Coordinating Committee, 140 Social Hall Ave., Salt Lake City, Utah 84111. Phone: (801) 533-2028.

Vermont

Chief, Research and Statistics, Department of Employment and Training, P.O. Box 488, Montpelier, Vt. 05602. Phone: (802) 229-0311.

Director, Vermont Occupational Information Coordinating Committee, P.O. Box 488, Montpelier, Vt. 05602. Phone: (802) 229-0311.

Virginia

Chief, Research and Analysis, Employment Commission, P.O. Box 1358, Richmond, Va. 23211. Phone: (804) 786-7496.

SOICC Director, Vocational and Adult Education, Department of Education, P.O. Box 6Q, Richmond, Va. 23216. Phone: (804) 225-2735.

Washington

Chief, Research and Statistics, Employment Security Department, 212 Maple Park, Olympia, Wash. 98504. Phone: (206) 753-5224.

SOICC Director, Commission for Vocational Education, Bldg. 17, Airdustrial Park, Mail Stop LS-10, Olympia, Wash. 98504. Phone: (206) 754-1552.

West Virginia

Chief, Division of Labor and Security, Department of Employment Security, 112 California Ave., Charleston, W. Va. 25305. Phone: (304) 348-2660.

Executive Director, West Virginia State Occupational Information Coordinating Committee, 1600 1/2 Washington St., E., Charleston, W. Va. 25305. Phone: (304) 348-0061.

Wisconsin

Chief, Labor Market Information, Department of Industry, Labor and Human Relations, P.O. Box 7944, Madison, Wis. 53707. Phone: (608) 266-5843.

Director, Wisconsin Occupational Information Coordinating Committee, Educational Sciences Bldg., Room 952, 1025 W. Johnson, Madison, Wis. 53706. Phone: (608) 263-1048.

Wyoming

Chief, Research and Analysis, Employment Security Commission, P.O. Box 2760, Casper, Wyo. 82602. Phone: (307) 237-3701.

Director, Wyoming Occupational Information Coordinating Committee, Hathaway Bldg.—Basement, 2300 Capitol Ave., Cheyenne, Wyo. 82002. Phone: (307) 777-7177 or 7178.